Living a Supernatural Life

Volume 3

Pastor M. F. Olumbo
Foreword written by Pastor E. A. Adeboye
General Overseer RCCG

This is the REAL SECRET that you have wanted to know for so long

LIVING A SUPERNATURAL LIFE

VOLUME 3

Copyright © 2008 by:

PASTOR MICHAEL F. OLUMBO

ISBN-13: 9789780857004
ISBN-10: 9780857001

First Published in Nigeria by:
EXTRA TIME COMMUNICATIONS LTD.

All rights reserved.
No portion of this book may be reproduced or transmitted in any form or by any means, electronics or mechanical, including photocopy, recording, or any information storage and retrieval system, without the written permission of the author
michaeolumbo@outlook.com

For further information or permission address:
Pastor Michael F Olumbo, The Apostolic Church,
Olorunda Ketu, Lagos, Nigeria.
Tel +234 816 526 5668
Tel +234 802 310 3275
First Print May 2008

Foreword written by Pastor E. A. Adeboye General Overseer
Redeemed Christian Church of God
All Scripture quotations are from the King James Version of the
Bible, except otherwise stated

DEDICATION

To God who ordered me to write the two books series titled *"Living a Supernatural life"* and *"You are a New Creature"* even when I knew next to nothing in the Word. It is He who stood by me, taught me and encouraged me throughout the course of writing the eight volumes that make up these two books series. Whenever it looked like I could no longer go forward with the writing because of my lack of enough knowledge of the Word, He would point me to the right Word in the Scriptures and give me the necessary revelation of the Word to fire me on. He has used the writing of these books to build up my faith in Him and in His Word.

CONTENTS

ACKNOWLEDGEMENTS	7
PREFACE	11
FOREWORD BY PASTOR E.A. ADEBOYE	13
INTRODUCTION	15
1. FOLLOWING THE STEPS OF JESUS	33
2. WHO YOU ARE IN CHRIST	47
3. WHAT YOU ARE IN CHRIST	79
4. WHAT YOU HAVE IN CHRIST	161
5. WHAT YOU CAN DO IN CHRIST	373
6. WHERE YOU ARE IN CHRIST	463
7. WHAT WILL YOU DO ABOUT THESE?	501
8. BUILDING A SOUND SCRIPTURAL IMAGE	521
9. ARE YOU SICK?	547
10 TORMENTED BY AFFLICTIONS?	613
11 ARE YOU STRUGGLING WITH SIN?	651

12 NOT SURE OF ANSWER TO PRAYER?	675
13 FACED WITH IMPOSSIBLE SITUATION?	719
14 YOU MUST BE BORN AGAIN	751
OTHER VOLUMES IN THE SERIES	761
OTHER BOOKS BY THE SAME AUTHOR	764
REFERENCES	768
INDEX	770

Living a supernatural life (Volume 3)

ACKNOWLEDGEMENTS

I am thankful to God for giving me the opportunity to write these book series. He alone should take whatever glory accrues from the writing of these books.

I thank Pastor S. S. Jemigbon who is the Chairman of The Apostolic Church in the Lagos and Western/Northern Areas (LAWNA) Territory and the Vice President of The Apostolic Church, Nigeria for reviewing the book and passing it to the Chairman of the Literature Committee of the Church.

I also thank Pastor A. M. O. Oshinowo who is the Chairman of the Literature Committee of The Apostolic Church in the LAWNA Territory and also the Superintendent of the Abeokuta Area of The Apostolic Church in the LAWNA Territory for agreeing to review the book and sending it to Pastor G. A. Oyetunji.

My thanks also go to late Pastor E. O. Arokodare who was the Superintendent of the Agege Area of The Apostolic Church in the LAWNA Territory for the useful advice that he gave me concerning the publishing of these book series.

Thanks to Pastor G. A. Oyetunji formerly of the Literature Department of The Apostolic Church LAWNA Territory who was also the District Apostle of Coker District in Apapa Area of The Apostolic Church in the LAWNA Territory and now the Administrative Secretary for the LAWNA Territory of The Apostolic Church

Living a supernatural life (Volume 3)

I thank him for patiently reading this book series and making some very useful observations and corrections, which have been incorporated into the book series.

My thanks also go to my wife, Grace who keeps nudging me asking when the books will be published. She felt so concerned that the books were getting too big for easy reading and kept advising me to make them short.

I owe a debt of gratitude to my friend and advisor Pastor E. A. Adeboye who is the General Overseer of the Redeemed Christian Church of God worldwide who despite his very busy schedule accepted to review this book and write the Foreword, which he has done very beautifully. His revision of the book and his prayers for me on various occasions has encouraged me to pursue the publication of these book series.

I owe a big thank you to my precious friend Elder Francis O. Aisida of The Apostolic Church Surulere Area of the LAWNA Territory for his encouragement throughout the period of the writing of these book series. He keeps reminding me that these books need to be published as quickly as possible as they are written as a result of an injunction from the Lord. He even took me to a printer in Ibadan two years ago to explore the possibility of getting the printer to print and publish the books. He not only encouraged me throughout the period of the writing of these books but has joined me several times to pray concerning these books and other issues. He was the one who suggested the breaking up of the book into volumes for easy reading and so as to make them more appealing to readers.

I also thank all my friends and worshippers in the various Churches or Assemblies in which I have preached sermons based on some of the topics discussed in these books who have ceaselessly been asking me to get the printed version of the sermons published. This has encouraged me.

Finally I thank my children Foluso, Foluke, Ayodeji and Feyisayo who during the preparation for and writing of these books having observed that they always see me studying the Scriptures and jotting down notes for long periods day after day spanning several years kept asking me if I was writing a Bible Commentary. I thank them for bearing with me and for their encouragement.

PREFACE

LIVING A SUPERNATURAL LIFE

You can live above sickness and disease. You can live above failure. You can live above poverty and lack. You can live above every afflictions of life.

God created man to be a spirit being housed in a physical body and man is a supernatural being like Him. He made man in His own image. You are a spirit being, a supernatural being and you can live a supernatural life here on earth. You don't have to get to heaven before you start living a supernatural life. When you are born-again, you are given a new invisible nature in Christ. With that new invisible nature, living a supernatural life here on earth becomes easy. Basically supernatural living involves practicing the release of this your new invisible nature in Christ into your visible human nature. It is the application of the TRUTH to FACTS, where the TRUTH is what the Word of God says, and the FACTS are what your natural situations say.

How then do you live a supernatural life above sicknesses, above diseases, above failure, above lack, above poverty and above all the afflictions of life? The answer to that question is what this book series is all about. To live in the supernatural you must be convinced that you are what God says that you are, that you are who God says that you are, that you have what God says that you have.

Living a supernatural life (Volume 3)

You must also be convinced that you can do what God says that you can do and that you are where God says that you are. Once you are convinced of these truths and you live your life in the light of the truths, supernatural living then becomes very cheap for you.

You must note that you have been sent to this world just as Jesus was sent. You are an ambassador of heaven here on earth. You have been given the powers to do the same supernatural works that Jesus did when He came to this earth. You have been given the power to do even greater works than He did. You have been made a god to your enemies and to all the situations and circumstances around you. This must be your mentality all the time and if it is, then you must live your life like someone who is reigning over and on top of all the circumstances and situations of life. Nothing should be daunting to you. The greater One than he that is in the world now lives in you. Therefore stop seeing yourself as an ordinary human being. You are a spirit being and you are supposed to live conscious of this truth as a spirit being.

Once you can do these and realize that it is not you who will be doing the supernatural acts, but the greater One who lives in you without whom you can do nothing then living in the supernatural realm will become very cheap and even ordinary for you.

This book series *"Living a supernatural life" Volumes 1, 2, 3 and 4* have been written to help you do all of these and much more.

FOREWORD

You can live a supernatural life here on earth. If we have no expectation or hope of enjoying the supernatural here on earth, then heaven is to that extent irrelevant to us. The truth however is that there is a constant interaction between the physical and the spiritual. Jacob saw the angels ascending and descending, taking things up – be they prayers, worship, self-sacrifice or wickedness and bringing the answers or consequences (of things sowed) in the flesh back.

We need help to send the appropriate things up and empowerment to overcome the pull and power of our carnal nature.

"But you shall receive power after the Holy Ghost is come upon you." This proclamation admits no equivocation. The immediate and direct consequence of the presence of the Holy Spirit in a man's life is endowment of enormous power – to live the supernatural here on earth. Olumbo summarizes this beautifully "Supernatural living is therefore your heritage in Christ". The reality on the ground however, is that Christians are seeking out other Christians; searching every nook and corner for "powerful men of God". Every Christian is a powerhouse in Christ Jesus. Worse some search for the power outside Christ.

Living a supernatural life (Volume 3)

The battle is won or lost even before the first shot is fired – in the mind. What we believe, our faith, determines how much power flows through our lives. But then faith without works is dead. Living faith will produce dynamic words, which leads to action, reaction and release of spiritual power from on high.

The book is interlaced, copiously, with the living Word for the proper instruction of the reader.

The author is not dealing in the realm of precepts but in the reality of applied principles so ably set out in this book. The spiritual battle with the ganglion on his wrist, for example, though protracted, ended in a resounding and permanent victory of the power of God over the unnatural growth.

Flesh cannot of course understand the matter of the spirit. You need to tap into the source of all power in heaven and earth by accepting the Lord Jesus Christ as your personal Lord and Saviour and then you can receive power. Find out how in the last chapter of this wonderful book. Read on. God bless and empower you to do exploits – here on earth.

Adeboye

PASTOR E. A. ADEBOYE
General Overseer
Redeemed Christian Church of God

INTRODUCTION

Just before Jesus left this earth, He promised that those who believe in Him would be empowered to do supernatural acts. He said that they would live supernatural lives as supernatural beings here on earth. He said that supernatural power would be flowing out of them. He said that following them in their paths would be miracles, signs and wonders.

He said in Mark 16:17-18 that signs and wonders would follow them, that they would cast out devils in His Name, that they would speak with new tongues in His Name, that they would take up serpents in His Name, that if they drink any deadly thing it will not hurt them, that they would lay hands on the sick in His Name and they shall recover.

> *And these signs shall follow them that believe; In my name shall they cast out devils; they shall speak with new tongues;*
>
> *They shall take up serpents; and if they drink any deadly thing, it shall not hurt them; they shall lay hands on the sick, and they shall recover.*
> **Mark 16:17-18**

He said in Acts 1:8 that they would receive the power to do these after the Holy Ghost has come upon them. Therefore it is obvious that they needed this power in order to be able to do the supernatural.

Living a supernatural life (Volume 3)

> *But ye shall receive power, after that the Holy Ghost is come upon you: and ye shall be witnesses unto me both in Jerusalem, and in all Judaea, and in Samaria, and unto the uttermost part of the earth.*
>
> **Acts 1:8**

He had said earlier in John 7:38 that once they receive this power, which He called rivers of living water, it would be flowing out of them.

> *He that believeth on me, as the scripture hath said, out of his belly shall flow rivers of living water.*
>
> **John 7:38**

He also said in John 14:12 that equipped with this power, they would do the same works that He did and that they would even do greater works than He did.

> *Verily, verily, I say unto you, He that believeth on me, the works that I do shall he do also; and greater works than these shall he do; because I go unto my Father.*
>
> **John 14:12**

Now look at the works that He did as described by Him in Luke 4:18-19. Then you will see there what you are supposed to do as a believer in Christ. You would realize that you need power in order to be able to do these. Among the things that you are supposed to be doing are healing the sick, setting the captives free, restoring eyes to the blind and of course preaching the gospel of Christ to the poor to make them rich. You are given the power of God in order to be able to do these.

Introduction

The Spirit of the Lord is upon me, because he hath anointed me to preach the gospel to the poor; he hath sent me to heal the brokenhearted, to preach deliverance to the captives, and recovering of sight to the blind, to set at liberty them that are bruised,

To preach the acceptable year of the Lord.
Luke 4:18-19

But the sad thing is that most Christians who are believers in Christ are not mindful of this power that they are supposed to have and demonstrate to the world. Even most of those that are mindful of it are unable to demonstrate this power in their lives. They keep praying that God should empower them by sending down His power to them. But God had already sent down the Holy Spirit and He, the Holy Spirit, is supposed to be living inside every believer in Christ. It is the believer who now has to give the Holy Spirit the room to operate in His life. Secondly, Jesus Christ who is the power of God is also supposed to be living inside every believer in Christ. That is what Jesus Christ Himself told us in John 14:20. God also made us to understand this through Apostle John in 1 John 4:13 and also through Paul written in 1 Corinthians 1:24. Therefore as a believer in Christ, you are supposed to be loaded with the power of God. You are a carrier of the power of God. The power of God is living inside you. It is already inside you.

At that day ye shall know that I am in my Father, and ye in me, and I in you.
John 14:20

Living a supernatural life (Volume 3)

Hereby know we that we dwell in him, and he in us, because he hath given us of his Spirit.
1 John 4:13

But unto them which are called, both Jews and Greeks, Christ the power of God, and the wisdom of God.
1 Corinthians 1:24

As a believer in Christ, the rivers of living water, which is also the virtue and the power to work miracles, signs and wonders are supposed to be flowing out of you. If you are a true believer in Christ therefore, then this power of God is truly living inside you. ***Supernatural living is therefore your heritage in Christ***.

You need to be able to demonstrate this power of God in your life. This is so because the world is moving perilously towards the end-time. As a believer in Christ in this end-time, you will be required to demonstrate this power of God that is now residing in you. We are now in the last days that God described vividly for us written in Micah 4:1-8 through Prophet Micah and through Prophet Joel in Joel 2:28 and, which God told us through Apostle Peter in Acts 2:16-17 had already started on the day of Pentecost.

But in the last days it shall come to pass, that the mountain of the house of the LORD shall be established in the top of the mountains, and it shall be exalted above the hills; and people shall flow unto it.

Introduction

And many nations shall come, and say, Come, and let us go up to the mountain of the LORD, and to the house of the God of Jacob; and he will teach us of his ways, and we will walk in his paths: for the law shall go forth of Zion, and the word of the LORD from Jerusalem.

And he shall judge among many people, and rebuke strong nations afar off; and they shall beat their swords into plowshares, and their spears into pruning hooks: nation shall not lift up a sword against nation, neither shall they learn war any more.

But they shall sit every man under his vine and under his fig tree; and none shall make them afraid: for the mouth of the LORD of hosts hath spoken it.

For all people will walk every one in the name of his god, and we will walk in the name of the LORD our God for ever and ever.

In that day, saith the LORD, will I assemble her that halteth, and I will gather her that is driven out, and her that I have afflicted;

And I will make her that halted a remnant, and her that was cast far off a strong nation: and the LORD shall reign over them in mount Zion from henceforth, even for ever.

And thou, O tower of the flock, the strong hold of the daughter of Zion, unto thee shall it come, even the first dominion; the Kingdom shall come to the daughter of Jerusalem.
Micah 4:1-8

Living a supernatural life (Volume 3)

> *And it shall come to pass afterward, that I will pour out my spirit upon all flesh; and your sons and your daughters shall prophesy, your old men shall dream dreams, your young men shall see visions:*
>
> Joel 2:28
>
> *But this is that which was spoken by the prophet Joel;*
>
> *And it shall come to pass in the last days, saith God, I will pour out of my Spirit upon all flesh: and your sons and your daughters shall prophesy, and your young men shall see visions, and your old men shall dream dreams:*
>
> Acts 2:16-17

If the last days started on the day of Pentecost as confirmed by Peter above, then we must be in the deep of the last days now. If you are truly a believer in Christ in these last days, then as a last day saint, according to the Scriptures the power of God should be flowing out of you without any inhibitions at all. You should be living a supernatural life here on earth. Take a look at the description of the last day saints that God gave us through Prophet Micah in Micah 4:1-8 written above and through Prophet Joel in Joel 2:1-11 written below and you will see just how much of the power of God should be oozing out of you as a last day saint.

> *Blow ye the trumpet in Zion, and sound an alarm in my holy mountain: let all the inhabitants of the land tremble: for the day of the LORD cometh, for it is nigh at hand;*

A day of darkness and of gloominess, a day of clouds and of thick darkness, as the morning spread upon the mountains: a great people and a strong; there hath not been ever the like, neither shall be any more after it, even to the years of many generations.

A fire devoureth before them; and behind them a flame burneth: the land is as the garden of Eden before them, and behind them a desolate wilderness; yea, and nothing shall escape them.

The appearance of them is as the appearance of horses; and as horsemen, so shall they run.

Like the noise of chariots on the tops of mountains shall they leap, like the noise of a flame of fire that devoureth the stubble, as a strong people set in battle array.

Before their face the people shall be much pained: all faces shall gather blackness.

They shall run like mighty men; they shall climb the wall like men of war; and they shall march every one on his ways, and they shall not break their ranks:

Neither shall one thrust another; they shall walk every one in his path: and when they fall upon the sword, they shall not be wounded.

Living a supernatural life (Volume 3)

They shall run to and fro in the city; they shall run upon the wall, they shall climb up upon the houses; they shall enter in at the windows like a thief.

The earth shall quake before them; the heavens shall tremble: the sun and the moon shall be dark, and the stars shall withdraw their shining:

And the LORD shall utter his voice before his army: for his camp is very great: for he is strong that executeth his word: for the day of the LORD is great and very terrible; and who can abide it?

Joel 2:1-11

He said that the last day saints would be strong and great. The world has never seen anything that looks like them in greatness and in strength before. This means that as a last day saint you should be greater than Solomon and stronger than Samson. Anything that comes against the last day saints would be devoured and destroyed. No evil shall escape them unpunished. No devil can hide anywhere and escape them. They will run like horses and like mighty horsemen, they will leap and jump over walls and they will not be tired. Nothing shall escape them. Yet they will not break their ranks so the enemy cannot tempt them into breaching the commands of God. Neither will they thrust one another.

Introduction

Every one of them will walk in his own path, which means that all the artificial denominational divides and traditions will not be an obstacle to their unity and strength for they will all see themselves as one army of the Lord. That is what the last-days army of the Lord will be like.

When they fall they will not be wounded. The whole earth shall quake before them. Even the heavens shall tremble. Nothing shall make them afraid. They would be filled with the Holy Spirit and it is the Holy Spirit inside them that would lift up a standard against any opposition that comes against them. So, all oppositions would dissolve before them. Miracles, signs and wonders will be following them for as the army of the Lord, they shall be executing the Word of the Lord.

This is a description of what you are supposed to be as a last day saint. This is your heritage as a last day believer in Christ. If you are a believer in Christ, you are supposed to be in Christ and you are supposed to be a member of this last day army of the Lord. If you are not experiencing that surge in the power of God flowing through your life then you need to examine your life to look at what you are doing or not doing that has not allowed this power of God to be manifested through you and, which has not allowed you to live the supernatural life that you are supposed to live right here on earth as a believer in Christ. Don't look at your position. It does not matter whether you are a Pastor, a Reverend, a Bishop, a Prophet, an Evangelist, an Apostle, an Elder, an Overseer or just an ordinary member of the Church without a title.

Living a supernatural life (Volume 3)

As long as you are a believer in Christ in these last days, you are supposed to be demonstrating this Power of God in your life. Living in the miraculous is supposed to be a normal thing for you as a last day saint. It should be your way of life. If you are not living such a life then you need to find out why you are not doing so. *That is what this "Living a Supernatural Life" book series is all about.*

But if you want to live this supernatural life, which is followed by miracles, signs and wonders, then note what we have been told by God in Acts 2:22 that it was God that approved Jesus Christ such that miracles, signs and wonders could be done by Him. It is God that will also approve you such that miracles, signs and wonders could be done by you.

> *Ye men of Israel, hear these words; Jesus of Nazareth, a man approved of God among you by miracles and wonders and signs, which God did by him in the midst of you, as ye yourselves also know:*
> **Acts 2:22**

But how do you get this approval of God? What do you need to do to get God's approval so that you could do miracles, signs and wonders? God has given us the answer to these questions through Apostle Paul written in 2 Timothy 2:15. He said,

> *"Study to shew thyself approved unto God, a workman that needeth not to be ashamed, rightly dividing the word of truth."*
> **2 Timothy 2:15**

Introduction

It means that what you need to do is to study, to get the necessary knowledge so as to be approved of God. Whatever is currently blocking your way so that you have not received this approval of God it is knowledge that will deliver you from it.

Whatever is stopping you from flowing and living in the supernatural so that miracles, signs and wonders cannot flow out through you it is knowledge that would deliver you from it. This is so because as a believer in Christ, God has now justified you He has imputed His own righteousness to you so that you are as righteous as anybody else therefore you are now *"The Just"*. But as the just, it is through knowledge that you would be delivered. That is what God told us through King Solomon in Proverbs 11:9.

> *An hypocrite with his mouth destroyeth his neighbour: but through knowledge shall the just be delivered.*
> **Proverbs 11:9**

This book has been written to give you some basic knowledge that you require as a last day saint and believer in Christ. And once you gain this knowledge, armed with it you will be delivered from whatever has held you down and you will be able to live the supernatural life that you have been ordained and destined to live as a believer in Christ. The lack of knowledge is the bane of the problem that most Christians have, which is not allowing them to live the power-packed life that has been ordained for them. God himself had seen this and He has sent two of His prophets to us to let us know this. Through Prophet Isaiah in Isaiah 5:13 He said,

> *"Therefore my people are gone into captivity, because they have no knowledge: and their honourable men are famished, and their multitude dried up with thirst."*
>
> **Isaiah 5:13**

And through Prophet Hosea in Hosea 4:6, He said,

> *"My people are destroyed for lack of knowledge: because thou hast rejected knowledge, I will also reject thee, that thou shalt be no priest to me: seeing thou hast forgotten the law of thy God, I will also forget thy children."*
>
> **Hosea 4:6**

Therefore it is the lack of knowledge that has not allowed many of the believers in Christ who are sons of God to actually demonstrate the power of God in their lives. There are various categories of this lack of knowledge and I will give here a few of these.

Firstly, there are those who are not really born-again. I have emphasized in this book that it is the born-again Christian that can claim this right to live the supernatural life that we are talking about in this book.

There are many people who call themselves Christians, who go to Church regularly but who are not really born-again. Such people not only lack the knowledge but also lack the power that they require to live a supernatural power-packed life here on earth. In the last Chapter of this book I have listed what it takes to become a born-again Christian.

Introduction

If you know that you are not a born-again Christian or you are not convinced of your status in Christ and you will like to live a supernatural life with miracles, signs and wonders following you then I will advice that you first go through that Chapter so as to make your standing in Christ sure. **That is fundamental.**

Secondly, there are those people who are really born-again Christians but who do not know that they are supposed to have this power flowing out of them. Such Christians go through life being tossed about and oppressed by all types of trials and tribulations of life because they are not aware that they can live in a realm, which is far above the oppressions of the devil.

Thirdly, there are those people who are born-again Christians, who know that this power is available to them either through reading or having been told this. So, they know and they believe it is possible for them to have this power but at the same time they believe that it is most improbable that they would have the power. This is so because they believe that the power is meant for those people who are righteous enough before God and whom God had given the special gifts required for the working of miracles.

They don't know that the righteousness of God has been imputed to them, and that they are as righteous as anybody else before God. They don't know how to make this power of God flow out of them so that through them God can demonstrate this power to the world. So, they keep praying that God should send down His power to work miracles in their lives.

Living a supernatural life (Volume 3)

This book has been written to prove to you that if you are born-again then you are in Christ and supernatural living is your heritage. It is also written to show you what you have to do to attain this supernatural living and thus have the power of God flowing freely through you. In order to show you these effectively we first explained to you what the make-up of man is.

We showed in **Volume 1** that man is basically created as a spirit being and therefore ought to be more sensitive to the spiritual things, which are unseen than he is to the physical things that are seen. Then we talked about a law of the spirit, which is operating in man's life on a continuous basis and, which most men have not taken cognizance of. This law is very important in the scheme of things and any man that wants to live a supernatural life here on earth must not only be very conversant with the law but must also make use of it. We tried to show you that it is not only possible but also essential to live a supernatural life right now here on earth and we believe that to a great extent we were able to do this.

We also listed some of the things that you must be and that you must do if you want to successfully live a supernatural life.

Those things that we have listed here are not by any means all that you have to do but these will go a long way to getting you there. We showed how Jesus lived for the brief period that He came down to live here on earth as an example of how we are supposed to live our lives also.

Introduction

When you read this book you will discover that most Christians are actually struggling to be what they are already. They are already righteous before God but they are still struggling to be righteous. God has already given them His righteousness as a gift but they are still looking for righteousness. They are already sons of God but they are still struggling to be children of God. They are not only struggling to be what they are already they are also struggling to go where they already are.

They are already in the Kingdom of God but they are still struggling to go there. They are already there but because they don't know this they are still struggling to go there. Most Christians are also struggling to have what they already have.

They already have power, which has been given to them by Jesus Christ. But because they don't know this they are still struggling to have power instead of giving the Holy Spirit who is the power of God that is already in them the room to express Himself.

Most Christians are struggling to do what is already in their power to do. They don't really know what they are capable of doing.

The Scriptures make us to understand that we can do all things through Christ and that nothing shall be impossible to us yet they still struggle when they are faced with any task. They don't know that nothing is impossible to them when they tackle it with the living faith, which God has given them. They are oblivious of the truth that the One living in them is greater than the one who is in this world.

Living a supernatural life (Volume 3)

The average Christian is like the son of a very rich man whose father has given most of what he has. But because he doesn't know the extent of his father's estate, he who should be living in opulence is living in penury and even living a beggarly and indigent life. When you read this book you will be able to get a good Scriptural picture of yourself and that will help you to live the abundant life that you are supposed to live as a Christian.

It will help you to change the picture that you have of yourself as a weak, failure-prone, disease-prone individual that is not sure of his standing. It is the picture that you build in your mind of who you are that determines who you become because as we have explained in *Volume 1* of this *"Living a Supernatural Life"* book series written by the same author what you have in your mind is what determines what you become in life because the battle of life is fought in the mind. If you can win the battle in your mind then you will win it physically. Whether you will live a sickly epileptic life or you will live a sound, healthy and supernatural life, the battle must be fought and won in your mind first and the picture of yourself that you have in your mind will help you to do this.

Specifically in this *Volume 3* we showed how Jesus lived for the brief period that He came down to live here on earth as an example of how we are supposed to live our lives also. If we want to do the works that Jesus did and get the results that Jesus got then we must do them the way that Jesus did them. We must follow the footsteps of Jesus.

Introduction

If we follow His footsteps then the miracles, signs and wonders that followed Him will also follow us. If we are to do what Jesus did then just like Jesus we must know and continuously confess who we are in Christ, what we are in Christ, what we have in Christ, what we can do in Christ and where we are in Christ.

We must build pictures of these images in our mind and keep focusing our imagination function machine upon them if they are to become realities and manifest physically in our lives.

This our new identity in Christ and how to focus our mind on this and how to use the Scriptural image that we have built in our mind from this to tackle the various problems and situations of life that we come across is what this *Volume 3* of the *"Living a Supernatural Life"* book series is all about. The picture of yourself that you have in your heart will determine how you will approach and fight all the battles of life that you come across and in turn determine whether you can live a supernatural life above all the situations that you come against in life.

Whether you will live a supernatural life that is full of miracles, signs and wonders or an unexciting mediocre and epileptic life full of highs and lows you will first have to fight and win this in your mind. Many so-called Christians who claim to be born again mock other Christians when they see them attempting to heal the sick or do the miraculous. When they see fellow Christians doing miracles they quickly say it must have been done by some devilish power.

Living a supernatural life (Volume 3)

To them the devil can do miracles in this end-time but God is no longer disposed to doing so.

After reading through this book I am sure you will not only be convinced that you too can do miracles, you will actually start to do them.

It is time for us born-again Christians to wake up and be what we are meant to be here on earth. We are not meant to be like every one else. We are supposed to be walking in the miraculous. We are supposed to be the light of the world and we should be shining here on earth.

Finally you will note that in this book practically every Scripture verse quoted is also boldly written out. This is to make the reading of the book and referencing easier for you the reader. **Happy reading!**

CHAPTER 1

FOLLOWING THE FOOTSTEPS OF JESUS

God came in the form of man as Jesus Christ and lived as a spirit being with His body and soul completely under the control of the Spirit. This has proven to us that the man that God created as a spirit being having a soul and who is housed in a body could live as a spirit being as God had intended for him to live here on earth. Christ's coming as a man has proved that it is possible for man to face all the ups and downs of life here on earth and still live a triumphant and spiritual life above such ups and downs of life. He has shown that man could live a Spirit-led life that will glorify God, which was God's intention for creating man. Remember that even though Jesus Christ is God, He came in the form of man to live like a man. This is so that His life can show to us that it is possible for man to live above the circumstances around him, live a Spirit-led life here on earth and also live and walk in the Spirit. He did not come then to live as God. He came to live as man. Therefore whatever He could do then, we can also do now. We can see that He even told us so in John 14:12. He said,

Living a supernatural life (Volume 3)

"Verily, verily, I say unto you, He that believeth on me, the works that I do shall he do also; and greater works than these shall he do; because I go unto my Father."

John 14:12

We are supposed to be able to do whatever Jesus Christ can do. But if we are to be able to do so then one major thing that we have to learn from His life is that Jesus knew whom He was, where He was from, what work He came to do, as well as where He was going and He lived His life to achieve those goals and objectives. As a born-again Christian, you also have to know these facts about yourself as a newly created being and you must live to bring them into manifestation. Jesus was always boldly confessing these truths of His life. Perhaps you have not noticed that yet, but He did. Look at some of His confessions below.

Jesus said in:

John 6:35	I am the Bread of Life.
John 6:51	I am the Living Bread, which came down from Heaven. If any man eats of this Bread, he shall live forever.
John 7:28	I am not come of myself, but He that sent me is true.
John 8:12	I am the Light of the world.
John 8:23	I am from above; I am not of this world.
John 8:42	I proceeded forth and came from God.

John 8:58	Before Abraham was, I am.
John 10:9	I am the Door
John 10:1	I am the Good Shepherd.
John 11:25-26	I am the resurrection and the life and anyone that liveth and believeth in me shall never die.
John 14:6	I am the way, the truth, and the life. I am the only way to God.
John 14:10	I am in the Father and the Father is in me.
John 14:20	I am in the Father, and ye in me, and I in you.
John 15:1	I am the true Vine, without me you can do nothing.
John 16:32	I am not alone, the Father is with me.

Looking at these confessions of Jesus Christ about the truths concerning His life should help you to know how you also ought to confess into your life those truths that you believe concerning yourself as a newly-created being stating *whom you are, what you are, where you are, what you have, what you can do and where you are going.*

Jesus boldly confessed all these statements and many more about Himself when He was physically here on earth. Definitely, the people living at that time when Jesus was physically on earth would have said, on most occasions, that He was mad. They would have said so because of the type of statements that was coming out of His mouth. But that did not stop Him nor deter Him. For example, how will you feel if someone tells you that he is the bread that you should eat?

Living a supernatural life (Volume 3)

I believe that even His disciples sometimes would have been very confused and skeptical about some of His confessions at the earlier stage of His Ministry. To confirm this, look at what Thomas, one of His disciples said in John 11:14-16, when Jesus told them that they were going to Bethany, the town of Lazarus, after He had told them that Lazarus was dead.

> *Then said Jesus unto them plainly, Lazarus is dead.*
>
> *And I am glad for your sakes that I was not there, to the intent ye may believe; nevertheless let us go unto him.*
>
> *Then said Thomas, which is called Didymus, unto his fellowdisciples, Let us also go, that we may die with him.*
>
> **John 11:14-16**

Thomas said, *"Let us go that we may die with Him."* Thomas made this statement because earlier the Jews had wanted to stone Jesus and He escaped. But now Thomas believed that their going back there would probably lead to their death.

To Thomas, Jesus' going there would definitely lead to His being attacked and killed. He believed that if they go with Him, they would all be killed and therefore they would all end up dying with Lazarus. It was a sarcastic statement by Thomas. But it showed just how difficult it was for the people to understand Jesus' Words.

It is obvious that many of the confessions of Jesus seemed strange to the people. Look at these ones written below from John 2:19-21, John 5:17-18 as well as in John 6:41-42, John 6:51-52 and John 7:33-36.

1. HE SAID HE WOULD RAISE UP THE TEMPLE IN THREE DAYS IF DESTROYED

Jesus answered and said unto them, Destroy this temple, and in three days I will raise it up.

Then said the Jews, Forty and six years was this temple in building, and wilt thou rear it up in three days?

But he spake of the temple of his body.
John 2:19-21

He was actually talking of His body since His body was then a temple of God just as your body is now a temple of God, but they did not know this. They thought He was talking of the temple building in Jerusalem.

2. HE CALLED GOD HIS FATHER

But Jesus answered them, My Father worketh hitherto, and I work.

Therefore the Jews sought the more to kill him, because he not only had broken the sabbath, but said also that God was his Father, making himself equal with God.
John 5:17-18

Living a supernatural life (Volume 3)

This was strange to them because they had never seen God as their Father. They had always seen themselves in a Master-servant or Master-slave relationship with God. Therefore that Jesus called God Father was a strange teaching to them. To them it was more than blasphemy. How could He dare called Himself a Son of God?

3. HE SAID HE WAS THE BREAD FROM HEAVEN

The Jews then murmured at him, because he said, I am the bread which came down from heaven.

And they said, Is not this Jesus, the son of Joseph, whose father and mother we know? how is it then that he saith, I came down from heaven?

John 6:41-42

4. HE SAID HE WAS THE LIVING BREAD AND ANYMAN THAT EATS HIM SHALL LIVE FOREVER

I am the living bread which came down from heaven: if any man eat of this bread, he shall live for ever: and the bread that I will give is my flesh, which I will give for the life of the world.

The Jews therefore strove among themselves, saying, How can this man give us his flesh to eat?

John 6:51-52

They were physically looking at Him among them yet He was telling them that He was a bread to be eaten by them. That must have sounded strange to them; so strange that they must have concluded that He was mad. Surely they did not see themselves as cannibals that would be eating human flesh. Yet that in their carnal minds was what He was telling them to do.

5. HE SAID HE WOULD SHORTLY GO BACK AND THEY WOULD NOT SEE HIM ANYMORE

Then said Jesus unto them, Yet a little while am I with you, and then I go unto him that sent me.

Ye shall seek me, and shall not find me: and where I am, thither ye cannot come.

Then said the Jews among themselves, Whither will he go, that we shall not find him? will he go unto the dispersed among the Gentiles, and teach the Gentiles?

What manner of saying is this that he said, Ye shall seek me, and shall not find me: and where I am, thither ye cannot come?
John 7:33-36

Many of His statements seemed strange to them and they thought that He was mad. They even told Him that He had a devil because of the type of confessions that He was making. That is what we are told as written in John 8:45-48. Look at it below.

Living a supernatural life (Volume 3)

> *And because I tell you the truth, ye believe me not*
>
> *Which of you convinceth me of sin? And if I say the truth, why do ye not believe me?*
>
> *He that is of God heareth God's words: ye therefore hear them not, because ye are not of God.*
>
> *Then answered the Jews, and said unto him, Say we not well that thou art a Samaritan, and hast a devil?*
>
> **John 8:45-48**

They repeated the same thing in John 8:51-59 as is written below. They said that He had a devil because what He was saying to them looked impossible. They believed that only a mad man without his senses could make such statements. What they believed was that mad people are possessed with devils, hence their suggestion that He had a devil. But their insults and opposition did not stop Jesus from proclaiming what He was.

> *Verily, verily, I say unto you, If a man keep my saying, he shall never see death.*
>
> *Then said the Jews unto him, Now we know that thou hast a devil. Abraham is dead, and the prophets; and thou sayest, If a man keep my saying, he shall never taste of death.*

Following the Footsteps of Jesus

Art thou greater than our father Abraham, which is dead? and the prophets are dead: whom makest thou thyself?

Jesus answered, If I honour myself, my honour is nothing: it is my Father that honoureth me; of whom ye say, that he is your God:

Yet ye have not known him; but I know him: and if I should say, I know him not, I shall be a liar like unto you: but I know him, and keep his saying.

Your father Abraham rejoiced to see my day: and he saw it, and was glad.

Then said the Jews unto him, Thou art not yet fifty years old, and hast thou seen Abraham?

Jesus said unto them, Verily, verily, I say unto you, Before Abraham was, I am.

Then took they up stones to cast at him: but Jesus hid himself, and went out of the temple, going through the midst of them, and so passed by.

John 8:51-59

People will also insult you and oppose you and say the same things about you that were said about Christ when you start to proclaim what you are in Christ and who you are in Christ.

Living a supernatural life (Volume 3)

What people could say, or even what His disciples could say, did not stop Jesus from making His confessions and proclaiming what He was openly. Jesus spoke openly and boldly wherever He went. We ought to do likewise. If you want to have the type of results that Jesus had, you must do it the way He did it. He has said that you would do the works that He did and even greater works than He did. If you must do the works that Jesus Christ did, there are no two-ways about it, you must follow His footsteps. Therefore, just as Jesus did when He was here on earth, you should make it a normal thing in your life to confess what your new identity and inheritance is in Christ. You must find out the answers to the following questions about your own identity in Christ and start to make bold declaration of them into your life.

Who are you? What are you? Where are you in Christ? What do you have in Christ? What can you do in Christ?

Some of the answers to these questions have been made known to us by God and are well stated in the Scriptures. Some of these are listed in the next five chapters of this book. When you start to say openly and boldly who you are in Christ, what you are in Christ, where you are in Christ, what you have in Christ and what you can do in Christ as stated in the next few Chapters, then people will also start to say the same things that they said of Jesus about you. In particular they will say that you are mad because you will become strange to them. If they say the same thing of you that they said of Jesus then you should rejoice that you are counted among those people that are grouped with Jesus.

But if you can believe in your heart the statements about you that are written in the next five chapters, and continue to confess them openly and boldly with your mouth, then they will be effected and they will eventually manifest in your life. This is so because it is as you think in your heart that you will be. That is what God said in Proverbs 23:7 through Solomon.

For as he thinketh in his heart, so is he: Eat and drink, saith he to thee; but his heart is not with thee.
Proverbs 23:7

So if you think and meditate in your heart on the statements, which are listed in the following five Chapters concerning your new identity in Christ, and you believe and know that these are true for you, and that you have all the characteristics thus listed and you confess them openly with your mouth, then they will manifest and become a reality in your life. But if you think that you can never be all these, then they will not become a reality in your life. Therefore, just like Jesus did while on earth, you better start confessing these characteristics of your new identity in Christ into your life. Let them become real to you. Personalize them because they are yours. They are yours in Christ. You may not see them, you may not feel them but they are true of you. It is by faith in these truths of what the Word of God says concerning you that you can acquire these attributes and make them to manifest. Many of these statements may not even look real to you but remember that what we are talking about here are spiritual things.

Living a supernatural life (Volume 3)

Feelings have very little to do with these because feelings are of the soul. What we are talking about here has to do with who you are spiritually, what you are spiritually, where you are spiritually, what you have spiritually and what you can do spiritually. You cannot judge these by the way you feel about them. As a Christian remember once again that you have been advised in 2 Corinthians 4:18 not to look at the things which are seen because what you see may not necessarily be as real as what you do not see.

While we look not at the things which are seen, but at the things which are not seen: for the things which are seen are temporal; but the things which are not seen are eternal.
                              2 Corinthians 4:18.

GET THE RIGHT SELF-IMAGE

Don't go by your feelings. Don't judge any situation by what your senses are telling you about it. Don't limit yourself by what your senses are telling you or by what people think or say that you are. If you are to be able to make use of the power and all the other things that are attributed to you here, which now belong to you in Christ then a prerequisite is that you must have a right Scriptural image of yourself built up in your mind. ***Note that you cannot do or be anything above the image that you have in your mind of yourself.*** Continuous confession of what the Scriptures say that you are, that you have as well as where you are and what you can do will give you the right self-image.

Speaking out with authority who you are, what you are, what you have, what you can do and where you are is one of the basic acts and foundation of the Christian religion. That was why Apostle Peter and Apostle Paul laid so much emphasis on this in their Epistles to the Christians in the early Church. It is a pity that the significance of this has been lost in the present day Church. That is the reason why the present day Church has lost so much of the power of God that was experienced in the early Church. As you read through this book thoughtfully and meditatively let the importance of this aspect of Christianity which has not been taken cognizance of be rekindled in your life.

In the next five Chapters we have written down what should be your confessions of who you are in Christ, what you are in Christ, what you have in Christ, what you can do in Christ and where you are in Christ as given in the Scriptures. If you are a born-again Christian you will do well to study these because they are all supposed to be true of you and they will change your life.

If you want that right self-image, then you must start to confess these characteristics of yours as given in the Scriptures. You must make it a habit to confess this your new nature in Christ. You will see an example of the kind of Confessions that should be coming out of your mouth regularly at the end of Chapters 2-6., which you will find on pages 76-78, 153-160, 359-372, in Pages 457-462 and 497-500.

Living a supernatural life (Volume 3)

If on the other hand you are not a born-again Christian you can see what you are missing, which you can gain if you are willing to accept Jesus Christ into your life as your Saviour.

How to accept Jesus Christ into your life and become a born-again Christian so that you too can enjoy all these is very simple and this is discussed in the last Chapter of this book. You will do well to first read that Chapter if you are not a born-again believer.

CHAPTER 2

WHO YOU ARE IN CHRIST

The problem with us Christians for the most part is that we do not know who we really have become after our new birth. Many claim to be a new creation but they still believe that they are who they used to be. They still behave as they used to do before their new birth experience. This is because they do not really know what has happened to them. They cannot physically comprehend what has happened to them spiritually. Please take your time to read the confessions in this Chapter of who you really are now. It will help you to get a true Scriptural image of yourself because they can all be true of you if you are truly born again. Here then are some confessions of who you are in Christ. You need to change your mindset, to train your spiritual eyes to see these, get a revelation of them and believe them if you are to enjoy the abundant life and power that you should now have as a born-again Christian. Here then are some statements of who you are in Christ.

YOU ARE A CHILD OF ABRAHAM

You are a child of Abraham. That is what you should see from what God said through Paul in Galatians 3:7.

Living a supernatural life (Volume 3)

> *Know ye therefore that they which are of faith, the same are the children of Abraham.*
>
> **Galatians 3:7**

Many Christians say this; they sing it like a parrot. But they don't understand the deep meaning of this. You must know that since you are a child of Abraham what it means therefore is that as Isaac was to Abraham so are you to Abraham now. Consequently you are also a child of promise. That is what God made us to see from what He said through Paul to us in Galatians 4:28.

> *Now we, brethren, as Isaac was, are the children of promise.*
>
> **Galatians 4:28**

But remember that Jesus told the physical children of Abraham after the flesh in John 8:39 that if they are truly children of Abraham they will do the works of Abraham.

> *They answered and said unto him, Abraham is our father. Jesus saith unto them, If ye were Abraham's children, ye would do the works of Abraham.*
>
> **John 8:39**

The same is true of you who God has declared to be a child of Abraham after the Spirit. If you are truly to be Abraham's child and you want to enjoy the privileges that come with that title then you must do the works that Abraham did, which includes standing in faith. The privileges that now accrue to you as Abraham's child are what we refer to as Abraham's blessing.

Who you are in Christ
THE BLESSINGS OF ABRAHAM ARE YOURS

Because you are a child of Abraham the blessings of Abraham are now yours. Just like the Israelites who are the natural, physical descendants of Abraham are entitled to the blessing of Abraham so are we who are the spiritual Israelites entitled to these blessing of Abraham. Christ died to redeem you so that these blessing of Abraham can also be yours. That is what God said through Apostle Paul in Galatians 3:13-14. This means that just as the Lord said to Abraham in Genesis 12:2-3, the Lord will bless you but you must also be a blessing to others. He will make your name great and make you a great nation. He will bless them that bless you and curse them that curse you.

> *Christ hath redeemed us from the curse of the law, being made a curse for us: for it is written, Cursed is every one that hangeth on a tree:*
>
> *That the blessing of Abraham might come on the Gentiles through Jesus Christ; that we might receive the promise of the Spirit through faith.*
>
> **Galatians 3:13-14**
>
> *And I will make of thee a great nation, and I will bless thee, and make thy name great; and thou shalt be a blessing:*
>
> *And I will bless them that bless thee, and curse him that curseth thee: and in thee shall all families of the earth be blessed.*
>
> **Genesis 12:2-3**

Living a supernatural life (Volume 3)
YOU ARE A TEMPLE OF GOD

You are a temple of God because the Spirit of God now lives in you. That is what God said through Apostle Paul in 1 Corinthians 3:16. This means that God Himself lives in you. Because your body is God's temple where He now lives He will make sure that anything that defiles your body will be destroyed since He had also said through Paul in 1 Corinthians 3:17 that He will destroy anything that defiles His temple. You should therefore make sure that you are not doing anything that can defile your body.

> *Know ye not that ye are the temple of God, and that the Spirit of God dwelleth in you?*
> **1 Corinthians 3:16**

> *If any man defile the temple of God, him shall God destroy; for the temple of God is holy, which temple ye are.*
> **1 Corinthians 3:17**

Therefore anything that defiles your body whether it originates from a physical being or from a spirit being will be destroyed by God. You don't have to worry yourself when anything attempts to defile your body because you ought to know that God Himself will defend the body because it is where He lives now. To confirm that God lives in your body He has also told you that you are His habitation through the Spirit. That is what He said through Paul in Ephesians 2:22.

> *In whom ye also are builded together for an habitation of God through the Spirit.*
> **Ephesians 2:22**

Who you are in Christ

You may ask; how can you know this? You can know this because you received this Spirit of God through faith according to what God said through Apostle Paul in Galatians 3:14. Therefore you know this by faith. Practically everything that you have through Salvation is obtained from God by faith. It is therefore very important that a Christian must be a man of faith. Without faith you cannot get anything from God nor can you interact well with God. Abraham's blessings are yours. Yes! But you can only receive these by faith.

> *That the blessing of Abraham might come on the Gentiles through Jesus Christ; that we might receive the promise of the Spirit through faith.*
> **Galatians 3:14**

Since you are now a habitation of God in your body it follows that your body should no longer harbour diseases. It cannot harbour God and at the same time be harbouring diseases because God has said that He will destroy whatever defiles His temple and any disease in your body is obviously defiling it.

Diseases may come and try to lodge in your body but if you know in your heart who you really are in Christ then they cannot stay. They must leave because from Isaiah 59:19, you can see that when such diseases come in like a flood the Spirit of God that lives in you will lift up a standard against them. Diseases are of the devil and it is written in James 4:7 that if you resist the devil he will flee from you. Therefore resist them with the Word of God and they will bow out.

> *So shall they fear the name of the Lord from the west, and his glory from the rising of the sun. When the enemy shall come in like a flood, the Spirit of the Lord shall lift up a standard against him.*
> **Isaiah 59:19**

According to what God said in 1 Corinthians 3:9 you are God's building. Therefore you should know and be sure that God will defend His own building and will not allow it to be defiled. You are a labourer together with God. You are God's husbandry. You are God's building. God will defend and protect you. God is your manager and He is the One guarding you. Therefore you need not worry about your protection.

> *For we are labourers together with God: ye are God's husbandry, ye are God's building.*
> **1 Corinthians 3:9**

YOU ARE BORN OF GOD

In this new birth, you are born of God. You are not born of blood. You are not born of the will of man but of God. Since you are not born of blood, you don't have to suffer from the blood diseases that the people born of blood suffer from. In fact, since you are born of God it follows that you are a son of God. That is what we can see from John 1:12-13. It therefore follows that you have divine blood running through your veins now. This may seem far-fetched but it is true because you are now a partaker of the divine nature.

Who you are in Christ

> *But as many as received him, to them gave he power to become the sons of God, even to them that believe on his name:*
>
> *Which were born, not of blood, nor of the will of the flesh, nor of the will of man, but of God.*
> **John 1:12-13**

Not only that, because you are now begotten of God according to 1 John 5:18, the wicked one can no longer touch you. You are now insulated from the wicked one. This is because according to what God said through John which is written below in 1 John 5:4 whatsoever is born of God overcomes the world. Therefore have the overcomer's mentality since you are now born of God. Therefore believe that nothing can overcome or defeat you anymore.

> *We know that whosoever is born of God sinneth not; but he that is begotten of God keepeth himself, and that wicked one toucheth him not.*
> **1 John 5:18**
>
> *For whatsoever is born of God overcometh the world: and this is the victory that overcometh the world, even our faith.*
> **1 John 5:4**

Since you are now born of God it follows that you have overcome the world. Your spiritual rebirth is complete because you are born of God the Father, you are born of the Word, who is Christ and you are born of the Holy Spirit

Living a supernatural life (Volume 3)

Therefore every member of the Trinity was involved in your spiritual rebirth. That is what we can see from what is written by Apostles John and Peter respectively in 1 John 5:1, John 3:6 and 1 Peter 1:23.

> *Whosoever believeth that Jesus is the Christ is born of God: and every one that loveth him that begat loveth him also that is begotten of him.*
>
> **1 John 5:1**

> *That which is born of the flesh is flesh; and that which is born of the Spirit is spirit.*
>
> **John 3:6**

> *Being born again, not of corruptible seed, but of incorruptible, by the word of God, which liveth and abideth for ever.*
>
> **1 Peter 1:23**

Everything produces after its kind. If that is the case then because like begets like. You are begotten of God, God is not a failure, you are a son of God therefore you are not born to be a failure. Because like begets like, God is the Most High, you are a son of God therefore you are born to be in the upper echelon of society. You are not born to be among the lowest echelon of society. Because like begets like, God is great, you are a son of God therefore you are born to be great. Because like begets like, God is a bright and morning star, you are a son of God therefore you are born to be a star that shines brightly. Because like begets like, God is a creator, you are a son of God therefore you are born to be a creator.

Because like begets like, God is all powerful, you are a son of God therefore you are not born to be a weakling. Because like begets like, God is all knowing and wise, you are a son of God therefore you are not born to be a fool. Because like begets like, God is in control of every situation, you are a son of God therefore you are born to be in control of and have dominion over all situations. Because like begets like, God is the King of kings and reigns you are a son of God therefore you are born to be a king and reign in life.

YOU ARE A SPIRIT-BEING

We have said that likes begets likes. You are born of God and according to John 4:24 God is a Spirit. Therefore you are a spirit-being because you are born of the Spirit. This is further confirmed by Apostle John in John 3:6. To live as a spirit being you must allow the spirit that you are now to take absolute control of your total self, which includes your soul and your body.

> *God is a Spirit: and they that worship him must worship him in spirit and in truth.*
> **John 4:24**

> *That which is born of the flesh is flesh; and that which is born of the Spirit is spirit.*
> **John 3:6**

That was the way God created man to function originally before man's fall. This means that as a spirit being your soul and your body should now be under the spirit's control.

Living a supernatural life (Volume 3)

We discussed in detail the truth and proof that you are a spirit being in *Chapter 1* of the *Volume 1* of this *"Living a Supernatural life"* book series. As a spirit-being born of God, the forces of darkness can no longer discern your actions nor can they know your movements unless of course you divulge these to them either consciously or unconsciously. They can only see the effects of whatever actions you take. Therefore your ways, your movements and also your destiny cannot be found out and tampered with or blocked by anything or anybody. That is what you can see from what Jesus said in John 3:8.

> *The wind bloweth where it listeth, and thou hearest the sound thereof, but canst not tell whence it cometh, and whither it goeth: so is every one that is born of the Spirit.*
> **John 3:8**

Therefore you no longer have to worry yourself about any evil forces aborting or disturbing your plans. This is true because you are now born of God. Your ways, your plans and your destiny are no longer open to the forces of darkness. Therefore you should no longer be intimidated by anybody telling you that some forces are blocking your plans or your destiny. It is just not possible if you live as a spirit being that you are. You are a spirit-being therefore from what Apostle Paul wrote in Romans 8:9 you are no longer in the flesh but in the Spirit. You should no longer think, feel, live and act in the flesh. You should think, feel, live and act in the Spirit.

> *But ye are not in the flesh, but in the Spirit, if so be that the Spirit of God dwell in you. Now if any man have not the Spirit of Christ, he is none of his.*
> **Romans 8:9**

Because you are born of God, as written in 1 John 3:9, the seed of God remains in you, and therefore you cannot be sinning as a habit any longer. The new nature of God that you now have imparted to you makes the continuous practice of sin impossible for you. You may fall into temptation occasionally but you can no longer make sin a habit. As written by John in 1 John 2:9 because you are born of God, doing righteousness has become your habitual practice therefore sinning should no longer be habitual to you. If you are still enjoying sin then you have not yet received from God the free gift of righteousness, which He has offered you through Christ.

> *Whosoever is born of God doth not commit sin; for his seed remaineth in him: and he cannot sin, because he is born of God.*
> **1 John 3:9**

> *He that saith he is in the light, and hateth his brother, is in darkness even until now.*
> **1 John 2:9**

Because you are born anew, old things are passed away, all things are become new. That is how it is supposed to be with you now as we can see in 2 Corinthian 5:17 from what Paul the Apostle wrote.

Living a supernatural life (Volume 3)

Therefore if any man be in Christ, he is a new creature: old things are passed away; behold, all things are become new.
2 Corinthians 5:17

You are a totally new spirit-being and you have been given a new soul, which now habours the mind of Christ as you can see from what God said through the same Apostle Paul in 1 Corinthians 2:16.

For who hath known the mind of the Lord, that he may instruct him? But we have the mind of Christ.
1 Corinthians 2:16

This means that your old thoughts, old ideas, old choices, old purposes, old affections and old goals should go away and you should now have new thoughts, new ideas, new choices, new purposes, new affections and new goals, which should be more in line with God's thoughts, God's ideas, God's choices, God's purposes, God's affections and God's goals.

YOU ARE A VICTOR

You are a victor and you have overcome the world. Because you are born of God you have overcome the world and you got this victory through the faith you have in the work of redemption that Jesus Christ did. That is what you now know from what God told us through John the Apostle in 1 John 5:4.

For whatsoever is born of God overcometh the world: and this is the victory that overcometh the world, even our faith.
1 John 5:4

Your victory over Satan and his forces is established through the Blood of the Lamb and the words of your testimony. That is what you can see from what God revealed to John in Revelation 12:11. Therefore as you take cover under the Blood of Jesus Christ and confess the Word of God in testimony against all the forces of the enemy your victory over them is assured. Both the Blood and the Word are required for victory.

And they overcame him by the blood of the Lamb, and by the word of their testimony; and they loved not their lives unto the death.
Revelation 12:11

The Blood of the Lamb guarantees you God's mercy and gives you complete insurance for your protection and needs. It also cleanses you from all your sins. This is because Jesus has cut an everlasting Blood Covenant with God through which you have been cleansed and His righteousness imparted unto you.

Therefore you can boldly tell Satan what the Blood of Jesus speaks on your behalf. The Blood speaks freedom for you that you are free. According to what is written in 1 Corinthians 6:11 you are washed, you are justified, you are redeemed, you are sanctified and you now have peace with God because you now have eternal victory over the enemy.

> *And such were some of you: but ye are washed, but ye are sanctified, but ye are justified in the name of the Lord Jesus, and by the Spirit of our God.*
>
> **1 Corinthians 6:11**

The word of your testimony, which is the confession of your faith in the Word of God and everything it says concerning you guarantees you victory over the enemy at all times. You are a victor since you have overcome all the forces that the devil can put against you because the Overcomer who is the greater One than the one that is in the world now lives in you. That is what you can see from 1 John 4:4. Therefore your victory over sin, sickness, failure, barrenness, poverty, over all afflictions and any weapon that the enemy may form against you is a sure thing. None of them can prosper against you. Your victory over them is certain. That is your heritage now as a servant of God as you can see in Isaiah 54:17. ***This should be your mindset.***

> *Ye are of God, little children, and have overcome them: because greater is he that is in you, than he that is in the world.*
>
> **1 John 4:4**

> *No weapon that is formed against thee shall prosper; and every tongue that shall rise against thee in judgment thou shalt condemn. This is the heritage of the servants of the Lord, and their righteousness is of me, saith the Lord.*
>
> **Isaiah 54:17**

Who you are in Christ

You now have in your heart the peace of God that passeth all understanding. That is what God made us to see from what He said through Apostle Paul in Philippians 4:7. Therefore you cannot be worried about anything because the end of every matter is now sure to you. It must always end for your good if you love God. That is what God said in Romans 8:28 and His Words cannot be broken. Therefore you don't have to worry yourself about anything. God is on your side. He is with you like a mighty warrior. Therefore relax! Live the full and abundant life that you are supposed to live here on earth.

> *And the peace of God, which passeth all understanding, shall keep your hearts and minds through Christ Jesus.*
> **Philippians 4:7**

> *And we know that all things work together for good to them that love God, to them who are the called according to his purpose.*
> **Romans 8:28**

Through Jesus Christ you have even overcome death because death has no more power over you. Now you can say as written in 1 Corinthians 15:55, *"O death, where is thy sting? O grave, where is thy victory?"* This is because as He promised to do in Hosea 13:14, He has redeemed you from death and He has ransomed you from the power of the grave. You no longer need to fear death. We showed this clearly in *Volume 1* of this *"Living a Supernatural Life"* book series.

> *O death, where is thy sting? O grave, where is thy victory?*
>
> **1 Corinthians 15:55**

> *I will ransom them from the power of the grave; I will redeem them from death: O death, I will be thy plagues; O grave, I will be thy destruction: repentance shall be hid from mine eyes.*
>
> **Hosea 13:14**

YOU ARE A CHILD OF LIGHT YOU ARE LIGHT

The Scripture says in 1 John 1:5 that God is Light. Since you are born of God it follows that you are a child of Light. That is what God said through Paul the Apostle in 1 Thessalonians 5:5. Because like begets like, you are a child of Light therefore you are light. The child of a goat is a goat. The child of a sheep is a sheep. The child of Light is light. Therefore you are light. That is why Jesus said in Matthew 5:14 that you are the light of the world.

> *This then is the message which we have heard of him, and declare unto you, that God is light, and in him is no darkness at all.*
>
> **1 John 1:5**

> *Ye are all the children of light, and the children of the day: we are not of the night, nor of darkness.*
>
> **1 Thessalonians 5:5**

Ye are the light of the world. A city that is set on an hill cannot be hid.
Matthew 5:14

Now because you are a child of Light and therefore light, darkness can no longer hang around you neither can any works of darkness hang around you. No matter how thick the darkness may be your light will overcome it and shine through it. This is so because as we are made to understand by what Paul said in Ephesians 5:8 you are not of the night or darkness any longer. It is obvious therefore that wherever you are darkness must give way and light must shine forth. Because your light has now come you must arise and shine. Even though darkness covers the whole earth and gross darkness covers the people but according to Isaiah 60:1-2 the Lord has arisen upon you and His glory can be seen upon you. You are destined to shine; that is now your heritage in Christ. But you must arise before you can shine. If you do not arise you will not shine. The ball is in your court.

For ye were sometimes darkness, but now are ye light in the Lord: walk as children of light:
Ephesians 5:8

Arise, shine; for thy light is come, and the glory of the Lord is risen upon thee.

For, behold, the darkness shall cover the earth, and gross darkness the people: but the Lord shall arise upon thee, and his glory shall be seen upon thee.
Isaiah 60:1-2

Living a supernatural life (Volume 3)
YOU ARE A SON OF GOD

You are a son of God. You have been empowered to become one. You can see this from what we are told through Apostle John in John 1:12.

> *But as many as received him, to them gave he power to become the sons of God, even to them that believe on his name:*
>
> **John 1:12**

As a son of God you are now supposed to be led by the Spirit of God from what is written in Romans 8:14. The Spirit Himself should bear witness with your spirit that you are now a son of God. That is what we are told in Romans 8:16. Think seriously about this. You are a son of the Almighty God. Get this mindset fully established in your mind.

> *For as many as are led by the Spirit of God, they are the sons of God.*
>
> **Romans 8:14**

> *The Spirit itself beareth witness with our spirit, that we are the children of God:*
>
> **Romans 8:16**

Now look at this, since you are a son of God you are entitled to all the privileges and benefits of a son of God. Therefore you are entitled to provision, protection, defense, teaching and advice from God your Father and from His Spirit. You are not a son of God by accident. You have been predestinated to be adopted as a son of God by Jesus Christ according to the good pleasure of God's will.

That is what He made us to know through Paul in Ephesians 1:5. From what God further said through Paul in Romans 8:29 you have been predestinated to be conformed to the image of Jesus Christ the Son of God through which you have also become a son of God.

> *Having predestinated us unto the adoption of children by Jesus Christ to himself, according to the good pleasure of his will,*
> **Ephesians 1:5**

> *For whom he did foreknow, he also did predestinate to be conformed to the image of his Son, that he might be the firstborn among many brethren.*
> **Romans 8:29**

To make sure that you are not just a son of God by title but that you can live and perform like a son of God, He has sent the Spirit of His Son into your heart according to Galatians 4:6.

> *And because ye are sons, God hath sent forth the Spirit of his Son into your hearts, crying, Abba, Father.*
> **Galatians 4:6**

His Spirit in you is the One that empowers you to become His son. This is so that you can have an intimate relationship with Him and not a servant-master relationship. As a son of God you have become a member of the family of God. It is a great mystery but true that the God who fills heaven and earth and yet can still live inside a human body is now your Father.

Living a supernatural life (Volume 3)

How can you have the God, Almighty, Omnipotent, Omniscient and Unchanging God as your Father and still be suffering under the bondage of any enemy oppression? How can you have the God who owns all things in heaven and earth as your Father and still suffer from lack and poverty? How can you have a Father who owns all power in heaven and in earth and still be a weakling? As a son of God your heritage is power, prosperity, wisdom, success and victory. As a son of God anything that you lay your hands upon if it is according to the will of your Father it is bound to be successful. Therefore seek His will for you.

YOU ARE A KING AND A PRIEST UNTO GOD

You are not only a son of God but God has made you a king to reign here on earth. You are a king and a priest unto God. That is what God made us to see in Revelation 5:10.

And hast made us unto our God kings and priests: and we shall reign on the earth.
Revelation 5:10

As a king unto God it is obvious that you are supposed to be reigning here on earth. As someone who is reigning here on earth you cannot suffer here on earth. That you are reigning here on earth means that you have power, dominion and control over all the circumstances and situations of life that you come across.

This means that as a king when you give orders or commands they have to be obeyed because where the word of a king is there is power and nobody can say what sayest thou to the king. That is what God made us to see from what is written in Ecclesiastes 8:4. That is why Jesus promised to give you a mouth and wisdom, which nobody can gainsay or resist according to what He said in Luke 21:15.

> *Where the word of a king is, there is power: and who may say unto him, What doest thou?*
> **Ecclesiastes 8:4**

> *For I will give you a mouth and wisdom, which all your adversaries shall not be able to gainsay nor resist.*
> **Luke 21:15**

Therefore there is power in the words that you speak. It is obvious that when you give orders and commands to the forces of darkness whenever you come across them they must bow and obey you. If you want to know the reasons why you have been given a mouth and wisdom you don't have to search for these. This is because you can see that you need the mouth to give commands. You also need the wisdom to reign as a king here on earth. This is because as a king you not only reign by your words you also reign by wisdom. That is what wisdom says according to what we are told by God through Solomon in Proverbs 8:15. Wisdom speaking here said,

> *"By me kings reign, and princes decree justice."*
> **Proverbs 8:15**

Living a supernatural life (Volume 3)

In order that you can reign by wisdom Christ who is the wisdom of God and the power of God who now lives in you has been made wisdom unto you so that you now have the wisdom of God and the power of God available to you as the major resources for your reigning here on earth. That is what we can infer from the combination of what God said through Apostle Paul in 1 Corinthians 1:24 and 1 Corinthians 1:30 and you need both power and wisdom to reign in life.

> *But unto them which are called, both Jews and Greeks, Christ the power of God, and the wisdom of God.*
> **1 Corinthians 1:24**

> *But of him are ye in Christ Jesus, who of God is made unto us wisdom, and righteousness, and sanctification, and redemption:*
> **1 Corinthians 1:30**

Because you are a king the following statements that are true of kings should all be true of you if you are on the Lord's side:

The Lord will lose your bonds. **(Job 12:18)**

The Lord gives you salvation. **(Psalm 144:10)**

Your heart will be unsearchable. **(Proverbs 25:3)**

There is power in your word and nobody can oppose it successfully. **(Ecclesiastes 8:4)**

The Lord will give you strength. **(1Samuel 2:10)**

Who you are in Christ

Mercy and truth will preserve you. **(Proverbs 20:28)**

You should not be drunk on wine and you should not give your strength to women. **(Proverbs 31:3-4)**

As a king you are supposed to reign by wisdom and you have been given the necessary wisdom with which to reign. **(Proverbs 8:15) (Luke 21:15)**

As a king you are supposed to reign by the words that you speak from your mouth and you have been given the necessary mouth, which no adversary can gainsay or resist. This means that whatever you say, when you speak it out with that mouth it is bound to be established. Whether you will reign or not depends on the words that come out of your mouth. Therefore you must speak out positive words that will confirm your dominion not words that will subjugate or enslave you and put you in any form of bondage of the enemy. **(Luke 21:15) (Ecclesiastes 8:4) (Proverbs 6:2).**

Be conscious of all these statements which are all true of you now and have this mindset:

You are a king unto the Lord and a son of the King of kings therefore the divine royal blood is running through your veins but you have to learn how to live like, think like, talk like and act like a king. A king's word is supreme. A king's word is full of authority. Therefore stop talking out of fear. Talk like someone who is in perfect control of every situation. When a king commands it is final. Your mindset has to be changed to believe that these are all true about you.

Living a supernatural life (Volume 3)

The Holy Spirit in you will be teaching you how to live like a king and how to talk like a king. Therefore listen to His teaching and direction. You must start to exercise the authority that you now have as a king over all the circumstances and situations of life that you come across. The Holy Spirit is supposed to give you boldness because He is a Spirit of power, of love and of a sound mind. He is not a spirit of fear. Therefore as a king you must do away with all thoughts of fear and anxiety.

A true king does not fear. Your thoughts and behavior of the past must change. You must start to speak as a king with authority not necessarily shouting because you must know that there is power in anything that you speak out and the power does not depend on how loud you speak. The power only depends on the authority of your position as a king and the confidence that you have in exercising that authority. All you have to do is to speak and believe in the authority that is in whatever you speak out as a king. You are ruling here on earth not by your own right but as a son and representative of God here on earth. According to Proverbs 16:12 as a king you are established in righteousness and doing wickedness should be an abomination to you.

> *It is an abomination to kings to commit wickedness: for the throne is established by righteousness.*
> **Proverbs 16:12**

Even in this earthly realm children born into royal families are taught right from their childhood days how to live and act like a king.

They are brainwashed so that they can see themselves not as ordinary persons. They are taught to behave in a manner that befits kings. They are taught how to walk like a king majestically with no fear or inferiority complex. They are taught how to talk like a king with authority not necessarily shouting. They are taught how to eat like a king in a manner that befits kings. They are taught how to sit down and stand in a posture that befits a king. If the people of this earthly realm can go to that extent to train their kings so as to be able to live their lives with the authority of a king then we can see that it is much more necessary for us who are children of the King of kings in the Kingdom of God to learn to live like kings.

The pity of it all is that most Christians do not even know that they are kings. How then can they live like one? We need to be taught and learn how to do so. That is the work that the Holy Spirit does in the life of the Christian. He is the One that teaches the Christian all things about the Kingdom of Heaven and how to make sure that the Christian can live to his full potential as a king and a citizen of the Kingdom of Heaven living in this earthly realm. Many Christians have been able to become citizens of the Kingdom of Heaven as a result of their salvation but they have not been able to learn how to live the abundant life that is available to them in that Kingdom. They are yet to experience the realities of the Kingdom of Heaven. They are still living with the slave mentality that they used to have even before they became citizens of the Kingdom of Heaven. They need to have the Kingdom mindset before they can start to enjoy the full benefits and privileges that they now have as citizens of the Kingdom of Heaven as kings.

Living a supernatural life (Volume 3)

They are in the Kingdom but they are at a loss as to what to do. On the other hand many born-again Christians do not even know that they are already citizens of the Kingdom of Heaven. They are still praying and hoping that they will not miss the flight to the Kingdom. They are still at the hoping stage therefore they require faith to turn their hope into reality since the Scriptures say in Hebrews 11:1 that faith is what turns hope into reality. It is faith that gives hope substance. The next point tops it all.

> *Now faith is the substance of things hoped for, the evidence of things not seen.*
> **Hebrews 11:1**

YOU ARE A GOD

To top it all do you know that you are not only a son of the Almighty God but you are actually a god? That is the truth. You are actually a god. I know that many people will say that this is blasphemy. However I did not say this or invent it. Jesus Himself said so as written in John 10:34-35. He said that those of us to whom the Word of God came are gods. This includes you. This is the dominion Scripture of the saints. This means that you are not just an ordinary human being any longer but a spirit being; you are a god and you should see yourself as a god.

> *Jesus answered them, Is it not written in your law, I said, Ye are gods?*
>
> *If he called them gods, unto whom the word of God came, and the scripture cannot be broken;*
> **John 10:34-35**

Who you are in Christ

Therefore you don't have to fear under any situation. This is what the devil does not want you to know because he knows that once you know this and the spirit of this dominion Scripture enters into you then your dominion on earth is sure. You are supposed to be reigning as a god and a king over every circumstance of life that you come across. You are a god. That is what the Scriptures said in Psalm 82:6. Just like God made Moses a god to Pharaoh in Exodus 7:1, He has also made you a god to all your enemies and adversaries. Therefore you have been given the power to reign over them, have dominion over them and subdue them through your commands. Whenever you command them believe that they must obey your commands.

> *I have said, Ye are gods; and all of you are children of the most High.*
> **Psalm 82:6**

> *And the LORD said unto Moses, See, I have made thee a god to Pharaoh: and Aaron thy brother shall be thy prophet.*
> **Exodus 7:1**

You have that authority now therefore use it to claim your freedom from all the forces of darkness. With the Spirit of God that is now living in you, which you have received by faith according to Galatians 3:14 no enemy or circumstance has any power over you anymore. This is because you have been given a mouth and wisdom which they cannot gainsay or resist. That is what Jesus said in His promise to you in Luke 21:15.

Living a supernatural life (Volume 3)

> *That the blessing of Abraham might come on the Gentiles through Jesus Christ; that we might receive the promise of the Spirit through faith.*
>
> **Galatians 3:14**

> *For I will give you a mouth and wisdom, which all your adversaries shall not be able to gainsay nor resist.*
>
> **Luke 21:15**

To make sure that you can live and reign as a god over all the circumstances, adversaries and enemies of your life God has also made you a partaker of His divine nature. That is what He made us to see through Peter in 2 Peter 1:4. This means that your feelings, your thoughts, your views and the basis for any action that you take should be brought in line with that of God. By so doing you have also become partakers of His holiness. That is what we now know from what is written in Hebrews 12:10.

> *Whereby are given unto us exceeding great and precious promises: that by these ye might be partakers of the divine nature, having escaped the corruption that is in the world through lust.*
>
> **2 Peter 1:4**

> *For they verily for a few days chastened us after their own pleasure; but he for our profit, that we might be partakers of his holiness.*
>
> **Hebrews 12:10**

Who you are in Christ

If you are a partaker of His divine nature and you are a partaker of His holiness then it follows that you have what it takes to be god to your adversaries and to all your circumstances and situations.

This then is a summary of who you are in Christ. This is who God says that you are in Christ. Do you believe that you are who God says that you are in Christ? If you do, then start acting who you are in Christ from today and start confessing who you are in Christ as follows on the next three pages:

THIS IS WHO I AM IN CHRIST

"I am a child of Abraham. The blessing of Abraham are mine. I am a Temple of God. The Spirit of God lives in me. ANYTHING that defiles my body, God will destroy it whether it originates from a physical being or a spirit being.

Because I am not born of blood but I am now born of the Spirit it follows that I am a spirit-being. As a spirit-being my ways and my actions cannot be discerned by anybody therefore the forces of darkness can no longer truncate my destiny since they cannot discern my actions. They can only see the effects of my actions. I am begotten of God so the wicked one can no longer touch me. Therefore I am insulated from the wicked. Since I am not born of blood and I am not born of the will of man but of the will of God it follows therefore that I do not need to suffer from the blood diseases that the people born of blood suffer from. Instead because I am born of God I have overcome the world and its diseases and I got this victory through my faith in the work of redemption of our Lord Jesus Christ.

God my Father is Light therefore I am a child of Light. Because like begets like it follows therefore that I am light and consequently darkness can no longer hang around me. I am not of the night or darkness anymore. Wherever I am darkness must give way and the light must shine forth. The forces of darkness must give way wherever I am. I cannot be inconsequential anywhere I am.

Who you are in Christ

I am not only born of the Spirit I am actually a son of God because I have been empowered to become one. Therefore I am entitled to all the privileges and benefits of a son of God.

I am entitled to provision, protection, defense, teaching and advice from God, who is now my Father and from His Spirit who now lives in me and I am getting these on a continuous basis every day. I have actually been predestinated to be adopted as a son of God by Jesus Christ according to the good pleasure of God's will. I know and I am convinced that I am a son of God because I am led by the Spirit of God. The Spirit Himself beareth witness with my spirit that I am a son of God.

I have been washed cleaned and sanctified. I am a vessel unto honour sanctified, set apart and meet for Christ's use and I am prepared unto every good work. I am sanctified and set apart by the Holy Ghost, the Spirit of our God.

I am also a king and a priest unto my Father God and I am reigning here on earth. Therefore I cannot suffer here on earth. Because I am reigning, I have the power, the dominion and the control over all the circumstances of life that comes my way. As a king, I reign by my words and I have been given a mouth to speak out words and commands that no adversary can resist. Therefore when I give orders and commands they have to be obeyed because where the word of a king is there is power and nobody can say what sayest thou to me.

Living a supernatural life (Volume 3)

As a king I also reign by wisdom and Christ who is the wisdom of God and the power of God now lives in me and He has been made wisdom unto me. Therefore I have the wisdom of God and the power of God available to me with which to reign. I have all the necessary resources for reigning here on earth. I cannot be enslaved by any force of darkness.

In order that I can reign here on earth I have been given a mouth coupled with the wisdom with which to give orders so that nobody can resist it whenever I give a command. The forces of darkness must be subject to whatever command I give them in the Name of Jesus.

I belong to Christ therefore I am Abraham's seed and an heir according to the promise that God made to Abraham. As an heir there is no difference between me and anybody else who is an heir. I am just as much an heir as any other heir. I am even a joint-heir of God with Christ.

As a son of God I am a child of the Most High and therefore I am a god. I am not just an ordinary human being, I am a god. Like begets like; My Father is God therefore I am a god. Therefore I don't have to fear in any situation. I do not have to fear the fear of men. Neither do I need the pity of anybody." Because I am a god I am now capable of the supernatural since I now have the supernatural powers and attributes of God."

CHAPTER 3

WHAT YOU ARE IN CHRIST

YOU ARE A NEW CREATURE

You are a new creature. That is what we are told by God through Apostle Paul in 2 Corinthians 5:17. The spirit-being that you now are is not a modification or amendment of what you used to be. You are totally recreated. Your old self is dead and passed away, everything is now new. All your old habits should be gone. You are not what the world says you are any longer. You are what the Word of God says you are. This means that you have to change your mindset from what it used to be. You have to believe in the new spirit-being that you are.

> *Therefore if any man be in Christ, he is a new creature: old things are passed away; behold, all things are become new.*
> *2 Corinthians 5:17*

From what we are further told by God through Apostle John and Apostle Paul in 1 John 3:14, Ephesians 2:1,4,5 as well as in Romans 12:2 you can see that as a result of your new life, you have passed from death into life.

Living a supernatural life (Volume 3)

> *We know that we have passed from death unto life, because we love the brethren. He that loveth not his brother abideth in death.*
> **1 John 3:14**

> *And you hath he quickened, who were dead in trespasses and sins;*
>
> *But God, who is rich in mercy, for his great love wherewith he loved us,*
>
> *Even when we were dead in sins, hath quickened us together with Christ, (by grace ye are saved;)*
> **Ephesians 2:1,4,5**

> *And be not conformed to this world: but be ye transformed by the renewing of your mind, that ye may prove what is that good, and acceptable, and perfect, will of God.*
> **Romans 12:2**

The life of God has been imparted to you. God has given you eternal life and this life is in His Son. That is what we are told in 1 John 5:11.

> *And this is the record, that God hath given to us eternal life, and this life is in his Son.*
> **1 John 5:11**

With this new creature that you are, your mind has also been made new. The old you that was weak, sickly, poor and fearful that Satan used to torment is gone.

What you are in Christ

You have been totally recreated in Christ. The new you has the nature of God as we are told in 2 Peter 1:4. You now have the ability of God and the life of God in you because God who is the greater One is now living in you. That is what we can understand from what is written in 1 John 4:4.

> *Whereby are given unto us exceeding great and precious promises: that by these ye might be partakers of the divine nature, having escaped the corruption that is in the world through lust.*
> **2 Peter 1:4**

> *Ye are of God, little children, and have overcome them: because greater is he that is in you, than he that is in the world.*
> **1 John 4:4**

The greater One than he that is in the world is now living in you. This means that God's power is now resident in you. With the divine nature that you now have, you should become bold. This is so because according to the Scriptures in Romans 5:17, you have now been given righteousness as a gift and you are now declared righteous by God. Once you know this boldness will start answering to you because the Scripture says in Proverbs 28:1 that the righteous is as bold as a lion.

> *For if by one man's offence death reigned by one; much more they which receive abundance of grace and of the gift of righteousness shall reign in life by one, Jesus Christ.*
> **Romans 5:17**

Living a supernatural life (Volume 3)

> *The wicked flee when no man pursueth: but the righteous are bold as a lion.*
>
> **Proverbs 28:1**

Therefore you should now be bold. You were weak before but now you are strong. You have become strong through Jesus Christ as you rejoice in the truth that you have been redeemed because according to what is written in the Scriptures in Nehemiah 8:10 as well as in Philippians 4:13 the joy of the Lord is your strength and it is the strength of Jesus Christ that you now use therefore you can now do all things.

> *Then he said unto them, Go your way, eat the fat, and drink the sweet, and send portions unto them for whom nothing is prepared: for this day is holy unto our Lord: neither be ye sorry; for the joy of the LORD is your strength.*
>
> **Nehemiah 8:10**

> *I can do all things through Christ which strengtheneth me.*
>
> **Philippians 4:13**

According to 1 Peter 2:24 God has taken all sicknesses away from you and healed you of all of them therefore the newly created you have become healthy. You have also been enabled to become prosperous because according to 3 John 2 that is God's wish for you now but as you can see from that Scripture your mind must agree with God's wish before God can effect the prosperity in your life. You now have dominion and authority over the devil.

Who his own self bare our sins in his own body on the tree, that we, being dead to sins, should live unto righteousness: by whose stripes ye were healed.

1 Peter 2:24

Beloved, I wish above all things that thou mayest prosper and be in health, even as thy soul prospereth.

3 John 1:2

You are a totally new creature made in the likeness of God, being a partaker of the divine nature of God as we have earlier seen in 2 Peter 1:4.

Whereby are given unto us exceeding great and precious promises: that by these ye might be partakers of the divine nature, having escaped the corruption that is in the world through lust.

2 Peter 1:4

YOU ARE ONE SPIRIT WITH CHRIST

Your body is sanctified by union with Christ's body and you are one Spirit with Christ. That is what we are made to know by what God said through Apostle Paul in 1 Corinthians 6:17.

But he that is joined unto the Lord is one spirit.

1 Corinthians 6:17

Living a supernatural life (Volume 3)

Since you are one Spirit with Christ it follows that Christ dwells in you and you also dwell in Christ and your union with Christ makes you spiritual just as He is spiritual. That is what Jesus Himself said in John 17:21. How can you be One Spirit with Christ and still be in fear of anything? Christ's Spirit that you now have is not a spirit of fear but a Spirit of power, of love and of a sound mind. That is what we are made to see by Apostle Paul in 2 Timothy 1:7.

> *That they all may be one; as thou, Father, art in me, and I in thee, that they also may be one in us: that the world may believe that thou hast sent me.*
> **John 17:21**

> *For God hath not given us the spirit of fear; but of power, and of love, and of a sound mind.*
> **2 Timothy 1:7**

According to Ephesians 1:13 and Ephesians 5:30 you are now sealed with the Holy Spirit of promise together with Christ thereby becoming one Body with Him in which case your bones are now part of His bones and your flesh part of His flesh. You are now in Christ. Think about this, how can you be thus sealed with Christ and still be in any bondage?

> *In whom ye also trusted, after that ye heard the word of truth, the gospel of your salvation: in whom also after that ye believed, ye were sealed with that Holy Spirit of promise,*
> **Ephesians 1:13**

For we are members of his body, of his flesh, and of his bones.
                               Ephesians 5:30

YOU ARE A MEMBER OF THE BODY OF CHRIST

You are a member of the Body of Christ because your body has been sanctified by a union with the Body of Christ. That in essence is what we are again made to see by what God said in both 1 Corinthians 6:15 and also in Ephesians 5:30.

Know ye not that your bodies are the members of Christ? shall I then take the members of Christ, and make them the members of an harlot? God forbid.
                               1 Corinthians 6:15

For we are members of his body, of his flesh, and of his bones.
                               Ephesians 5:30

God is not speaking here of a hypothetical union with Christ. He is talking of a union that has made your flesh to become a member of Christ's flesh and your bones to become members of Christ's bones. Therefore if you are aware of this truth then you will realize that your flesh should no longer harbour any disease since it is a member of God's flesh. Similarly your bones should no longer harbour any disease since they are members of God's bones. When Christ was here on earth there was no record of His being sick.

Living a supernatural life (Volume 3)

Therefore if your body (your flesh and your bones) is now a member of His Body (His flesh and His bones) then it follows that sicknesses should not be able to turn your body into their homes. Do you not know that you have actually been sealed together with Christ and that you are now one with Him? That is what God made us to see through Paul the Apostle in 2 Corinthians 1:22. How can your body be part of His Body and still be harbouring diseases?

> *Who hath also sealed us, and given the earnest of the Spirit in our hearts.*
> **2 Corinthians 1:22**

If you can only know the significance of this union with Christ's Body that you now have your worries will be over. This is so because you will know that whatever may be happening to your body, since it is part of Christ's Body you can be sure that Christ will protect your body. Whatever it may be it cannot manifest any power before Christ who said in Matthew 28:18 that He now has all power in heaven and earth.

> *And Jesus came and spake unto them, saying, All power is given unto me in heaven and in earth.*
> **Matthew 28:18**

Jesus will protect your body since it is part of His own Body. After all, which man will not care for even the least part of his body if it is suffering or being attacked by the enemy? Even if it is the least of his fingers he will care and he will do something about it.

What you are in Christ

If man can be so concerned about even the least part of his body how much more so will Christ be for any part of His Body? Therefore relax and know that nothing can hurt you if you remain in the Body of Christ where you are supposed to be. Your mental attitude now should be that whatever could not attack the Body of Christ and stay there when Christ was here on earth should not be able to attack your body now and stay there. It should not be able to make your body its home. In fact even though you may not even see it yet, however from what God said through Apostle Paul in Romans 8:29 as well as in 1 Corinthians 3:18, you are gradually being made to look like and conform to the image of Christ. You are therefore being changed from glory to glory by the Spirit of God that is now living in you. God Himself had foreknown you and predestinated you to conform to His image of Christ who is the firstborn in the family of God of which you are now a member. As you conform to His image you change from glory to glory by the Holy Spirit that is now resident in you.

> *For whom he did foreknow, he also did predestinate to be conformed to the image of his Son, that he might be the firstborn among many brethren.*
> **Romans 8:29**

> *But we all, with open face beholding as in a glass the glory of the Lord, are changed into the same image from glory to glory, even as by the Spirit of the Lord.*
> **2 Corinthians 3:18**

Living a supernatural life (Volume 3)
YOU ARE A BELOVED OF THE LORD

You are a beloved of the Lord. That is what we know from what God said through John in 1 John 4:11. Because you are a beloved of the Lord you will dwell in safety. That is what God said in Deuteronomy 33:12. Therefore you don't have to worry yourself concerning any evil plan against you because no evil will befall you. Your safety is assured as a beloved of the Lord.

> *Beloved, if God so loved us, we ought also to love one another.*
>
> **1 John 4:11**

> *And of Benjamin he said, The beloved of the L<small>ORD</small> shall dwell in safety by him; and the L<small>ORD</small> shall cover him all the day long, and he shall dwell between his shoulders.*
>
> **Deut. 33:12**

As a beloved of the Lord what God wants above all things for you is that you should prosper and be in health as your soul prospereth. That is what He said through John in 3 John 2. It is obvious therefore that when any problem of sickness or disease surfaces in your life God is not the One behind it. You should now know all the time that what God wants for you is perfect health. Therefore don't let Satan convince you that any sickness or disease that you see in your body is from God. No!

> *Beloved, I wish above all things that thou mayest prosper and be in health, even as thy soul prospereth.*
>
> **3 John 2**

God wants you to prosper and be in good health. Your prospering is top priority for Him but it depends on what your mind accepts. God has already provided prosperity and good health for you but it is left for you to accept it in your mind. You will see that He said through Paul in Ephesians 1:3 that He **has blessed** you (not **will bless**) with **all** spiritual blessings in heavenly places in Christ. But your mind must accept this truth.

Blessed be the God and Father of our Lord Jesus Christ, who hath blessed us with all spiritual blessings in heavenly places in Christ:
Ephesians 1:3

We know that all things are first spiritual before they manifest physically. As we explained in *Chapter 1* of *Volume 1* of this *"Living a supernatural life"* book series even you as a man was first created as a spirit being to start with before God made you to manifest physically by providing a physical body for you to live in. Just as God made the spiritual you to appear physically you can also make the *"all spiritual blessings"* that God has given you to manifest physically when your mind agrees with that statement of God and acts on it. When you do this your prospering cannot be blocked by the devil. Once you receive the prosperity and the health in your soul your prosperity and health in the physical realm is assured. But your mind must be totally in agreement with God on this if it is to become a reality in your life for we can see in Proverbs 23:7 that it is as you think in your mind that you will be.

> *For as he thinketh in his heart, so is he: Eat and drink, saith he to thee; but his heart is not with thee.*
>
> **Proverbs 23:7**

YOU ARE A SAINT

You are sanctified in Christ and called to be a saint just like the Corinthian Christians that Apostle Paul wrote to in 1 Corinthians 1:2.

> *Unto the church of God which is at Corinth, to them that are sanctified in Christ Jesus, called to be saints, with all that in every place call upon the name of Jesus Christ our Lord, both theirs and ours:*
>
> **1 Corinthians 1:2**

Therefore you are a saint. See yourself as a saint and believe that whatever God said of saints now also applies to you. As a saint the Holy Spirit helps you to pray according to the will of God because as written in Roman 8:27 the Spirit makes intercession for the saints according to the will of God.

> *And he that searcheth the hearts knoweth what is the mind of the Spirit, because he maketh intercession for the saints according to the will of God.*
>
> **Romans 8:27**

What you are in Christ

Because you are a saint you know and you can therefore be confident that the Lord will keep your feet from falling. That is the assurance that you have as you can see from what is written in 1 Samuel 2:9. This should give you an assurance of your safety all the time. Anytime anything threatens your safety you should remember that you are a saint of God and that He will keep your feet from falling. You should therefore be confident that no evil can befall you.

> *He will keep the feet of his saints, and the wicked shall be silent in darkness; for by strength shall no man prevail.*
> **1 Samuel 2:9**

Because you are His saint God can never forsake you. He will preserve your soul, He will preserve your way and He will deliver you out of the hands of the wicked. That is what He said concerning His saints through David in Psalm 37:28, Proverbs 2:8 and Psalm 97:10.

> *For the LORD loveth judgment, and forsaketh not his saints; they are preserved for ever: but the seed of the wicked shall be cut off.*
> **Psalm 37:28**

> *He keepeth the paths of judgment, and preserveth the way of his saints.*
> **Proverbs 2:8**

> *Ye that love the LORD, hate evil: he preserveth the souls of his saints; he delivereth them out of the hand of the wicked.*
> **Psalm 97:10**

Living a supernatural life (Volume 3)

As a saint of the Lord you are a member of those chosen ones to whom God has revealed and made manifest the mystery behind redemption. You can see this from what He said through Apostle Paul in Colossians 1:26. You should therefore see yourself as a privileged one specifically chosen by God to be shown the mystery of salvation. Note that it is not everybody that is so privileged to be shown this mystery.

> *Even the mystery which hath been hid from ages and from generations, but now is made manifest to his saints:*
> **Colossians 1:26**

As a saint of God if you praise God you will have the honour of executing vengeance on the heathen and to bind their kings with chains and their nobles with fetters of iron. That is the promise of God to His saints through David in Psalm 149:5-9.

> *Let the saints be joyful in glory: let them sing aloud upon their beds.*
>
> *Let the high praises of God be in their mouth, and a twoedged sword in their hand;*
>
> *To execute vengeance upon the heathen, and punishments upon the people;*
>
> *To bind their kings with chains, and their nobles with fetters of iron;*
>
> *To execute upon them the judgment written: this honour have all his saints. Praise ye the Lord.*
> **Psalm 149:5-9**

YOU ARE A CITIZEN OF THE KINGDOM OF GOD

You are a citizen of the Kingdom of God. You are no more a stranger or a foreigner to God. You are now a fellow citizen of the household of God with the saints. That is what God made us to see by what He said through Paul in Ephesians 2:19 and Hebrews 12:22-23.

> *Now therefore ye are no more strangers and foreigners, but fellowcitizens with the saints, and of the household of God;*
> **Ephesians 2:19**

> *But ye are come unto mount Sion, and unto the city of the living God, the heavenly Jerusalem, and to an innumerable company of angels,*
>
> *To the general assembly and church of the firstborn, which are written in heaven, and to God the Judge of all, and to the spirits of just men made perfect,*
> **Hebrews 12:22-23**

You are now a member of the household of God. That is what God again said through Apostle Paul in Ephesians 2:19. In the Kingdom of God where you now are all the citizens of that Kingdom are kings. That is why God has said through John in Revelation 5:10 that He has made you a king unto Himself.

> *Now therefore ye are no more strangers and foreigners, but fellowcitizens with the saints, and of the household of God;*
>
> **Ephesians 2:19**

> *And hast made us unto our God kings and priests: and we shall reign on the earth.*
>
> **Revelation 5:10**

That is also why Christ your King is called the King of kings in 1 Timothy 6:15. As a citizen of the Kingdom of God you are entitled to all the privileges that accrue to its citizens. Among such privileges are divine provision, divine protection, divine direction and any other thing that will make your life comfortable here on earth. All the resources, authority and power of the Kingdom of God are now available to you to help you to live a victorious and abundant life here on earth. You are now a stranger and a pilgrim to this world. That is what God said through Apostle Peter in 1 Peter 2:11.

> *Which in his times he shall shew, who is the blessed and only Potentate, the King of kings, and Lord of lords;*
>
> **1 Timothy 6:15**

> *Dearly beloved, I beseech you as strangers and pilgrims, abstain from fleshly lusts, which war against the soul;*
>
> **1 Peter 2:11**

But the unfortunate thing is that many Christians live their life as citizens of this world do and they therefore cannot enjoy the benefits of the Kingdom of God to which they now belong.

What you are in Christ

There are many benefits that accrue to you, which you can enjoy right now here on earth as a citizen of that Kingdom. We have discussed some of these benefits in **Chapter 6** of this book titled, *"Where you are in Christ"*

YOU ARE GOD'S ANOINTED

You are God's anointed because from what God said through Paul in 2 Corinthians 1:21 He has anointed you. He also said the same thing through Apostle John in 1 John 2:27.

> *Now he which stablisheth us with you in Christ, and hath anointed us, is God;*
> **2 Corinthians 1:21**

> *But the anointing which ye have received of him abideth in you, and ye need not that any man teach you: but as the same anointing teacheth you of all things, and is truth, and is no lie, and even as it hath taught you, ye shall abide in him.*
> **1 John 2:27**

According to Isaiah 45:1-3 because you are God's anointed the Lord Himself can go before you to make all the crooked ways straight and the Lord can give you the hidden riches of secret places. That is what God will do for His anointed. God will not only do that but according to 1 Samuel 2:10 the Lord will also exalt your horn.

> *Thus saith the LORD to his anointed, to Cyrus, whose right hand I have holden, to subdue nations before him; and I will loose the loins of kings, to open before him the two leaved gates; and the gates shall not be shut;*
>
> *I will go before thee, and make the crooked places straight: I will break in pieces the gates of brass, and cut in sunder the bars of iron:*
>
> *And I will give thee the treasures of darkness, and hidden riches of secret places, that thou mayest know that I, the LORD, which call thee by thy name, am the God of Israel.*
>
> **Isaiah 45:1-3**
>
> *The adversaries of the LORD shall be broken to pieces; out of heaven shall he thunder upon them: the LORD shall judge the ends of the earth; and he shall give strength unto his king, and exalt the horn of his anointed.*
>
> **1 Samuel 2:10**

Because you are God's anointed nobody can stretch forth his hand against you and be guiltless. That is what God made us to see in 1 Samuel 26:9. Because you are God's anointed the Lord will not allow anybody to do you any harm. There is a *"touch- not decree"* upon you as we can see in Psalm 105:14-15.

> *And David said to Abishai, Destroy him not: for who can stretch forth his hand against the LORD'S anointed, and be guiltless?*
>
> **1 Samuel 26:9**

He suffered no man to do them wrong: yea, he reproved kings for their sakes;

Saying, Touch not mine anointed, and do my prophets no harm.
Psalm 105:14-15

Therefore as a truly born-again Christian you should not worry yourself about what people are doing to you. If you only believe in your God you will realize that they can not really hurt you. They may try but you should realize that there is a *"touch-not decree"* upon you. This divine standing order upon your life instructing that you should not be touched nor harmed should give you confidence that no matter what the enemy does he cannot harm you. The Lord will not allow anyone to do you wrong. Because you are God's anointed it follows according to Psalm 2:2-4 that when people set themselves against you the Lord shall laugh at them and set them in derision and from what is also written in Psalm 18:50 you can see that as God's anointed the Lord will always show mercy to you.

The kings of the earth set themselves, and the rulers take counsel together, against the LORD, and against his anointed, saying,

Let us break their bands asunder, and cast away their cords from us.

He that sitteth in the heavens shall laugh: the Lord shall have them in derision.
Psalm 2:2-4

> *Great deliverance giveth he to his king; and sheweth mercy to his anointed, to David, and to his seed for evermore.*
> **Psalm 18:50**

Furthermore from what David said in Psalm 20:6 you can see that as God's anointed the Lord will save you whenever you need help and He will hear you from His holy Heaven whenever you call and will answer you with the saving strength of His right hand because according to what David said in Psalm 28:8 the Lord is your saving strength.

> *Now know I that the Lord saveth his anointed; he will hear him from his holy heaven with the saving strength of his right hand.*
> **Psalm 20:6**

> *The LORD is their strength, and he is the saving strength of his anointed.*
> **Psalm 28:8**

As God's anointed the Lord has ordained a lamp for you. The Lord will clothe your enemies with shame but your crown will flourish. That is what David said in Psalm 132:17-18. No doubt therefore that as the anointed of God there can no longer be any yoke upon you. This is because as God made us to understand through Isaiah in Isaiah 10:27 the yoke shall be destroyed by the anointing and your enemy's burden shall be taken off your shoulder and his yoke from off your neck.

> *There will I make the horn of David to bud: I have ordained a lamp for mine anointed.*

His enemies will I clothe with shame: but upon himself shall his crown flourish.
Psalm 132:17-18

And it shall come to pass in that day, that his burden shall be taken away from off thy shoulder, and his yoke from off thy neck, and the yoke shall be destroyed because of the anointing.
Isaiah 10:27

YOU ARE GOD'S CHOSEN

You are chosen of God. You have been chosen in Christ even before the foundation of the world to be holy and without blame before God in love. God has chosen and predestinated you to be adopted as His son. That is what Apostle Paul made us to see by what he wrote in Ephesians 1:4-5. In truth just like God said of Jeremiah in Jeremiah 1:5, God had separated you and chosen you right from your mother's womb and called you by His grace. You should always remember this truth.

According as he hath chosen us in him before the foundation of the world, that we should be holy and without blame before him in love:

Having predestinated us unto the adoption of children by Jesus Christ to himself, according to the good pleasure of his will,
Ephesians 1:4-5

> *Before I formed thee in the belly I knew thee; and before thou camest forth out of the womb I sanctified thee, and I ordained thee a prophet unto the nations.*
>
> **Jeremiah 1:5**

YOU ARE THE SALT OF THE EARTH

You are the salt of the earth. That is what Jesus Himself called you in Matthew 5:13. As a salt of the earth it means that wherever you are you impart flavour and you spice the place.

> *Ye are the salt of the earth: but if the salt have lost his savour, wherewith shall it be salted? it is thenceforth good for nothing, but to be cast out, and to be trodden under foot of men.*
>
> **Matthew 5:13**

As a salt you are also a preservative of that which is good. You are a preservative of the values and the dignity of the creation of God. As a salt sorrow and depression must be far from you.

YOU ARE A LIGHT

You are the light of the world. That is what Jesus also called you in Matthew 5:14.

> *Ye are the light of the world. A city that is set on an hill cannot be hid.*
>
> **Matthew 5:14**

Wherever there is light even if it is dim darkness must give way therefore darkness and all the forces of darkness should not hang around you any longer if you really know that *you are light* in Christ. Wherever you are they must feel very uncomfortable. You are supposed to be shining here on this earth therefore no darkness should be able to cover your light. You are like a city set on a hill, which cannot be hidden. This means that you can no longer be hidden. This also means that you are supposed to be a pacesetter and you have to be recognized wherever you go as a leader and someone to be followed. You are light and a child of Light. You cannot be suppressed or repressed any longer. Wherever you are you must be relevant and you must excel. Your presence must be recognized anywhere you go. Wherever you find yourself people must know that you are there because wherever you are you must make impact there because light cannot be hidden. Wherever you pass through people must know that someone has gone through the place. As a light you are born to be outstanding. Anywhere you pass through the tracks of your footprints must be visible.

Therefore nobody should be able to sideline you. No! Not even the devil. If your achievement is below this level then you are not achieving the destiny that God has ordained for you. Therefore you must change your mindset so that you can attain the destiny that God has ordained for you. You are a light therefore wherever you are you must be shining and the forces of darkness must be in subjection to you there. In fact they must leave if they know that you really know what you are and the authority that you have and they are sure that you are ready to use that authority.

Living a supernatural life (Volume 3)

You are not only shining but according to what Paul the Apostle wrote in 1 Corinthians 6:11 you are now also justified therefore you are supposed to shine more and more.

> *And such were some of you: but ye are washed, but ye are sanctified, but ye are justified in the name of the Lord Jesus, and by the Spirit of our God.*
> **1 Corinthians 6:11**

This is so because since you are justified you are now **"the just"** and if you are **"the just"** then you are actually supposed to be shining more and more everyday unto the perfect day. That is what the Scriptures say in Proverbs 4:18.

> *But the path of the just is as the shining light, that shineth more and more unto the perfect day.*
> **Proverbs 4:18**

This means that every day of your life must now be better than the previous day. All your tomorrows must be better than your todays. This means that your future is bound to be a glorious one. Wherever you are today you must believe that you will be better off tomorrow. If that is not happening to you then you need to sit down and re-examine yourself and your mind's alignment to the Word to see if there is need for you to readjust so as to be properly aligned to Christ. This should be your mental attitude. You must believe that every day of your life as you enter a new day must be better than the previous day.

YOU ARE "THE JUST"

As we mentioned in the last section you are *the just* that God is talking about whenever He talks about *the just*. This is so because as we have explained in the last section He said through Paul in 1 Corinthians 6:11 that you are justified in the Name of the Lord Jesus Christ and by the Spirit of our God.

> *And such were some of you: but ye are washed, but ye are sanctified, but ye are justified in the name of the Lord Jesus, and by the Spirit of our God.*
> **1 Corinthians 6:11**

You are justified by faith in Jesus Christ and by the Blood of Jesus Christ having believed the work of redemption done by His Blood. That is what Paul made us to see in Roman 5:1,9. You have not only been justified you have been predestinated and called to be justified and glorified from what God said through Paul in Romans 8:30. Because you are justified, it follows that you have also been glorified. Therefore nothing can reproach you anymore.

> *Therefore being justified by faith, we have peace with God through our Lord Jesus Christ:*
>
> *Much more then, being now justified by his blood, we shall be saved from wrath through him.*
> **Romans 5:1, 9**

> *Moreover whom he did predestinate, them he also called: and whom he called, them he also justified: and whom he justified, them he also glorified.*
> **Romans 8:30**

But as ***the just*** you must know that you are supposed to live by faith. That is a rule given to ***the just*** written in Romans 1:17. It is the rule that you must follow if you are to live as ***the just*** and you want to enjoy the benefits that God has prepared for ***the just***. As ***the just*** you are not only to live by faith but you are also supposed to walk by faith and not by sight. That is what God commanded you to do in 2 Corinthians 5:7.

> *For therein is the righteousness of God revealed from faith to faith: as it is written, The just shall live by faith.*
> **Romans 1:17**

> *For we walk by faith, not by sight:*
> **2 Corinthians 5:7**

So that you can live and walk by faith God has given you the measure of faith that you require to do these. That is what we can see from what God said through Paul in Romans 12:3.

> *For I say, through the grace given unto me, to every man that is among you, not to think of himself more highly than he ought to think; but to think soberly, according as God hath dealt to every man the measure of faith.*
> **Romans 12:3**

What you are in Christ

The pity of it all is that despite these instructions from God and the measure of faith that they have been given, most Christians are still living by sight allowing the devil to intimidate them by what they can see, taste, smell, hear and feel. They allow the symptoms that the devil brings to dictate their judgments and actions. That is why many of them pray and come out believing that their prayers have not been answered. They want to see evidence of the answer before they believe. Of course as a result of their living by sight through their senses they are unable to reap the benefits that should now be theirs as *"the just"* and they do not get the answers to their prayers. One of the benefits that now accrue to you as *"the Just"* is that your path is as a shining light that shineth more and more everyday until the perfect day. That is what we have seen earlier from what God said through Solomon in Proverbs 4:18. Therefore your today should always be better than your yesterday and your tomorrow should always be better than your today for every day of your life. You go from glory to glory every day. This must be your mindset and if you believe it, so shall it be.

Because you have been justified by faith, you have peace with God through Christ Jesus. No man can lay any charge against you or condemn you any longer because it is God Himself who has justified you. That is what we are made to know by God through Apostle Paul in Romans 5:1

> *Therefore being justified by faith, we have peace with God through our Lord Jesus Christ:*
> **Romans 5:1**

Living a supernatural life (Volume 3)

There is therefore no more condemnation for you before God and no one can lay any charge against you since God has justified you. Every record against you has been wiped out. God reckons nothing against you anymore. That is what we are made to know by Paul in Romans 8:1. All the ordinances against you which were contrary to you have been taken out of the way and nailed to the cross. That is what we are also made to see by what Paul wrote in Colossians 2:14.

> *There is therefore now no condemnation to them which are in Christ Jesus, who walk not after the flesh, but after the Spirit.*
> **Romans 8:1**

> *Blotting out the handwriting of ordinances that was against us, which was contrary to us, and took it out of the way, nailing it to his cross;*
> **Colossians 2:14**

Since God no longer condemns you no one can condemn you anymore because you have been justified by God. You are also saved from the wrath of God. That is what God told us through Apostle Paul in Romans 8:33-34 and Romans 5:9. Therefore do not let Satan torment you by accusing you of sins that you have committed, which you have confessed and which have been forgiven you by God. You must shed all those guilt-conscience that you have so that your communion and fellowship with God will not be impeded.

> *Who shall lay any thing to the charge of God's elect? It is God that justifieth.*

What you are in Christ

Who is he that condemneth? It is Christ that died, yea rather, that is risen again, who is even at the right hand of God, who also maketh intercession for us.
Romans 8:33-34

Much more then, being now justified by his blood, we shall be saved from wrath through him.
Romans 5:9

You must be convinced in your mind of your right-standing with God if you want your prayers to Him to have no hindrance. There are other benefits that accrue to you because you are justified and you have become *"the just"* before God. We shall look at some of the statements made concerning *"the just"* in the Scriptures, which are now true of you. One of such statements is what God said through Solomon in Proverbs 10:6 that the blessings of God are now upon your head.

Blessings are upon the head of the just: but violence covereth the mouth of the wicked.
Proverbs 10:6

The blessings are not only on your head but God will also bless your habitation. That is what He said through Solomon in Proverbs 3:33. Even your memory will be blessed and your children will be blessed after you. That is what He said again through Solomon in Proverbs 10:7 and Proverbs 20:7. In Proverbs 13:22 God made us to know that as *"the just"* the wealth of the sinners is laid up for you. Therefore do not fret.

> *The curse of the LORD is in the house of the wicked: but he blesseth the habitation of the just.*
>
> **Proverbs 3:33**
>
> *The memory of the just is blessed: but the name of the wicked shall rot.*
>
> **Proverbs 10:7**
>
> *The just man walketh in his integrity: his children are blessed after him.*
>
> **Proverbs 20:7**
>
> *A good man leaveth an inheritance to his children's children: and the wealth of the sinner is laid up for the just.*
>
> **Proverbs 13:22**

It follows therefore that as the just you are now entitled to God's blessings. But if you are to get these blessings of God then you must have a good knowledge of the Word. This is so because God said through Apostle Peter in 2 Peter 1:3 that God has given unto you all things that pertain unto life and godliness but it is through the knowledge of Him *(The Word)* that you will get these.

> *According as his divine power hath given unto us all things that pertain unto life and godliness, through the knowledge of him that hath called us to glory and virtue:*
>
> **2 Peter 1:3**

What you are in Christ

Similarly no matter what anybody may be planning or doing against you, since you are now *"the just"* because you have been justified there is an assurance that you will be delivered from it. But again it is through knowledge that you will be delivered for that is what we are made to see by God in Proverbs 11:9 through King Solomon as written below.

> *An hypocrite with his mouth destroyeth his neighbour: but through knowledge shall the just be delivered.*
> **Proverbs 11:9**

Because you are now *"the just"* that God is talking about in the Scriptures you are now also entitled to God's protection. For example God said as written in Psalm 37:12-13 that when the wicked plan evil against you as *"the just"* the Lord will laugh at him and his plan will be frustrated by the Lord. Not only that, when you enter into any trouble there is an assurance that you will come out of the trouble. That is what God made us to see through King Solomon in Proverbs 12:13. In fact, according to the Scriptures in Proverbs 12:21, no evil will happen to you. God has said in Proverbs 24:16 that no matter what you may be going through even if you fall seven times you can rest assured that you will rise again. This is your heritage as *"the just"*.

> *The wicked plotteth against the just, and gnasheth upon him with his teeth.*
>
> *The Lord shall laugh at him: for he seeth that his day is coming.*
> **Psalm 37:12-13**

> *The wicked is snared by the transgression of his lips: but the just shall come out of trouble.*
> **Proverbs 12:13**

> *There shall no evil happen to the just: but the wicked shall be filled with mischief.*
> **Proverbs 12:21**

> *For a just man falleth seven times, and riseth up again: but the wicked shall fall into mischief.*
> **Proverbs 24:16**

As *"the just"* those people or things that attempt to make you inconsequential will themselves become inconsequential. That is what God made us to see in Isaiah 29:20-21. Anyone that tries to deride you, mock you, ridicule you, scorn or put you down will be consumed and brought to nothing by God. This should be your understanding of the type of being that you now are.

> *For the terrible one is brought to nought, and the scorner is consumed, and all that watch for iniquity are cut off:*
>
> *That make a man an offender for a word, and lay a snare for him that reproveth in the gate, and turn aside the just for a thing of nought.*
> **Isaiah 29:20-21**

I know that you may be thinking in your mind that being just must mean that you are an upright and holy person without any sin.

In that case you may be thinking that since you are not sinless these promises of God are not true of you. But God has said in Ecclesiastes 7:20 that there is no just man on earth that doeth good and does not sin. God justified you by grace not because of any good work that you did. Therefore you can rest assured that all of the above promises of God are for you.

> *For there is not a just man upon earth, that doeth good, and sinneth not.*
> **Ecclesiastes 7:20**

YOU ARE RIGHTEOUS

As someone who is justified and as we have seen earlier from what God said through Paul in Romans 5:17 that you are also given freely the gift of the righteousness. The righteousness that you are given is that of Christ. You are supposed to receive this righteousness of God as a gift and once you receive it then you are covered by the righteousness of Christ and you are supposed to be reigning in life. Once you receive it, as far as God is concerned you are righteous and you are supposed to be reigning in life through the Lord Jesus Christ.

> *For if by one man's offence death reigned by one; much more they which receive abundance of grace and of the gift of righteousness shall reign in life by one, Jesus Christ.*
> **Romans 5:17**

Living a supernatural life (Volume 3)

If you do not know that you have been given this righteousness as a gift then you will be struggling to be righteous through your works and you will not be able to reign in this life. You have not only received this righteousness as a gift but you have actually been made the righteousness of God in Christ. That is what we can understand from what God said through Apostle Paul in 2 Corinthians 5:21. If that is true then as a righteous person, your prayers are supposed to avail much with God. You can see this from what Apostle James said in James 5:16.

> *For he hath made him to be sin for us, who knew no sin; that we might be made the righteousness of God in him.*
> **2 Corinthians 5:21**

> *Confess your faults one to another, and pray one for another, that ye may be healed. The effectual fervent prayer of a righteous man availeth much.*
> **James 5:16**

Therefore whenever you pray to God you should have the confidence that since you are using the righteousness of Christ to approach God and not your own because you have none anyway your prayer will be answered by God. Therefore you must jettison any guilt or sin complex when you approach God because those are weights that you must lay aside as advised in Hebrews 12:1 if you want your prayer to be answered.

What you are in Christ

Wherefore seeing we also are compassed about with so great a cloud of witnesses, let us lay aside every weight, and the sin which doth so easily beset us, and let us run with patience the race that is set before us,
Hebrews 12:1

Furthermore as written in Malachi 4:2 we know that Christ is the Sun of righteousness and according to Paul in 1 Corinthians 1:30 Christ has been made to be righteousness unto us.

But unto you that fear my name shall the Sun of righteousness arise with healing in his wings; and ye shall go forth, and grow up as calves of the stall.
Malachi 4:2

But of him are ye in Christ Jesus, who of God is made unto us wisdom, and righteousness, and sanctification, and redemption:
1 Corinthians 1:30

Therefore you do not have to approach God with your own righteousness anymore. You now approach Him with the righteousness of Christ, which has been given to you. When you approach God to ask for any thing now, have the mental attitude that you are doing so with the righteousness of Christ and that God will always honour the righteousness of Christ.

Living a supernatural life (Volume 3)

We have discussed in detail the method of receiving this gift of righteousness in *Chapter 3* of *Volume 1* of this *"Living a Supernatural life"* book series in the section titled *"You are Righteous" on Page 104.*

You are now free. You are Christ's servant. That is what you can see from what Paul said which is written in 1 Corinthians 7:22. From what we are also told in Acts 13:39 you are now justified from all things in Christ. The moment you believed and accepted Christ, you became united with Him. From that point on, His righteousness was imputed unto you and God reckons the righteousness of Christ to you. Therefore you can go to God without any guilt-conscience because you can now approach God with Christ's righteousness. That is what God made us to further see through what Apostle Paul said in Romans 4:11,22-24.

> *For he that is called in the Lord, being a servant, is the Lord's freeman: likewise also he that is called, being free, is Christ's servant.*
> **1 Corinthians 7:22**

> *And by him all that believe are justified from all things, from which ye could not be justified by the law of Moses.*
> **Acts 13:39**

> *And he received the sign of circumcision, a seal of the righteousness of the faith which he had yet being uncircumcised: that he might be the father of all them that believe, though they be not circumcised; that righteousness might be imputed unto them also:*

And therefore it was imputed to him for righteousness.

Now it was not written for his sake alone, that it was imputed to him;

But for us also, to whom it shall be imputed, if we believe on him that raised up Jesus our Lord from the dead;
Romans 4:11,22-24

AS THE RIGHTEOUS THE FOLLOWINGS ARE TRUE OF YOU

1. It shall be well with you because the Scripture says that in Isaiah 3:10. Therefore no matter what happens you should relax and know that it shall be well with you.

   Say ye to the righteous, that it shall be well with him: for they shall eat the fruit of their doings.
   Isaiah 3:10

2. Your salvation is of the Lord, He is your strength in time of trouble. He will save you and deliver you from the wicked because you trust Him. That is what the God says in Psalm 37:39-40 about you as a righteous person.

Living a supernatural life (Volume 3)

But the salvation of the righteous is of the LORD: he is their strength in the time of trouble.

And the LORD shall help them and deliver them: he shall deliver them from the wicked, and save them, because they trust in him.
Psalm 37:39-40

3. Your fervent prayers can now avail much because the Scripture says so in James 5:16. Therefore you can rest assured that when you pray fervently it can move mountains. Jesus even said in Matthew 17:20 that if you will only say that the mountain should move and not doubt what you say in your mind it must move. For you, if you have the righteousness-complex instead of the guilt-complex it will be easy to give such a command and not doubt in your mind that your command will be obeyed. It is this complex of unworthiness that is making most Christians to have doubts in their mind as to whether their prayer has been answered or not when they pray. If you must have the assurance of answer to your prayer then it is imperative therefore that you approach God with a righteousness-complex.

Confess your faults one to another, and pray one for another, that ye may be healed. The effectual fervent prayer of a righteous man availeth much.
James 5:16

And Jesus said unto them, Because of your unbelief: for verily I say unto you, If ye have faith as a grain of mustard seed, ye shall say unto this mountain, Remove hence to yonder place; and it shall remove; and nothing shall be impossible unto you.
Matthew 17:20

4. Whenever you cry the Lord hears and delivers you because that is what the God said in Psalm 34:17 through David. Therefore you should know that when you cry to the Lord He hears you and since He said through Apostle John in 1 John 5:15 that if you know that He hears you then you can rest assured that He has given you what you desired of Him. Your problem therefore is to know that He hears you and as a righteous man that is now settled. It is obvious therefore that as a righteous man whenever you cry unto the Lord you will get whatever you ask of Him since you know that He hears you.

   The righteous cry, and the LORD heareth, and delivereth them out of all their troubles.
   Psalm 34:17

   And if we know that he hear us, whatsoever we ask, we know that we have the petitions that we desired of him.
   1 John 5:15

5. According to Psalm 34:19-20 you will have many afflictions but the Lord will deliver you from **them all** and He will keep your bones so that not one of them will be broken.

Therefore no matter what afflictions may come your way you should rest assured that you will be delivered from them all. They cannot overcome you. They will come but the Lord will not allow them to overcome you. As a believer in Christ if this does not give you confidence I cannot imagine what else will do.

Many are the afflictions of the righteous: but the LORD delivereth him out of them all.

He keepeth all his bones: not one of them is broken.
Psalm 34:19-20

6. Because you are righteous, the Lord will never suffer you to be moved. That is what He said through David in Psalm 55:22. Therefore you must know that you are on a solid ground. Nothing can move you. God is your refuge and He will protect you. If you can only believe this and act on it you will not have to worry anymore about all those problems that Satan brings your way. That is a promise of protection for you by God. You must have the mind that no matter what may be happening to you the Lord is there to protect you.

Cast thy burden upon the LORD, and he shall sustain thee: he shall never suffer the righteous to be moved.
Psalm 55:22

What you are in Christ

7. As a righteous man, your horn shall be exalted. You will flourish like the palm tree and grow like the cedars of Babylon. That is what God said through King David in Psalm 75:10 and in Psalm 92:12. Therefore your success is assured in anything that you lay your hands upon. Looking at these statements of God concerning the righteous it should be obvious to you that you are on a much more solid ground than you had thought. God has imputed His righteousness to you it follows therefore that all the promises and statements concerning the righteous are now true of you. That should be your mental attitude all the time. It is imperative that your mind must be fixed on these truths.

   All the horns of the wicked also will I cut off; but the horns of the righteous shall be exalted.
   Psalm 75:10

   The righteous shall flourish like the palm tree: he shall grow like a cedar in Lebanon.
   Psalm 92:12

8. As a righteous man you must know that no wicked man can lay his hands on you and get away with it. The Scripture says in Psalm 125:3 that the rod of the wicked shall not rest upon the righteous. Therefore you should rest assured that you are safe and that no oppressive force can put you in any form of bondage.

   For the rod of the wicked shall not rest upon the lot of the righteous; lest the righteous put forth their hands unto iniquity.
   Psalm 125:3

Living a supernatural life (Volume 3)

9. As a righteous man you cannot lack wisdom because the Scripture says in Proverbs 2:7 that the Lord layeth up sound wisdom for you. Therefore you only need to ask for wisdom from God and you will have it. In fact according to Paul the Apostle in 1 Corinthians 1:24,30 Christ who is the wisdom of God is now living in you and He has been made wisdom unto you. Therefore the wisdom of God is at your disposal. How can you have the wisdom of God available to you and still be operating in the realm of the foolish? If that is the case then it must be either that you have not yet received this gift of righteousness or you have not allowed this wisdom of God that is now living in you to manifest His full potential.

He layeth up sound wisdom for the righteous: he is a buckler to them that walk uprightly.
　　　　　　　　　　　　　　　　Proverbs 2:7

But unto them which are called, both Jews and Greeks, Christ the power of God, and the wisdom of God.

But of him are ye in Christ Jesus, who of God is made unto us wisdom, and righteousness, and sanctification, and redemption:
　　　　　　　　　　　　　　　1 Corinthians 1:24,30

10. Whatever you desire of the Lord shall be granted to you because you are righteous. That is what God made us to understand from what He said through Solomon in Proverbs 10:24. Therefore you must be very confident that your request will be granted when you ask God for anything.

The fear of the wicked, it shall come upon him: but the desire of the righteous shall be granted.
Proverbs 10:24

You should no longer be one of those who believe that their prayers have not been answered when they pray. If you have the righteousness mentality you will know that all your prayers or requests to God will be answered. This is so because as you can see above the Lord will grant you whatever you desire of Him. Therefore pray with the mentality of someone that is sure to be answered. Therefore ask with confidence.

11. When enemies plan against your children, even though they may join hands against them, your children will be delivered. That is what God promised you as a righteous man in Proverbs 11:21. Therefore even the safety of your family is taken care of by God if you are one of those Christians who have accepted His gift of righteousness. This means that as a man now declared righteous by God His protection is not only for you but even for your family. It is not only that God will frustrate the plans of the wicked against your children and deliver them but He will also make sure that the wicked people that plan against your children will not go unpunished. Therefore you don't have to plan and scheme your own revenge. Let God avenge for you.

Though hand join in hand, the wicked shall not be unpunished: but the seed of the righteous shall be delivered.
Proverbs 11:21

12. Now that you are righteous, when afflictions come and the enemies are all over you, there is a place of refuge that the Lord has prepared for you. That place of refuge is the Name of the Lord for He said in Proverbs 18:10 that the Name of the Lord is a strong tower for you as a righteous man, when you come against any opposition or attacks of the enemy if you run into this tower as a righteous man you will be saved no matter what comes up against you. This is a great promise for you because what God is saying here is that His Name is your protection. All you have to do when trouble comes is to call upon the Name of the Lord and you will be saved. We have discussed the importance and use of the Name of the Lord in ***Chapters 3 and 4*** of the ***Volume 2*** of this ***"Living a supernatural life"*** book series.

The name of the LORD is a strong tower: the righteous runneth into it, and is safe.
Proverbs 18:10

13. As a righteous man you cannot be defeated in any situation. You may fall once or twice or even many more times but that is not the end of the matter for you. God has promised you in Proverbs 24:17 that even if you fall seven times you will rise up again.

Rejoice not when thine enemy falleth, and let not thine heart be glad when he stumbleth:
Proverbs 24:17

What you are in Christ

14. As a righteous man you cannot fear under any situation. Fear is no longer a problem to you because He told you through Paul in 2 Timothy 1:7 that you no longer have the spirit of fear. Therefore as He said through King Solomon in Proverbs 28:1 you should be as bold as a lion since you are no longer troubled by any guilt-conscience. The fact that you know that God considers you righteous should give you boldness when you approach Him.

For God hath not given us the spirit of fear; but of power, and of love, and of a sound mind.
2 Timothy 1:7

The wicked flee when no man pursueth: but the righteous are bold as a lion.
Proverbs 28:1

15. Because you are righteous anybody that causes you to go astray shall fall into his own pit. That is what God promised you in Proverbs 28:10. Therefore you must know that nobody can deceive or trick you into making a mistake and get away with it. He is bound to fall into his own trap. This should embolden you when you come against all kinds of scheming and tricks of the enemy planned against you and you should know that such schemers and tricksters against you will lose.

Whoso causeth the righteous to go astray in an evil way, he shall fall himself into his own pit: but the upright shall have good things in possession.
Proverbs 28:10

16. As a righteous man no doubt many afflictions will be trying to overtake you and many will rise up against you but as advised in Isaiah 51:7 you should not fear the reproach of men or be afraid of their reviling. You know that in the end it will come to nothing. This is because the Lord has also promised you through Isaiah in Isaiah 54:14 that you will be far from oppression and that you will not fear any terror for it will not come near you. He also said that when people gather against you, they will fall for your sake. He went on to say in Isaiah 54:17 that no weapon fashioned against you shall prosper and any tongue that rises up in judgment against you will be condemned by you.

Hearken unto me, ye that know righteousness, the people in whose heart is my law; fear ye not the reproach of men, neither be ye afraid of their revilings.
Isaiah 51:7

In righteousness shalt thou be established: thou shalt be far from oppression; for thou shalt not fear: and from terror; for it shall not come near thee.
Isaiah 54:14

No weapon that is formed against thee shall prosper; and every tongue that shall rise against thee in judgment thou shalt condemn. This is the heritage of the servants of the LORD, and their righteousness is of me, saith the LORD.
Isaiah 54:17

Note here that it is you who will have to condemn those tongues that rise up in judgment against you. These are great promises that should build up your confidence no matter what the opposition may be. No wonder the Scripture says as we have seen earlier in Proverbs 28:1 that the righteous is as bold as a lion. How can you have all these promises to fall back upon and not be as bold as a lion? With the assurance that there is peace between you and God and that God is holding nothing against you it is now possible for you to approach God with a clear conscience without any guilt-complex. You should be free to approach God to ask boldly for anything that you want and your mind should be at rest having total assurance that you will be answered. The righteousness of Christ that you have been given should embolden you to come before God without any guilt-conscience to ask for whatsoever you want from Him. These are all yours because you are now righteous. The Righteousness of Christ has all these rewards yet God gave it to us freely. Accept this free gift!

YOU ARE HOLY

We have noted previously that you are a temple of God and the temple of God is holy therefore you are meant to be holy. That is what God said through Apostle Paul in 1 Corinthians 3:16-17. I know that most Christians believe that holiness is beyond them and that it is for God alone. But I am not saying this on my own here. I am telling you what the Word of God says.

> *Know ye not that ye are the temple of God, and that the Spirit of God dwelleth in you?*

Living a supernatural life (Volume 3)

> *If any man defile the temple of God, him shall God destroy; for the temple of God is holy, which temple ye are.*
> **1 Corinthians 3:16-17**

If you are a temple of God then you can rest assured that whatever defiles you will be destroyed by God for that is what He promised in the Scripture above. I am surprised that many Christians see things such as diseases defiling their bodies that are supposed to be temples of God and they get afraid and just virtually yield to the disease when God has already promised them that He will deal with such defilers of their bodies Himself. If you are not convinced that you are supposed to be holy then look at the following as a further proof of this. Jesus Christ is the true vine and you are now a branch of the vine. Christ who is the lump of the vine is holy and since the tree is holy the branches of which you are one are also holy. Therefore you are holy. That is what we can infer from what Apostle Paul wrote in Romans 11:16. God chose you in Christ before the foundation of the world that you should be holy and without blame before Him in love. Therefore you are chosen to be holy. That is what Paul the Apostle wrote in Ephesians 1:4.

> *For if the firstfruit be holy, the lump is also holy: and if the root be holy, so are the branches.*
> **Romans 11:16**

> *According as he hath chosen us in him before the foundation of the world, that we should be holy and without blame before him in love:*
> **Ephesians 1:4**

What you are in Christ

Sin is the main thing that can stop you from being holy but as written in 1 John 3:9 your new nature as one born of God does not sin because His seed remains in you. When you consider this together with what is written in Hebrews 12:10 as well as in 1 Thessalonians 5:27 you will see that you are now a partaker of God's holiness; You are a partaker of the heavenly calling and you are a member of the people that God referred to as holy brethren therefore you are supposed to be holy. You now belong to a holy nation of God and you are supposed to be showing forth the praises of God. That is what God made us to see by what He said through Peter in 1 Peter 2:9.

> *Whosoever is born of God doth not commit sin; for his seed remaineth in him: and he cannot sin, because he is born of God.*
> **1 John 3:9**

> *For they verily for a few days chastened us after their own pleasure; but he for our profit, that we might be partakers of his holiness.*
> **Hebrews 12:10**

> *I charge you by the Lord that this epistle be read unto all the holy brethren.*
> **1 Thessalonians 5:27**

> *But ye are a chosen generation, a royal priesthood, an holy nation, a peculiar people; that ye should shew forth the praises of him who hath called you out of darkness into his marvellous light:*
> **1 Peter 2:9**

Living a supernatural life (Volume 3)

You are holy. That is why you have been called a member of the Holy nation in 1 Peter 2:9 above. The One who has called you is holy and has instructed you to be holy therefore you can be holy. That is what we know through Peter in 1 Peter 1:15.

> *But as he which hath called you is holy, so be ye holy in all manner of conversation;*
> **Peter 1:15**

YOU ARE AN HEIR OF GOD

You are an heir of God through Christ. You are an heir of all that God is and all that God has. That is what God made us to know through Paul in Galatians 4:7. You are not only an heir you are a joint-heir of God with Christ. As a joint-heir with Christ it does not mean that you are sharing the estate proportionately with Christ. What it means is that both you and Christ have access to and own the whole estate together. This means that you now have a birthright to whatever God owns. You are therefore entitled to all the power and resources that the Father has. You are now a partaker of His glory. This again was also made known to us by Paul the Apostle in Romans 8:17.

> *Wherefore thou art no more a servant, but a son; and if a son, then an heir of God through Christ.*
> **Galatians 4:7**

What you are in Christ

And if children, then heirs; heirs of God, and joint-heirs with Christ; if so be that we suffer with him, that we may be also glorified together.
Romans 8:17

Peter also made us to understand in 1 Peter 3:9 that you have been called to inherit a blessing not a curse, therefore you have no inherited curse. That is no longer your portion since you are in Christ. Many Christians of nowadays claim that they are being tormented by all types of afflictions which they claim are as a result of curses that had been pronounced on them or on their ancestors. But God is telling you here that you have inherited a blessing and not a curse. Get this Scriptural image of yourself. It should be your mental attitude all the time. You must believe that you cannot inherit a curse and that your portion now can only be blessings.

Not rendering evil for evil, or railing for railing: but contrariwise blessing; knowing that ye are thereunto called, that ye should inherit a blessing.
1 Peter 3:9

You should believe that you can never be under any curse. As a truth according to Galatians 3:13-14 Christ has redeemed you from the curse of the Law therefore you no longer have to suffer from the curse of the Law. As someone who is justified by grace, you are made an heir according to the hope of eternal life. As an heir you are now entitled to everything that God has in His kingdom.

> *Christ hath redeemed us from the curse of the law, being made a curse for us: for it is written, Cursed is every one that hangeth on a tree:*
>
> *That the blessing of Abraham might come on the Gentiles through Jesus Christ; that we might receive the promise of the Spirit through faith.*
>   **Galatians 3:13-14**

That is why He said in 1 Corinthians 3:21-23 that *all* things are yours now since He owns all things and you are now one in union with Him. You also belong to Him. If *all* things are yours then it follows that you cannot suffer from lack anymore. If you are suffering from lack then it means that you do not know the truth that since you now belong to Christ *all* things are yours because Christ owns all things.

> *Therefore let no man glory in men. For all things are yours;*
>
> *Whether Paul, or Apollos, or Cephas, or the world, or life, or death, or things present, or things to come; all are yours;*
>
> *And ye are Christ's; and Christ is God's.*
>   **1 Corinthians 3:21-23**

How can you be an heir of the God who owns all things in heaven and in earth and who says He has given you all things and still lack anything?

Note that He also said in Ephesians 1:3 that He has blessed you with *all* spiritual blessings in heavenly places in Christ Jesus. He said with *all* not with *some.*

> ***Blessed be the God and Father of our Lord Jesus Christ, who hath blessed us with all spiritual blessings in heavenly places in Christ:***
> **Ephesians 1:3**

So how can you be an heir of all that God, who owns all things in earth and in heaven, has and be blessed with *all* spiritual blessings in the heavenly realm and still be suffering from lack in this earthly physical realm? It must be that you don't know that *all* things are first spiritual or appear in the spiritual realm before they manifest in the physical realm. For example the house in which you are currently sitting down to read this book was first a spiritual object or design in somebody's mind before it was brought to appear in the physical realm through the effort of some people.

Therefore when God says that He has given you *all spiritual blessings* what He is saying is that you have been blessed with *all things* spiritually but you have to make them to manifest physically through the use of your faith and work. You need to do the works of faith to direct your faith towards any particular blessing that you want to appear physically. Once you do this you can get the blessing to become a physical reality. You are an heir of God. You have been blessed with *all* things. You only need to know how to draw the blessing with your faith from God's spiritual bank in heaven.

Living a supernatural life (Volume 3)

Because you are an heir of salvation one of your great heritages is that you have the angels of God to minister to your needs. Angels are supposed to minister to you. That is what God has made known to you from what is written in Hebrews 1:13-14.

> *But to which of the angels said he at any times, Sit on my right hand, until I make thine enemies thy footstool?*
>
> *Are they not all ministering spirits, sent forth to minister for them who shall be heirs of salvation?*
>
> **Hebrews 1:13-14**

Therefore as of right you can send the angels of God to minister to your needs. Where the need arises you can even send for as many as twelve legions of angels, that is seventy two thousands angels, to come to your aid just as Jesus said that He could do in Matthew 26:53. I said this because according to what Jesus said also in John 20:21 He says that He is sending you to the world as He was sent by the Father, which means that you are entitled, to whatever help He was entitled to when He came. Therefore if He could call for the services of that many angels it means that you too can do the same.

> *Thinkest thou that I cannot now pray to my Father, and he shall presently give me more than twelve legions of angels?*
>
> **Matthew 26:53**
>
> *Then said Jesus to them again, Peace be unto you: as my Father hath sent me, even so send I you.*
>
> **John 20:21**

What you are in Christ

From what God said through Paul in Colossians 1:12 He has made you meet to be a partaker of the inheritance of the saints in light. You were predestinated to obtain this inheritance in Jesus Christ. That again was made known by Apostle Paul in Ephesians 1:11. But what assets are you an heir to? You should try to find out the contents of the will to which you are heir. Some elements of the will are what we covered in this book.

> *Giving thanks unto the Father, which hath made us meet to be partakers of the inheritance of the saints in light:*
> **Colossians 1:12**

> *In whom also we have obtained an inheritance, being predestinated according to the purpose of him who worketh all things after the counsel of his own will:*
> **Ephesians 1:11**

Finally from what God said through Paul the Apostle in Galatians 3:28-29, you belong to Christ, You are Abraham's seed and you are an heir according to the promise that God made to Abraham. Note that as an heir there is no difference between you and anybody else who is an heir. You are just as much an heir as any other heir. Therefore you are entitled to have whatever support any other Christian has. But it all depends on your mindset.

> *There is neither Jew nor Greek, there is neither bond nor free, there is neither male nor female: for ye are all one in Christ Jesus.*

Living a supernatural life (Volume 3)

> *And if ye be Christ's, then are ye Abraham's seed, and heirs according to the promise.*
>
> **Galatians 3:28-29**

YOU ARE A VICTOR

You are a victor. You are a conqueror. You are even more than a conqueror through Christ who loves you. That is what you can see from Romans 8:37. Also from 1 John 5:4-5 you can see that nothing can defeat you anymore if you know who you really are in Christ. In any battle you should come out the winner. This is so because your winning is already assured. You have already won the battle before it even starts. What God is letting you know here is that every battle that you will have to fight in life is a fixed battle in which the winner is already fixed to be you. This means that you are not supposed to loose any battle. Therefore you have no cause to be anxious about any battle that you may be currently going through or fighting. You are bound to come out the winner unless of course you ignorantly decide to throw in the towel. It is fixed.

> *Nay, in all these things we are more than conquerors through him that loved us.*
>
> **Romans 8:37**

> *For whatsoever is born of God overcometh the world: and this is the victory that overcometh the world, even our faith.*

> *Who is he that overcometh the world, but he that believeth that Jesus is the Son of God?*
>
> **1 John 5:4-5**

Because you are now born of God you are not expecting victory, you already have victory because you have already overcome the world. What this means is that even though you may be currently fighting a battle and you can even see the scars of the battle you need not worry yourself because you are already living the victory and enjoying it. The Scriptures says and it is written in 1 John 4:4 that you have already won because the One living in you now is greater than the one in this world. Therefore you cannot loose.

Ye are of God, little children, and have overcome them: because greater is he that is in you, than he that is in the world.
                              1 John 4:4

YOU ARE AN AMBASSADOR FOR CHRIST HERE ON EARTH

You are an ambassador for Christ here on earth. That is what you can see from what Paul the Apostle wrote as written in 2 Corinthians 5:20. You cannot be appointed to be an ambassador for a kingdom that you are not a citizen of. So it follows therefore that since you have been made an ambassador of heaven here on earth you must be a citizen of the Kingdom of God. This is confirmed by what Paul wrote in Ephesians 2:19. As an ambassador of heaven here on earth you cannot suffer in this your host kingdom because your home Kingdom will not allow that. You can see this from what happens here on earth. You cannot find an ambassador of any country suffering in the host country. No country will allow its ambassador to suffer.

Living a supernatural life (Volume 3)

> *Now then we are ambassadors for Christ, as though God did beseech you by us: we pray you in Christ's stead, be ye reconciled to God.*
> **2 Corinthians 5:20**

> *Now therefore ye are no more strangers and foreigners, but fellowcitizens with the saints, and of the household of God;*
> **Ephesians 2:19**

In Proverbs 13:17 God said something through King Solomon that we have to take cognizance of as an ambassador. He said that *a faithful ambassador is health.*

> *A wicked messenger falleth into mischief: but a faithful ambassador is health.*
> **Proverbs 13:17**

Because you are now an ambassador it follows therefore that if you are faithful in your job then you are health personified, which means that you cannot even be sick at all. You are not allowed to be sick for how can health falls sick? How can health be praying for healing or to be healed? Therefore it is very important that you find out what you have to do to be a faithful ambassador so that you can be health personified. You should remember that you are no longer of this world. As an ambassador of Heaven here on earth you have the backing of the resources of heaven to tackle all your problems here on earth. Whatever needs you may have now will be met from the resources of heaven. Your home Kingdom will meet your needs. You ought to find out how you have been sent. So how did God send you into this world as an ambassador?

What you are in Christ

What was your letter of credence that shows that you are now sent by the Kingdom of God? In John 20:21 Jesus said that He has sent you to the world just as the Father sent Him when He came. This means that you are sent by Jesus Christ just as the Father sent Him. Therefore once you know how Jesus was sent you can know how you have been sent.

> *Then said Jesus to them again, Peace be unto you: as my Father hath sent me, even so send I you.*
>
> **John 20:21**

From what is written in Luke 1:31-33 as well as in Revelation 22:16 you can see that Jesus was sent to reign and to be a star here on earth and He reigned and shined. Therefore you are also sent to reign here on earth. Jesus was sent to be a star, a bright and morning star. Therefore since you are sent as He was sent it follows that you should be shining as a bright star here on earth.

> *And, behold, thou shalt conceive in thy womb, and bring forth a son, and shalt call his name JESUS.*
>
> *He shall be great, and shall be called the Son of the Highest: and the Lord God shall give unto him the throne of his father David:*
>
> *And he shall reign over the house of Jacob for ever; and of his kingdom there shall be no end.*
>
> **Luke 1:31-33**

Living a supernatural life (Volume 3)

I Jesus have sent mine angel to testify unto you these things in the churches. I am the root and the offspring of David, and the bright and morning star.
Revelation 22:16

Since you are sent as Jesus was sent the same power that backed Jesus up is backing you up. Therefore potentially you are just as loaded with power as Jesus was because you are now operating from the same source with Him. You are now driven by the same power that was driving Him. Whatever Jesus could handle you also have the potential to handle now because God is the One that is actually working in you. That is what we are made to see in Philippians 2:13.

For it is God which worketh in you both to will and to do of his good pleasure.
Philippians 2:13

Jesus said in Matthew 26:53 as we have noted earlier that if the need arose He could send to the Father and ask for more than twelve legions of angels to come to His aid and they would be sent instantly. Because you are sent as He was sent you are entitled to what He was entitled to. Therefore should the need arise you too can also pray to our Father and He will give you instantly more than twelve legions of angels *(that is 72,000)* to come and fight on your behalf just like Jesus said of Himself. As we have discussed earlier you are now an heir of the Kingdom therefore according to what God made us to see in Hebrews 1:13-14 angels are supposed to be ministering to you.

> *Thinkest thou that I cannot now pray to my Father, and he shall presently give me more than twelve legions of angels?*
> **Matthew 26:53**

> *But to which of the angels said he at any times, Sit on my right hand, until I make thine enemies thy footstool?*
>
> *Are they not all ministering spirits, sent forth to minister for them who shall be heirs of salvation?*
> **Hebrews 1:13-14**

Jesus said in John 15:5-7 that He is the vine and you are a branch. Therefore you are operating from the same tap root that Jesus operated from. As long as you abide in Jesus you will bear much fruit because whatever you ask of God you will get.

> *I am the vine, ye are the branches: He that abideth in me, and I in him, the same bringeth forth much fruit: for without me ye can do nothing.*
>
> *If a man abide not in me, he is cast forth as a branch, and is withered; and men gather them, and cast them into the fire, and they are burned.*
>
> *If ye abide in me, and my words abide in you, ye shall ask what ye will, and it shall be done unto you.*
> **John 15:5-7**

Living a supernatural life (Volume 3)

As an ambassador of the Kingdom of God the Kingdom of God is actually in you. You will find this difficult to believe but it is true. Therefore wherever you go here on earth the influence of the Kingdom of God automatically extends to the place and as long as you are there it represents an embassy of the Kingdom of God here on earth. Therefore such a place becomes a part of the territory and property of the Kingdom of God. The embassies of countries here on earth have diplomatic immunity and protection against any atrocities in their host countries. Similarly wherever you are at any particular time becomes an embassy of the Kingdom of God here on earth and is out of bound to the devil if you know your right as an ambassador. The devil and his forces of the kingdom of darkness have no jurisdiction over such a place. Therefore we can say that on earth here you have what we can refer to as a heavenly derived diplomatic immunity. This means that as an ambassador of the Kingdom of God here on earth, you should be immune from the teething problems and afflictions of this kingdom of darkness. Therefore you should not suffer from the afflictions that are buffeting the citizens of this world. You have absolute protection from your home Kingdom when you seek first and foremost the interests and things of your home Kingdom provided that you are faithful as an ambassador of your home Kingdom here on earth. As written in Matthew 6:33 Jesus said that if you seek first the things of your Kingdom here on earth all other things will be added unto you. In order to do this successfully you have to seek and get the righteousness of God, which you have been given as a gift because you require this righteousness in order to be a faithful ambassador of the Kingdom of God.

What you are in Christ

But seek ye first the Kingdom of God, and his righteousness; and all these things shall be added unto you.
Matthew 6:33

But the problem with most Christians is that it is those things, which are to be added that they seek first and completely neglect the things of their own Kingdom and its righteousness. Many do not even know that they have been given and they are to receive righteousness as a gift. They are trying to work for it.

As an ambassador of the Kingdom of God you represent and speak for your home Kingdom of God therefore whatever you say here on earth, the authority of your home Kingdom of God that you now represent is backing you up. Your words in this kingdom of darkness in which you are as an ambassador should always represent the views and opinions of your home Kingdom. You should never speak of your own or act on your own but you should express the views of your home Kingdom and act as directed by your home Kingdom through the Holy Spirit who directs you and intimates you of the views of your home Kingdom of God. That was what Jesus Christ did when He was sent as He made us to know in John 12:49-50, as well as in John 5:19 and John 5:30. Since you are sent as He was sent you are supposed to act as He did. But the trouble with most Christians today is that they don't wait for the Holy Spirit to direct their views and opinions. They just form their views and opinions based on what their senses dictate to them.

> *For I have not spoken of myself; but the Father which sent me, he gave me a commandment, what I should say, and what I should speak.*
>
> *And I know that his commandment is life everlasting: whatsoever I speak therefore, even as the Father said unto me, so I speak.*
> **John 12:49-50**
>
> *Then answered Jesus and said unto them, Verily, verily, I say unto you, The Son can do nothing of himself, but what he seeth the Father do: for what things soever he doeth, these also doeth the Son likewise.*
> **John 5:19**
>
> *I can of mine own self do nothing: as I hear, I judge: and my judgment is just; because I seek not mine own will, but the will of the Father which hath sent me.*
> **John 5:30**

Satan knows this and that is why he tries to control their senses by supplying them with his own images and pictures so as to control their views, opinions and even thoughts. For example when people see symptoms of diseases on a person, in this kingdom of darkness where you are now serving as an ambassador the people of this kingdom of darkness normally say that such a person is sick. But the view of your own Kingdom that you now represent here on earth is that such a person cannot be sick since he had been healed already.

What you are in Christ

Whoever has that symptom has been healed more than two thousand years ago by the stripes that Jesus took when He died for our sins and carried our diseases as we are told by God through Peter in 1 Peter 2:24. That is the view of your home Kingdom and that is the view that you must express. This means that no matter what sickness a man can have as far as you are concerned in your Kingdom he has been healed of the sickness even before he got sick. As an ambassador of the Kingdom of Heaven you also have to express the policy of your home Kingdom to them in this kingdom of darkness.

> *Who his own self bare our sins in his own body on the tree, that we, being dead to sins, should live unto righteousness: by whose stripes ye were healed.*
> **1 Peter 2:24**

A major policy of your home Kingdom which has been handed over and committed to you is the policy of reconciliation as is written in 2 Corinthians 5:19 by Paul the Apostle, which is shown below.

> *To wit, that God was in Christ, reconciling the world unto himself, not imputing their trespasses unto them; and hath committed unto us the word of reconciliation.*
> **2 Corinthians 5:19**

It is obvious therefore that if you are to be a successful ambassador that the Scripture refers to as a faithful ambassador then your link with your heavenly country or Kingdom must be intact.

Living a supernatural life (Volume 3)

There must be no communications gap between you and your home Kingdom. You must be receiving instructions and information from your home Kingdom. You must also be sending your requests and information back to your home Kingdom on a daily basis. You must know the opinion of your home Kingdom about every issue and situation that you come across in the place where you are serving as ambassador so that you can communicate this to your host kingdom. That is how to be a faithful ambassador.

It is so that this communication link between you and your home Kingdom will not break that you have been given the Holy Spirit who is living inside you. That is the basic work of the Holy Spirit as stated by Jesus in John 14:16-17, John 15:26 and John 16:13-14.

> *And I will pray the Father, and he shall give you another Comforter, that he may abide with you for ever;*
>
> *Even the Spirit of truth; whom the world cannot receive, because it seeth him not, neither knoweth him: but ye know him; for he dwelleth with you, and shall be in you.*
> **John 14:16-17**
>
> *But when the Comforter is come, whom I will send unto you from the Father, even the Spirit of truth, which proceedeth from the Father, he shall testify of me:*
> **John 15:26**

What you are in Christ

Howbeit when he, the Spirit of truth, is come, he will guide you into all truth: for he shall not speak of himself; but whatsoever he shall hear, that shall he speak: and he will shew you things to come.

He shall glorify me: for he shall receive of mine, and shall shew it unto you.
John 16:13-14

As a citizen of the Kingdom of Heaven your citizenship comes freely with power, authority, peace, joy and eternal life. If you use these you have the capacity to live an abundant life to the maximum here on earth. But if you must enjoy these then your loyalty to your home Kingdom must not be in doubt or questionable. It must be absolute and impeccable. You derive all your power and authority from your home Kingdom and if you attempt to do anything outside the authority of your home Kingdom then you are on your own. Come to think of it God must have placed much trust in you to be able to say that you should be representing His interests here on earth. Now He said in Luke 12:48 that to whom much is given much is expected. Therefore having put so much trust in you God will be expecting much from you also.

But he that knew not, and did commit things worthy of stripes, shall be beaten with few stripes. For unto whomsoever much is given, of him shall be much required: and to whom men have committed much, of him they will ask the more.
Luke 12:48

YOU ARE PECULIAR

You are peculiar. You are a member of the chosen generation. You are of the royal priesthood. You belong to a holy nation. You have obtained the mercy of God. You belong to the holy priesthood. That is what you can see from what Apostle Peter said in 1 Peter 2:9-10. As a priest you have a privilege and immediate access to God in Jesus Christ and you can intercede for others before God. You belong to an elect race. That should give you confidence and make you bold.

> *But ye are a chosen generation, a royal priesthood, an holy nation, a peculiar people; that ye should shew forth the praises of him who hath called you out of darkness into his marvellous light:*
>
> *Which in time past were not a people, but are now the people of God: which had not obtained mercy, but now have obtained mercy.*
> **1 Peter 2:9-10**

From what Apostle Paul wrote in Romans 12:2 it is obvious that you are being transformed outwardly by the inward renewing of your mind and as this is happening you will see that you are no longer fashioned according to this world because your thoughts will no longer be determined by what is happening around you but by the Word of God. Apart from this you can also see from what Paul wrote in Colossians 3:10 that you are being made new into the likeness of God your creator in knowledge and you will see that your mind is being brought into conformity with that of God on a daily basis.

What you are in Christ

> *And be not conformed to this world: but be ye transformed by the renewing of your mind, that ye may prove what is that good, and acceptable, and perfect, will of God.*
> **Romans 12:2**

> *And have put on the new man, which is renewed in knowledge after the image of him that created him:*
> **Colossians 3:10**

It is obvious therefore that you belong to a peculiar creed of people who are already citizens of the Kingdom of God. You cannot believe all that the Scripture says that you are and not agree that you must be peculiar.

YOU ARE A SWEET SAVOUR OF JESUS CHRIST

You are unto God a sweet savour of Jesus Christ. This means that it is Jesus Christ that God smells in you. God sees you through Jesus Christ. That is what Paul the Apostle made us to realize from what he wrote through inspiration in 2 Corinthians 2:15.

> *For we are unto God a sweet savour of Christ, in them that are saved, and in them that perish:*
> **2 Corinthians 2:15**

Living a supernatural life (Volume 3)

Therefore when you stand before God to pray or ask for anything you should realize this because it will help you to know that God is not seeing your own righteousness, because you have none anyway. What God sees is the righteousness of Jesus Christ that is covering you and therefore to God you are just as righteous as Christ before Him. That is the way God sees you now through Christ. You are now one with Christ and Christ sees you as His brother. You are gradually being conformed to Christ's image who is the firstborn in your new family, the family of God. That is what the Scriptures confirm as written by Paul in Hebrews 2:11 and Romans 8:29.

> *For both he that sanctifieth and they who are sanctified are all of one: for which cause he is not ashamed to call them brethren,*
> **Hebrews 2:11**

> *For whom he did foreknow, he also did predestinate to be conformed to the image of his Son, that he might be the firstborn among many brethren.*
> **Romans 8:29**

The first time the Scriptures talked of the Lord smelling a sweet savour was in Genesis 8:21. This was after the flood in Noah's time when Noah built an altar and made sacrifices unto the Lord. When the Lord smelt the sweet savour then it moved Him to make a promise not to curse the ground anymore for man's sake. That was what led Him to make the Covenant promise written in Genesis 8:22 that while the earth remaineth, seedtime and harvest, and cold and heat, and summer and winter, and day and night shall never cease.

And the LORD smelled a sweet savour; and the LORD said in his heart, I will not again curse the ground any more for man's sake; for the imagination of man's heart is evil from his youth; neither will I again smite any more every thing living, as I have done.
Genesis 8:21

While the earth remaineth, seedtime and harvest, and cold and heat, and summer and winter, and day and night shall not cease.
Genesis 8:22

In fact it was what led God to make the Covenant in Genesis Chapter 9 with Noah and with his seed after him in Genesis 9:9-17.

And I, behold, I establish my covenant with you, and with your seed after you;

And with every living creature that is with you, of the fowl, of the cattle, and of every beast of the earth with you; from all that go out of the ark, to every beast of the earth.

And I will establish my covenant with you; neither shall all flesh be cut off any more by the waters of a flood; neither shall there any more be a flood to destroy the earth.

And God said, This is the token of the covenant which I make between me and you and every living creature that is with you, for perpetual generations:

> *I do set my bow in the cloud, and it shall be for a token of a covenant between me and the earth.*
>
> *And it shall come to pass, when I bring a cloud over the earth, that the bow shall be seen in the cloud:*
>
> *And I will remember my covenant, which is between me and you and every living creature of all flesh; and the waters shall no more become a flood to destroy all flesh.*
>
> *And the bow shall be in the cloud; and I will look upon it, that I may remember the everlasting covenant between God and every living creature of all flesh that is upon the earth.*
>
> *And God said unto Noah, This is the token of the covenant, which I have established between me and all flesh that is upon the earth.*
> **Genesis 9:9-17**

Therefore as you can see when God smelt a sweet savour it pleased Him so much that it provoked Him to make a Covenant with man. Because you are now a sweet savour of Christ unto God your fellowship with God should please God so much that even if it will not provoke Him to make a Covenant promise to you it should at least provoke Him to remember you for good and remember the Covenant promises that He has made for your protection, your prosperity, your fruitfulness and guidance..

What you are in Christ

That should be your mindset concerning your relationship with God. That you are a sweet savour of Jesus Christ unto God means that you are now sweet incense unto God acceptable and well pleasing to God. This means that you have become acceptable unto God. That was what He promised concerning the sweet savour of the Israelites of the flesh in Ezekiel 20:41. Their sweet savour invoked God's mercy and change of heart towards them. You are an Israelite after the spirit. As an Israelite after the spirit His promise also stands for your sweet savour, which should also invoke God's mercy towards you.

> *I will accept you with your sweet savour, when I bring you out from the people, and gather you out of the countries wherein ye have been scattered; and I will be sanctified in you before the heathen.*
> **Ezekiel 20:41**

Because you are born of God, you are supposed to love all others that are born of God regardless of their race, country, denomination or background. Love is part of the nature of Christ that is now your portion as you can see in 1 John 4:7. You are now a partaker of the divine nature of God therefore you are supposed to behave like God. This means that love which is one the attributes of God should now be your attribute also.

> *Beloved, let us love one another: for love is of God; and every one that loveth is born of God, and knoweth God.*
> **1 John 4:7**

Living a supernatural life (Volume 3)

This then is a summary of what you are in Christ. This is what God says that you are in Christ. Do you believe that you are what God says that you are in Christ? If you do, then start acting what you are in Christ from today on. Start living what you are in Christ. Start using these characteristics that are now yours in your day-to-day life and start confessing as follows on the next eight pages:

THIS IS WHAT I AM IN CHRIST

"I am a new creation, a spirit-being. The spirit-being that I am is not a modification or amendment of what I used to be. No! I am totally recreated. My old self is dead and passed away, everything is now new. As a result of my new life, I have passed from death unto life. The life of God has been imparted to me. With this new creation that I am, my mind has also been made new. I now have a new mind, the mind of Christ. My spiritual rebirth is complete because I am born of God, I am born of Christ and I am born of the Holy Spirit. Therefore every member of the Trinity manifestations of God was involved in my spiritual rebirth. Because I am born of the Spirit, therefore I am a spirit being.

I am also a habitation of God through the Spirit. This means that God lives in me. Therefore my body can no longer harbour diseases. It cannot harbour God and at the same time harbour diseases. I received the Spirit of God through faith. I am one spirit with Christ.

My body is a member of Christ. My flesh is a member of His flesh and my bones are members of His bones. Therefore my flesh and my bones cannot harbour any disease. Sickness can no longer rule in my body.

I am gradually being made to look like and conform to the image of Christ from glory to glory by the Spirit of the Lord who is in me. God had foreknown me and predestinated me to conform to His image even before I was created.

Living a supernatural life (Volume 3)

I am beloved of the Lord. Therefore as a beloved of the Lord I shall dwell in safety. Though I walk through the valley of the shadow of death I know that I am safe. I am a saint. I am called to be a saint. I am no more a stranger or a foreigner to God. I am now a fellow citizen of the household of God with the saints. I am now a stranger and a pilgrim to the world.

God has anointed me. I am God's anointed. Because I am God's anointed nobody can stretch forth his hand against me and be guiltless. He will be guilty before God. Because I am God's anointed, the Lord will go before me to make all the crooked ways straight and the Lord will give me the hidden riches of secret places. Because I am God's anointed, the Lord will not allow anybody to do me harm.

I am chosen of God. I have been chosen in Christ before the foundation of the world to be holy and without blame before God in love. Therefore God will not allow any harm to come to me. I am not only chosen of God He actually separated me right from my mother's womb and called me by His grace.

I am the salt of the earth. As a salt of the earth wherever I am, I impart flavour and spice it up. I am also a preservative of that which is good. I am a preservative of the values and the dignity of the creation of God.

I am the light of the world. I am shinning on this earth. I cannot be hidden. I am a city set on a hill, which cannot be hidden. Therefore I am supposed to be a pacesetter. I have to be recognized wherever I go as someone to be followed.

What you are in Christ

I cannot be suppressed or repressed. Wherever I am the forces of darkness must leave. I am born to be outstanding. I am not only shining but I am shining more and more everyday unto the perfect day. I am a labourer together with God. I am God's husbandry. I am God's building. Therefore God will defend and protect me. God is my manager and He is the One guarding me.

I am justified in the Name of the Lord Jesus Christ and the Spirit of our God. I am justified by faith in Jesus Christ and by the Blood of Jesus Christ having believed the work of redemption done by His Blood. Therefore I am "The Just". I have been predestinated to be called, justified and glorified. Because I am justified it follows therefore that I have also been glorified. Therefore nothing can reproach me anymore. Because I am justified I know that I am supposed to live by faith and not by my senses, symptoms or my experiences.

As "the Just" my path is as a shining light that shinneth more and more every day until the perfect day. Therefore my today will always be better than my yesterday and my tomorrow will always be better than my today. I go from glory to glory and from victory to victory everyday. Because I have been justified by faith, I have peace with God through Christ Jesus. No man can lay any charge against me or condemn me because it is God Himself who has justified me.

As someone who is justified, God has freely imputed the righteousness of Christ to me. I received this righteousness of God as a gift. Therefore God sees me as righteous. Therefore I am righteous.

Living a supernatural life (Volume 3)

As the righteous I am supposed to be reigning in life through the Lord Jesus Christ. I have been made the righteousness of God in Christ. Because I am righteous, my prayers now avail much with God since I am using God's righteousness and not my own because I have none of my own. Christ is the Sun of righteousness to me because He has been made to be righteousness unto me. God no longer sees my own righteousness because I now reflect the righteousness of Christ, which has been imputed to me and it is this righteousness of Christ that God sees when I approach Him.

The moment I believed and accepted Christ, I became united with Him and from that point on, God reckons the righteousness of Christ to me. Therefore I can now go to God without any guilt-conscience because when I go to God I now approach Him with the righteousness of Christ.

There is no more condemnation for me before God and no one can lay any charge against me since God has justified me. Every record against me has been wiped out. God reckons nothing against me anymore. God has blotted out every handwriting of ordinances that were against me, which was contrary to me. He took them out of my way and nailed them to the Cross. Since God no longer condemns me no one can condemn me. Because I have been justified by God I am also saved from the wrath of God. I am free. I am Christ's servant. In Christ, I am justified from all things.

I am a temple of God and the temple of God is holy therefore I am supposed to be holy. Jesus Christ is the true vine and I am a branch of the vine.

Christ who is the lump of the vine is holy and since the tree is holy the branches of which I am one are also holy. Therefore I am holy. God chose me in Christ before the foundation of the world that I should be holy and without blame before Him in love. Therefore I am chosen to be holy. My new nature as one born of God does not sin. I am a partaker of God's holiness. I am a partaker of the heavenly calling and I am a member of the holy brethren therefore I am holy. The One who has called me is holy and He called me to be holy therefore I can be holy. I am supposed to be holy because I am a member of the Holy Priesthood built up as a spiritual house by God.

I am an heir of God through Christ. I am an heir of all that God is and all that God has. I am a joint-heir of God with Christ. Because I am now born of God I have a birthright to whatever God owns. I am therefore entitled to all the power and resources that the Father has. Because I am an heir of salvation, angels are supposed to minister to me. As of right I can ask for the services of as many as seventy two thousand angels of God to minister to my needs.

God has made me meet to be a partaker of the inheritance of the saints in light. I was predestinated to obtain this inheritance in Jesus Christ. I have been called to inherit a blessing not a curse, therefore I have no inherited curse. That is no longer my portion since I am in Christ. As someone who is justified by grace, I am made an heir according to the hope of eternal life.

Living a supernatural life (Volume 3)

As an heir I am now entitled to everything that God has in His Kingdom. That is why He said that all things are mine now since He owns all things and I am now one in union with Him.

Jesus Christ is the vine and I am a branch of the vine. Therefore I am operating from the same tap root that Jesus operated from. As long as I abide in Jesus I will bear much fruit because whatever I ask of Christ shall be done for me.

I am more than a conqueror through Christ who loves me. Nothing can defeat me. In any battle I will come out the winner no matter who the opponent is. This is so because my winning is already assured. I have already won the battle and overcome the opposition before it even starts. I am not expecting victory because my faith in the victory, which Jesus has already won, is my victory. I am already living the victory and enjoying it.

I am an ambassador for Christ here on earth. Once I am a faithful ambassador faithful to my home Kingdom, then I am health personified in which case I cannot be sick since health cannot be sick. How can health falls sick? I am no longer of this world. As an ambassador here I now have the backing of the resources of Heaven to tackle all my challenges here on earth. Whatever needs I may have now will be met from the resources of Heaven. I am sent by Jesus Christ just as the Father sent Him. He was sent to be a star and to reign therefore I shall reign here on earth and I will be a star. The same power that backed Jesus up is backing me up. Therefore I am just as loaded with power as Jesus was because I am now operating from the same source with Him.

What you are in Christ

I am now driven by the same power that was driving Him. Whatever Jesus could handle I too can now also handle because He is the One that actually works in me. Because I am sent as Jesus was sent I can pray to my Father God if the need arises and He will give me instantly more than twelve legions of *(7200)* angels to come and fight on my behalf just like Jesus said of Himself.

I am peculiar. I am of the chosen generation. I am of the royal priesthood. I belong to a holy nation. I have obtained the mercy of God. I am a priest unto God. As a priest I have a privilege of immediate access to God in Jesus Christ and I can intercede for others before God. I belong to an elect race. I am one with Christ and Christ sees me as His brother. I am now conformed to Christ's image who is the firstborn in our family, the family of God. I am being transformed outwardly by the inward renewing of my mind so that I am no longer fashioned according to this world. My thoughts are not determined by what is happening around me but by the Word of God.

I am being made new into the likeness of God my creator in knowledge. My mind is being brought into conformity with that of God on a daily basis. I am unto God a sweet savour of Jesus Christ. It is Jesus Christ that God sees and smells in me. God now sees me through Jesus Christ so when I approach God for anything I have the assurance that He hears me and therefore that I have received what I requested of Him.

Living a supernatural life (Volume 3)

Because I am now born of the Spirit my ways, my movements and also my destiny cannot be found out, tampered with or blocked by anything or anybody. This is because my ways are past finding out. I am not in the flesh anymore but in the Spirit. I no longer think, feel, live and act in the flesh. I think, feel, live and act in the Spirit. Because I am born of God, the seed of God remains in me, and therefore I cannot be sinning as a habit. The new nature of God that I now have imparted to me makes the habitual practice of sin impossible for me now.

Because I am born of God, doing righteousness has become my habitual practice. Because I am born of God, I love all others that are born of God regardless of their race, country, denomination or background. Because I am born anew, I have said earlier that old things are passed away, all things are become new. This means that my old thoughts, old ideas, old choices, old purposes, old affections and old goals are gone away and I now have new thoughts, new ideas, new choices, new purposes, new affections and new goals, which are more in line with God's. Because I am a son of God, He has sent the Spirit of His Son into my heart.

Finally as I have said earlier I am a god. Just like God made Moses a god to Pharaoh, He has made me a god to all my enemies and my adversaries, therefore I am given the power to reign over them and subdue them through my commands. They have no power over me. This is so because the dominion that God gave man, which man lost through Adam has now been restored by Jesus to man. I received the Spirit of God that is now living in me through faith."

CHAPTER 4

WHAT YOU HAVE IN CHRIST

YOU HAVE THE MARKS OF JESUS CHRIST

You have the marks of Jesus Christ in your body. Because you bear these marks of Jesus Christ in your body no man should trouble you anymore. You can see this from what Paul said in Galatians 6:17 concerning himself. What he said of himself is also true of you. These marks are the proofs that you belong to Jesus Christ. They could be physical marks that you have received as a result of the afflictions that you have passed through in the service of our Lord Jesus Christ. On the other hand they could also be spiritual marks, which the devil and all others in the spiritual world can see and recognize. When they see such marks they know that whoever has such marks belongs to the Kingdom of light and they know that they have no power over such a person. Such marks establish the *"touch not"* decree, which King David referred to in Psalm 105:15.

Living a supernatural life (Volume 3)

> *From henceforth let no man trouble me: for I bear in my body the marks of the Lord Jesus.*
> **Galatians 6:17**

> *Saying, Touch not mine anointed, and do my prophets no harm.*
> **Psalms 105:15**

As soon as you are born-again you are branded by Christ so that wherever you go it will be seen that you belong to Christ. Therefore whatever enemy wants to afflict you such an enemy will know that you belong to someone and will be careful not to touch you except with the permission of God to whom you now belong. It was for this reason that Satan had to first ask for God's permission in Job 1:10-12 before he could afflict Job.

> *Hast not thou made an hedge about him, and about his house, and about all that he hath on every side? thou hast blessed the work of his hands, and his substance is increased in the land.*
>
> *But put forth thine hand now, and touch all that he hath, and he will curse thee to thy face.*
>
> *And the LORD said unto Satan, Behold, all that he hath is in thy power; only upon himself put not forth thine hand. So Satan went forth from the presence of the LORD.*
> **Job 1:10-12**

What you have in Christ

From the above Scriptures you can see that Satan recognized that Job had a hedge of God's protection around him, around his house and around all that he had. Satan knew that he could not break the hedge except with the permission of God who built the hedge. In order to break the hedge what he did was to plant fear in the mind of Job so that Job can speak out words that will break the hedge as in Job 1:5 below.

> *And it was so, when the days of their feasting were gone about, that Job sent and sanctified them, and rose up early in the morning, and offered burnt offerings according to the number of them all: for Job said, It may be that my sons have sinned, and cursed God in their hearts. Thus did Job continually.*
>
> **Job 1:5**

You can see the consequences of what fear brings from Job's negative confessions by what Job himself said in Job 3:25-26.

> *For the thing which I greatly feared is come upon me, and that which I was afraid of is come unto me.*
>
> *I was not in safety, neither had I rest, neither was I quiet; yet trouble came.*
>
> **Job 3:25-26**

It is the same thing that is happening to you today. God has also given you a hedge of protection around you, your house and all that you have.

Living a supernatural life (Volume 3)

The various promises of God to you including these characteristics that come with the new identity and status that He has now given you are the hedge of protection that He has built around you, around your house and around all that you have. Satan cannot break that hedge without God's permission. Even after that you will have to use your own mouth or action to break it before Satan can enter and do you any harm.

Whenever you say or do anything that contradicts what God has said about you then you are breaking the hedge that God has built around you. The Bible says in Ecclesiastes 10:8 that whoever breaks a hedge a serpent would bite him. Therefore if you allow your hedge to be broken the serpent, the devil, will come in and bite you.

> *He that diggeth a pit shall fall into it; and whoso breaketh an hedge, a serpent shall bite him.*
> **Ecclesiastes 10:8**

What Satan does to get you to break your hedge is that he brings thoughts of fear and doubts into your mind. He does this mainly through your senses. When he brings such thoughts, which contradicts God's promises if you accept them and start to confess them with your own mouth then you have used your own mouth to break the hedge of protection that God has built around you. You then leave the gap open for Satan to come in and afflict you. So whatever Satan is doing to you must have been consciously or unconsciously permitted by you.

What you have in Christ

That is why it is very important that you do not make any confession out of fear and you should jettison fear out of your mind because just like it happened to Job as he said in Job 3:25 which we have looked at earlier whatever you fear will come upon you. No matter what Satan brings to you via your senses or thoughts you don't have to fear anymore because you no longer have the spirit of fear in you but that of power, of love and of a sound mind. That is what we are told by God through Paul in 2 Timothy 1:7.

> *For God hath not given us the spirit of fear; but of power, and of love, and of a sound mind.*
> **2 Timothy 1:7**

YOU HAVE A BUILDING OF GOD

You have a heavenly body to house you waiting for you. This is a house not made with hands, which is eternal and is in the heavens. That is what God told us in 2 Corinthians 5:1 through Paul. Jesus also said in John 14:2-3 that He was going back to heaven to prepare a place for us. Therefore it should not be surprising to you that you are told by Paul that you have a building of God waiting for you in the heavens.

> *For we know that if our earthly house of this tabernacle were dissolved, we have a building of God, an house not made with hands, eternal in the heavens.*
> **2 Corinthians 5:1**

> *In my Father's house are many mansions: if it were not so, I would have told you. I go to prepare a place for you.*
>
> *And if I go and prepare a place for you, I will come again, and receive you unto myself; that where I am, there ye may be also.*
>
> **John 14:2-3**

YOU HAVE THE KEYS OF THE KINGDOM

You have the keys of the Kingdom of Heaven. You have been given the keys of the Kingdom of Heaven by Jesus Christ. That is what Jesus Christ promised to give you in Matthew 16:19.

> *And I will give unto thee the keys of the Kingdom of Heaven: and whatsoever thou shalt bind on earth shall be bound in heaven: and whatsoever thou shalt loose on earth shall be loosed in heaven.*
>
> **Matthew 16:19**

With these keys you have the power to bind and loose anything. This means that anything you bind on earth would be bound in Heaven and anything you loose on earth would be loosed in Heaven. What this further means is that you have been given power to effect things in the spiritual realm right from here on earth. These are great weapons given to you in order to be able to put every situation that you find yourself under very cheap control.

What you have in Christ

This is so regardless of whether that situation is a physical or a spiritual situation. Therefore you don't have to be anxious or worry yourself anymore about any situation that is working contrary to you. You have the authority to bind whatever is behind any situation that is working contrary to you. You also have the authority to set loose whatever will make the situation work for your good. You not only have the authority to do these you also have the **keys** with which to effect them. Note that He said *keys* not *key* so there are many of them.

Another thing you should note about this promise of Christ is that it is you who will first bind or loose anything that you want bound or loosed before it is done in Heaven. If you don't bind it here on earth it will not be bound in Heaven. Similarly if you do not loose it here on earth it will not be loosed in Heaven. The binding or loosing of anything starts with you. What you have not bound or loosed don't ask God to bind or loose.

You can therefore see that what God is saying to you here is this, "I have given you power. If you want to bind or loose anything here on earth don't ask me to do it for you. Do it yourself then I will confirm what you have done." But this is not what most Christians do. What they do is ask God to do everything for them. Yes! God can do it but He has transferred the authority for doing this to you. Use this authority and the power of attorney that you have been given to effect the changes that you want to see in the situations around you.

<u>Living a supernatural life (Volume 3)</u>
YOU HAVE A COMFORTER

You have a Comforter, the Holy Spirit, who is the Spirit of truth. Jesus made the promise to send Him to you in His Name in John 14:16-18, John 14:26 and also in John 16:13-15. He said that this Comforter will guide you and teach you. This Spirit will abide with you, dwell with you and be in you forever. He will bring all things that Jesus Christ has taught you to your remembrance and guide you into all truth. Jesus said that this Spirit will teach us ***all things***. This means that there is no topic that you need to be enlightened about that this Spirit cannot handle.

> *And I will pray the Father, and he shall give you another Comforter, that he may abide with you for ever;*
>
> *Even the Spirit of truth; whom the world cannot receive, because it seeth him not, neither knoweth him: but ye know him; for he dwelleth with you, and shall be in you.*
>
> *I will not leave you comfortless: I will come to you.*
>
> John 14:16-18
>
> *But the Comforter, which is the Holy Ghost, whom the Father will send in my name, he shall teach you all things, and bring all things to your remembrance, whatsoever I have said unto you.*
>
> John 14:26

What you have in Christ

Howbeit when he, the Spirit of truth, is come, he will guide you into all truth: for he shall not speak of himself; but whatsoever he shall hear, that shall he speak: and he will shew you things to come.

He shall glorify me: for he shall receive of mine, and shall shew it unto you.

All things that the Father hath are mine: therefore said I, that he shall take of mine, and shall shew it unto you.
John 16:13-15

You have received this Comforter who is the Holy Spirit, the Spirit of truth and He now abides with you, He is supposed to teach you all things and bring all things that Jesus has said, which you have read or heard to your remembrance. He will guide you into all truths and show you the things to come. He will also show you the things that are of God. He lives in you therefore He is with you all the time as a helper and an advocate to give you help and advice especially when you need to defend yourself against the wiles and trials from the enemy. If you are truly born again there can be no doubt that you have received the Holy Spirit and He abides in you and teaches you all things thereby confirming what God promised through Apostle John in 1 John 2:27. But the problem with most Christians is that they do not give the Holy Spirit the room to operate in their lives. They don't even recognize the voice of the Holy Spirit. How then can they listen to Him, whose voice they can not even recognize?

Living a supernatural life (Volume 3)

> *But the anointing which ye have received of him abideth in you, and ye need not that any man teach you: but as the same anointing teacheth you of all things, and is truth, and is no lie, and even as it hath taught you, ye shall abide in him.*
>
> **1 John 2:27**

Such Christians are not directed by the Holy Spirit. Because of this they run from one pitfall in life to another and live an epileptic life unable to take absolute control of their lives. Whenever you are delivered for trial either by accusation or through a burden, an ordeal or an adversity you don't have to think of what to say. What you will say will be given to you that same hour because you are not the one who will do the speaking. The Spirit of your Father who is in you is the One that will normally speak through you if you give Him the chance to do so. That is what Jesus Himself told us that the Holy Spirit will do for us in Matthew 10:19-20 and the Holy Spirit is constantly doing this in your life. Therefore you must be sensitive to the Holy Spirit that now lives in you.

> *But when they deliver you up, take no thought how or what ye shall speak: for it shall be given you in that same hour what ye shall speak.*
>
> *For it is not ye that speak, but the Spirit of your Father which speaketh in you.*
>
> **Matthew 10:19-20**

What you have in Christ

This was the secret behind the success of Jesus' ministry when He came to this world. He never did anything on His own. He listened to the Holy Spirit and followed only the instructions given to Him by the Holy Spirit. That is basically the meaning of what He said in John 5:30.

> *I can of mine own self do nothing: as I hear, I judge: and my judgment is just; because I seek not mine own will, but the will of the Father which hath sent me.*
> **John 5:30**

From what God said through Paul in 1 Corinthians 1:5 and through Apostle John in 1 John 2:20 you can see that you are enriched by Christ in all utterances and in all knowledge through the work of the Holy Spirit who is now abiding in you.

> *That in every thing ye are enriched by him, in all utterance, and in all knowledge;*
> **1 Corinthians 1:5**

> *But ye have an unction from the Holy One, and ye know all things.*
> **1 John 2:20**

Through the work of the Holy Spirit you also have the unction from God that can make all things known to you so that you can no longer be in the dark about any situation. Therefore you now have the right words and the right knowledge for every situation through the work of the Holy Spirit. There can be no more surprises for you anymore.

Living a supernatural life (Volume 3)

With this Spirit living in you it means that you have put on the new man and you can now be renewed and enriched in knowledge and in likeness to God because you now have a heart to know God that He is the Lord. That is what God made us to see through Paul the Apostle in Colossians 3:10 and also through Jeremiah in Jeremiah 24:7.

> *And have put on the new man, which is renewed in knowledge after the image of him that created him:*
> **Colossians 3:10**

> *And I will give them an heart to know me, that I am the LORD: and they shall be my people, and I will be their God: for they shall return unto me with their whole heart.*
> **Jeremiah 24:7**

Another function of the Holy Spirit that should comfort you and give you confidence all the time is that the Holy Spirit also fights your battles for you when the need arises because as written in Isaiah 59:19, whenever the enemy comes surging at you like a flood wanting to engulf you or drown you and it seems as if you are being submerged and overwhelmed, then the Holy Spirit will lift up a standard against the enemy.

> *So shall they fear the name of the LORD from the west, and his glory from the rising of the sun. When the enemy shall come in like a flood, the Spirit of the LORD shall lift up a standard against him.*
> **Isaiah 59:19**

Therefore when you are inundated with all types of afflictions and it looks like you are being overwhelmed; relax! When it looks like you are sinking and defeat is looking imminent; don't worry! When it looks like you are being subdued, trounced and overpowered by the enemy and the enemy is beginning to think that he has conquered or crushed you and that you are vanquished, you don't have to worry yourself. Instead you should be happy and start praising God because you know that it is time for the Holy Spirit to work and lift up the standard against the enemy. After all you know that when the Holy Spirit starts to work no enemy has the ability or capacity to stand against Him and stop Him. Believe me, He has never failed me and He will never fail you if you will only entrust your problems to Him. What the Holy Spirit does is written in Isaiah 59:18. He repays fury to your adversaries and repays recompence to your enemies and He does these at all times for you. So you can always rest assured that no affliction can bow your head unless you decide to bow it yourself. Nothing the enemy does can win against you unless you decide to give up and hand over the victory to the enemy yourself, which is what many Christians are doing.

> *According to their deeds, accordingly he will repay, fury to his adversaries, recompence to his enemies; to the islands he will repay recompence.*
> **Isaiah 59:18**

Jesus never did anything without getting instructions from the Holy Spirit. You should also do the same thing. Get your instructions from the Holy Spirit.

Living a supernatural life (Volume 3)

It will help you to live the abundant life that you are supposed to live here on earth. The Holy Spirit will teach you what to do all the time.

YOU HAVE LIFE
YOU HAVE ETERNAL LIFE

According to 1 John 5:11-13 you have life; you have eternal life. God has given you eternal life and this eternal life is in His Son. Therefore once you have the Son you have eternal life.

And this is the record, that God hath given to us eternal life, and this life is in his Son.

He that hath the Son hath life; and he that hath not the Son of God hath not life.

These things have I written unto you that believe on the name of the Son of God; that ye may know that ye have eternal life, and that ye may believe on the name of the Son of God.
1 John 5:11-13

You have everlasting life because you believe on the Son, Jesus Christ. That is what Jesus Himself has assured us by His statement in John 3:36.

He that believeth on the Son hath everlasting life: and he that believeth not the Son shall not see life; but the wrath of God abideth on him.
John 3:36

What you have in Christ

Therefore the real you, the spirit-being can never die. We are not talking of your body here. That is just the physical house that you are living in and when it can no longer support you, then you will have to leave it and it will go back to dust from which it was made in the beginning. But the real you, the spirit-being cannot die.

It is not only that you cannot die, but your life is now actually hidden with Christ in God. That is what God made us to see in Colossians 3:3. This is because you have already died and risen with Christ and you have been recreated and translated to heaven to be with Jesus Christ. That is what you should understand by what God said in Ephesians 2:5-6.

> *For ye are dead, and your life is hid with Christ in God.*
> **Colossians 3:3**
>
> *Even when we were dead in sins, hath quickened us together with Christ, by grace ye are saved;*
>
> *And hath raised us up together, and made us sit together in heavenly places in Christ Jesus:*
> **Ephesians 2:5-6**

Even though you cannot see your translation physically since it is a spiritual one you should be able to see the effects of the translation just as Jesus explained by what He said in John 3:8. People will not be able to discern what has happened to you but they will see the effects of what has happened to you.

Living a supernatural life (Volume 3)

The wind bloweth where it listeth, and thou hearest the sound thereof, but canst not tell whence it cometh, and whither it goeth: so is every one that is born of the Spirit.
John 3:8

You should realize that we are talking of spiritual things here so the translation that we are talking about is a spiritual translation. You have life. You have eternal life. Christ is your life now. That is what God said through Paul in Colossians 3:4. The One who has conquered death is now your life. He has delivered you from the power of death because He now has the keys of hell and death, having taken the keys from the devil who used to have them. That is what we can see from the combination of what God said through Paul in Hebrews 2:14 and through John in Revelation 1:18. The devil no longer has the keys of hell and death; therefore do not let him harass you pretending to have them. He cannot decide when you die unless you agree to relinquish that authority to him.

When Christ, who is our life, shall appear, then shall ye also appear with him in glory.
Colossians 3:4

Forasmuch then as the children are partakers of flesh and blood, he also himself likewise took part of the same; that through death he might destroy him that had the power of death, that is, the devil;
Hebrews 2:14

What you have in Christ

I am he that liveth, and was dead; and, behold, I am alive for evermore, Amen; and have the keys of hell and of death.
Revelation 1:18

Therefore you should no longer fear death because you know that the real you will never die. You now have eternal life. Death is no longer your problem. You are now divinely protected. In any case you are a spirit-being and your body is just an earth-suit that you are supposed to be wearing while still here on earth in order to be able to interact with this physical environment. A time will come when you will have to change or leave this earth-suit or tabernacle for an eternal suit, your heavenly suit, which is your glorified body just like Apostle Peter said of himself in 2 Peter 1:13-14.

Yea, I think it meet, as long as I am in this tabernacle, to stir you up by putting you in remembrance;

Knowing that shortly I must put off this my tabernacle, even as our Lord Jesus Christ hath shewed me.
2 Peter 1:13-14

But you will never die because death has no more power over you. It can no longer sting you. As is written by Apostle Paul in 1 Corinthians 15:55, you can now say with confidence, *"O death, where is thy sting? O grave, where is thy victory?"* You are a spirit-being and as such to you physical death merely means leaving this your physical body.

> *O death, where is thy sting? O grave, where is thy victory?*
> **1 Corinthians 15:55**

Therefore whether you are in this earthly body or you leave this earthly body, which you call death, should mean nothing to you. Because for you to live in this earthly body is Christ and for you to drop this earthly body which you call death is gain to you since you will then take up your heavenly, glorified body to be with Christ forever. We know this from what Apostle Paul said in Philippians 1:21.

> *For to me to live is Christ, and to die is gain.*
> **Philippians 1:21**

YOU HAVE FREEDOM

You have freedom from the law of sin and death. The law of the Spirit of life in Christ has made you free from the law of sin and death. That is what God made us to know from what He said through Apostle Paul in Romans 8:2. You should no longer walk after the flesh but after the Spirit. You are now free to live and walk in the Spirit. You are no longer the devil's business. You have been bought by God and He washed you clean not for your sake but for His own sake.

> *For the law of the Spirit of life in Christ Jesus hath made me free from the law of sin and death.*
> **Romans 8:2**

What you have in Christ

When you live and walk in the Spirit you will be totally free from the death that sin brings. You now have the power to live above sin and this power to live a holy life comes from the Holy Spirit. The physical constraint that the natural man has does not disturb a man that walks and lives in the Spirit. You have your liberty now because you have the Spirit of the Lord in you and where the Spirit of the Lord is, there is liberty. That is what God said through Paul in 2 Corinthians 3:17.

> *Now the Lord is that Spirit: and where the Spirit of the Lord is, there is liberty.*
> **2 Corinthians 3:17**

Therefore you are free. You should be free. You are free therefore seize your liberty from the enemy. Don't allow the enemy to intimidate you with any form of bondage. You are free from all bondages of the enemy. You must resist the enemy violently if he attempts to put you in any form of bondage through a guilt-complex or sin-complex. You should be liberated completely from all the bondages and captivities of the enemy.

If you are Spirit-controlled and also Spirit-led then the Spirit of God will take control of your whole person, spirit, soul and body and your mind will be taking the dictates of, and instruction from, the Spirit. There is no load or burden upon you that the Spirit cannot handle. If you allow the Spirit to take control of your whole self you will be absolutely free. Because you have believed you have actually entered into rest. That is what we know from what is written in Hebrews 4:3.

Living a supernatural life (Volume 3)

> *For we which have believed do enter into rest, as he said, As I have sworn in my wrath, if they shall enter into my rest: although the works were finished from the foundation of the world.*
>
> **Hebrews 4:3**

Nothing should disturb you anymore unless you allow it. You are totally freed from the snares of Satan. No sin can have any dominion over you anymore. Fear can no longer torment you. You are totally free of all encumbrances. You don't have to worry about anything anymore. You are free because you are now complete in Christ. Nothing can mock, shame or reproach you anymore. Reproaches are not your portion in Christ.

You have not been called for reproach and shame. You have been called unto glory and virtue. Your portions now are virtue and glory. You should be moving from glory to glory. Let that be your mindset because that is what God said through Peter in 2 Peter 1:3 as well as through Paul in Colossians 2:10.

> *According as his divine power hath given unto us all things that pertain unto life and godliness, through the knowledge of him that hath called us to glory and virtue:*
>
> **2 Peter 1:3**

> *And ye are complete in him, which is the head of all principality and power:*
>
> **Colossians 2:10**

What you have in Christ

Jesus was raised from the dead because of you so that you can receive your justification. That is what the Scripture says in Romans 4:25. Now that you have been justified, you are free. Since you are justified by the Father no one can condemn you anymore. The Scriptures say so in Romans 8:33-34. Therefore don't let Satan have access to your mind to put any guilt or sin-complex there so as to frighten you. Don't let Satan take you on a guilt-trip. You are no longer in bondage to sin.

> *Who was delivered for our offences, and was raised again for our justification.*
> **Romans 4:25**

> *Who shall lay any thing to the charge of God's elect? It is God that justifieth.*

> *Who is he that condemneth? It is Christ that died, yea rather, that is risen again, who is even at the right hand of God, who also maketh intercession for us.*
> **Romans 8:33-34**

Let Satan know that you have confessed your sins and God has forgiven you of all the sins and washed you clean of all your unrighteousness as He promised you as written in 1 John 1:9. Therefore God is not holding anything against you anymore. The Son has made you free because you now know the truth; therefore you are free indeed. God said so in John 8:32,36.

> *If we confess our sins, he is faithful and just to forgive us our sins, and to cleanse us from all unrighteousness.*
>
> **1 John 1:9**

> *And ye shall know the truth, and the truth shall make you free.*
>
> *If the Son therefore shall make you free, ye shall be free indeed.*
>
> **John 8:32,36**

You have now escaped from the snare of the fowlers. As written in Psalm 124:7 the snare is broken and you have escaped. You are free. Therefore don't allow yourself to be re-enslaved or re-snared by the devil.

> *Our soul is escaped as a bird out of the snare of the fowlers: the snare is broken, and we are escaped.*
>
> **Psalm 124:7**

You are justified because you believe in Jesus Christ and in the work of redemption that He did. Your justification has nothing to do with any works of the law, which you have done. You can see that clearly from Acts 13:39, Romans 3:20, Romans 4:5 and also in Galatians 2:16, Romans 3:24 as well as Romans 5:9. Therefore it is totally as a result of God's grace that you are justified.

> *And by him all that believe are justified from all things, from which ye could not be justified by the law of Moses.*
>
> **Acts 13:39**

What you have in Christ

Therefore by the deeds of the law there shall no flesh be justified in his sight: for by the law is the knowledge of sin.
Romans 3:20

But to him that worketh not, but believeth on him that justifieth the ungodly, his faith is counted for righteousness.
Romans 4:5

Knowing that a man is not justified by the works of the law, but by the faith of Jesus Christ, even we have believed in Jesus Christ, that we might be justified by the faith of Christ, and not by the works of the law: for by the works of the law shall no flesh be justified.
Galatians 2:16

Being justified freely by his grace through the redemption that is in Christ Jesus:
Romans 3:24

Much more then, being now justified by his blood, we shall be saved from wrath through him.
Romans 5:9

It is because you believe in Jesus that you can claim your justification through faith in Him. Even though you have no works of the law the justification is freely given to you by God's grace and you got it through the redemption work that Christ did. Your justification is also by the Blood of Christ that was shed on the Cross.

Living a supernatural life (Volume 3)

Through this justification you have now therefore been counted to be righteous through the shed Blood of Jesus Christ. You have been freely given the righteousness of Christ. You are now counted to be righteous.

From what God said through Paul in Galatians 2:16, which is written on the previous page and also in Galatians 3:10-13, which is written below you can see that you are no longer under the curse therefore every one of the curses in the Curse of the Law should no longer apply to you unless you put yourself under it.

> *For as many as are of the works of the law are under the curse: for it is written, Cursed is every one that continueth not in all things which are written in the book of the law to do them.*
>
> *But that no man is justified by the law in the sight of God, it is evident: for, The just shall live by faith.*
>
> *And the law is not of faith: but, The man that doeth them shall live in them.*
>
> *Christ hath redeemed us from the curse of the law, being made a curse for us: for it is written, Cursed is every one that hangeth on a tree:*
>
> **Galatians 3:10-13**

This is so because you are justified by faith in the work of redemption, which Christ did. Christ has redeemed you from the Curse of the Law.

What you have in Christ

It follows therefore that you are now dead to the law so that you may live unto God. Therefore you no longer live to be justified by the works of the Law. You live by faith and you have been justified by the faith of Jesus Christ. You have been set free by Jesus Christ who is the Son of God. As Jesus said in John 8:32, this truth will make you free when you know it and when you are thus free you are really free indeed because the Son is the One that has set you free. Jesus said in John 8:36 that if the Son has made you free then you are free indeed. We have previously looked at these two verses of the Scripture. You have been freed by the Son therefore agree in your heart that you are truly free indeed. Let that be your mental attitude all the time and refuse to go back into the bondage of Satan.

> *And ye shall know the truth, and the truth shall make you free.*
>
> **John 8:32**

> *If the Son therefore shall make you free, ye shall be free indeed.*
>
> **John 8:36**

YOU HAVE RECONCILIATION WITH GOD

Since you have been justified by God it follows that you have been reconciled to God by Jesus Christ. All obstacles between you and God have been removed. That is what we are told by Paul the Apostle that Jesus did in 2 Corinthians 5:18. Therefore you can now approach God with confidence without any inhibition. You have been cleansed from all sins by the blood of Jesus Christ, the Son of God. Therefore you are free from all accusations.

Living a supernatural life (Volume 3)

And all things are of God, who hath reconciled us to himself by Jesus Christ, and hath given to us the ministry of reconciliation;
2 Corinthians 5:18

You should no longer sin as a habit because you now have power over sin but if you fall into sin you have the assurance that your sins will be forgiven you by God if you confess them. He has promised that He will also cleanse you from all your unrighteousness. That is what God said through Apostle John in both 1 John 1:7 and in 1 John 1:9. According to what Jesus said written in John 8:12, you now have complete freedom having been moved from darkness into complete light.

But if we walk in the light, as he is in the light, we have fellowship one with another, and the blood of Jesus Christ his Son cleanseth us from all sin.
1 John 1:7

If we confess our sins, he is faithful and just to forgive us our sins, and to cleanse us from all unrighteousness.
1 John 1:9

Then spake Jesus again unto them, saying, I am the light of the world: he that followeth me shall not walk in darkness, but shall have the light of life.
John 8:12

You now have peace with God through our Lord Jesus Christ. That is what you can see from what God said through Apostle Paul in Romans 5:1.

What you have in Christ

> *Therefore being justified by faith, we have peace with God through our Lord Jesus Christ:*
> **Romans 5:1**

Therefore you should feel free to express yourself to God without any inhibition. Speak to God like a son will speak to his Father. Cast out all the guilt and unworthy feelings that Satan brings into your mind. There is nothing standing between you and God to worry about that you cannot confess and be forgiven. So relax! God loves you.

According to the Scripture and as explained by Paul to the Colossians in Colossians 1:20 the peace that you have with God came through the Blood of Jesus Christ that was shed on the Cross for you.

> *And, having made peace through the blood of his cross, by him to reconcile all things unto himself; by him, I say, whether they be things in earth, or things in heaven.*
> **Colossians 1:20**

What this means is that you have been reconciled to God. You are no longer under any condemnation of sin. You are no longer in a state of enmity with God. You now have access to the favour of God. From what God said through Apostle Paul in Philippians 4:7, you can see that it is this peace of God, which passeth all understanding, which is now keeping your heart and mind through Christ Jesus. You are now totally at peace with God. Therefore approach God with confidence.

> *And the peace of God, which passeth all understanding, shall keep your hearts and minds through Christ Jesus.*
>
> **Philippians 4:7**

Your views, your feelings, your desires should all be changed and aligned with God's views, God's feelings and God's desires. Once that is done you can rest assured that you now have God's divine protection. Therefore you have no cause to fear anymore. You don't have to struggle to do the right things. Doing the right things should come naturally to you because the nature that you had, which tended to do evil things have been changed. You now have a new nature in Christ, the divine nature.

YOU HAVE GOD'S DIVINE PROTECTION

You have God's protection. ANYBODY or anything that defiles your body would be destroyed by God because you are a habitation of God. God dwells in you. Your body is His temple, where He lives. God cannot leave His dwelling place unprotected. You ought to know that God will not allow His dwelling place to be defiled. Therefore anybody or anything that attempts to defile or destroy your body will incur the wrath of God and that includes you. That is what God made us to know through Apostle Paul in 1 Corinthians 3:16-17.

> *Know ye not that ye are the temple of God, and that the Spirit of God dwelleth in you?*

What you have in Christ

If any man defile the temple of God, him shall God destroy; for the temple of God is holy, which temple ye are.
1 Corinthians 3:16-17

It follows that no sickness can defile your body and get away with it. You are now a member of the Body of Christ, the Church. You have been sealed with Christ and have become one with Him. This is not a hypothetical union but a real union. What this means is that your flesh is now part of His flesh and your bones are now part of His bones. That is what God made us to see in Ephesians 5:30. God Himself will not want any part of His body to be hurt. No one will hurt any part of his own body willingly. Therefore no matter what part of the Body of Christ you may be, God will not allow anything to defile or damage you because it will not please Him at all that a part of His Body is damaged or hurt. Be assured therefore that you don't have to fear in any situation that you find yourself.

For we are members of his body, of his flesh, and of his bones.
Ephesians 5:30

If a battle has to be fought to get over the situation you should not worry because the battle is not yours to fight. God Himself will take over the battle and fight it to defend His own temple. No matter how terrible the situation may be all you have to do is just stand firm and not be afraid. That is what He told the physical children of Israel in 2 Chronicles 20:15.

> *And he said, Hearken ye, all Judah, and ye inhabitants of Jerusalem, and thou king Jehoshaphat, Thus saith the LORD unto you, Be not afraid nor dismayed by reason of this great multitude; for the battle is not yours, but God's.*
>
> **2 Chronicles 20:15**

But now you belong to the spiritual Israel and this promise of God is just as true for you today. If He would do that for the physical children of Israel who are the children of Abraham His friend how much more so will He do for you, who is not only a spiritual child of Abraham His friend but who He has also adopted and empowered to become His own son as we are told in John 1:12? Not His friend's son but His own son!

> *But as many as received him, to them gave he power to become the sons of God, even to them that believe on his name:*
>
> **John 1:12**

Therefore wake up and let this sink into you. All you need to do is put your trust in God, stand still under all situations and you will see the salvation of the Lord. God has bought you with a price therefore you are now His property. You no longer belong to yourself. That is what we are made to see from what Apostle Paul wrote in 1 Corinthians 6:19-20. This means that you are now God's responsibility.

> *What? know ye not that your body is the temple of the Holy Ghost which is in you, which ye have of God, and ye are not your own?*

What you have in Christ

For ye are bought with a price: therefore glorify God in your body, and in your spirit, which are God's.
1 Corinthians 6:19-20

You don't need to fret or fume at all about anything. God is the One that is in charge in your life. Put Him in the driver's seat of your life and your protection will be absolutely sure. No matter how impossible the situation may be, if you just put all your trust in God, rejoice even under the situation and not try to fight the battle by yourself you will definitely see the salvation of the Lord because that is what God Himself promised you in 2 Chronicles 20:17. You know that His Word can never fail because it is settled in heaven forever. His Word cannot be broken. That is what Jesus said in John 10:35.

Ye shall not need to fight in this battle: set yourselves, stand ye still, and see the salvation of the LORD with you, O Judah and Jerusalem: fear not, nor be dismayed; to morrow go out against them: for the LORD will be with you.
2 Chronicles 20:17

If he called them gods, unto whom the word of God came, and the scripture cannot be broken;
John 10:35

After all He is your strong hold in the day of trouble as He made us to see in Nahum 1:7. You have and you can enjoy absolute protection because God will contend with whatever is contending your possessions or your destiny with you.

Living a supernatural life (Volume 3)

> *The LORD is good, a strong hold in the day of trouble; and he knoweth them that trust in him.*
>
> **Nahum 1:7**

No matter how strong the contender may be; no matter how powerful the contender may be, the promise of God is that He will contend with him. That is His promise in Isaiah 49:25.

> *But thus saith the LORD, Even the captives of the mighty shall be taken away, and the prey of the terrible shall be delivered: for I will contend with him that contendeth with thee, and I will save thy children.*
>
> **Isaiah 49:25**

God will contend with everyone that contends with you and get you back whatever he might have stolen from you. Because you believe God you should know that you have entered into rest. That is what we are told in Hebrews 4:3. Therefore you should not be disturbed under any situation. You have entered into rest because your protection under all situations is assured. As a Christian you are supposed to have your mind at rest because that shows that your confidence is in God and only God. If you are afraid it means that you do not have explicit trust in God.

> *For we which have believed do enter into rest, as he said, As I have sworn in my wrath, if they shall enter into my rest: although the works were finished from the foundation of the world.*
>
> **Hebrews 4:3**

What you have in Christ

Even if a situation becomes so hot that it looks as if your enemies are getting the upper hand against you and your world seems to be crumbling around you it is imperative that you must not worry yourself or be anxious. In fact it is then that you should rejoice the more and show absolute confidence. This is because it is in such a situation that the Spirit of the Lord, who now lives in you, will lift up a standard against your enemies. That is what God promised you through Isaiah in Isaiah 59:19. Therefore you have absolute assurance that no situation can knock you down. You are well protected under all situations.

> *So shall they fear the name of the LORD from the west, and his glory from the rising of the sun. When the enemy shall come in like a flood, the Spirit of the LORD shall lift up a standard against him.*
> **Isaiah 59:19**

You have absolute protection from God because He monitors every situation that you have to go through to make sure that you are quite capable of going through and withstanding the situation and that the situation cannot overwhelm you no matter what the conditions are. Therefore you can rest assured that whatever you are going through you have the capability to withstand it and that in the end you will come out the winner. Even when it looks like a situation may overwhelm you or box you into a corner God has made sure that a way of escape from the situation is provided for you. God will always provide a way of escape for you. That is what He promised. That is the essence of what God said through Paul in 1 Corinthians 10:13.

Living a supernatural life (Volume 3)

> *There hath no temptation taken you but such as is common to man: but God is faithful, who will not suffer you to be tempted above that ye are able; but will with the temptation also make a way to escape, that ye may be able to bear it.*
>
> **1 Corinthians 10:13**

Therefore you can see that you are absolutely secured in Christ. This is why God Himself said through John in 1 John 4:4 that you have already overcome whatever may be attacking you. You have already been declared the winner even before the battle begins. So you are really fighting a pre-fixed battle in which you are already declared the winner. That is the way God sees your fights. He knows that He has made all the provision for your victory under all situations. That is why He is so confident that you cannot loose. No matter what the enemy does as long as you stay where you are supposed to be in Christ, the enemy can never win. You actually have absolute security in Christ. You are now born of God and God told you through John in 1 John 5:4-5 that whatsoever is born of God overcomes the world. He also told you that the victory that overcomes the world is your faith because you believe that Jesus Christ is the Son of God. Therefore you have the assurance that anytime you walk in faith no matter what may come against you, your victory is assured.

> *Ye are of God, little children, and have overcome them: because greater is he that is in you, than he that is in the world.*
>
> **1 John 4:4**

For whatsoever is born of God overcometh the world: and this is the victory that overcometh the world, even our faith.

Who is he that overcometh the world, but he that believeth that Jesus is the Son of God?
1 John 5:4-5

YOU HAVE ABSOLUTE SECURITY IN CHRIST

You have absolute security in Christ. As long as you walk in the truth as given by the Word of God, Satan can no longer harm you. Nobody can harm you. You are absolutely secured in Christ. As long as you do good, eschew evil, seek peace and ensue peace, nobody can harm you. That is what we can see from what God said through Peter in 1 Peter 3:10-13. This is so because as written by Peter in 1 Peter 1:5, you are now kept by the power of God through faith. Therefore nothing can attack you and win against you. Think about this, if the power of God is keeping you how can anything attack you and win against you? It is just not possible unless you agree to be defeated.

For he that will love life, and see good days, let him refrain his tongue from evil, and his lips that they speak no guile:

Let him eschew evil, and do good; let him seek peace, and ensue it.

> *For the eyes of the Lord are over the righteous, and his ears are open unto their prayers: but the face of the Lord is against them that do evil.*
>
> *And who is he that will harm you, if ye be followers of that which is good?*
> **1 Peter 3:10-13**

> *Who are kept by the power of God through faith unto salvation ready to be revealed in the last time.*
> **1 Peter 1:5**

In fact anybody that troubles you God considers it a righteous thing to recompense tribulation to him. That is what God said in 2 Thessalonians 1:6. That should make you feel secured.

> *Seeing it is a righteous thing with God to recompense tribulation to them that trouble you;*
> **2 Thessalonians 1:6**

You are absolutely secured because you are of God and Satan cannot touch you anymore unless you give him the room. He can make the attempt but he can no longer win against you. You are now protected from Satan's devices. That is what God made us to see from what is written in 1 John 5:18-19.

> *We know that whosoever is born of God sinneth not; but he that is begotten of God keepeth himself, and that wicked one toucheth him not.*

What you have in Christ

And we know that we are of God, and the whole world lieth in wickedness.
1 John 5:18-19

In fact, no matter what Satan may bring your way you need not be perturbed and you should not be disturbed because you now know that all things work together for good to you because you love God and He has called you according to His purpose. Therefore from what God said through Paul in Romans 8:28, you know that all things must work together for good for you unless of course you do not love God.

And we know that all things work together for good to them that love God, to them who are the called according to his purpose.
Romans 8:28

Even for many of the situations in your life that look very terrible and give a bleak picture at the onset you will find that by the time the full course of events unfolds they will actually work out for your good. Every situation will always eventually work out for your good when you look at the overall effect critically. You have God's assurance and you know that under all situations you are absolutely secured because whatever the situation may be it will turn out for your good eventually. What God promised in Isaiah 49:24-26 is now applicable to you.

Shall the prey be taken from the mighty, or the lawful captive delivered?

> *But thus saith the LORD, Even the captives of the mighty shall be taken away, and the prey of the terrible shall be delivered: for I will contend with him that contendeth with thee, and I will save thy children.*
>
> *And I will feed them that oppress thee with their own flesh; and they shall be drunken with their own blood, as with sweet wine: and all flesh shall know that I the LORD am thy Saviour and thy Redeemer, the mighty One of Jacob.*
>
> **Isaiah 49:24-26**

No body, no matter how mighty, powerful or terrible can now lord it over you or prey upon you and hold your goods or heritage captive. No! God is telling you here that He will not allow that. He is saying that He will contend with whoever contends your goods or your belongings with you and He will take them away from whosoever has taken them captive and give them back to you. What an assurance you have there! God is saying here that even if that your adversary has legal right either through what you have done or not done consciously or unconsciously to take your possessions captive, God says that He will still get them for you.

With that promise of God if you cannot see just how secured you are then I don't know what else will make you see it. As we have discussed earlier there is a hedge of protection that God has built around you, around your house and around all that you have on every side just like He did for Job as Satan discovered and said in Job 1:10. Satan knows this but do you?

Hast not thou made an hedge about him, and about his house, and about all that he hath on every side? thou hast blessed the work of his hands, and his substance is increased in the land.
Job 1:10

All the various good promises that God made to you are what constitute the hedge of protection around you. Once you keep this hedge of protection that God has built around you intact you will be secured. But if you break the hedge by speaking negative words that contradict the promises of God then of course the enemy will have a way into your life to torment you. The Scripture says in Ecclesiastes 10:8 and we repeat it here again that whosoever breaks a hedge a serpent will bite him.

He that diggeth a pit shall fall into it; and whoso breaketh an hedge, a serpent shall bite him.
Ecclesiastes 10:8

Therefore if you break the hedge of protection that God's promises have put around you through negative and lousy talk with your mouth then you can be sure that the most wicked serpent of them all, the devil, will come in and bite you. That was what Job did that made Satan to have the opportunity to come and afflict him. He used his own mouth to break the hedge that God had built around him by saying negative things such as not been sure of his protection for himself and for his children.

YOU HAVE ENRICHED KNOWLEDGE

The Scriptures say in Colossians 3:10 that you are renewed in knowledge and in likeness to God. That is what we know from what God said through Apostle Paul. You have put on the new man and you now have a heart, which God promised you in Jeremiah 24:7 to know God and to know that He is the Lord.

> *And have put on the new man, which is renewed in knowledge after the image of him that created him:*
> **Colossians 3:10**

> *And I will give them an heart to know me, that I am the LORD: and they shall be my people, and I will be their God: for they shall return unto me with their whole heart.*
> **Jeremiah 24:7**

You are enriched by Jesus Christ in all utterance and in all knowledge. That is what 1 Corinthians 1:5 says. You now have unction from God and you know all things. That is the potential that God says you now have as we are made to see through John in 1 John 2:20. This may look too far-fetched to you but that is the potential that you now have in Christ. Because you have the anointing of the Holy Spirit you can now comprehend the mysteries of the Kingdom of God.

> *That in every thing ye are enriched by him, in all utterance, and in all knowledge;*
> **1 Corinthians 1:5**

But ye have an unction from the Holy One, and ye know all things.

What you have in Christ

1 John 2:20

YOU HAVE THE LAWS OF GOD IN YOUR HEART

You have the laws of God in your heart. God has written them in your mind and He no longer remembers your sins.

The Law of God no longer needs to irritate you. Because of the new Covenant that God has with Christ for man God has promised in Hebrews 10:16-17 to do this for you and He has already done it. Your delight should now be in the law of God after the inward man just like Paul said of himself in Romans 7:22.

> *This is the covenant that I will make with them after those days, saith the Lord, I will put my laws into their hearts, and in their minds will I write them;*
>
> *And their sins and iniquities will I remember no more.*
>
> **Hebrews 10:16-17**
>
> *For I delight in the law of God after the inward man:*
>
> **Romans 7:22**

YOU HAVE A REGENERATED SPIRIT

You have been saved by the washing of regeneration and the renewing of the Holy Spirit, which is a total rebirth of your spirit. That is what we are told by God in Titus 3:5.

> *Not by works of righteousness which we have done, but according to his mercy he saved us, by the washing of regeneration, and renewing of the Holy Ghost;*
>
> **Titus 3:5**

This means that you have a regenerated spirit. It is this regenerated spirit that you now have that can harbour the Holy Spirit of God. You have therefore been *re-gene-rated*. We can say your *genes* are now totally *re-rated*. You now have super divine genes that cannot be subject to any genetic disorder or malfunction because of the purifying work of the Holy Spirit, through whom the rivers of living water is now flowing out of your belly according to what Jesus said in John 7:38.

> *He that believeth on me, as the scripture hath said, out of his belly shall flow rivers of living water.*
>
> **John 7:38**

God is the fountain of these living waters. That is what God told us through Prophet Jeremiah in Jeremiah 2:13 and Jeremiah 17:13. The rivers of living water that is now supposed to be flowing out of your belly is the same thing that came out of Jesus in Luke 6:19 to heal all people, which Jesus called virtue in Luke 8:46.

For my people have committed two evils; they have forsaken me the fountain of living waters, and hewed them out cisterns, broken cisterns, that can hold no water.
Jeremiah 2:13

O LORD, the hope of Israel, all that forsake thee shall be ashamed, and they that depart from me shall be written in the earth, because they have forsaken the LORD, the fountain of living waters.
Jeremiah 17:13

And the whole multitude sought to touch him: for there went virtue out of him, and healed them all.
Luke 6:19

This virtue has healing power and can flow out of you to heal. That is what came out of Jesus to heal the lady with the issue of blood as narrated in Luke 8:43-48. Jesus said virtue came out of Him to heal this woman with the issue of blood. You have the same virtue in you also. Therefore if you open up your mind and allow the Spirit of God in you to work through you, then healing can also be performed through you.

And a woman having an issue of blood twelve years, which had spent all her living upon physicians, neither could be healed of any,

Came behind him, and touched the border of his garment: and immediately her issue of blood stanched.

Living a supernatural life (Volume 3)

> *And Jesus said, Who touched me? When all denied, Peter and they that were with him said, Master, the multitude throng thee and press thee, and sayest thou, Who touched me?*
>
> *And Jesus said, Somebody hath touched me: for I perceive that virtue is gone out of me.*
>
> *And when the woman saw that she was not hid, she came trembling, and falling down before him, she declared unto him before all the people for what cause she had touched him and how she was healed immediately.*
>
> *And he said unto her, Daughter, be of good comfort: thy faith hath made thee whole; go in peace.*
>
> **Luke 8:43-48**

When the lady touched the garment of Jesus virtue went out of Jesus to heal the lady. The same virtue is what Jesus called rivers of living water, which is now supposed to be flowing out of your innermost being. These rivers of living water are also supposed to be continuously doing a healing and quickening work in your body. That is what we can understand by what Paul the Apostle wrote in Romans 8:11. There he said that the Spirit of God from whom the rivers of living water oozes out was the One that quickened Jesus and raised Him up from the dead. That virtue, rivers of Living water should now be coming out of you to heal. That is why it is wrong for Christians to be ***praying power down*** when the power actually resides in them and what they need to do is to ***pray the power out.***

What you have in Christ

But if the Spirit of him that raised up Jesus from the dead dwell in you, he that raised up Christ from the dead shall also quicken your mortal bodies by his Spirit that dwelleth in you.
Romans 8:11

Paul's argument is that since the same Spirit is now living in you He is supposed to be quickening your mortal body on a continuous basis. If you know and believe this then obviously you will realize that sicknesses and diseases and anything that defiles your body can no longer hang around your body if you allow the Spirit of God in you to have His full expression. From Isaiah 59:19 you can see that the Spirit will normally raise a standard against whatever seeks to defile you.

So shall they fear the name of the LORD from the west, and his glory from the rising of the sun. When the enemy shall come in like a flood, the Spirit of the LORD shall lift up a standard against him.
Isaiah 59:19

What God wants for you is that sickness and disease should no longer be able to oppress you in any way. That is what God wants for you but your mind must agree with God on this because He has said in 3 John 2 and Proverbs 23:7 that it is your mind that will decide what happens to you. Even if God wants you healthy but your mind is telling you that you are sick God will do nothing to change what your mind has accepted.

Living a supernatural life (Volume 3)

> *Beloved, I wish above all things that thou mayest prosper and be in health, even as thy soul prospereth.*
> **3 John 2**

> *For as he thinketh in his heart, so is he: Eat and drink, saith he to thee; but his heart is not with thee.*
> **Proverbs 23:7**

With this regeneration a new life was commenced in you. You were recreated anew as a new creature and you are now a totally new person different from what you used to be as explained by God through Apostle Paul in 2 Corinthians 5:17.

> *Therefore if any man be in Christ, he is a new creature: old things are passed away; behold, all things are become new.*
> **2 Corinthians 5:17**

You should not see yourself in the light of who you used to be. The new you is not a weakling but strong in Christ Jesus. The new you is no longer foolish but wise with the mind of Christ operating in you. You must change the image that you have of yourself in your mind to align with your true Scriptural image. You have been delivered from the bondage of corruption into a glorious liberty. Your past sins have been cleansed by the washing of this regeneration and the renewing of the Holy Spirit has changed your old nature. You now have the spiritual life with which you can do God's will. By this regeneration your soul which was dead has been replaced with a new one, which is given eternal life by God.

What you have in Christ

This has given you a new life power of divine origin to glorify God because your regeneration is for the glory of God. That is what God made us to see through Isaiah in Isaiah 43:7. Therefore you must make sure that whatever you do it is done to the glory of God.

> *Even every one that is called by my name: for I have created him for my glory, I have formed him; yea, I have made him.*
> **Isaiah 43:7**

Your regeneration and new creation has now made it possible for you to partake in the divine nature and that is what we are going to discuss in the next section.

YOU HAVE THE DIVINE NATURE

You are now a partaker of the divine nature of God. God's own nature has been imparted to you. That is what we are told by God through Peter in 2 Peter 1:4.

> *Whereby are given unto us exceeding great and precious promises: that by these ye might be partakers of the divine nature, having escaped the corruption that is in the world through lust.*
> **2 Peter 1:4**

Many Christians do not know the gravity of this statement by God through Peter. When God says that you are now a partaker of the divine nature, He is saying that you are now totally recreated and in this new creation you now have God's nature.

Living a supernatural life (Volume 3)

This means that you have His life, His power, His glory, His strength, His health, His wisdom and His ability. These are all available to you now. The totality of this is that you are now united with deity. You are now a partaker of the glory of God. You are a partaker of His virtue. You are a partaker of His righteousness. According to what is written in Hebrews 12:10 you are also a partaker of God's holiness. Your passion now should be to know the God whose nature you now partake of.

> *For they verily for a few days chastened us after their own pleasure; but he for our profit, that we might be partakers of his holiness.*
> **Hebrews 12:10**

You are not only a partaker of God's divine nature; you are also a partaker of His material nature. That is why it is said that you are now a member of the Body of Christ.

This is not a hypothetical union but your mortal body is now a member of the Body of Christ; which means that your flesh is a member of His flesh and your bones are members of His bones. That in essence is what God is letting us know through Paul in 1 Corinthians 12:27 and Ephesians 5:30.

> *Now ye are the body of Christ, and members in particular.*
> **1 Corinthians 12:27**

> *For we are members of his body, of his flesh, and of his bones.*
> **Ephesians 5:30**

What you have in Christ

The same Spirit that quickened Jesus Christ from the dead is now living in you to quicken you also. The Spirit is doing the same thing in you that He did in Christ. That is what God made us to know from what Apostle Paul said in Romans 8:11. Whatever worked for Christ will now also work for you because the same Spirit is working in you because as He is so are you in this world. That is what God said in 1 John 4:17.

> *But if the Spirit of him that raised up Jesus from the dead dwell in you, he that raised up Christ from the dead shall also quicken your mortal bodies by his Spirit that dwelleth in you.*
> **Romans 8:11**

> *Herein is our love made perfect, that we may have boldness in the day of judgment: because as he is, so are we in this world.*
> **1 John 4:17**

Because you are a partaker of the divine nature it follows that just like Jesus said in John 6:63 of His words that they are spirit and they are life the words that you speak are also spirit and they are life. That means that the words that come from your mouth are very powerful and have creative life in them. Therefore because you are now a partaker of the divine nature of God, whatever commands you speak out with your mouth, no adversary can oppose it. They have to be obeyed. That is the power that Jesus has promised to give you in Luke 21:15.

> *It is the spirit that quickeneth; the flesh profiteth nothing: the words that I speak unto you, they are spirit, and they are life.*
>
> **John 6:63**

> *For I will give you a mouth and wisdom, which all your adversaries shall not be able to gainsay nor resist.*
>
> **Luke 21:15**

In fact, the power of life and death are in the words that you speak out of your mouth. That is what God made us to see through Solomon in Proverbs 18:21. Now we know according to Hebrews 11:3, that the worlds were framed by the Word of God. Because you now have the divine nature you too should realize that you are also continuously framing what happens in your world by the words that you speak.

> *Death and life are in the power of the tongue: and they that love it shall eat the fruit thereof.*
>
> **Proverbs 18:21**

> *Through faith we understand that the worlds were framed by the word of God, so that things which are seen were not made of things which do appear.*
>
> **Hebrews 11:3**

You have the ability to also frame your own world with the words that you speak out. Therefore you can command any condition that is contrary to you and it must obey you. This means that you can command sickness and disease and they must obey you. You can command failure and it must obey you.

What you have in Christ

You can command poverty and lack and they must obey you. Therefore you have the power to change anything that is working contrary to you. From what is written by Apostle Paul in 2 Corinthians 5:5, you can see that you are now joined with God and have become one with Him through Christ because you now have the earnest pledge of the Spirit. You are one Spirit with the Lord because you are now joined with the Lord and you are sealed together with Him. That is what God made us to see through Apostle Paul in Ephesians 1:13 and also in 1 Corinthian 6:17.

> *Now he that hath wrought us for the selfsame thing is God, who also hath given unto us the earnest of the Spirit.*
> **2 Corinthians 5:5**

> *In whom ye also trusted, after that ye heard the word of truth, the gospel of your salvation: in whom also after that ye believed, ye were sealed with that holy Spirit of promise,*
> **Ephesians 1:13**

> *But he that is joined unto the Lord is one spirit.*
> **1 Corinthians 6:17**

According to what God said through the same Apostle Paul in 2 Corinthians 3:18, you are being changed more and more into the image of God in which you are made on a daily basis.

> *But we all, with open face beholding as in a glass the glory of the Lord, are changed into the same image from glory to glory, even as by the Spirit of the Lord.*
> **2 Corinthians 3:18**

Because you are now a partaker of the divine nature of God, there is no problem that is too much for you to solve anymore. There is no enemy that is too powerful for you to overcome. Whatever the divinity of God can surmount or go through you can now surmount or go through.

Whatever the divinity of God can conquer, prevail against, or triumph over, you too can now conquer, prevail against and triumph over. You have also escaped the corruption that is in this world through lust as we have seen earlier in 2 Peter 1:4. Whatever cannot defeat God can no longer defeat you. This should be your understanding of your position now because it is God that is now working in you. That is what we are made to see in Philippians 2:13.

> *Whereby are given unto us exceeding great and precious promises: that by these ye might be partakers of the divine nature, having escaped the corruption that is in the world through lust.*
> **2 Peter 1:4**

> *For it is God which worketh in you both to will and to do of his good pleasure.*
> **Philippians 2:13**

What you have in Christ

The divine nature that you now have carries greatness with it. Therefore greatness is now your portion. It carries glory, honour and favour with it. Therefore you should be swimming in divine favour and moving from glory to glory every day. That should be your mindset all the time. Your new nature carries strength with it because God is now your strength and because Christ strengthens you there is nothing that you cannot do. You can now do all things through Christ who strengthens you. You can see that these are all true of you from what God made us to know through His servants in Exodus 15:2, and also in 2 Samuel 22:33 and in Philippians 4:13.

> *The LORD is my strength and song, and he is become my salvation: he is my God, and I will prepare him an habitation; my father's God, and I will exalt him.*
> **Exodus 15:2**

> *God is my strength and power: and he maketh my way perfect.*
> **2 Samuel 22:33**

> *I can do all things through Christ which strengtheneth me.*
> **Philippians 4:13**

Your new nature also carries health and prosperity with it because that is God's wish for you according to what is written in 3 John 1:2. Therefore you can swim in divine health and divine blessing. You don't have to be looking for healing because as we have explained earlier that as an ambassador for Christ if you are faithful then you are now health personified.

> *Beloved, I wish above all things that thou mayest prosper and be in health, even as thy soul prospereth.*
>
> **3 John 1:2**

YOU HAVE THE POWER OF GOD IN YOU

The divine nature that you now have carries power with it. Actually you are now an embodiment of the power of God because you now have the power of God living in you. The power of God has been given to you to tread upon serpents and scorpions and over all the power of the enemy and nothing can hurt you anymore. That is what Jesus said that He has given to you as written in Luke 10:19. If you have power over *all* the power of your enemies it means that no enemy can harass you anymore unless you don't know that you have power over the power of that enemy.

> *Behold, I give unto you power to tread on serpents and scorpions, and over all the power of the enemy: and nothing shall by any means hurt you.*
>
> **Luke 10:19**

He said *all the power of the enemy* so there is none excluded. If you can only know the power that you now have you can tell any enemy where to go. You can even tell him to get lost.

What you have in Christ

Jesus Christ is the power of God. That is what God made us to see from what He said through Apostle Paul in 1 Corinthians 1:24. The same Jesus Christ who is the power of God now lives in you. That is what He said in John 14:20. Therefore the power of God is now living in you. The power of God is in you. The power of life Christ is living in you and He will lead you to glory. That is what God made us to see through Apostle Paul in Colossians 1:27.

> *But unto them which are called, both Jews and Greeks, Christ the power of God, and the wisdom of God.*
> **1 Corinthians 1:24**

> *At that day ye shall know that I am in my Father, and ye in me, and I in you.*
> **John 14:20**

> *To whom God would make known what is the riches of the glory of this mystery among the Gentiles; which is Christ in you, the hope of glory:*
> **Colossians 1:27**

Therefore reproaches are a thing of the past for you. Nothing can reproach you anymore. You have received the power of God by the anointing of the Holy Spirit. This anointing that you now have breaks every yoke according to what God said through Prophet Isaiah in Isaiah 10:27. Because you have received this anointing of the Holy Spirit, you have therefore received the power of God that Jesus said that you will receive after the Holy Ghost comes upon you in Acts 1:8.

> *And it shall come to pass in that day, that his burden shall be taken away from off thy shoulder, and his yoke from off thy neck, and the yoke shall be destroyed because of the anointing.*
>
> **Isaiah 10:27**

> *But ye shall receive power, after that the Holy Ghost is come upon you: and ye shall be witnesses unto me both in Jerusalem, and in all Judaea, and in Samaria, and unto the uttermost part of the earth.*
>
> **Acts 1:8**

This power in you is the power that created all things. With this power of the Holy Spirit in you, nothing can stop you or be an obstacle in your way that the Holy Spirit cannot take care of. Therefore you can no longer be intimidated by any situation.

You have this great exceeding power of God available to you. In the position in which you are now everything should be possible for you. You can no longer think of impossibilities. The power of God towards you is exceedingly great and mighty and there are great riches and glory in the inheritance that you now have in Christ. That is what God said in Ephesians 1:18-19.

> *The eyes of your understanding being enlightened; that ye may know what is the hope of his calling, and what the riches of the glory of his inheritance in the saints,*

What you have in Christ

And what is the exceeding greatness of his power to us-ward who believe, according to the working of his mighty power,
Ephesians 1:18-19

It follows therefore that as we have noted earlier, no situation can intimidate you anymore. This is so because the spirit that is now living in you is the Spirit of power, which cannot be intimidated by anything. You don't have to fear or worry under any circumstance because you no longer have the spirit of fear. That is what the Scripture says in 2 Timothy 1:7.

For God hath not given us the spirit of fear; but of power, and of love, and of a sound mind.
2 Timothy 1:7

You are not just a son of God you have been given the power to become a son of God. This means that you have actually been empowered to become a son of God so that you can act as one. That is what the Scripture says in John 1:12.

But as many as received him, to them gave he power to become the sons of God, even to them that believe on his name:
John 1:12

Because you are empowered to become a son of God it means that your sonship comes with power. Therefore when you call yourself a son of God it will not be by just the words of your mouth but also by the demonstration of the power of God that you will be able to exhibit.

Living a supernatural life (Volume 3)

As we had shown earlier in Philippians 2:13, it is God that is working in you to do His will. You don't have to rely on your own strength to do His will. If it is God that is working in you, do you not also know that you can get God to do exceeding and abundantly above all that you ask or think with the power of God that is now working in you? That is what God told us through Paul in Ephesians 3:20. This means that you have access to that enormous power of God.

> *For it is God which worketh in you both to will and to do of his good pleasure.*
> **Philippians 2:13**

> *Now unto him that is able to do exceeding abundantly above all that we ask or think, according to the power that worketh in us,*
> **Ephesians 3:20**

You have the power to cast out unclean spirits and to heal *all* manner of sickness and disease. That is the promise of Jesus to you as a believer in Matthew 10:1. You will say that this promise was for His disciples. Yes! But He said in Mark 13:37 that what He said to them also applies to you.

> *And when he had called unto him his twelve disciples, he gave them power against unclean spirits, to cast them out, and to heal all manner of sickness and all manner of disease.*
> **Matthew 10:1**

> *And what I say unto you I say unto all, Watch.*
> **Mark 13:37**

What you have in Christ

To confirm that the statement of Jesus also applies to you look at what Jesus said in Mark 16:17. He said that one of the signs that will be following you because you believe is that you will cast out devils. The signs are meant to follow every believer. If you are a Christian but not a believer the signs will not follow you. They are meant only for believers. Are you a believer?

> *And these signs shall follow them that believe;*
> *In my name shall they cast out devils; they shall speak with new tongues;*
> **Mark 16:17**

Jesus said in Luke 10:19 that He has given you power over *all* the powers of your enemies. Nothing can hurt you anymore.

> *Behold, I give unto you power to tread on serpents and scorpions, and over all the power of the enemy: and nothing shall by any means hurt you.*
> **Luke 10:19**

This means that you have divine protection. It follows therefore that you are not defenseless against any type of affliction such as sickness, accident, robbery etc. You have immunity from all afflictions provided you stay in Christ where you are supposed to be now. Therefore you cannot be afraid of any situation anymore. You have divine authority over all the power of the devil. You no longer care about what the devil can do or is doing.

Living a supernatural life (Volume 3)

All you have to focus on is what God is doing or what God has called you to do since you know that nothing can stop what God is doing through you unless you consciously or unconsciously cooperate with it. You do not have to spend your time thinking about, talking about or listening to what the enemy can do or is doing anymore. It is not a good testimony. You should now spend your time listening to or reading the Word of God because as written in Romans 10:17 that is the way that you can get faith or increase your faith with which you can tackle whatever the enemy brings your way.

> *So then faith cometh by hearing, and hearing by the word of God.*
> **Romans 10:17**

You have unlimited power in God and nothing is impossible to you now. That is what we can see from the combination of what Jesus said in Mark 9:23 and Matthew 17:20. Many Christians read this but do not really believe it because they feel inadequate. Your only limitation is your faith.

> *Jesus said unto him, If thou canst believe, all things are possible to him that believeth.*
> **Mark 9:23**

> *And Jesus said unto them, Because of your unbelief: for verily I say unto you, If ye have faith as a grain of mustard seed, ye shall say unto this mountain, Remove hence to yonder place; and it shall remove; and nothing shall be impossible unto you.*
> **Matthew 17:20**

What you have in Christ

You have the power to destroy the works of the devil whenever you come across these. Why do I say this? I say this because Jesus said in John 14:12 that you would do the works that He did and do even greater works than He did. But the main work that He came to do was to destroy the works of the devil. That is what we are told by Apostle John in 1 John 3:8.

> *Verily, verily, I say unto you, He that believeth on me, the works that I do shall he do also; and greater works than these shall he do; because I go unto my Father.*
> **John 14:12**

> *He that committeth sin is of the devil; for the devil sinneth from the beginning. For this purpose the Son of God was manifested, that he might destroy the works of the devil.*
> **1 John 3:8**

Jesus also said in John 20:21 that He is sending you as the Father had sent Him.

> *Then said Jesus to them again, Peace be unto you: as my Father hath sent me, even so send I you.*
> **John 20:21**

Since the Father sent Him to come and destroy the works of the devil it follows that you have also been sent to destroy the works of the devil. This is so because we are further made to see in 1 John 4:17 that as Jesus was so are we now in the world.

Living a supernatural life (Volume 3)

> *Herein is our love made perfect, that we may have boldness in the day of judgment: because as he is, so are we in this world.*
> **1 John 4:17**

In Acts 10:38 we are told that Jesus went about healing all that were oppressed of the devil. If you are sent as He was sent, and you are in the world as He is then you too now have the power to go about healing all that are oppressed of the devil. You must believe that whatever power supported Him you have the same power supporting you now.

> *How God anointed Jesus of Nazareth with the Holy Ghost and with power: who went about doing good, and healing all that were oppressed of the devil; for God was with him.*
> **Acts 10:38**

You have and can exercise power and authority over all devils and cure diseases. That is what Jesus said in Luke 9:1. However from what God also said through Peter in 2 Peter 1:4 Jesus Christ has healed all your diseases by the stripes that He took when He died. But it is through your faith that you will receive your healing and also help others to receive theirs.

> *Then he called his twelve disciples together, and gave them power and authority over all devils, and to cure diseases.*
> **Luke 9:1**

Whereby are given unto us exceeding great and precious promises: that by these ye might be partakers of the divine nature, having escaped the corruption that is in the world through lust.

2 Peter 1:4

Therefore when you come face to face with any disease or sickness all you have to do is to bind the strong man behind the disease using the keys that Jesus promised to give us in Matthew 16:19 and cast out the disease in the Name of Jesus.

And I will give unto thee the keys of the Kingdom of Heaven: and whatsoever thou shalt bind on earth shall be bound in heaven: and whatsoever thou shalt loose on earth shall be loosed in heaven.

Matthew 16:19

You do this by commanding the spirit behind the sickness or disease to come out and then command that the healing, which Jesus Christ has already done should manifest. If you do not doubt in your heart whatever command you give will be obeyed and you will get the healing. You have the power to do the works that Jesus Christ did and to do even greater works than He did. I know that you may say that what I have said is profane or blasphemous but I want you to note that Jesus Himself was the One who said this. So that you will be able to do the works that He did or even greater works than He did He has promised you by what He said in John 14:12-14 where He said that whatever you ask to be done in His Name He will do it.

Living a supernatural life (Volume 3)

> *Verily, verily, I say unto you, He that believeth on me, the works that I do shall he do also; and greater works than these shall he do; because I go unto my Father.*
>
> *And whatsoever ye shall ask in my name, that will I do, that the Father may be glorified in the Son.*
>
> *If ye shall ask any thing in my name, I will do it.*
>
> John 14:12-14

So it is not you who is really doing the work. Christ is the One who will do the work. All you need to do is to command that the work be done in His Name and you can leave the doing to Him.

Jesus also said in John 16:23 that whatever resources you need to do the work if you ask the Father in His Name, the Father will give it to you.

> *And in that day ye shall ask me nothing. Verily, verily, I say unto you, Whatsoever ye shall ask the Father in my name, he will give it you.*
>
> John 16:23

One of the resources that you need in order to be able to do the works that Jesus did is boldness, therefore you can ask for this resource from the Father. Now in order for you to be bold He has given you as written in Romans 5:17 the righteousness of Christ as a gift knowing that once you know that you are righteous you can be as bold as a lion.

What you have in Christ

For if by one man's offence death reigned by one; much more they which receive abundance of grace and of the gift of righteousness shall reign in life by one, Jesus Christ.
Romans 5:17

That is what we know from Proverbs 28:1. We have discussed in detail the above verse, your need for boldness and how to get it in **Chapter 13** of the **Volume 2** of this *"Living a Supernatural life"* book series.

The wicked flee when no man pursueth: but the righteous are bold as a lion.
Proverbs 28:1

You have the power to control the elements, to cast out devils and do all types of miracles. Because you believe, whenever you lay your hands on any sick person he will recover. You have the power of immunity from poison as well as the power to control wild beasts and devils.

You have the capability and the potential to do these in the Name of Jesus. That is the promise that Jesus made to you in Mark 16:17-18. This should be your mental attitude. You should believe that whatever the Scriptures say about you is the truth and nothing else.

And these signs shall follow them that believe; In my name shall they cast out devils; they shall speak with new tongues;

Living a supernatural life (Volume 3)

> *They shall take up serpents; and if they drink any deadly thing, it shall not hurt them; they shall lay hands on the sick, and they shall recover.*
>
> **Mark 16:17-18**

You have the potential for a greater anointing and therefore a greater power potential to do miracles than that of any Old Covenant saint. You have the potential to work more miracles than Elijah or Elisha did, to have more wisdom and riches than Solomon had and to exhibit more power than Samson did. You have more power inside you than Elijah and Elisha had inside them. That is the essence of what Jesus said concerning you as a New Covenant saint in Matthew 11:11, Matthew 12:41-42 and also in John 14:12. That you have more wisdom inside you than Solomon had inside him is not surprising because from what God said through Paul in 1 Corinthians 1:24,30 you can see that Jesus Christ who is the wisdom and power of God now lives in you and has been made wisdom to you.

> *Verily I say unto you, Among them that are born of women there hath not risen a greater than John the Baptist: notwithstanding he that is least in the Kingdom of Heaven is greater than he.*
>
> **Matthew 11:11**

> *The men of Nineveh shall rise in judgment with this generation, and shall condemn it: because they repented at the preaching of Jonas; and, behold, a greater than Jonas is here.*

What you have in Christ

The queen of the south shall rise up in the judgment with this generation, and shall condemn it: for she came from the uttermost parts of the earth to hear the wisdom of Solomon; and, behold, a greater than Solomon is here.
Matthew 12:41-42

But unto them which are called, both Jews and Greeks, Christ the power of God, and the wisdom of God.

But of him are ye in Christ Jesus, who of God is made unto us wisdom, and righteousness, and sanctification, and redemption:
1 Corinthians 1:24,30

YOU HAVE A GOODLY HERITAGE

You have an inheritance in the Lord. That is what we are told by God through Paul in Ephesians 1:11. Your inheritance in Christ is sure, incorruptible and cannot fade away. That is what God also made us to know from what He said through Peter in 1 Peter 1:3-4.

In whom also we have obtained an inheritance, being predestinated according to the purpose of him who worketh all things after the counsel of his own will:
Ephesians 1:11

Living a supernatural life (Volume 3)

> *Blessed be the God and Father of our Lord Jesus Christ, which according to his abundant mercy hath begotten us again unto a lively hope by the resurrection of Jesus Christ from the dead,*
>
> *To an inheritance incorruptible, and undefiled, and that fadeth not away, reserved in heaven for you,*
> **1 Peter 1:3-4**

Because according to Ephesians 1:13 you are now sealed with God you are now a part of God and you now have His divine nature as previously explained. Therefore you can confidently say like David said in Psalm 16:5-6 that the Lord is your inheritance therefore you have a goodly heritage.

> *In whom ye also trusted, after that ye heard the word of truth, the gospel of your salvation: in whom also after that ye believed, ye were sealed with that holy Spirit of promise,*
> **Ephesians 1:13**
>
> *The LORD is the portion of mine inheritance and of my cup: thou maintainest my lot.*
>
> *The lines are fallen unto me in pleasant places; yea, I have a goodly heritage.*
> **Psalm 16:5-6**

Therefore diseases, malfunctioning genes as well as genetically derived problems are not your inheritance. You have been regenerated according to Titus 3:5.

What you have in Christ

Not by works of righteousness which we have done, but according to his mercy he saved us, by the washing of regeneration, and renewing of the Holy Ghost;

Titus 3:5

This means spiritually that your genes have been re-rated. *(re-gene-rated)*

Therefore you cannot have any genetically based problem because your *genes* have now been *re-rated*. You now have divine genes. Since you are a member of the Body of Christ it means that your flesh is now part of His flesh and your bones part of His bones therefore you now have running through your veins *the divine Blood of Jesus Christ*.

Therefore your blood can no longer be diseased. This may sound too far-fetched to you but the Scriptures say in Proverbs 23:7 that it is as you think in your mind that you will be so get this into your mind.

For as he thinketh in his heart, so is he: Eat and drink, saith he to thee; but his heart is not with thee.

Proverbs 23:7

I am convinced in my mind that I can no longer have a diseased gene. You must also be convinced in your mind that you can no longer have a diseased gene because you now have divine genes. Your genes have been re-rated because they are now *divine genes* and you can no longer have an abnormal or malfunctioning genes.

YOU HAVE ALL THINGS THAT PERTAIN TO LIFE

You have been given all things that pertain unto life and godliness through the knowledge of Christ. This is what God made us to know through Peter in 2 Peter 1:3. You will say that this is a wide statement and be pondering how it can be possible. But these are spiritual things and you will only get to understand this spiritually.

> *According as his divine power hath given unto us all things that pertain unto life and godliness, through the knowledge of him that hath called us to glory and virtue:*
> **2 Peter 1:3**

This means that even though you have been given all things it is only through the knowledge that you have of Christ that you will get them. Since Christ is the Word of God what this means is that it is through the knowledge of the Word of God that you will have all the things that you have been given.

Therefore the more knowledge you have of the Word of God concerning those things that you have been given, the more the possibility of your getting them becomes. This is so because according to Romans 10:17 the more of the Word of God you hear and absorb the more your faith increases and it is by faith that you will receive those things that have been given to you.

> *So then faith cometh by hearing, and hearing by the word of God.*
> **Romans 10:17**

What you have in Christ

The Scripture says that you have been called unto glory and virtue not to shame and reproach therefore excellence is now your portion in anything that you lay your hands on. All things are yours now and you are Christ's. This means that nothing can make you a proverb or a byword among your peers. Whether life or death, things present or things to come; all are yours now. That is what we are made to see from what is written in 1 Corinthians 3:21-23.

> *Therefore let no man glory in men. For all things are yours;*
>
> *Whether Paul, or Apollos, or Cephas, or the world, or life, or death, or things present, or things to come; all are yours;*
>
> *And ye are Christ's; and Christ is God's.*
> **1 Corinthians 3:21-23**

You have all things. This means that anything that you can imagine or think you can have. The greatest possession that you have is that God is now yours. He is your Father. You are His son. You are in Him. He is all around you. You are joined to Him. You are sealed in Him with the Holy Spirit according to what the Scripture says in Ephesians 1:13.

> *In whom ye also trusted, after that ye heard the word of truth, the gospel of your salvation: in whom also after that ye believed, ye were sealed with that Holy Spirit of promise,*
> **Ephesians 1:13**

Living a supernatural life (Volume 3)

Therefore God is for you and if God be for you nobody can be against you and win. I am not saying that they cannot be against you but they cannot win. Nobody can lay any charge against you and succeed anymore because God has already justified you. That is the implication of what God said through Apostle Paul in Romans 8:31 and Romans 8:33. Since God is for you, nothing adverse should disturb or upset you anymore.

> *What shall we then say to these things? If God be for us, who can be against us?*
> **Romans 8:31**

> *Who shall lay any thing to the charge of God's elect? It is God that justifieth.*
> **Romans 8:33**

This is so because you should know that whatever may be the circumstance or situation that you are going through, God is the One that will decide what happens to you; not the situation or the circumstance. That should be your mental attitude now. Therefore stop worrying yourself when you see disturbing symptoms. When Satan brings his symptoms to you let him know that you are not moved by them at all because you know that you are far above any symptom that he can bring and you can put any symptom that he brings under absolute control.

YOU HAVE VICTORY OVER THE WORLD

You have victory over the world because you have overcome the world. That is what God said through John in 1 John 5:4-5.

What you have in Christ

> *For whatsoever is born of God overcometh the world: and this is the victory that overcometh the world, even our faith.*
>
> *Who is he that overcometh the world, but he that believeth that Jesus is the Son of God?*
> **1 John 5:4-5**

It is your faith that brings you the victory. In fact, faith is the victory. Note that you have been given the measure of faith that you require to live and that measure of faith is not smaller than the measure given to any other person. It is the same for all. That is the understanding that we have of what God said through Paul in Romans 12:3. Therefore what you need to do is to grow the measure that you have been given by applying it and exercising it. We are not talking about the gift of faith here. That is a gift of the Holy Spirit given to some people at a particular time for a specific purpose in order that they can do something that requires great faith. But such a gift is not necessarily permanent. It may come and go as the Spirit wills.

> *For I say, through the grace given unto me, to every man that is among you, not to think of himself more highly than he ought to think; but to think soberly, according as God hath dealt to every man the measure of faith.*
> **Romans 12:3**

With faith, you can stand up to any challenge now and you will always win. Faith has never lost any battle. With faith defeats and failures are no longer your portion. You have the faith that can overcome the world. Nothing can overcome you now.

Living a supernatural life (Volume 3)

This is not a victory being expected. No! It is a victory that you already have. From what is written by Apostle Paul in 2 Corinthians 2:14 and in 2 Corinthians 15:57, you can see that you have victory all the time because no matter the problem God always makes sure that you triumph in Jesus Christ who is the Word of God.

> *Now thanks be unto God, which always causeth us to triumph in Christ, and maketh manifest the savour of his knowledge by us in every place.*
> **2 Corinthians 2:14**

> *But thanks be to God, which giveth us the victory through our Lord Jesus Christ.*
> **1 Corinthians 15:57**

What a great assurance you have there? What God is telling you here is that with the Word of God in your heart coming out of your mouth you are assured of victory all the time. You have victory through our Lord Jesus Christ who is the Word of God. It is God that causes you to triumph always.

This means that with the use of the Word you can always triumph over any situation. No matter what the situation may be you will triumph over it with the Word. You can change any situation and force it to align itself with what the Word of God says by applying the Word of God to the situation. Whatever tests or trials Satan may bring, you will always triumph in Christ because God wants to manifest the savour of His knowledge through you.

What you have in Christ

That way, people will be able to know through you just how sweet the knowledge of God is. That is what He said through Paul in 2 Corinthians 2:14 as we have seen above. You have victory over *all* the power of the enemy not just some of the power of the enemy. That is what Jesus Himself promised in Luke 10:19. You received absolute victory in Jesus Christ as soon as you accept Jesus Christ. It is very important that you know that you are not trying to obtain victory. No! You already have victory. That should always be your mental attitude

> *Behold, I give unto you power to tread on serpents and scorpions, and over all the power of the enemy: and nothing shall by any means hurt you.*
> **Luke 10:19**

Since Jesus said in John 8:32 that when we know the truth it will set us free, knowing this truth about your victory over the enemy has set you free. You received your victory as a result of the completed work of redemption that Jesus did. That is why you are told as written in Romans 8:37 that you are more than a conqueror. You are not just a victor. You are more than a victor. You are now free from the fear of any enemy. You can no longer be intimidated by any enemy because you know that whatever the enemy may bring your victory is sure.

> *And ye shall know the truth, and the truth shall make you free.*
> **John 8:32**

> *Nay, in all these things we are more than conquerors through him that loved us.*
>
> **Romans 8:37**

You can win over every opposition. You can win every battle now. You don't have to loose any battle anymore. The Jesus that is now in you is the One that is wining all the victory through you. No matter the opposition your victory is assured. Even death can no longer intimidate you because you know that it cannot win against you. The Jesus in you has defeated the devil that used to have the power of death according to what is written in Hebrews 2:14.

> *Forasmuch then as the children are partakers of flesh and blood, he also himself likewise took part of the same; that through death he might destroy him that had the power of death, that is, the devil;*
>
> **Hebrews 2:14**

Jesus has taken the keys of hell and death from the devil according to Revelation 1:18. Whatever the devil may be using against you need not worry you anymore. Jesus has blotted out **all** the handwriting of ordinances that was against you, which was contrary to you. He has taken it out of your way and nailed it to the Cross. He then spoiled all principalities and powers and made an open show of them triumphing over them in it. That is what we are made to see from Colossians 2:14-15.

> *I am he that liveth, and was dead; and, behold, I am alive for evermore, Amen; and have the keys of hell and of death.*
>
> **Revelation 1:18**

Blotting out the handwriting of ordinances that was against us, which was contrary to us, and took it out of the way, nailing it to his cross;

And having spoiled principalities and powers, he made a shew of them openly, triumphing over them in it.
Colossians 2:14-15

Having done all these, Jesus declared after He rose up from the grave in Matthew 28:18 that all power in heaven and in earth has been given unto Him.

And Jesus came and spake unto them, saying, All power is given unto me in heaven and in earth.
Matthew 28:18

If Jesus has *all* power in heaven and in earth, it is obvious then that the devil has no power of his own. Where then do you get the power that you attribute to the devil? Jesus has disarmed the devil and all his forces and He has dismantled their arsenal and stripped them of all power and authority. Just like it used to be done by victors to their captives in the days of the Roman Empire, He has shown and demonstrated His victory by exhibiting openly in the heavens His conquered foes in the spiritual realm together with the captured gains of war from the defeated hosts of Satan. It was after wresting the power that the devil had and taking away from him the keys of hell and death that Jesus said that all power in heaven and in earth has been given to Him.

Living a supernatural life (Volume 3)

Therefore Satan and his forces have absolutely no power over you anymore. They can no longer hold you down or dominate you. They can only pretend to have power. But since you now know the truth that you are free you can always tell them to shut up. This is so because you already know the secret that they are already defeated and do not really have any power over you anymore. This truth that you know has completely freed you from Satan's hold since Jesus said as written in John 8:32 that when you know the truth the truth will make you free. Now you know the truth about Satan so you are free.

> *And ye shall know the truth, and the truth shall make you free.*
> **John 8:32**

Satan can no longer dominate you because you know the truth about his defeat. Jesus said in Luke 10:19 that He, who is now the owner of power has given you power over the power of your enemies, therefore you can now dominate them and put them under your control. You can free whoever is being oppressed by them. They no longer have any power over you.

> *Behold, I give unto you power to tread on serpents and scorpions, and over all the power of the enemy: and nothing shall by any means hurt you.*
> **Luke 10:19**

You have absolute victory over them through your faith in Jesus Christ and in the victory that He has obtained for you.

__What you have in Christ__

You don't even have to fight them because your battles against them are not yours to fight but God's. That is what God made us to see by what He said which is written in 2 Chronicles 20:15. So stop wasting your time.

And he said, Hearken ye, all Judah, and ye inhabitants of Jerusalem, and thou king Jehoshaphat, Thus saith the L<small>ORD</small> unto you, Be not afraid nor dismayed by reason of this great multitude; for the battle is not yours, but God's.
2 Chronicles 20:15

God has already fought and won the victory for you. Yours is just to know this and enforce the victory that is already won. You cannot be afraid or dismayed under any situation because God is committed to fight for you and God will always win. You can now have the understanding of this truth because God can reveal by His Spirit to you all the things that He has done for you because His Spirit searches all things even the deep things of God.

That is what we know from what God said through Paul in 1 Corinthians 2:9-10 and in 1 Corinthians 2:12. Therefore there is no hiding place for the devil and his forces anymore. Nothing can be hidden from you anymore. You can always know the truth about any situation that you come across. You know the truth now because the Spirit of the Lord in you guides you into all truths and the truth has set you free.

> *But as it is written, Eye hath not seen, nor ear heard, neither have entered into the heart of man, the things which God hath prepared for them that love him.*
>
> *But God hath revealed them unto us by his Spirit: for the Spirit searcheth all things, yea, the deep things of God.*
> **1 Corinthians 2:9-10**
>
> *Now we have received, not the spirit of the world, but the spirit which is of God; that we might know the things that are freely given to us of God.*
> **1 Corinthians 2:12**

YOU HAVE A QUICKENED BODY

You have been quickened together with Christ and forgiven all your sins. This is so because the Spirit of God that raised up Jesus from the dead now lives in you and it is by that same Spirit that God is quickening your mortal body. This is what God said through Paul the Apostle in Colossians 2:13 and Romans 8:11

> *And you, being dead in your sins and the uncircumcision of your flesh, hath he quickened together with him, having forgiven you all trespasses;*
> **Colossians 2:13**

<u>What you have in Christ</u>

But if the Spirit of him that raised up Jesus from the dead dwell in you, he that raised up Christ from the dead shall also quicken your mortal bodies by his Spirit that dwelleth in you.
Romans 8:11

You now have the rivers of living waters flowing out of your belly because you believe in the work of redemption that Jesus did. We know this from what Jesus Himself said in John 7:38. These rivers of living waters in you is the virtue that Jesus said came out of Him in Mark 5:30-34, which healed the woman with the issue of blood.

He that believeth on me, as the scripture hath said, out of his belly shall flow rivers of living water.
John 7:38

And Jesus, immediately knowing in himself that virtue had gone out of him, turned him about in the press, and said, Who touched my clothes?

And his disciples said unto him, Thou seest the multitude thronging thee, and sayest thou, Who touched me?

And he looked round about to see her that had done this thing.

But the woman fearing and trembling, knowing what was done in her, came and fell down before him, and told him all the truth.

Living a supernatural life (Volume 3)

> *And he said unto her, Daughter, thy faith hath made thee whole; go in peace, and be whole of thy plague.*
>
> **Mark 5:30-34**

It is that same virtue that Jesus called the rivers of living water that is supposed to be flowing out of your belly now. Therefore you also have the healing virtue, which is supposed to be flowing out of you. You can therefore see the reason why Jesus said in Mark 16:18 that you will lay hands on the sick and they shall recover. This is because the healing virtue will be flowing through your hand into the sick person. This is a spiritual phenomenon. This is the spiritual power that Jesus said you will receive after the Holy Ghost has come upon you. The same power was the one that Jesus had when He was here on earth. He has made the same power available to you now for you to wrought signs and wonders with. The same power is given to you so that you can live a life of victory here on earth.

> *They shall take up serpents; and if they drink any deadly thing, it shall not hurt them; they shall lay hands on the sick, and they shall recover.*
>
> **Mark 16:18**

Please note that Jesus did not say here that you ***shall lay hands on the sick, pray for him*** and then he will recover. The laying of the hands transfers the healing virtue into the sick person and this should heal him even if prayer is not offered for him. But today what most Christians do is lay hands on the sick then pray and pray and pray to try and get the sick person healed.

The reason for this is that they do not realize that the healing virtue that Jesus called the rivers of living water is what will flow through their hands to heal the sick man. I know that prayer can solve any problem but Jesus did not say that you should pray here. The easy way is what Jesus has given you but it requires you to know and believe that you have the healing virtue and that it will flow out of you to do the healing. What we Christians should do is to spend time with God seeking the full baptism of the Holy Spirit and the power that Jesus instructed His disciples to get before going out to witness the Gospel. You are in Christ and you should no longer walk after the flesh but after the Spirit. God has said that there is no more condemnation for you if you do so. Therefore you should make it a point of utmost importance to receive the full baptism of the Holy Spirit and feel free to let this virtue flow out of you.

YOU HAVE THE MIND OF CHRIST

You have the mind of Christ. That is what God said through Paul in 1 Corinthians 2:16. Do you know what this means? What God is telling you here is that the most developed mind, the perfect mind of God is what you now have. You have the omniscient mind of the King of kings and the Lord of lords. That is the mind that created all things, without which there was not anything created as we are made to know from what John said in John 1:1-3,14.

> *For who hath known the mind of the Lord, that he may instruct him? But we have the mind of Christ.*
>
> **1 Corinthians 2:16**

> *In the beginning was the Word, and the Word was with God, and the Word was God.*
>
> *The same was in the beginning with God.*
>
> *All things were made by him; and without him was not any thing made that was made.*
>
> *And the Word was made flesh, and dwelt among us, and we beheld his glory, the glory as of the only begotten of the Father, full of grace and truth.*
>
> **John 1:1-3,14**

This means that the creative mind of God is now at your disposal. With such a mind nothing should be daunting to you any longer. Judging by what Jesus said in Matthew 12:42 the mind of Christ that you now have gives you the capability to have more wisdom inside you than Solomon had inside him. This is true because as written in the Scriptures in John 6:56 Christ now lives in you. But from Colossians 2:3 you can see that the Christ that lives in you has all the treasures of wisdom and knowledge hidden in Him. With the One that has all the treasures of knowledge and wisdom living in you it is obvious that you are bound to be wise. Can you not see this?

> *The queen of the south shall rise up in the judgment with this generation, and shall condemn it: for she came from the uttermost parts of the earth to hear the wisdom of Solomon; and, behold, a greater than Solomon is here.*
>
> **Matthew 12:42**

What you have in Christ

He that eateth my flesh, and drinketh my blood, dwelleth in me, and I in him.
John 6:56

In whom are hid all the treasures of wisdom and knowledge.
Colossians 2:3

What this means is that you have all the treasures of wisdom and knowledge hidden in you. This means that you have the potential to have more ideas inside you than any earthly person has inside him because you have the keeper of the treasure of wisdom and knowledge living right inside you. It is obvious therefore that you are a genius waiting to explode with great inventions. You have the capability to create things. This means that wherever you are you cannot be inconsequential among your peers.

That you have the capability to have more wisdom inside you than Solomon had inside him is not surprising because Jesus Christ who is the wisdom of God and the power of God whose mind you now have and who lives in you has been made wisdom to you. You can see this from what God said through Apostle Paul in 1 Corinthians 1:24,30. So it is not only that you have His mind but He actually now lives in you to make sure that you can make positive use of that mind if you allow Him.

But unto them which are called, both Jews and Greeks, Christ the power of God, and the wisdom of God.

Living a supernatural life (Volume 3)

But of him are ye in Christ Jesus, who of God is made unto us wisdom, and righteousness, and sanctification, and redemption:
1 Corinthians 1:24,30

From what Jesus Himself said in John 15:16 you can see that He has chosen you and ordained you so that you can go and bring forth fruit and that your fruit should remain.

Ye have not chosen me, but I have chosen you, and ordained you, that ye should go and bring forth fruit, and that your fruit should remain: that whatsoever ye shall ask of the Father in my name, he may give it you.
John 15:16

Whatever you ask of the Father in the Name of Jesus Christ the Father will give it to you so that you can bear fruit. You can therefore ask and receive whatever you want in order to bear fruit. From what Jesus said in Luke 21:15 He has given you a mouth and a wisdom, which no adversary can resist or gainsay. You therefore have the ability to speak rightly all the time so that nobody can resist whatever you say if you are willing to allow the wisdom of God living in you to take control. Therefore in anything that you lay your hands upon now your success is sure. No enemy can stop or overcome you anymore.

For I will give you a mouth and wisdom, which all your adversaries shall not be able to gainsay nor resist.
Luke 21:15

What you have in Christ
YOU HAVE THE MEASURE OF FAITH

You have *the necessary measure* of faith to walk with so that you don't have to walk by sight. God has given each one of us believers *the same measure* of faith with which to walk. That is our understanding of what God said through Apostle Paul in Romans 12:3. Nobody has been given any measure greater than what you have been given. We all have *the same measure*. What makes the difference is that some people have exercised their own more than others and as a result their faith has increased. The more you exercise and practice the use of *the measure* given to you the more your faith will increase. You have to use your faith over very little things or problems and thereby gradually develop it to the point where it can cope with bigger problems and demands.

> *For I say, through the grace given unto me, to every man that is among you, not to think of himself more highly than he ought to think; but to think soberly, according as God hath dealt to every man the measure of faith.*
> **Romans 12:3**

With the measure of faith that you now have you should walk by faith not by sight. That is what God said that you should do in 2 Corinthians 5:7. As you practice walking by faith on a daily basis your faith will start to increase. If you walk by faith then you will not walk by your senses. You will not base your reactions to situations on what you see, hear, smell, taste or feel. You will not follow symptoms to decide your reactions to any situation.

Living a supernatural life (Volume 3)

For we walk by faith, not by sight:
                            2 Corinthians 5:7

For example you should not conclude that you have a fever or you are sick because your body is hot and the temperature is higher than normal. Your temperature is very high. Yes! But the Word of God says that you have been healed by the stripes that Jesus took. That is what you should base your decision on. You should only walk by faith based on whatever the Word of God says about any situation.

You must not look at things which are seen and base your decisions on them because you know that the physical things, which you can see, hear, taste, feel or smell, are temporal. But the spiritual things which you cannot see, hear, taste, feel or smell are eternal. That is what God said through Paul in 2 Corinthians 4:18. When you base your decisions in life on physical things that you can see then you are walking by sight. But when you base your decisions on faith in what the Word of God says then you are walking and living by faith. When you do so as we are advised to do by God in Romans 1:17 then those spiritual things, which you cannot see, hear, taste, feel or smell would be more real to you than the physical things, which you can see, hear, taste, feel or smell and will manifest.

While we look not at the things which are seen, but at the things which are not seen: for the things which are seen are temporal; but the things which are not seen are eternal.
                            2 Corinthians 4:18

What you have in Christ

For therein is the righteousness of God revealed from faith to faith: as it is written, The just shall live by faith.
Romans 1:17

You should not be directed by your feeling, seeing, hearing, tasting or smelling. You should only be directed by what the Word of God says. Whatever your natural senses say about any issue should not be taken as the conclusive evidence on that issue unless what they say agree with what the Word of God says on the issue. You must imbibe the spirit of faith so that, even though you cannot see, hear, taste, feel or smell those things that you want, you will still speak them out as if they already exist because that is the spirit of faith according to what God said through Paul the Apostle in 2 Corinthians 4:13. The Spirit in you is a Spirit of faith, therefore allow that Spirit of faith to work in you and express Himself fully through you.

We having the same spirit of faith, according as it is written, I believed, and therefore have I spoken; we also believe, and therefore speak;
2 Corinthians 4:13

You must be willing to stand upon the Word of God in faith until you get what you want. Even though the devil and the symptoms he brings may be saying something else to you, if you stand, securely resting on what the Word of God says without any doubt in your mind you will get whatever you want. Jesus has said in Matthew 17:20 that if you have faith and do not doubt in your mind nothing shall be impossible to you and you will get whatever you say. The ball is in your court. God has given you the faith that you need. Use it!

Living a supernatural life (Volume 3)

> *And Jesus said unto them, Because of your unbelief: for verily I say unto you, If ye have faith as a grain of mustard seed, ye shall say unto this mountain, Remove hence to yonder place; and it shall remove; and nothing shall be impossible unto you.*
> **Matthew 17:20**

He has also said in Mark 11:24 that whatever you desire, when you pray you should believe that you receive it, and you shall have it.

> *Therefore I say unto you, What things soever ye desire, when ye pray, believe that ye receive them, and ye shall have them.*
> **Mark 11:24**

I want you to particularly note what Jesus said about our prayers here. What He is saying here is that if you are to pray in faith then you must believe that you receive what you pray for as you are praying. This means that when you prayed you received what you prayed for. If your belief whenever you pray is that you will receive what you prayed for then you are praying in hope not in faith and that is not what Jesus is talking about here. But we know that it is the prayer prayed in faith that gets answered. I know that most Christians pray in hope because that is natural. But you should start practicing praying in faith if you want quick answers to your prayers. A true test that you prayed in faith when you prayed is that you will not go back to God in prayer asking for the same thing a second time.

What you have in Christ

This is because if you believe that you received it when you prayed for it the first time then there will be no need going back to God to ask for the same thing again. All you need to do from that point on is to be thanking God for having received it when you prayed even though you cannot physically see it yet. Therefore you should have no doubt whenever you pray that you received what you prayed for. This is so because you should know that God hears you whenever you pray.

He has said through John in 1 John 5:15 that if you can know that He heard you when you prayed to Him then you can be sure that you have gotten whatever you desired of Him.

> *And if we know that he hear us, whatsoever we ask, we know that we have the petitions that we desired of him.*
> **1 John 5:15**

But you can know that He always hears you if you make sure that whatever you ask for you do so according to His will, for He has said in 1 John 5:14 that if you ask for anything according to His will He hears you. So what is His will?

> *And this is the confidence that we have in him, that, if we ask any thing according to his will, he heareth us:*
> **1 John 5:14**

Anything you ask for according to His Word you can rest assured that it is also according to His will. And whatever you as according to His will you will get.

Living a supernatural life (Volume 3)

This is because His Word is a revelation of His will and He said in His Word in 3 John 2 that His will for you is to be prosperous and to be in health.

> *Beloved, I wish above all things that thou mayest prosper and be in health, even as thy soul prospereth.*
>
> 3 John 2

The measure of faith that you have been given is meant for you to do your spiritual warfare with because faith is a fight. If you do not use your faith to fight it will not develop. We have said earlier that the more you use your faith to fight the stronger it becomes. Therefore use your faith to fight. God has instructed us through Paul in 1 Timothy 6:12 to fight the good fight of faith. That is the only fight that you should fight because it is the only fight that God has instructed you as a Christian to fight, **the good fight of faith.**

> *Fight the good fight of faith, lay hold on eternal life, whereunto thou art also called, and hast professed a good profession before many witnesses.*
>
> 1 Timothy 6:12

Also through the same Paul, in 1 Corinthians 16:13, God has instructed us to stand fast in faith and to be strong. As you do these, what God says in His Word will get fulfilled in your life and the enemy's plans will be shattered. With your stand in faith therefore you can always overcome the enemy. You should know that your enemy the devil and his forces are lurking round the corner always seeking to devour you.

What you have in Christ

Watch ye, stand fast in the faith, quit you like men, be strong.
1 Corinthians 16:13

It is only your steadfast resistance in faith that will make your victory to manifest. That is what we are made to see from what God said through Apostle Peter in 1 Peter 5:8-9. It is your faith that will give you the victory, which is already yours according to Apostle John in 1 John 5:4. Now that you know that you have been given the measure of faith that you need for victory and that it is your faith that will always give you the victory you will do well to use that measure of faith that you have been given by exercising it to develop it if you want to be victorious in life.

Be sober, be vigilant; because your adversary the devil, as a roaring lion, walketh about, seeking whom he may devour:

Whom resist stedfast in the faith, knowing that the same afflictions are accomplished in your brethren that are in the world.
1 Peter 5:8-9

For whatsoever is born of God overcometh the world: and this is the victory that overcometh the world, even our faith.
1 John 5:4

Practicing the use of your faith whenever the chance or opportunity arises should be your major preoccupation as a Christian. That is the way you will increase your faith and make it stronger.

YOU HAVE THE RIGHTEOUSNESS OF CHRIST

You now have the righteousness of God because you have been given the righteousness of God as a gift and you are supposed to receive it by faith. That is what God said through Apostle Paul in Romans 5:17.

For if by one man's offence death reigned by one; much more they which receive abundance of grace and of the gift of righteousness shall reign in life by one, Jesus Christ.
Romans 5:17

When you receive this gift of the righteousness of God you are made the righteousness of God in Christ. That is the reason why Christ who knew no sin was made sin for you. This is what God said through Apostle Paul in 2 Corinthians 5:21. It follows therefore that when you receive this righteousness Christ then becomes the Sun of righteousness to you as stated in Malachi 4:2. You are then taken to be righteous by God because it is the righteousness of Christ that you are reflecting and that is what God sees when He looks at you.

For he hath made him to be sin for us, who knew no sin; that we might be made the righteousness of God in him.
2 Corinthians 5:21

But unto you that fear my name shall the Sun of righteousness arise with healing in his wings; and ye shall go forth, and grow up as calves of the stall.
Malachi 4:2

What you have in Christ

To explain this to you I want you to see that what really happens when you accept this righteousness in faith is that when you approach God it is the reflection of this Christ's righteousness that God sees. Just like the moon reflects the light of the sun to the earth at night even though it has no light of its own so likewise you now also reflect the righteousness of Christ even though you have no righteousness of your own.

In that case before God you are just as righteous as Christ because you are now united with Christ such that God now sees you in Christ and reckons Christ's righteousness to you since it is His righteousness that you are reflecting. That is what God said again through Paul in Philippians 3:9 as well as in 1 Corinthians 1:30. You have therefore become unto God a sweet savour of Jesus Christ. That is what God now makes you to be from what He said through Paul in 2 Corinthians 2:15. We have explained this earlier in *Chapter 3* of this book.

> *And be found in him, not having mine own righteousness, which is of the law, but that which is through the faith of Christ, the righteousness which is of God by faith:*
> **Philippians 3:9**

> *But of him are ye in Christ Jesus, who of God is made unto us wisdom, and righteousness, and sanctification, and redemption:*
> **1 Corinthians 1:30**

> *For we are unto God a sweet savour of Christ, in them that are saved, and in them that perish:*
>
> **2 Corinthians 2:15**

Since you are in-Christ it is Jesus Christ that God sees whenever you approach Him. Whenever you approach God for anything you can go to Him now with full confidence and no guilt-conscience knowing that what God sees is a righteous man who is approaching Him with the righteousness of Christ. Therefore you know from what He said in James 5:16 that whenever you approach Him your effectual fervent prayers to Him avail much and you should be convinced that you receive whatever you ask of Him whenever you approach Him.

> *Confess your faults one to another, and pray one for another, that ye may be healed. The effectual fervent prayer of a righteous man availeth much.*
>
> **James 5:16**

The truth that you now have the righteousness of Christ and what this means to you is well covered in *Chapter 3* of this book in the section titled *"You are righteous"*.

YOU HAVE SANCTIFICATION

You have sanctification because you are sanctified and set apart by the Holy Ghost, the Spirit of our God. You have been washed, you have been sanctified and *set apart for God* and you have been justified in the Name of our Lord Jesus Christ and by the Spirit of our God.

What you have in Christ

That is what we are made to know from what God said through Paul in 1 Corinthians 6:11.

> *And such were some of you: but ye are washed, but ye are sanctified, but ye are justified in the name of the Lord Jesus, and by the Spirit of our God.*
> **1 Corinthians 6:11**

The purpose of your sanctification is to empower you to live a righteous life having been declared righteous by God by the imputation of Christ's righteousness unto you. God gave you the righteousness of Christ as a gift and declared you righteous. But the fact that He declared you righteous does not mean that you can live a righteous life and do the works of righteousness. Yet what the Scriptures say in 1 John 3:7 is that he that doeth righteousness is righteous. It is for the purpose of empowering you to be able to do righteousness that He has sanctified you.

> *Little children, let no man deceive you: he that doeth righteousness is righteous, even as he is righteous.*
> **1 John 3:7**

Since God says that you are righteous it follows that you need to do the works of righteousness and it is sanctification that empowers you to be able to do the works of righteousness. Therefore sanctification is what perfects your righteousness because even though you are declared to be righteous by God with the righteousness of Christ given to you as a gift.

Living a supernatural life (Volume 3)

It is sanctification that actually empowers you to be able to live a righteous life. Without sanctification it is not possible for you to live a righteous life and the gift of the righteousness of Jesus Christ that God gave you will be useless to you because you will not be able to make use of it. The gift will therefore be a dormant gift not useable for the purpose for which God gave it.

According to what God said in 1 Corinthians 1:30 through Paul Christ has been made sanctification unto you. It is in Jesus Christ that you received your sanctification and from what God said through the same Paul to Timothy in 2 Timothy 2:19-21 you are a vessel unto honour sanctified, set apart and meet for Christ's use and you are prepared unto every good work. Therefore sanctification prepares you and sets you apart as a vessel to be used by Christ to do good works. From what God also said in Jude 1:1 you are also sanctified by God the Father and you are preserved in Jesus.

> *But of him are ye in Christ Jesus, who of God is made unto us wisdom, and righteousness, and sanctification, and redemption:*
> *1* **Corinthians 1:30**

> *Nevertheless the foundation of God standeth sure, having this seal, The Lord knoweth them that are his. And, Let every one that nameth the name of Christ depart from iniquity.*

> *But in a great house there are not only vessels of gold and of silver, but also of wood and of earth; and some to honour, and some to dishonour.*

If a man therefore purge himself from these, he shall be a vessel unto honour, sanctified, and meet for the master's use, and prepared unto every good work.
2 Timothy 2:19-21

Jude, the servant of Jesus Christ, and brother of James, to them that are sanctified by God the Father, and preserved in Jesus Christ, and called:
Jude 1:1

Because you have been sanctified, Jesus Christ has perfected you forever by the one offering, which He made of Himself for your sins. Because of this total sanctification that you received you have been separated from the guilt of sin. What this means is that you no longer need to allow the sin-complex conscience or the guilt-complex conscience to weigh you down. You can therefore approach God with a righteous-complex conscience having absolute confidence that God will not only give ear to what you have to say but will also accede to whatever request you make of Him. This establishes your standing before God as guiltless. That is what God said in Romans 8:1

There is therefore now no condemnation to them which are in Christ Jesus, who walk not after the flesh, but after the Spirit.
Romans 8:1

Jesus Christ sanctified you and you are now one with Him. He is not ashamed to call you His brother because you have become a member of the family of God.

Living a supernatural life (Volume 3)

That is what God made us to see in Hebrews 2:11. It is through sanctification that you have become a member of the family of God.

> *For both he that sanctifieth and they who are sanctified are all of one: for which cause he is not ashamed to call them brethren,*
> **Hebrews 2:11**

Without sanctification you cannot be accepted into the family of God. Salvation gives you the *passport* to be able to go into the Kingdom of God but sanctification is the entry *visa* that will allow or give you entry into the kingdom. A sanctified Christian will live a consecrated life *separated from sin*. Because you are now sanctified you know therefore that you are now *separated from sin* and made pure in heart to be *separated holy unto God* thus empowering you to be able to live a righteous and holy life. You therefore know that you shall see the Lord because without holiness and a pure heart no man can see the Lord. That is what God has made us to see in Hebrews 12:14 and also in Matthew 5:8.

> *Follow peace with all men, and holiness, without which no man shall see the Lord:*
> **Hebrews 12:14**

> *Blessed are the pure in heart: for they shall see God.*
> **Matthew 5:8**

You are sanctified through the Blood of Jesus Christ and through the Word of God, which is truth. That is what God said again in Hebrews 13:12 and John 17:17.

What you have in Christ

Wherefore Jesus also, that he might sanctify the people with his own blood, suffered without the gate.
Hebrews 13:12

Sanctify them through thy truth: thy word is truth.
John 17:17

From what God said in Acts 26:18 and Acts 20:32, it follows that because you have been sanctified by having faith in Christ Jesus, you have inheritance among the saints who are sanctified through the faith that you have in Christ Jesus. The inheritance is meant only for saints that are sanctified. So now that you are sanctified you have become a partaker of this inheritance of the saints who are sanctified. This makes you an heir of God and a joint-heir with Jesus Christ as stated by God in Romans 8:17.

To open their eyes, and to turn them from darkness to light, and from the power of Satan unto God, that they may receive forgiveness of sins, and inheritance among them which are sanctified by faith that is in me.
Acts 26:18

And now, brethren, I commend you to God, and to the word of his grace, which is able to build you up, and to give you an inheritance among all them which are sanctified.
Acts 20:32

> *And if children, then heirs; heirs of God, and joint-heirs with Christ; if so be that we suffer with him, that we may be also glorified together.*
>
> **Romans 8:17**

You should note that sanctification is not a once and for all thing. It is a process of perfecting holiness in you in the fear of God. Your sanctification is continuously being improved and is being perfected daily as you separate yourself from all filthiness of the flesh and the spirit. That is what God made us to realize from what He said through Apostle Paul in 2 Corinthians 6:17 and also in 2 Corinthians 7:1.

> *Wherefore come out from among them, and be ye separate, saith the Lord, and touch not the unclean thing; and I will receive you,*
>
> **2 Corinthians 6:17**

> *Having therefore these promises, dearly beloved, let us cleanse ourselves from all filthiness of the flesh and spirit, perfecting holiness in the fear of God.*
>
> **2 Corinthians 7:1**

As we have noted earlier it is the righteousness of Jesus Christ that you are now using because Christ is made unto you wisdom, righteousness, redemption and sanctification. That is what we are made to know from what God said through Paul in 1 Corinthians 1:30. You are therefore given the potential to use God's wisdom and God's righteousness through Jesus Christ.

What you have in Christ

> *But of him are ye in Christ Jesus, who of God is made unto us wisdom, and righteousness, and sanctification, and redemption:*
> **1 Corinthians 1:30**

Your sanctification is not by accident. You have been separated and called by God to be sanctified even before you were born. Before God even formed you in the belly, He already knew you. Before you came forth out of the womb, He sanctified you and set you apart.

Just as this was true for Prophet Jeremiah as is stated in Jeremiah 1:5, it is also true for you now. That God separated you right from your mother's womb and called you by His grace is also confirmed by what Apostle Paul said of himself in Galatians 1:15 because what he said here is also true of you.

> *Before I formed thee in the belly I knew thee; and before thou camest forth out of the womb I sanctified thee, and I ordained thee a prophet unto the nations.*
> **Jeremiah 1:5**

> *But when it pleased God, who separated me from my mother's womb, and called me by his grace,*
> **Galatians 1:15**

YOU HAVE DIVINE HEALTH AND HEALING

You have been healed by the stripes that Jesus Christ took on the Cross. That is what we got to know from what is written in 1 Peter 2:24.

Living a supernatural life (Volume 3)

Who his own self bare our sins in his own body on the tree, that we, being dead to sins, should live unto righteousness: by whose stripes ye were healed.

1 Peter 2:24

Note that He said *"ye were healed"* not *"ye will be healed"*. This is past tense, which means that the healing has already taken place in the spiritual realm. Therefore you cannot be sick and be praying for healing. You cannot be asking for healing in prayer. You have been healed therefore you just take your healing, which is already done, by faith. You have to command your healing to manifest in the physical realm in the Name of Jesus Christ. If you pray to God asking Him to heal you or anyone else for that matter then you are making God a liar. How will you feel if you tell your child that you have done something for him and he keeps coming back to you begging you that you should please come and do it for him even though you have told him that you have done it? Will you not think that he is making you a liar? That is the way God sees us when we pray asking Him to heal us. This is one of the most misapplied verses of the Scriptures. I know that many Christians find it difficult to believe that they are already healed since they cannot see the healing. They go by symptoms.

In order that you can have divine health God has made you an ambassador of the Kingdom here on earth knowing that if you are faithful as an ambassador then you will be health personified. We can infer this from what is written in 2 Corinthians 5:20 combined with what is written in Proverbs 13:17.

What you have in Christ

Now then we are ambassadors for Christ, as though God did beseech you by us: we pray you in Christ's stead, be ye reconciled to God.
2 Corinthians 5:20

A wicked messenger falleth into mischief: but a faithful ambassador is health.
Proverbs 13:17

This because the Scriptures also said in Proverbs 13:17 written above that a faithful ambassador is health. Therefore if you are faithful as an ambassador for Christ, which God has appointed you to be then you should be health personified. If you are health personified then it follows that you cannot be sick. How can health be sick? How can health be asking for healing? That is just not possible. Being faithful is therefore your route to divine health. As a result of your belief in Jesus Christ you have become a born-again Christian. But Jesus Christ has said in John 7:38 that whoever believes in Him out of that person's belly shall flow rivers of living water. Therefore if you truly believe in Him then you have the rivers of living water flowing out of your belly. These rivers of living water that Jesus talked about here are the healing virtue that He said came out of Him to heal the lady with the issue of blood in the story of Mark 5:28-30. What this means is that you also have this healing virtue.

He that believeth on me, as the scripture hath said, out of his belly shall flow rivers of living water.
John 7:38

> *For she said, If I may touch but his clothes, I shall be whole.*
>
> *And straightway the fountain of her blood was dried up; and she felt in her body that she was healed of that plague.*
>
> *And Jesus, immediately knowing in himself that virtue had gone out of him, turned him about in the press, and said, Who touched my clothes?*
>
> **Mark 5:28-30**

This means that you are not only health personified but you also have the healing virtue, which according to Romans 8:11 is also supposed to be quickening your mortal body. If your mortal body is being continually quickened it means that you can live in divine health.

> *But if the Spirit of him that raised up Jesus from the dead dwell in you, he that raised up Christ from the dead shall also quicken your mortal bodies by his Spirit that dwelleth in you.*
>
> **Romans 8:11**

Jesus Christ has been made perfect. That is what God said through Paul in Hebrews 5:9. Since He has been made perfect, He has perfected for ever them that are sanctified. That is what God also said as written in Hebrews 10:14. If I understand what God is saying here about being perfected then I can say that you are supposed to be living a holy life in which case you can live the life of a faithful ambassador for Christ.

And being made perfect, he became the author of eternal salvation unto all them that obey him;

Hebrews 5:9

For by one offering he hath perfected for ever them that are sanctified.

Hebrews 10:14

Since Christ has perfected you there should be no further inhibition to your living a perfect life before God. If that is the case and you know this truth and imbibe it then you cannot be tormented by diseases and any form of sickness any longer, which means that you can live in divine health.

How can you be perfected and still be moribund due to sickness or any form of disease? That is just not possible. God cannot be saying that you have been perfected if sicknesses and diseases are still making your body their home. Since you have been perfected everything in your life must carry honour.

From what God said through Paul in Romans 8:11 which we discussed in the last page you have the Spirit of God who is quickening and making alive your mortal body. Therefore sickness cannot put you in bondage. Jesus has blotted out and taken out of the way all the things that were against you and contrary to you and He has nailed them to the Cross. That is what God said in Colossians 2:14

Living a supernatural life (Volume 3)

> *Blotting out the handwriting of ordinances that was against us, which was contrary to us, and took it out of the way, nailing it to his cross;*
>
> **Colossians 2:14**

Definitely diseases, sicknesses, failures, poverty, lack and barrenness are all against you and contrary to you. If that is the case it means that they have been nailed to the Cross and taken out of your way. Therefore your mindset should be that you cannot be sick. Remember that God said through Solomon in Proverbs 23:7 that it is as you think in your heart that you will be. Therefore if your mindset is that you cannot be sick and you believe it and live as a faithful ambassador so will it be with you. But remember that your thoughts must also lead you to corresponding actions. Therefore if your mindset is that you cannot be sick you will not be doing things or eating things that can make you sick. You will run from them. By the same reasoning you can build up the mindset that you cannot fail and you will not fail. You can also have the mindset that you cannot be poor and you will not be poor. You can also develop the mindset that you cannot lack any good thing and you will not lack anything. You can also develop the mindset that you cannot be barren and you will not be barren. It is in your mind that you will fight the battles between light and darkness

> *For as he thinketh in his heart, so is he: Eat and drink, saith he to thee; but his heart is not with thee.*
>
> **Proverbs 23:7**

What you have in Christ

Every disease and every sickness or affliction that comes upon you comes as a result of the Curse of the Law. But the Scriptures say in Galatians 3:13-14 that you have been redeemed from the Curse of the Law by Jesus Christ.

> *Christ hath redeemed us from the curse of the law, being made a curse for us: for it is written, Cursed is every one that hangeth on a tree:*
>
> *That the blessing of Abraham might come on the Gentiles through Jesus Christ; that we might receive the promise of the Spirit through faith.*
>
> **Galatians 3:13-14**

If you have been redeemed from the Curse of the Law then it follows that you have also been redeemed from the consequences of the Curse of the Law. Therefore you have been redeemed from sicknesses and diseases. By inference therefore we can say that you have been healed of all sicknesses, diseases and all afflictions since all of these are part of the consequences of the Curse of the Law. Therefore no affliction can hold you down any longer. Healing is your heritage in Christ. You can see this from what Jesus said concerning the lady with the spirit of infirmity that He healed recorded in Luke 13:16. He said that the woman was entitled to healing because she was a daughter of Abraham who was God's friend. Even though you are also Abraham's son, you are much more than that. You are actually a son of God Himself not just a son of His friend Abraham.

> *And ought not this woman, being a daughter of Abraham, whom Satan hath bound, lo, these eighteen years, be loosed from this bond on the sabbath day?*
>
> **Luke 13:16**

Therefore it is obvious that if that woman with the spirit of infirmity was entitled to healing from God because she was a daughter of Abraham then you are even more entitled to the healing as a son of God, which is better than being the son of His friend.

Another thing to note is that God said through Apostle Paul in 1 Corinthians 6:20 that you are supposed to glorify God in your body and in your spirit. Definitely you cannot glorify God in your body if your body is riddled with sickness and all sorts of afflictions. That is not possible. Therefore sicknesses and afflictions are not supposed to be housed in your body.

> *For ye are bought with a price: therefore glorify God in your body, and in your spirit, which are God's.*
>
> **1 Corinthians 6:20**

YOU HAVE A ROYAL PRIESTLY OFFICE

You are of the Royal Priesthood. You belong to the elect race of the Holy nation of God that is meant to proclaim the praises of God. You are of the chosen generation. That is what God said through Apostle Peter in 1 Peter 2:9.

What you have in Christ

But ye are a chosen generation, a royal priesthood, an holy nation, a peculiar people; that ye should shew forth the praises of him who hath called you out of darkness into his marvellous light:
                                                    1 Peter 2:9

Therefore anything that will not proclaim the praises of God should not hang around you. Anything that will not proclaim the praises of God should not be part of you. Definitely such things as diseases, lack, poverty, failure and barrenness will not proclaim the praises of God in your life unless they are in your life to be healed in a miraculous way to show the power of God.

As a priest, you have a ministry of reconciliation. That is what God said through Paul in 2 Corinthians 5:18-19. This means that it is your business to show to all people the plan of God with which He has reconciled us to Himself. It also means that you can go to God to plead men's cases. You can also go to men to give them God's views and speak God's heart to them. You can hear from God directly. You don't need any human intermediary between you and God. You can go directly to the Father through the Son. God is your Father and you are his son. You now belong to His family. Speak to Him as your Father.

And all things are of God, who hath reconciled us to himself by Jesus Christ, and hath given to us the ministry of reconciliation;

Living a supernatural life (Volume 3)

> *To wit, that God was in Christ, reconciling the world unto himself, not imputing their trespasses unto them; and hath committed unto us the word of reconciliation.*
> **2 Corinthians 5:18-19**

You are also a king and a priest unto God. That is what God made us to know from what He said through John the Apostle in his revelation in Revelation 5:10. You have the divine royal blood in you because you are now a son of God and you have been made a partaker of the divine nature of God.

> *And hast made us unto our God kings and priests: and we shall reign on the earth.*
> **Revelation 5:10**

As a king therefore there is power in the words that you speak because just like Jesus said of His words as written in John 6:63, your words are also spirit and they are life. As a king nobody can say no to your words and commands. That is what we can see from what is written in Ecclesiastes 8:4. We have discussed your royal priestly role in greater detail in *Chapter 2* in the section titled, *"You are a king and a priest."*

> *It is the spirit that quickeneth; the flesh profiteth nothing: the words that I speak unto you, they are spirit, and they are life.*
> **John 6:63**

You are a priest. Yes! But you have a High Priest. Jesus Christ who is set on the right hand of God in the heavens is your High Priest who is pleading your case.

What you have in Christ

That is what the Scriptures say in Hebrews 8:1. This means that Christ our High Priest is very near to God in a position of the highest honour and respect with God. In fact we know that He is God. In Hebrews 3:1 Jesus Christ is called the High Priest of our confession and He is a faithful High Priest who will make sure that what you confess gets fulfilled once they are done in faith.

> *Now of the things which we have spoken this is the sum: We have such an high priest, who is set on the right hand of the throne of the Majesty in the heavens;*
> **Hebrews 8:1**

> *Wherefore, holy brethren, partakers of the heavenly calling, consider the Apostle and High Priest of our profession, Christ Jesus;*
> **Hebrews 3:1**

YOU HAVE THE GREATER ONE IN YOU

Because you are born of God you have overcome the world and it is your faith that gets you this victory that overcomes the world. That is what God said through John in 1 John 5:4. Jesus acting as your substitute has defeated the enemy and this victory has been counted in your favour. As far as God is concerned now He has credited that victory to you and taken you to be the winner over Satan. Therefore in the Name of Jesus you are now Satan's master and Satan is aware of this truth. But the truth is that many Christians don't know this. They don't know that Christ's victory was credited to them.

For whatsoever is born of God overcometh the world: and this is the victory that overcometh the world, even our faith.
1 John 5:4

Satan can still be pretending through his tricks and wiles to have power over you but you now know the truth that he has no power over you. *All* power belongs to God. That is what we are made to see in Psalm 62:11 and Romans 13:1. Not only that, Jesus also said in Matthew 28:18 that He has now been given all power in heaven and in earth. So if Jesus has *all* power, which one do you have left that you ascribe to Satan? What Satan now has are wiles and tricks, not power. But the manifold or many-sided wisdom of God, Jesus Christ, who is living in you now answers to you to debunk all of Satan's wiles and tricks. Once you know this truth you can no longer fall into Satan's tricks unless you refuse to tackle him with wisdom?

God hath spoken once; twice have I heard this; that power belongeth unto God.
Psalm 62:11

Let every soul be subject unto the higher powers. For there is no power but of God: the powers that be are ordained of God.
Romans 13:1

And Jesus came and spake unto them, saying, All power is given unto me in heaven and in earth.
Matthew 28:18

What you have in Christ

It is you who now has power over Satan and Satan knows this truth also. But if you don't know this Satan will hoodwink you into believing the opposite. He will then use your lack of the knowledge of the truth to continue to oppress you. If you give the wisdom of God room He should now answer to you all the time since Christ who is this wisdom is now living in you. Satan knows that he cannot do anything against you to hurt you since you now have total immunity from all his works provided you are aware of this truth. Nothing can hurt you anymore unless you decide to allow it through a lack of knowledge or other means. That is what Jesus said in Luke 10:19. We have discussed the weakness of Satan on **Pages 92-110** in **Chapter 2** of **Volume 1** of this **"Living a supernatural life"** book series.

> *Behold, I give unto you power to tread on serpents and scorpions, and over all the power of the enemy: and nothing shall by any means hurt you.*
> **Luke 10:19**

Jesus Christ now lives in you. That is what we are made to see by Paul in both Galatians 2:20 as well as in 2 Corinthian 13:5. But you know that this Christ that is now living in you is greater than whatever you may be going through. Therefore nothing should make you tremble anymore.

> *I am crucified with Christ: nevertheless I live; yet not I, but Christ liveth in me: and the life which I now live in the flesh I live by the faith of the Son of God, who loved me, and gave himself for me.*
> **Galatians 2:20**

Living a supernatural life (Volume 3)

> *Examine yourselves, whether ye be in the faith; prove your own selves. Know ye not your own selves, how that Jesus Christ is in you, except ye be reprobates?*
>
> **2 Corinthians 13:5**

Because Christ now lives in you your glorious destiny is certain. His living in you gives you the hope for this glory; "Christ in you, the hope of glory". That is what we are made to understand from what God said through Apostle Paul in Colossians 1:27.

> *To whom God would make known what is the riches of the glory of this mystery among the Gentiles; which is Christ in you, the hope of glory:*
>
> **Colossians 1:27**

You are of God and you have overcome the world as well as every spirit that is not of God because Jesus Christ who is the One in you is greater than anything in the world. That is what God also made us to know from what He said in 1 John 4:4 through Apostle John. God is in you. The One in you is greater than anything that you can come across in this world. Therefore you need not fear or have any anxiety no matter what you come across. With the greater One who is in you it follows that you have become a supernatural person too hot for Satan to handle. With the greater One in you it is obvious that your Christian journey cannot be impotent or unproductive.

What you have in Christ

Ye are of God, little children, and have overcome them: because greater is he that is in you, than he that is in the world.
1 John 4:4

You must know and keep in mind always that Christ dwells in you by faith. It is by faith that you know this. That is what Paul said in Ephesians 3:17. He is not only in you He is your life and you are in Him. He has also been made wisdom to you. That is what we have seen earlier from what God said through Paul the Apostle in both 1 Corinthians 1:30 and Colossians 3:4.

That Christ may dwell in your hearts by faith; that ye, being rooted and grounded in love,
Ephesians 3:17

But of him are ye in Christ Jesus, who of God is made unto us wisdom, and righteousness, and sanctification, and redemption:
1 Corinthians 1:30

When Christ, who is our life, shall appear, then shall ye also appear with him in glory.
Colossians 3:4

You know that Christ is the power behind all creation therefore the power behind all creation is now living inside you. That should excite you. It should make you feel on top of the world and on top of all situations that you can come across. Satan's dominion has ended in your life. Jesus, who is the greater One, now has dominion over your life.

Living a supernatural life (Volume 3)

Since the greater One dwells in you than is in the world, you should know therefore that there is nothing that you can see in this world that is greater than who is in you. This should be your mindset at all times. If you can have this Scriptural image of yourself you will never find anything daunting to you anymore because no matter what it is you will know that the One you have in you is greater than it. This will put your mind at rest so that fear and anxiety will be far from you. Come what may you will know that you will overcome in the end. You must have *the greater One mentality*.

YOU HAVE REDEMPTION IN CHRIST

You have been redeemed from all iniquity and purified unto Christ as a peculiar person who is zealous of good works. That is what God made us to see in Titus 2:14. This redemption that Jesus Christ bought for us is an eternal redemption which He obtained for us with His Blood. That is what the Scriptures say in Hebrews 9:12. Be conscious of this truth all the time.

> *Who gave himself for us, that he might redeem us from all iniquity, and purify unto himself a peculiar people, zealous of good works.*
> **Titus 2:14**

> *Neither by the blood of goats and calves, but by his own blood he entered in once into the holy place, having obtained eternal redemption for us.*
> **Hebrews 9:12**

What you have in Christ

Because you have accepted Jesus Christ into your life you have been redeemed and if we go by what Jesus said in John 7:37-38 we can conclude that you have taken of the water of life therefore you can no longer thirst. Instead, the rivers of living water are now supposed to be flowing out of your belly.

> *In the last day, that great day of the feast, Jesus stood and cried, saying, If any man thirst, let him come unto me, and drink.*
>
> *He that believeth on me, as the scripture hath said, out of his belly shall flow rivers of living water.*
> **John 7:37-38**

Because you have redemption in Christ you now have absolute liberty because Jesus has brought you into a glorious liberty. That is what God said through Apostle Paul in Romans 8:21. Therefore you can no longer be held in any type of bondage and there should be no more sorrows for you. There should be no more fears for you. Your life has been changed for ever. You are redeemed to become a blessing to all around not a curse. Whatever you do now should result in blessing because you are redeemed to bless. Your redemption has brought you out of the pit of hell into a glorious liberty in Christ.

> *Because the creature itself also shall be delivered from the bondage of corruption into the glorious liberty of the children of God.*
> **Romans 8:21**

Living a supernatural life (Volume 3)

You are redeemed to shine. You are redeemed to be a star. You are not redeemed to suffer. You are redeemed to reign over all the circumstances of life that you come across. Nothing should be able to reproach you anymore. You are redeemed to stand out. Don't you know that Jesus called you a light that is supposed to be shinning in this world? That is what the redemption that you have in Christ should do for you.

YOU HAVE THE ABUNDANT LIFE

Jesus came so that you may have the abundant life. That is what He said in John 10:10. You have accepted Him into your life therefore you have the potential for the abundant life because the abundant life is what God plans for every believer.

> *The thief cometh not, but for to steal, and to kill, and to destroy: I am come that they might have life, and that they might have it more abundantly.*
>
> **John 10:10**

Once you receive this abundant life it follows that you cannot live in poverty anymore. You should not be in want because Jesus Christ then becomes your shepherd and therefore your experience should be like that of King David, which He wrote through God's inspiration in Psalm 23:1. That is you can no longer be in want. Receive this abundant life and those things that are causing the promises of God to fail in your life will go.

What you have in Christ

The LORD is my shepherd; I shall not want.
Psalm 23:1

According to Joshua 1:8 if you have the Word of God in you and you do not allow the Word to depart from your mouth but meditate in it day and night with the mind of Christ that you now have according to what we are told by Paul in 1 Corinthians 2:16 then you must be prosperous and successful.

> *This book of the law shall not depart out of thy mouth; but thou shalt meditate therein day and night, that thou mayest observe to do according to all that is written therein: for then thou shalt make thy way prosperous, and then thou shalt have good success.*
> **Joshua 1:8**

> *For who hath known the mind of the Lord, that he may instruct him? But we have the mind of Christ.*
> **1 Corinthians 2:16**

Poverty is of the devil but you are now extremely rich because you have all things stored for you in Christ Jesus. According to the Scriptures as written by Paul in 1 Corinthians 3:21-22 all things are now yours but you get them through the knowledge of Christ as we are told in 2 Peter 1:3. That means through the knowledge of the Word of God. God's plan for you is that you live a prosperous, abundant and healthy life in which you have more than enough. He said this in 3 John 2. But as you can see it is what your soul accepts that you will have.

Living a supernatural life (Volume 3)

Therefore let no man glory in men. For all things are yours;

Whether Paul, or Apollos, or Cephas, or the world, or life, or death, or things present, or things to come; all are yours;
1 Corinthians 3:21-22

According as his divine power hath given unto us all things that pertain unto life and godliness, through the knowledge of him that hath called us to glory and virtue:
2 Peter 1:3

Beloved, I wish above all things that thou mayest prosper and be in health, even as thy soul prospereth.
3 John 2

It is what your mind accepts that you will be able to bring out in your life. Once your mind accepts prosperity and health spiritually then you have the assurance that the prosperity as well as the health will manifest physically in your life. Failure, sickness or poverty cannot have any place in your life if you do not accept them in your mind.

You are here on earth to live a good life that is full of riches and all the good things of life because you have God as your supplier. Christ who is your Shepherd is supplying all your needs but you have to know this in order to enjoy that benefit. The reason why many Christians are not enjoying this benefit is that they don't know what they really have in Jesus Christ.

Even when they do know they are timid to claim them as of right. They go to God in a beggarly manner asking God to give them what He says that they already have or to do for them what He says that He has already done. They do this because they do not know that God has already given them those things that they are asking of Him.

God is supplying all your needs and you have an abundant provision of all things in life because according to what Paul said in Philippians 4:19 God will supply all your needs according to His riches in Christ Jesus. But we do know that God has gathered together all things which are in heaven and which are in earth and put them in Christ. That is what God made us to see through Paul in Ephesians 1:10.

> *But my God shall supply all your need according to his riches in glory by Christ Jesus.*
> **Philippians 4:19**

> *That in the dispensation of the fulness of times he might gather together in one all things in Christ, both which are in heaven, and which are on earth; even in him:*
> **Ephesians 1:10**

If all things in heaven and in earth have been put in Christ it follows that there is nothing that you can need that is not in Christ Jesus. It is obvious therefore that if God will supply your needs according to His riches in Christ then you cannot lack anything.

Living a supernatural life (Volume 3)

This means that you cannot be in want of anything unless you don't know how to ask for it or you are asking for it just for the purpose of satisfying your own lusts. That is what James referred to as asking amiss in James 4:3. God will always supply your needs. That should be your mindset and if it is then that will also be your experience.

> *Ye ask, and receive not, because ye ask amiss, that ye may consume it upon your lusts.*
> **James 4:3**

In fact, God will bless you with much more than you need so that you can also be a blessing to others. I say this because when God promised Abraham as recorded in Genesis 12:2 that He was going to bless him He said He was blessing him so that he could become a blessing. I want you to note that if you are not willing to be a blessing to others then you should not expect God to bless you. Abraham's blessing was given to him so that he could be a blessing to others but from what Paul wrote in Galatians 3:13-14 you can see that you are redeemed so that you could also partake of Abraham's blessing.

> *And I will make of thee a great nation, and I will bless thee, and make thy name great; and thou shalt be a blessing:*
> **Genesis 12:2**

> *Christ hath redeemed us from the curse of the law, being made a curse for us: for it is written, Cursed is every one that hangeth on a tree:*

__What you have in Christ__

That the blessing of Abraham might come on the Gentiles through Jesus Christ; that we might receive the promise of the Spirit through faith.
Galatians 3:13-14

You are now a child of Abraham not after the flesh as Paul wrote in 1 Corinthians 10:18 but after the Spirit as implied in Galatians 3:7. Therefore the blessing of Abraham now applies to you. It follows therefore that just as in the case of Abraham, God is blessing you so that you can be a blessing. God's riches cannot be imagined because God owns everything so there is nothing that you want that you cannot get from God.

Behold Israel after the flesh: are not they which eat of the sacrifices partakers of the altar?
1 Corinthians 10:18

Know ye therefore that they which are of faith, the same are the children of Abraham.
Galatians 3:7

In the case of what you will eat or drink you don't even have to worry yourself about it because you have the assurance that this will always be provided and it is being provided if you will only trust in God for it. That is what He Himself promised in Matthew 6:25 and His promises never fail.

Living a supernatural life (Volume 3)

> *Therefore I say unto you, Take no thought for your life, what ye shall eat, or what ye shall drink; nor yet for your body, what ye shall put on. Is not the life more than meat, and the body than raiment?*
>
> **Matthew 6:25**

You have the unsearchable riches of Christ available to you now and you have been freely given all things. That is what God said in Ephesians 3:8 as well as Romans 8:32. Therefore according to 2 Corinthians 3:5 you have sufficiency. But this sufficiency is not of yourself; your sufficiency is of God. Jesus has told you in Matthew 6:33 that if you can only seek first the Kingdom of God and its righteousness then everything that you are asking for will be added unto you. You will not even need to ask for them. They are just appendages and they will be given to you as the need arises.

> *Unto me, who am less than the least of all saints, is this grace given, that I should preach among the Gentiles the unsearchable riches of Christ;*
>
> **Ephesians 3:8**

> *He that spared not his own Son, but delivered him up for us all, how shall he not with him also freely give us all things?*
>
> **Romans 8:32**

> *Not that we are sufficient of ourselves to think any thing as of ourselves; but our sufficiency is of God;*
>
> **2 Corinthians 3:5**

What you have in Christ

But seek ye first the kingdom of God, and his righteousness; and all these things shall be added unto you.
Matthew 6:33

But the problem with most Christians is that it is those things that God said would be added that they actually seek first and they put seeking the Kingdom of God and its righteousness last. Of course they get neither the Kingdom of God nor the additions that God promised. They are so eager to get wealth and struggle so much for it that they relegate seeking the Kingdom of God to the background and of course they only get poverty. If only they could just take Jesus at His Word they would have found out how easy it is to get wealth without struggling. As a born-again Christian you don't have to struggle to get wealth. In fact you have been blessed with every spiritual blessing in heavenly places in Christ. That is what God made us to see from what Paul said in Ephesians 1:3.

Blessed be the God and Father of our Lord Jesus Christ, who hath blessed us with all spiritual blessings in heavenly places in Christ:
Ephesians 1:3

Everything that you can ever need has been provided for you and stored in the heavenly bank spiritually. You have all things given to you in the spiritual realm. All you need to do is to make whatever you need to appear or manifest physically. How do you do this? To do this you must first realize that all things first manifest in the spiritual realm before they manifest in the physically realm.

Living a supernatural life (Volume 3)

But as a spirit-being that you are the spiritual things should be more real to you. That is the essence of what Paul is telling you in 2 Corinthians 4:18.

> *While we look not at the things which are seen, but at the things which are not seen: for the things which are seen are temporal; but the things which are not seen are eternal.*
> **2 Corinthians 4:18**

As we have explained earlier even the building in which you are currently seating down and reading this book was first at one time a spiritual object in somebody's mind before it was brought out to manifest in the physical to become what you now see today. Something had to be done to move it from the spiritual realm and get it to appear in the physical realm.

When you do the correct things your spiritual blessings that God said that He has given you will manifest as physical blessings. Therefore we can actually say that since you have been blessed with all spiritual blessings, it means that you have been blessed with all possible physical blessings. You only have to convert the spiritual blessings to physical blessings as and at when desired through the use of your faith coupled with works. It is through the use of your faith coupled with the appropriate work that you can make the spiritual blessings, which has been stored in Christ for you to appear or manifest physically. Therefore as a redeemed Christian who knows his rights in Christ, you cannot be poor. This may sound far-fetched to most Christians and may sound too simple to be true to them.

What you have in Christ

But remember what Paul said in 2 Corinthians 11:3. He said that you should not allow the devil to corrupt your mind from the simplicity that is in the Gospel of Christ.

> *But I fear, lest by any means, as the serpent beguiled Eve through his subtilty, so your minds should be corrupted from the simplicity that is in Christ.*
>
> **2 Corinthians 11:3**

This means that you should not let the devil put the thought in your mind that it is too simple therefore it cannot be true. Who says that it must be difficult for it to be true? Don't make things more difficult than God wants them to be for you. God said that He has blessed you with all blessings in the spiritual realm. Believe this and find out how to make your blessings in the spiritual realm to manifest in this physical realm.

You cannot suffer any lack because you have been given all spiritual blessings in heavenly places. Since these blessings are stored in Christ for you in heavenly places it means that they are very safe. They cannot be stolen, tampered with or destroyed by the enemy. They are not affected by any fire disaster, rain, economic downturn or any type of disaster. They are safe in Christ and absolutely secured. You can always go and collect them if you know what you have to do to claim them because they are there for you. They are yours. The Word of God as water in your lips can make every desert of your life to become a fertile ground blossoming with all types of beautiful flowers and fruit trees once you plant the appropriate seed of the Word of God.

Living a supernatural life (Volume 3)

When you do this then you can say as written by David in Psalm 103:5 that God satisfies your mouth with good things so that your youth is renewed as the eagle.

> *Who satisfieth thy mouth with good things; so that thy youth is renewed like the eagle's.*
> **Psalm 103:5**

Whatever you do now must prosper. As King David noted in Psalm 1:1-3 if you delight in and meditate on the Word of God day and night and walk in God's counsel following His Word, you will be like a tree planted by the rivers of water that bringeth forth his fruits in his season whose leaf never withers and everything that you lay your hands upon will prosper.

> *Blessed is the man that walketh not in the counsel of the ungodly, nor standeth in the way of sinners, nor sitteth in the seat of the scornful.*
>
> *But his delight is in the law of the LORD; and in his law doth he meditate day and night.*
>
> *And he shall be like a tree planted by the rivers of water, that bringeth forth his fruit in his season; his leaf also shall not wither; and whatsoever he doeth shall prosper.*
> **Psalm 1:1-3**

Even the economic downturn or recession in your country will not affect you. Natural and unnatural disasters will not affect you.

What you have in Christ

There will be no drought period for you. No matter the situations and trials that you may be going through, the blessing of the Lord will just follow you around if you have God's Word in your heart and you do them. Not only that, if you walk uprightly before God there is no good thing that the Lord will withhold from you as He said in Psalm 84:11.

> *For the LORD God is a sun and shield: the LORD will give grace and glory: no good thing will he withhold from them that walk uprightly.*
> **Psalm 84:11**

As you can see therefore your potential for blessing is far beyond what you can imagine. That you can have and live an abundant life is not in any doubt.

You are created in God's image and one nature of God that you ought to emulate is what Paul told us in Romans 4:17 through Apostle Paul. It is the truth that God calls those things which be not as though they were and then they appear. That is the way that you should call your spiritual blessing to appear. Even though you cannot see them, call them as though they were and they will appear.

> *As it is written, I have made thee a father of many nations, before him whom he believed, even God, who quickeneth the dead, and calleth those things which be not as though they were.*
> **Romans 4:17**

Living a supernatural life (Volume 3)
YOU HAVE STRENGTH

You have strength because the Lord is the strength of your life. That is what we are told in Psalm 27:1. Since the Lord is the strength of your life it means that everything that makes up God's strength is now yours to claim.

> *The LORD is my light and my salvation; whom shall I fear? the LORD is the strength of my life; of whom shall I be afraid?*
> **Psalm 27:1**

Therefore you have God's power, God's might, God's energy, God's force and God's ability at your disposal. That was why Apostle Paul said in Philippians 4:13 that he could do all things through Christ who strengthened him. You too can do all things through Christ who strengthens you. You now have Christ's ability therefore you don't need to fear anything. Nothing can stop you from doing whatever God lays in your heart to do. The divine strength of God is now available to you for doing whatever you are called upon to do.

> *I can do all things through Christ which strengtheneth me.*
> **Philippians 4:13**

You should be rejoicing because Jesus, who now lives in you, has overcome the world. That is what He said in John 16:33. Therefore since He has overcome the world you have also overcome the world. That should always be your mindset and your mentality. That must be the image that you have in your mind of yourself.

What you have in Christ

> *These things I have spoken unto you, that in me ye might have peace. In the world ye shall have tribulation: but be of good cheer; I have overcome the world.*
> **John 16:33**

If you really want to enjoy the use of this strength of God then you should have the joy of the Lord in your heart and rejoice always in the Lord. You must be a happy man. This is because as you know *the joy of the Lord is your strength*. You can see this from what is written in Nehemiah 8:10. You are in Zion and as written in Psalm 84:7, you will go from strength to strength every day.

> *Then he said unto them, Go your way, eat the fat, and drink the sweet, and send portions unto them for whom nothing is prepared: for this day is holy unto our Lord: neither be ye sorry; for the joy of the LORD is your strength.*
> **Nehemiah 8:10**

> *They go from strength to strength, every one of them in Zion appeareth before God.*
> **Psalm 84:7**

If you have the joy of the Lord in you there is no doubt that you will have strength. Therefore it is imperative that you must be joyful all the time if you want to enjoy the strength of God that is now available to you. With the joy of the Lord in you, it is not only the strength of God that is available to you but from what God said through Prophet Isaiah in Isaiah 12:3, it is with joy that you can draw the benefits accruing to you as a result of your salvation out of the well of salvation.

Living a supernatural life (Volume 3)

Therefore with joy shall ye draw water out of the wells of salvation.
Isaiah 12:3

This means that if you have joy in your heart then you can draw out the benefits that accrue to you as a result of your salvation just like you draw water out of a well. One of such benefits that you can draw out of the well of your salvation is strength; the strength of God because once you are saved the strength of God becomes your portion. When you do this you will have so much strength that nothing can conquer you anymore because you will be using the strength of Christ and with that on your side you will be more than a conqueror through Christ as written by Apostle Paul in Romans 8:37.

Nay, in all these things we are more than conquerors through him that loved us.
Romans 8:37

Through the strength of the Lord that you now have, you have triumphed over all your enemies. You have won the victory. Your enemies and your adversaries have been totally defeated. You have overcome every opposition of the enemy. These are truths that have to be effected by you. No doubt Satan will try to prove to you that you have no strength and that you are weak before him. He will manifest in all sorts of ways to try and prove himself strong and try to show that you are weak. But let him know that your strength is in Christ and as written in Philippians 4:13 you can do all things through Christ who strengthens you.

What you have in Christ

I can do all things through Christ which strengtheneth me.
Philippians 4:13

Satan will continue to try and prove to you that you are weak and that he can push you around. If he continues to torment you with thoughts of weakness then tell him what God said in Philippians 2:13 that it is God that works in you and you don't need to use your own strength. Then let him know also what is written in the Scriptures in 2 Corinthians 12:9 which says that the strength of God which you are now using is made perfect in weakness. Therefore the weaker you are the more perfect the strength of God that you are using becomes. Tell him that you can therefore say as it is written by Apostle Paul in 2 Corinthians 12:10 that when you are weak it is then that you are strong. Therefore the weaker you seem in the flesh the stronger you are spiritually so Satan should not frighten you with weakness. This is true because the more you make the flesh weaker the easier it becomes for you to subject it to the control of the spirit.

For it is God which worketh in you both to will and to do of his good pleasure.
Philippians 2:13

And he said unto me, My grace is sufficient for thee: for my strength is made perfect in weakness. Most gladly therefore will I rather glory in my infirmities, that the power of Christ may rest upon me.
2 Corinthians 12:9

Living a supernatural life (Volume 3)

> *Therefore I take pleasure in infirmities, in reproaches, in necessities, in persecutions, in distresses for Christ's sake: for when I am weak, then am I strong.*
> **2 Corinthians 12:10**

Therefore do not let Satan torment you with any thought that you are weak. The weaker he thinks that you are the stronger you really are. Therefore know and be convinced that you have strength. Let that be the image that you have of yourself. Let that be your mindset. Let the devil do anything or manifest in any form you know and you are sure that you have power above whatever he can manifest. You are using the strength of Christ therefore nothing the devil does should move you. No matter what the devil does now, no matter what problems or afflictions he may bring, the result is already known because as written by John in 1 John 4:4 you have already won the battle through Christ who is the greater One that is in you and nothing can change that. God has made you a conqueror through Jesus Christ. You are even more than a conqueror as written in Romans 8:37 unless you sell in to the devil.

> *Ye are of God, little children, and have overcome them: because greater is he that is in you, than he that is in the world.*
> **1 John 4:4**

> *Nay, in all these things we are more than conquerors through him that loved us.*
> **Romans 8:37**

What you have in Christ

Note that Christ has already won the victory and you are now living in the victory. You are supposed to be enjoying the fruit of that victory now. But as is done in the physical realm even when you have defeated an enemy and disarm him he can start a guerrilla warfare against you, that is a hit and run type of attack. That is exactly what the devil is doing with you. He knows that he is a defeated foe but do you know that? He knows that if you do not know this truth then he can take advantage of you and that is what he is doing with most Christians.

You need not worry yourself about his attacks because if you know what you now have in Christ you will know that you can put the devil and his forces of darkness under control. To top it all God Himself is now with you and once you are with God nothing shall be impossible for you according to Jesus in Luke 1:37.

> *For with God nothing shall be impossible.*
> **Luke 1:37**

Therefore nothing is impossible to you now because God lives in you as written by Paul in Galatians 2:20. You have God's strength and ability therefore there is no limitation for you anymore if you are living a life of sanctity.

> *I am crucified with Christ: nevertheless I live; yet not I, but Christ liveth in me: and the life which I now live in the flesh I live by the faith of the Son of God, who loved me, and gave himself for me.*
> **Galatians 2:20**

Living a supernatural life (Volume 3)

Every Red Sea on your way must give way to you and swallow up whatever is pursuing you. Every wall of Jericho on your path must now fall for you. Every bitter waters of Marah on your path will now automatically become sweetened. Every Pharaoh holding you or your heritage captive that you come into combat with must bow for you and let go of you and all that belong to you. Nobody can hold you in bondage any longer.

Live as you are supposed to live by faith and stop focusing your sight on symptoms of diseases and afflictions and things which you can see with your senses and which are brought to you by the devil. You don't have to allow space in your mind for any picture that Satan throws into your mind. If you can do this and apply the Word of God that you now have to anything that Satan brings you will find all the threatening of Satan to be just illusions and ephemeral. Satan has no power to permanently hang anything on you anymore.

With the strength of God that you now have, living a supernatural life full of miracles, signs and wonders will become a reality and the normal way of life for you.

YOU HAVE GOD WITH YOU ALWAYS

You have the Lord with you always, even unto the end of the world. So wherever you may go the Lord Jesus Christ is with you at any time and always. That is what Jesus said that He would do in Matthew 28:18-20. Whatever storm you may be going through know that God is there with you.

What you have in Christ

And Jesus came and spake unto them, saying, All power is given unto me in heaven and in earth.

Go ye therefore, and teach all nations, baptizing them in the name of the Father, and of the Son, and of the Holy Ghost:

Teaching them to observe all things whatsoever I have commanded you: and, lo, I am with you alway, even unto the end of the world. Amen.
Matthew 28:18-20

Knowing this should give you the confidence that you need at all times. He had said that He would never leave you nor forsake you. Therefore you can boldly say as it is written in Hebrews 13:5-6 that the Lord is your helper and you will not fear what man shall do unto you. If the Lord God is with you what can you fear? You should fear nothing.

Let your conversation be without covetousness; and be content with such things as ye have: for he hath said, I will never leave thee, nor forsake thee.

So that we may boldly say, The Lord is my helper, and I will not fear what man shall do unto me.
Hebrews 13:5-6

Living a supernatural life (Volume 3)

Therefore you know that wherever you are God is there. No matter what you may be going through God is there with you. He is there and He is for you and if God be for you nobody can be against you and win. That is the essence of the question that God is asking us through Paul in Romans 8:31.

> *What shall we then say to these things? If God be for us, who can be against us?*
> **Romans 8:31**

Obviously the enemies will come against you but the truth is that they can never win against you. It is sure that they will come but they cannot win. Since God is for you, it is not necessary for you to border yourself about what the enemy is doing to you anymore because whatever the enemy does should not be a deciding factor in the decisions that you take. You should not in any way allow it to affect your destiny.

Your mind must be set on the truth that no enemy can come against you and win. You don't have to worry yourself anymore about what the enemy is doing. With God on your side, nothing can stand against you and win. That should be the understanding that you have of your position now in Christ. Therefore you should no longer fear no matter what the situation may be.

When some Christians pray you hear them **asking God to come down and join them or sing, "Pass me not oh gentle Saviour."** That kind of prayer lacks understanding. They pray with much zeal but not according to knowledge just like the Roman Christians that Paul talked about in Romans 10:2 who he said had the zeal of God but not according to knowledge.

What you have in Christ

> *For I bear them record that they have a zeal of God, but not according to knowledge.*
> **Romans 10:2**

To show you just how much of a mistake such Christians are making and their lack of knowledge when they pray asking God to come down and join them let us look at what the Word of God has to say about this.

What we can see from the Word of God is that God is with you always because God is in front of you, God is behind you, God is underneath you, God is above you, God is around you, God is living inside you and you are inside God. That is what the Scriptures make us to understand. Let us look at each of these statements in the light of what the Scriptures say.

GOD IS IN FRONT OF YOU

This is true because we are told in Isaiah 52:12, also in Isaiah 45:2 and Deuteronomy 31:8 that the Lord will go before you.

> *For ye shall not go out with haste, nor go by flight: for the LORD will go before you; and the God of Israel will be your rereward.*
> **Isaiah 52:12**

> *I will go before thee, and make the crooked places straight: I will break in pieces the gates of brass, and cut in sunder the bars of iron:*
> **Isaiah 45:2**

Living a supernatural life (Volume 3)

> *And the LORD, he it is that doth go before thee; he will be with thee, he will not fail thee, neither forsake thee: fear not, neither be dismayed.*
>
> **Deuteronomy 31:8**

God was in front of the children of Israel in their journey after they were freed by the Pharaoh of Egypt.

The God going before them was the One that David was talking about in Psalm 114:3-7 when he referred to something that the sea saw in front of the Israelites and fled. He said it was the presence of the God of Jacob that the sea saw that made the sea to flee, the mountains to skip like rams and the hills like lambs. God was in front of them but they did not know.

> *The sea saw it, and fled: Jordan was driven back.*
>
> *The mountains skipped like rams, and the little hills like lambs.*
>
> *What ailed thee, O thou sea, that thou fleddest? thou Jordan, that thou wast driven back?*
>
> *Ye mountains, that ye skipped like rams; and ye little hills, like lambs?*
>
> *Tremble, thou earth, at the presence of the Lord, at the presence of the God of Jacob;*
>
> **Psalm 114:3-7**

Even though they could not see God He was there in front of them. Look at the way David described the scene above. God is also going in front of you in your journey through life even though you cannot see Him. It is the same thing with you today. God is in front of you but most people don't know this. Get to know and believe this so that your confidence can increase.

GOD IS BEHIND YOU

God is not only in front of you He is behind you. This is true because we are told in Isaiah 58:8 that the glory of the Lord shall be your rereward and in Isaiah 52:12 that God is your rereward. What this actually means is that God and the glory of the Lord shall be your rear guard. This means that God is behind you and the glory of the Lord is behind you.

> *Then shall thy light break forth as the morning, and thine health shall spring forth speedily: and thy righteousness shall go before thee; the glory of the LORD shall be thy rereward.*
> **Isaiah 58:8**

> *For ye shall not go out with haste, nor go by flight: for the Lord will go before you; and the God of Israel will be your rereward.*
> **Isaiah 52:12**

As stated through Prophet Isaiah in Isaiah 30:21 the God that is behind you is the One that will talk into your ears from behind you whenever you need instruction or direction. You should realize therefore that even though you cannot see your back, you should know that God is there.

> *And thine ears shall hear a word behind thee, saying, This is the way, walk ye in it, when ye turn to the right hand, and when ye turn to the left.*
>
> **Isaiah 30:21**

That should give you an assurance that whatever may come at you from your back even though you cannot see it God who can see it is there to protect you. You therefore have security even behind you.

GOD IS UNDERNEATH YOU

This is true because as you can see from what we are told by God in Deuteronomy 33:27 that the everlasting arm of the Lord is underneath you. With His hand underneath you it is sure that you are safe because He will thrust out every enemy before you. He will destroy every enemy that comes against you.

> *The eternal God is thy refuge, and underneath are the everlasting arms: and he shall thrust out the enemy from before thee; and shall say, Destroy them.*
>
> **Deuteronomy 33:27**

GOD IS ABOVE YOU

This is also true because from what King Solomon wrote in the Songs of Solomon 2:4 we are told that God's love is the banner over His saints among which you are now one. His banner is over you.

> *He brought me to the banqueting house, and his banner over me was love.*
> **Songs of Solomon 2:4**

God is the God in heaven above. He is also the God in the earth beneath. That is what we are made to understand from what is written in Deuteronomy 4:39. Therefore God is above you and God is beneath you. The fact that you cannot see Him with your physical eyes does not mean that He is not above you or beneath you. The truth is that He has stretched His banner over you. Therefore you can be confident and know assuredly that you are secured.

> *Know therefore this day, and consider it in thine heart, that the LORD he is God in heaven above, and upon the earth beneath: there is none else.*
> **Deuteronomy 4:39**

We have shown so far that God is before you in front of you, behind you; above you and underneath you.

Living a supernatural life (Volume 3)
GOD IS AROUND YOU

This means that God surrounds you completely. That is what we are made to understand by what David the king said in Psalm 125:2.

> *As the mountains are round about Jerusalem, so the LORD is round about his people from henceforth even for ever.*
> **Psalm 125:2**

What this means is that God surrounds you completely. God not only surrounds you but according to what is written in Zechariah 2:5 He is actually a wall of fire around you. This means that whatever attempts to attack you will be burnt.

> *For I, saith the LORD, will be unto her a wall of fire round about, and will be the glory in the midst of her.*
> **Zechariah 2:5**

If you are where God placed you in-Christ nothing can attack you and not be burned.

GOD IS IN YOU

In order that you can have absolute confidence that God is always with you and for you, He has decided to actually dwell in you. So, you have God dwelling in you and walking in you. That is what God said through Paul in 2 Corinthians 6:16.

What you have in Christ

> *And what agreement hath the temple of God with idols? for ye are the temple of the living God; as God hath said, I will dwell in them, and walk in them; and I will be their God, and they shall be my people.*
> **2 Corinthians 6:16**

From what Jesus said in John 14:23 and what Paul the Apostle wrote in Romans 8:9, you have God the Father, the Son and the Holy Ghost dwelling in you; therefore the fullness of the Godhead dwells in you spiritually. This is very significant and you must be very conscious of this truth. If you are conscious of it you will then know that it is God that now works in you to do His will. That is what he made us to know from what He said through Paul in Philippians 2:13.

> *Jesus answered and said unto him, If a man love me, he will keep my words: and my Father will love him, and we will come unto him, and make our abode with him.*
> **John 14:23**

> *But ye are not in the flesh, but in the Spirit, if so be that the Spirit of God dwell in you. Now if any man have not the Spirit of Christ, he is none of his.*
> **Romans 8:9**

> *For it is God which worketh in you both to will and to do of his good pleasure.*
> **Philippians 2:13**

Living a supernatural life (Volume 3)

It is quite difficult for most Christians to comprehend this truth that God lives in them. They say it but they don't really believe what they are saying. This is because they try to comprehend this truth physically with their minds. But this is not a physical phenomenon. This is a spiritual phenomenon. If you can only remember the truth that you are a spirit being then this will not be difficult for you to comprehend. God is in you through His Spirit. He lives in you. His Spirit lives in your spirit. This means that you have become His tabernacle. You have become His temple where He lives. That is what He told us through John in 1 John 3:24 and through Paul in 1 Corinthians 3:16.

And he that keepeth his commandments dwelleth in him, and he in him. And hereby we know that he abideth in us, by the Spirit which he hath given us.
1 John 3:24

Know ye not that ye are the temple of God, and that the Spirit of God dwelleth in you?
1 Corinthians 3:16

Since you are now His temple, His house where He lives, it follows that He will take care of you and not let anything defile you. That is what we are told by God through Paul the Apostle in 1 Corinthians 3:17. He knows that it is when your body is in good shape that it will be a convenient abode for Him so He will do anything necessary to protect it.

What you have in Christ

If any man defile the temple of God, him shall God destroy; for the temple of God is holy, which temple ye are.
1 Corinthians 3:17

You should therefore be confident and rest assured that God Himself is the One looking out for whatever attempts to pollute or defile you. That God is in you is further confirmed by God by what He said through Apostle Paul in 1 Corinthians 6:19.

What? know ye not that your body is the temple of the Holy Ghost which is in you, which ye have of God, and ye are not your own?
1 Corinthians 6:19

You can see from what we are told here that it is not only that God is living in you but that you actually belong to Him.

You are His property and from what He said written in 1 Corinthians 6:20 He bought you with a price, which is the Blood of Jesus Christ His only begotten Son. Therefore you are priceless and precious to Him. You are worth much more than you think to Him.

For ye are bought with a price: therefore glorify God in your body, and in your spirit, which are God's.
1 Corinthians 6:20

Living a supernatural life (Volume 3)

You can therefore see that any apprehensions about what may be happening to you are baseless. This is because God who owns you and sees you as His house will obviously protect what belongs to Him and where He lives. With the revelation of this truth that your body is a temple of God, where God lives and that it belongs to God all your worries should be over. God is capable of protecting His own house. Let this be your mindset about your body all the time. Believe that you are God's and nothing can happen to you without Him knowing about it. You need not be afraid of any situation anymore because you know that God is living in you. The God that is living in you is greater than anything that you can come across in this world. Therefore you can always overcome anything that comes against you. The power to do this is living right inside of you. That is what God is making you to see in 1 John 4:4.

> *Ye are of God, little children, and have overcome them: because greater is he that is in you, than he that is in the world.*
> **1 John 4:4**

No matter what may be the intensity of the attack of the enemy or adversary against you, your victory is assured. In fact, it is when the intensity becomes much that the Spirit of God that lives in you will raise up a standard against the enemy. That is the essence of what God is making us to see from what He said through Prophet Isaiah in Isaiah 59:19. What an assurance that is for you to know that nothing can come against you and win unless you agree in your mind to be defeated. You can now always win in every battle of life you get involved in.

So shall they fear the name of the Lord from the west, and his glory from the rising of the sun. When the enemy shall come in like a flood, the Spirit of the Lord shall lift up a standard against him.

Isaiah 59:19

YOU ARE HIDDEN IN GOD

To make absolutely sure that you are well protected God now puts you in Himself so that you are hidden in Him. This is a mystery that cannot be comprehended with the ordinary human mind but it is the truth for that is what the Bible says in Colossians 3:3. This can only be spiritually discerned. The God that is so big He can fill the universe can also live inside man! Meditate on this.

For ye are dead, and your life is hid with Christ in God.

Colossians 3:3

How can you be hidden in God, have God in front of you, behind you, underneath you, above you, also surrounding you, in you, and you in Him and with all these still be praying that God should come and join you or pass you not?

If you do that it means that you have not gotten the revelation of God's presence with you. Read the Word of God; meditate on it until you get that revelation. God is with you all the time and everywhere. There is an all-round protection for you because God is always around you. That should be your mindset.

Living a supernatural life (Volume 3)

Remember how Jacob awoke from his sleep in Bethel in Genesis 28:16 to realize that God was there with him and he did not know it? So it is with many of the Christians of today. It is obvious that God is with them and they do not know it. God is not only with you He is actually with you like a mighty terrible One as written in Jeremiah 20:11. It is obvious therefore that ***God is always with you.***

> *And Jacob awaked out of his sleep, and he said, Surely the Lord is in this place; and I knew it not.*
> **Genesis 28:16**

> *But the LORD is with me as a mighty terrible one: therefore my persecutors shall stumble, and they shall not prevail: they shall be greatly ashamed; for they shall not prosper: their everlasting confusion shall never be forgotten.*
> **Jeremiah 20:11**

Just like God built a hedge around Job as stated even by Satan in Job 1:10 and Job did not know it God has also built a hedge around you to protect you and all that belongs to you but you don't know this. His many promises to you form the hedge of protection that He has built around you, around your house and all that you have.

> *Hast not thou made an hedge about him, and about his house, and about all that he hath on every side? thou hast blessed the work of his hands, and his substance is increased in the land.*
> **Job 1:10**

It is obvious therefore that God is always with you. He is not only with you; He surrounds you with Himself like a hedge, which is a wall of fire. He is above you, He is underneath you, He is in front of you and He is behind you. Just as He said in Zechariah 2:5 through Prophet Zechariah that He would be unto Jerusalem a wall of fire around her so is He now supposed to be a wall of fire around you.

> *For I, saith the Lord, will be unto her a wall of fire round about, and will be the glory in the midst of her.*
> **Zechariah 2:5**

Wherever you turn God is there. How can you still be praying that He should come and join you or pass you not? God is already with you and is for you and if God be for you who can be against you and win? Nobody according to Romans 8:31.

> *What shall we then say to these things? If God be for us, who can be against us?*
> **Romans 8:31**

It is this realization that God is always with us and that there is no where that we are that God is not there that made David to write about God's omnipresence with us in Psalm 139:1-14. In that Scripture David made us to realize that we cannot hide ourselves from God because He knows all our movements and He is always with us. Wherever we are He is there with us.

> *O LORD, thou hast searched me, and known me.*

Thou knowest my downsitting and mine uprising, thou understandest my thought afar off.

Thou compassest my path and my lying down, and art acquainted with all my ways.

For there is not a word in my tongue, but, lo, O LORD, thou knowest it altogether.

Thou hast beset me behind and before, and laid thine hand upon me.

Such knowledge is too wonderful for me; it is high, I cannot attain unto it.

Whither shall I go from thy spirit? or whither shall I flee from thy presence?

If I ascend up into heaven, thou art there: if I make my bed in hell, behold, thou art there.

If I take the wings of the morning, and dwell in the uttermost parts of the sea;

Even there shall thy hand lead me, and thy right hand shall hold me.

If I say, Surely the darkness shall cover me; even the night shall be light about me.

Yea, the darkness hideth not from thee; but the night shineth as the day: the darkness and the light are both alike to thee.

> *For thou hast possessed my reins: thou hast covered me in my mother's womb.*
>
> *I will praise thee; for I am fearfully and wonderfully made: marvellous are thy works; and that my soul knoweth right well.*
>
> **Psalm 139:1-14**

You now have the capability to see beyond the natural. Set your mind and your spiritual eyes to see this revelation that God is with you everywhere you go all the time. Therefore nothing should move you anymore. If you can only see this you will never feel lonely again.

We are made to know through Proverbs 15:3 that the eyes of the Lord are in every place. It follows therefore that no matter where you are God is there. God's presence is there and He can see what is happening to you.

> *The eyes of the LORD are in every place, beholding the evil and the good.*
>
> **Proverbs 15:3**

God is not only in every place and His eyes in every place where you are but you actually live and move in Him. That is what we are told in Acts 17:28.

> *For in him we live, and move, and have our being; as certain also of your own poets have said, For we are also his offspring.*
>
> **Acts 17:28**

Living a supernatural life (Volume 3)

As written in Isaiah 43:2 therefore whatever trouble or danger you may go through God will be there with you to protect you. It doesn't matter whether you are going through the waters, the rivers of affliction, through the fire of hardship and torments the Lord God will be there with you so that the waters will not overflow you neither will the fire burn you.

> *When thou passest through the waters, I will be with thee; and through the rivers, they shall not overflow thee: when thou walkest through the fire, thou shalt not be burned; neither shall the flame kindle upon thee.*
> **Isaiah 43:2**

YOU HAVE POWER OVER THAT OF THE ENEMY

Jesus has been given all authority and power both in Heaven and on earth and even under the earth and He in return has given you this power and authority over any power that wants to oppose you.

This include power over any power that opposes you while carrying out His order to evangelize the world as He commanded in Matthew 28:18-20. Jesus Christ who is the Lord of Heaven and earth has been given absolute and total authority over every spirit-being in Heaven, on earth and under the earth. Therefore your authority is not a fake one. You can see this from what Paul said in Philippians 2:9-11. It is obvious therefore that if He gives you power then you truly have real power indeed.

And Jesus came and spake unto them, saying, All power is given unto me in heaven and in earth.

Go ye therefore, and teach all nations, baptizing them in the name of the Father, and of the Son, and of the Holy Ghost:

Teaching them to observe all things whatsoever I have commanded you: and, lo, I am with you alway, even unto the end of the world. Amen.
Matthew 28:18-20

Wherefore God also hath highly exalted him, and given him a name which is above every name:

That at the name of Jesus every knee should bow, of things in heaven, and things in earth, and things under the earth;

And that every tongue should confess that Jesus Christ is Lord, to the glory of God the Father.
Philippians 2:9-11

What He has done in delegating this authority that He has to us amounts to giving us the power of attorney to use the authority. He has not only given you the right to use His authority but He is with you always to support you in its use even unto the end of this age. Christ gave us this order to go and preach the good news to the world but in order that you can do this

Living a supernatural life (Volume 3)

He has recreated you in Him as you can see in Ephesians 2:10. You are now a totally new creature in Christ and you are now a member of the Body of Christ. Your flesh is a member of His flesh and your bones are members of His bones. That is what we are told by Paul in 2 Corinthians 5:17 and Ephesians 5:30.

> *For we are his workmanship, created in Christ Jesus unto good works, which God hath before ordained that we should walk in them.*
> **Ephesians 2:10**

> *Therefore if any man be in Christ, he is a new creature: old things are passed away; behold, all things are become new.*
> **2 Corinthians 5:17**

> *For we are members of his body, of his flesh, and of his bones.*
> **Ephesians 5:30**

He has said in Mark 9:23 that all things are possible to them that believe. If all things are possible to you then you cannot be subdued by any enemy or adversary because you can always put their plans and actions against you under control. Because you believe in Christ, all things are now possible to you. You have life now because you have Christ the Son of God living in you and He is life. You have eternal life. That is what we see from what is written in 1 John 5:11-12.

> *Jesus said unto him, If thou canst believe, all things are possible to him that believeth.*
> **Mark 9:23**

What you have in Christ

And this is the record, that God hath given to us eternal life, and this life is in his Son.

He that hath the Son hath life; and he that hath not the Son of God hath not life.
                              1 John 5:11-12

Since Christ is the power of God and the wisdom of God as we are told in 1 Corinthians 1:24 it follows that you have the wisdom of God in you and you have the power of God living in you. From what is written by Apostle Paul in 1 Corinthians 1:30 Christ has also been made wisdom and righteousness and sanctification and redemption unto you.

But unto them which are called, both Jews and Greeks, Christ the power of God, and the wisdom of God.
                              1 Corinthians 1:24

But of him are ye in Christ Jesus, who of God is made unto us wisdom, and righteousness, and sanctification, and redemption:
                              1 Corinthians 1:30

This means that Christ has been made your wisdom, your righteousness, your sanctification and your redemption. His wisdom has become your wisdom. His ability has become your ability. Therefore there is no trick or wiles that the enemy can use that Christ who is the manifold wisdom of God cannot overcome. You now have the authority to do the works that Christ did by using His Name because He authorized you to do this from what He said in John 14:12. In His Name you have been authorized to cast out devils, heal the sick and speak in a new tongue.

Living a supernatural life (Volume 3)

> *Verily, verily, I say unto you, He that believeth on me, the works that I do shall he do also; and greater works than these shall he do; because I go unto my Father.*
>
> **John 14:12**

In His Name you have been authorized to take up serpents and they shall not hurt you. Even if you drink any deadly thing it shall not hurt you. In His Name you have been authorized to lay hands on the sick and they shall recover. He gave us this authority from what He said in Mark 16:15-18. In order for you to be able to do these and to successfully establish the authority that He has given you, He has given you the power to tread upon serpents and scorpions and over all the power of any enemy. He said this in Luke 10:19. This means that no enemy can stop you. Can you see this?

> *And he said unto them, Go ye into all the world, and preach the gospel to every creature.*
>
> *He that believeth and is baptized shall be saved; but he that believeth not shall be damned.*
>
> *And these signs shall follow them that believe; In my name shall they cast out devils; they shall speak with new tongues;*
>
> *They shall take up serpents; and if they drink any deadly thing, it shall not hurt them; they shall lay hands on the sick, and they shall recover.*
>
> **Mark 16:15-18**

Behold, I give unto you power to tread on serpents and scorpions, and over all the power of the enemy: and nothing shall by any means hurt you.

Luke 10:19

This assures you that no power of the enemy can overcome you. Whatever powers the enemy can demonstrate the power in you is greater. No enemy can resist you if you know where you are and you stay there.

If you know what power you now have in-Christ you will realize that no opposition can stop you. When you give commands to the enemy it must be obeyed. That should be your mental attitude and mindset at all times and in all situations.

YOU HAVE THE ABILITY TO OVERCOME TEMPTATIONS

You have the ability to face all temptations or trials and triumph over them. God has given you the ability and power to overcome every temptation that comes your way. Trials will come. They may bring pains and all kinds of negative effects but you will surely come on top of them in the end. That should be your mentality. Therefore you don't have to worry yourself about trials and temptation. This is because God has said that He would not allow any temptation or trial that is bigger than you can cope with to come your way. That is what God said through Paul in 1 Corinthians 10:13.

Living a supernatural life (Volume 3)

> *There hath no temptation taken you but such as is common to man: but God is faithful, who will not suffer you to be tempted above that ye are able; but will with the temptation also make a way to escape, that ye may be able to bear it.*
> **1 Corinthians 10:13**

From what God said here you know that whatever temptation or trial comes your way it is because God knows that you are quite capable of coping with it. That is why He has allowed it to come your way. Not only that, God even said that should in case you have to struggle with it then He has provided a way of escape for you. If God finds that you are finding it difficult to cope with He has provided a way of escape for you.

When I see a Christian depressed when he is being afflicted I know that such a Christian is one of God's people that He referred to as being destroyed for lack of knowledge in Hosea 4:6.

> *My people are destroyed for lack of knowledge: because thou hast rejected knowledge, I will also reject thee, that thou shalt be no priest to me: seeing thou hast forgotten the law of thy God, I will also forget thy children.*
> **Hosea 4:6**

This is because I know that as a Christian it is obvious that you can never be boxed in by any trial or temptation. This should give you absolute confidence in any trial.

What you have in Christ

In fact you should count it all joy and rejoice in the Lord when you fall into such trial and temptations because the testing of your faith produces patience and patience will eventually lead you to your perfection so that you can be complete and lacking in nothing. That is what we are told in James 1:2-4. Therefore you should be thanking God for His ability that He has given you to face temptations whenever you fall into divers' temptations and rejoice because you know that the joy of the Lord is your strength. That is what God said in Nehemiah 8:10. We also know from what we are told in 1 Peter 1:7 that as the trial of your faith works patience in you it will eventually lead you into praise, honour, glory and fruitfulness in the knowledge of Christ. As you steadfastly allow patience to have its perfect work in you, it will lead you more and more to perfection thereby putting you in a position where you are in want of nothing.

> *My brethren, count it all joy when ye fall into divers temptations;*
>
> *Knowing this, that the trying of your faith worketh patience.*
>
> *But let patience have her perfect work, that ye may be perfect and entire, wanting nothing.*
> **James 1:2-4**
>
> *Then he said unto them, Go your way, eat the fat, and drink the sweet, and send portions unto them for whom nothing is prepared: for this day is holy unto our Lord: neither be ye sorry; for the joy of the LORD is your strength.*
> **Nehemiah 8:10**

> *That the trial of your faith, being much more precious than of gold that perisheth, though it be tried with fire, might be found unto praise and honour and glory at the appearing of Jesus Christ:*
>
> 1 Peter 1:7

YOU HAVE THE GLORY THAT JESUS HAD

Just before Jesus Christ left this earth He said as written in John 17:22 that He has given you the glory that God gave to Him so that you could be one with the other believers in Christ. You have that potential.

> *And the glory which thou gavest me I have given them; that they may be one, even as we are one:*
>
> John 17:22

Therefore you should make sure that as much as is possible you try to be one with all other believers in Christ.

This is necessary because from what Jesus said above you know that as long as you do this you are entitled to the same glory that God gave to Jesus Christ when He came to this world. But if you are one of the Christians that will not cooperate with other Christians because they do not belong to the same denomination with you or for any other reason then you should not expect to partake of this glory that Christ has given to us who are believers.

This is so because the glory is given to you so that you can be one with the other believers in Christ. You can see that day by day you are being changed on a continuous basis into the same image as the Lord Jesus Christ from glory to glory by the Spirit of the Lord that now lives in you. That is the essence of what God is making us to know in 2 Corinthians 3:18.

> *But we all, with open face beholding as in a glass the glory of the Lord, are changed into the same image from glory to glory, even as by the Spirit of the Lord.*
> **2 Corinthians 3:18**

YOU HAVE THE SUPPORT THAT JESUS HAD

We have said earlier that you are here on earth as an ambassador of Jesus Christ. That is what God has made us to understand from what He said through Paul the Apostle in 2 Corinthians 5:20. As an ambassador of Christ you have been sent by Jesus Christ and He has sent you just as the Father sent Him. That is what Jesus Himself said in John 20:21. Since you are sent as He was sent you now have available to you for your support everything that He had for His support when He was here on earth.

> *Now then we are ambassadors for Christ, as though God did beseech you by us: we pray you in Christ's stead, be ye reconciled to God.*
> **2 Corinthians 5:20**

Living a supernatural life (Volume 3)

Then said Jesus to them again, Peace be unto you: as my Father hath sent me, even so send I you.
                                                        John 20:21

Looking at the way that He was sent as listed and described in Isaiah 7:14-15, Luke 1:31-33 as well as in Revelation 22:16, you can see that He was sent to be great and He was great. He was sent to be prosperous and He was very prosperous. He was sent to be a star, a bright and morning star, to shine here on earth and He shone like a million stars.

Therefore the Lord himself shall give you a sign; Behold, a virgin shall conceive, and bear a son, and shall call his name Immanuel.

Butter and honey shall he eat, that he may know to refuse the evil, and choose the good.
                                                        Isaiah 7:14-15

And, behold, thou shalt conceive in thy womb, and bring forth a son, and shalt call his name Jesus.

He shall be great, and shall be called the Son of the Highest: and the Lord God shall give unto him the throne of his father David:

And he shall reign over the house of Jacob for ever; and of his kingdom there shall be no end.
                                                        Luke 1:31-33

I Jesus have sent mine angel to testify unto you these things in the churches. I am the root and the offspring of David, and the bright and morning star.
Revelation 22:16

He was sent to reign here on earth and He reigned over all the circumstances that He came across when He was here on earth. He reigned over diseases and sicknesses. He reigned over the wind, the waves and over all the elements. Even He talked to trees and trees obeyed Him. He talked and commanded both animate and in animate objects and they obeyed Him. He reigned over the demons and evil spirits. No demon was able to withstand Him. Since He has sent you as He was sent and you are in Him, it follows therefore that you are also sent to be great. You are sent to be prosperous. You are sent to be a star and you are supposed to be shining. You are sent to be reigning over all the circumstances of life. They are all supposed to be under your control. That is why He said in Revelation 5:10 that you have been made a king unto Him to reign here on earth.

And hast made us unto our God kings and priests: and we shall reign on the earth.
Revelation 5:10

Since He has sent you as He was sent, it means that you have the support that He had when He was here on earth. Whatever He could do when He was here on earth you are now enabled to do the same thing. Whatever facilities He had available to Him when He was on earth are now available to you also.

Living a supernatural life (Volume 3)

That was why He said that you will do the works that He did in John 14:12. He even said that you will do greater works. He is with you to help you do the works. He said in John 8:29, *"And he that sent me is with me."* The Father is also with you just as the Father that sent Him was with Him. That was His promise to you in Matthew 28:20. Because you are sent as He was sent whatever could not win against Him should not be able to win against you. If you stay in Him as you are supposed to do then whatever bowed for Him when He was here on earth must bow for you also. His enemies that attacked Him when He was here on earth will also be your enemies and they will attack you. Whatever He used to defeat such enemies is now available for you to use and will also defeat them.

> *Verily, verily, I say unto you, He that believeth on me, the works that I do shall he do also; and greater works than these shall he do; because I go unto my Father.*
> **John 14:12**

> *And he that sent me is with me: the Father hath not left me alone; for I do always those things that please him.*
> **John 8:29**

> *Teaching them to observe all things whatsoever I have commanded you: and, lo, I am with you alway, even unto the end of the world. Amen.*
> **Matthew 28:20**

What you have in Christ

Since Jesus Christ is the One that sent you, He is also with you. Therefore whenever you want to do the works that He did, He is there to do them. It follows that whatever Jesus could do when He was here on earth, you can now also do since He is the One that is working in you according to Philippians 2:13. This is true because the Spirit that was living in Him and supporting Him is now living in you and supporting you also. Since He has sent you as He was sent, it is not only that you can do what did, but you now have the same source and protection that He had when He was here on earth.

For it is God which worketh in you both to will and to do of his good pleasure.
Philippians 2:13

This means that whatever could not touch Him then cannot touch you now. Come to think of it, Jesus was never sick when He was here on earth so you have no business being sick. You are now health personified as an ambassador of Christ if you are faithful. You should not be looking for healing because you are health. You are health personified. How can health be sick? How can health be praying for health? How can health be praying for healing?

You are health because He has sent you to be an ambassador here on earth and if you are faithful as an ambassador then according to Proverbs 13:17 you are health personified and you will therefore not be looking for healing. Instead diseases will run from you. You must note this because it is very important. Diseases should be running away from you.

Living a supernatural life (Volume 3)

A wicked messenger falleth into mischief: but a faithful ambassador is health.

Proverbs 13:17

It is difficult to comprehend how one can be health personified yet you are sent to be one and you must be conscious of this. If you are faithful Christ will give you every support that you need to be health personified. One of the supports that Jesus made us to know that He had available to Him when He was here on earth was the services of the angels of God if ever the need arose. He said this when soldiers came to arrest Him and one of His disciples cut the ear of one of the soldiers Look at the story in Matthew 26:47-53. In particular look at His statement in verse 53.

> *And while he yet spake, lo, Judas, one of the twelve, came, and with him a great multitude with swords and staves, from the chief priests and elders of the people.*
>
> *Now he that betrayed him gave them a sign, saying, Whomsoever I shall kiss, that same is he: hold him fast.*
>
> *And forthwith he came to Jesus, and said, Hail, master; and kissed him.*
>
> *And Jesus said unto him, Friend, wherefore art thou come? Then came they, and laid hands on Jesus, and took him.*

What you have in Christ

And, behold, one of them which were with Jesus stretched out his hand, and drew his sword, and struck a servant of the high priest's, and smote off his ear.

Then said Jesus unto him, Put up again thy sword into his place: for all they that take the sword shall perish with the sword.

Thinkest thou that I cannot now pray to my Father, and he shall presently give me more than twelve legions of angels?
Matthew 26:47-53

This showed that Jesus had access to the services of God's angels if ever the need arose for Him. Now that he has sent you as the Father sent Him, it means you are entitled to the same support that He had when He was around. Therefore if He was entitled to call upon the Father to send Him angels if the need arose for Him to use their services then it means that you are also entitled now to call upon God to send you His angels if the need for them arises. God's angels are extremely powerful. One angel can destroy a whole city and Jesus said that He could call upon God to send Him more than twelve legions of angels, which means more than seventy-two thousand angels. This means that you too can call upon the services of more than seventy-two thousand angels to come to your aid if the need arises. God said in Hebrews 1:13-14 that angels are supposed to be ministering to you since you are an heir of salvation. They are supposed to minister to you so don't pray to them, just send them and they will obey you especially if you send or command them using the Name of Jesus.

Living a supernatural life (Volume 3)

> *But to which of the angels said he at any times, Sit on my right hand, until I make thine enemies thy footstool?*
>
> *Are they not all ministering spirits, sent forth to minister for them who shall be heirs of salvation?*
>
> **Hebrews 1:13-14**

You must also command them using the Word of God. This is because they only hearken to the *voice* of the Word of God. Therefore give *voice* to the Word of God and use this to send them. What an awesome power you now have available to you through this service of God's angels? Most Christians don't know about this power that is available to them. In fact when you talk of angels they see it as a taboo and they cannot comprehend their reality and their functions.

YOU HAVE GOD'S LOVE

God is love. That is what we are made to understand from what God said through John in 1 John 4:16. But you are a son of God because you have been empowered to become a son of God. That is what He said through John in John 1:12. You are also a partaker of God's divine nature. That is what God also made us to see through Apostle Peter in 2 Peter 1:4. Therefore since God is love and you are His son it follows that you have God's love in you. Since likes begets likes it follows that if God is love then you His son must be love also. Love is the major attribute of God. Since you are now a partaker of His divine nature, it follows that you must have God's love in you.

What you have in Christ

And we have known and believed the love that God hath to us. God is love; and he that dwelleth in love dwelleth in God, and God in him.
1 John 4:16

But as many as received him, to them gave he power to become the sons of God, even to them that believe on his name:
John 1:12

Whereby are given unto us exceeding great and precious promises: that by these ye might be partakers of the divine nature, having escaped the corruption that is in the world through lust.
2 Peter 1:4

In fact, you have the love of God shed abroad or poured out in your heart by the Holy Ghost, which has been given to you. If you are not radiating love you need to reexamine yourself. That is what God made us to see from what He said through Paul in Romans 5:3-5.

And not only so, but we glory in tribulations also: knowing that tribulation worketh patience;

And patience, experience; and experience, hope:

And hope maketh not ashamed; because the love of God is shed abroad in our hearts by the Holy Ghost which is given unto us.
Romans 5:3-5

Living a supernatural life (Volume 3)

Therefore whatever the situation may be, even if you are offended and you are hurt, you can always show love because God's love is inside you. No matter what is happening to you or around you God's love that is in you cannot be quenched unless you on your own do not allow the love to manifest in you. You have the love of God and just like Apostle Paul said in Romans 8:38-39, you can also say that nothing can separate you from that love of God.

For I am persuaded, that neither death, nor life, nor angels, nor principalities, nor powers, nor things present, nor things to come,

Nor height, nor depth, nor any other creature, shall be able to separate us from the love of God, which is in Christ Jesus our Lord.
Romans 8:38-39

Nothing can separate you from the love of God, which is in Christ; not death, not life, not angels, not principalities, not powers, not present things, not things to come, not height, not depth, not any other creature can separate you from that love of God. Therefore God's plans and purpose in your life cannot be stopped or frustrated by anything or anybody. His plans will be realized. That should make you bold and confident.

Because God the uncreated One is for you, no created thing can separate you from Him. Your security in Him and His love for you as well as in you are totally assured. Yet many Christians worry themselves over trivial matters whenever they are disturbed or whenever their comfort zone is attacked by the enemy.

What you have in Christ

They quickly forget the total and absolute security and the love of God that they now have in Christ. Because you love God, no matter what temptation or trials you may be going through you know that it will work out for your good in the end because He said as written in Romans 8:28 that if you love God all things will work together for good for you. You should no longer worry yourself or get nervous about any situation because you know that God is with you all the way no matter what the situation may bring. You know that it will eventually work out for your good. Just centre your love on God.

> *And we know that all things work together for good to them that love God, to them who are the called according to his purpose.*
> **Romans 8:28**

Your decision therefore should no longer be determined by what the situation says. It should no longer be determined by any symptoms that you may see or by anything for that matter. Your decision must be based on whatever the Word of God says and only that because you know that whatever the situation may be, when it is subjected to the Word of God in faith, it must change and align itself to whatever the Word of God says. Everything must bow to the Word. You cannot fear under any situation because you have God's love in you and the Scriptures say in 1 John 4:18 that there is no fear in love but perfect love casteth out fear.

> *There is no fear in love; but perfect love casteth out fear: because fear hath torment. He that feareth is not made perfect in love.*
> **1 John 4:18**

Living a supernatural life (Volume 3)

You must keep God's Word in your heart all the time and obey the Word so that the love of God can be perfected in you. Then you will know that you are in Him because you will walk as He walked. That is what He made us to know from what He said through John the Apostle in 1 John 2:5. You will know this because you will no longer have anger or hate or malice in your heart for anybody. You are free. Even where people show and treat you with hatred you will now prefer to love them in return.

> *But whoso keepeth his word, in him verily is the love of God perfected: hereby know we that we are in him.*
> **1 John 2:5**

You will do this because you know that it is a route for the opening up God's blessing for you. This is because God has said in 1 Peter 3:9 through Peter that if people do evil to you and you in return do good to them you will inherit a blessing.

> *Not rendering evil for evil, or railing for railing: but contrariwise blessing; knowing that ye are thereunto called, that ye should inherit a blessing.*
> **1 Peter 3:9**

Therefore you should see loving people as a route to your blessing. So when people do evil to you, there is an advantage in it for you. God's love was given to you and poured in your heart so that you may be able to do this without struggling.

YOU HAVE LIGHT AND UNDERSTANDING

You have the Spirit of God living in you, thereby making you a temple of the Holy Spirit. That is what we know from what God told us through Apostle Paul in 1 Corinthians 3:16. But wherever the Spirit of the Lord is you have liberty there. That is what we are made to see in 2 Corinthians 3:17. Therefore because you have the Spirit of the Lord in you it follows that you have complete liberty and you have Light in you.

> *Know ye not that ye are the temple of God, and that the Spirit of God dwelleth in you?*
> **1 Corinthians 3:16**

> *Now the Lord is that Spirit: and where the Spirit of the Lord is, there is liberty.*
> **2 Corinthians 3:17**

This Spirit of God that you have gives you light in your heart because God has commanded His light to shine out of darkness into your heart, to give you the light of the knowledge of the glory of God in the face of Jesus Christ. That is what God said in 2 Corinthians 4:6.

> *For God, who commanded the light to shine out of darkness, hath shined in our hearts, to give the light of the knowledge of the glory of God in the face of Jesus Christ.*
> **2 Corinthians 4:6**

Living a supernatural life (Volume 3)

With this light shed into your spirit God gives your spirit understanding through the inspiration that comes from His Spirit into your heart. That is what He made us to understand by what is said in Job 32:8.

> *But there is a spirit in man: and the inspiration of the Almighty giveth them understanding.*
> **Job 32:8**

From what God said in 1 Corinthians 2:12, your spirit is given this understanding so that you may know and be able to comprehend those things that have been freely given to you by God among which is the righteousness of Christ. Without this light from the Spirit it will not be possible for you to know those things that have been given to you freely by God. This is the reason why it is so difficult for many Christians to know that God has given them the righteousness of Christ as a gift, which they must accept and receive by faith.

> *Now we have received, not the spirit of the world, but the spirit which is of God; that we might know the things that are freely given to us of God.*
> **1 Corinthians 2:12**

Whoever has not received this light from God cannot know this nor comprehend it because it will be foolishness to him. According to 1 Corinthians 2:10 the Spirit of God that now lives in you is the One that can reveal these to you because the Spirit searches all things, even the deep things of God. The things of God can only be discerned spiritually. It cannot be clear to us through our natural senses.

What you have in Christ

> *But God hath revealed them unto us by his Spirit: for the Spirit searcheth all things, yea, the deep things of God.*
>
> **1 Corinthians 2:10**

With this Spirit of God in you it follows that you now have the unction from God that can make you to know all things. That is the implication of what Apostle John said in 1 John 2:20. Nothing is secret to you anymore. The light of God that you have in you can reveal all things to you.

> *But ye have an unction from the Holy One, and ye know all things.*
>
> **1 John 2:20**

YOU HAVE SPIRITUAL WEAPONS OF WARFARE

You have spiritual weapons of warfare that are not carnal but mighty through God to the pulling down of strong holds. That is the essence of what God is telling you through Paul the Apostle in 2 Corinthians 10:4-6. With the weapons now at your disposal, you can cast down every imagination or high thing that exalts itself against the knowledge of God. Since God and His Word are One and the same we can actually interpret this as saying every imagination or high thing that exalts itself against the knowledge of what the Word of God says. It is very important that you get this truth that **God, Christ and the Word are One and the same**. It is then that this Scripture will be very useful to you.

Living a supernatural life (Volume 3)

> *For the weapons of our warfare are not carnal, but mighty through God to the pulling down of strong holds;*
>
> *Casting down imaginations, and every high thing that exalteth itself against the knowledge of God, and bringing into captivity every thought to the obedience of Christ;*
>
> *And having in a readiness to revenge all disobedience, when your obedience is fulfilled.*
> **2 Corinthians 10:4-6**

With the spiritual weapons that you now have you can also force and bring into captivity every thought to the obedience of Christ. From what we are told by God in John 1:1-3,14 Jesus Christ is the Word of God. We can therefore interpret the above as saying that we can force and bring into captivity every thought to the obedience of what the Word of God says. Therefore you can always bring everything in subjection to the Word of God.

> *In the beginning was the Word, and the Word was with God, and the Word was God.*
>
> *The same was in the beginning with God.*
>
> *All things were made by him; and without him was not any thing made that was made.*
>
> *And the Word was made flesh, and dwelt among us, and we beheld his glory, the glory as of the only begotten of the Father, full of grace and truth.*
> **John 1:1-3,14**

What you have in Christ

Therefore you can see that the Word of God is one of the major spiritual weapons that you have. With the Word of God in you, there is nothing that can be hidden from you anymore. This is so because the Word of God is quick and powerful and sharper than any two-edged sword. It can pierce even to the dividing asunder of soul and spirit and of the joints and marrow. It is a discerner of the thoughts and intents of the heart. That is what we are made to see in Hebrews 4:12-13.

> *For the word of God is quick, and powerful, and sharper than any twoedged sword, piercing even to the dividing asunder of soul and spirit, and of the joints and marrow, and is a discerner of the thoughts and intents of the heart.*
>
> *Neither is there any creature that is not manifest in his sight: but all things are naked and opened unto the eyes of him with whom we have to do.*
> **Hebrews 4:12-13**

Therefore with the Word of God as a spiritual weapon in your heart and coming from your mouth there can be nothing too powerful for you to handle. There is no secret that cannot be revealed to you. Satan is no match for any born-again Christian armed with the Word of God. This is because as we are told by Paul the Apostle in 1 Corinthians 1:24 the Word of God is the power of God and the manifold wisdom of God, with which you can tackle any tricks of Satan.

Living a supernatural life (Volume 3)

But unto them which are called, both Jews and Greeks, Christ the power of God, and the wisdom of God.
1 Corinthians 1:24

The Word of God is your sword of the Spirit. When you are attacked you can defend yourself with it. But that is not all; you can also use the Word as a sword of the Spirit to go on the offensive against the enemy.

You can use the Word to root out, to pull down, to destroy, to throw down, to build and to plant. The Word is a great asset for the pulling down of Satan's strong holds. Those things that you can use the Word of God to pull down, to destroy, to throw down, to build and to plant are discussed in detail in **Chapter 15** of **Volume 2** of this *"Living a Supernatural life"* book series. The various other uses of the Word of God are also discussed in **Chapter 8** of **Volume 1** of this *"Living a Supernatural life"* book series.

Another weapon that you have with which you can protect yourself from the snares of the enemy is the Blood of Jesus. Anytime Satan comes trying to put you in any type of bondage If you take your cover under the Blood of Jesus you will be fully protected. The Blood of Jesus is our strong hold. It was the instrument used for the removal of our sins.

It was the blood that the children of Israel applied in Egypt so that the angel of death could pass over their houses. That blood that they applied was the last straw that broke Pharaoh's back. It was the last card that God used to free the children of Israel in Egypt.

After the blood they got their freedom. The angel of death had to pass over and hands off when he saw the blood in Egypt. Today you have a better Blood to apply, the Blood of Jesus Christ. That is the Blood of the New Covenant of God for man. This Blood of the New Covenant is your strong hold. In any bondage, pit or any affliction of the enemy, once you turn to the Blood your hope will be rekindled to get out of the pit of the enemy according to Zechariah 9:11-12.

> *As for thee also, by the blood of thy covenant I have sent forth thy prisoners out of the pit wherein is no water.*
>
> *Turn you to the strong hold, ye prisoners of hope: even to day do I declare that I will render double unto thee;*
> **Zechariah 9:11-12**

The Blood of Jesus is the Blood of the New Covenant. The importance of the Blood of Jesus can be seen from what God said in Leviticus 17:11. There, God made us to understand that the life of the flesh is in the blood. What this means is that whenever you call upon the Blood of Jesus, you are actually calling for the presence of Jesus Himself. Whenever you take cover under the Blood of Jesus, you are actually taking cover under Jesus Himself. ***The Blood of Jesus is your strong hold now.*** You can always take cover under the Blood and you will be saved.

Living a supernatural life (Volume 3)

For the life of the flesh is in the blood: and I have given it to you upon the altar to make an atonement for your souls: for it is the blood that maketh an atonement for the soul.
Leviticus 17:11

Just like it happened in Egypt so it is today, whenever you run under the cover of the Blood of Jesus, Satan must hands off. He must pass you over. The Blood of Jesus is the key to your freedom from every yoke of oppression. This Blood of the New Covenant always renders Satan impotent.

The Scripture says, unto God all things are possible. But we have said that calling the Blood of Jesus into any situation is equivalent to bringing Jesus into the situation. Therefore you can say if all things are possible unto God then unto the Blood all things are possible. When you take cover under the Blood, Satan and his forces of darkness cannot touch you therefore the Blood keeps Satan off your terrain. In Romans 5:9 the Scripture says that you are justified by the Blood. With your justification by the Blood, no force of darkness can condemn you anymore. Satan will try to do so by giving you the guilt-complex but he doesn't have the power to overcome the Blood.

Much more then, being now justified by his blood, we shall be saved from wrath through him.
Romans 5:9

What you have in Christ

Taking the Blood in Communion is like an inoculation that immunizes you against Satan and all the schemes of the enemy. The Scriptures say in Revelation 5:9-12 that Jesus Christ has redeemed you back to God by His Blood; that through the Blood He has received power. He has also received riches and wisdom and strength and honour and glory and blessing. He received all of these so that you may have them. Therefore with His Blood you have been restored back to the position of power, to riches, to wisdom, to strength, to honour, to glory and to blessing.

And they sung a new song, saying, Thou art worthy to take the book, and to open the seals thereof: for thou wast slain, and hast redeemed us to God by thy blood out of every kindred, and tongue, and people, and nation;

And hast made us unto our God kings and priests: and we shall reign on the earth.

And I beheld, and I heard the voice of many angels round about the throne and the beasts and the elders: and the number of them was ten thousand times ten thousand, and thousands of thousands;

Saying with a loud voice, Worthy is the Lamb that was slain to receive power, and riches, and wisdom, and strength, and honour, and glory, and blessing.
                                Revelation 5:9-12

Living a supernatural life (Volume 3)

One other major weapon that you have is divine boldness in Christ, which you have now obtained because you now have access to God with confidence by the faith of Christ.

This you can see from what God said through Paul in Ephesians 3:12. You have been baptized into Christ and because you have been so baptized you have put on Christ and He is the ultimate weapon. That is what God made us to see through Paul in Galatians 3:27.

> *In whom we have boldness and access with confidence by the faith of him.*
> **Ephesians 3:12**
>
> *For as many of you as have been baptized into Christ have put on Christ.*
> **Galatians 3:27**

YOU HAVE THE NAME OF JESUS

You have the Name of Jesus just like Peter said that He had the Name in Acts 3:6. The Name now belongs to you also if you are regenerated or born again. It is one of the keys of the Kingdom of Heaven that Jesus gave to us. You have been given authority by Jesus to use the Name to ask for whatever you want from God.

> *Then Peter said, Silver and gold have I none; but such as I have give I thee: In the name of Jesus Christ of Nazareth rise up and walk.*
> **Acts 3:6**

What you have in Christ

Jesus did so by the instructions that He gave that are written in John 14:13-14 and John 16:23-24.

> *And whatsoever ye shall ask in my name, that will I do, that the Father may be glorified in the Son.*
>
> *If ye shall ask any thing in my name, I will do it.*
>
> **John 14:13-14**

> *And in that day ye shall ask me nothing. Verily, verily, I say unto you, Whatsoever ye shall ask the Father in my name, he will give it you.*
>
> *Hitherto have ye asked nothing in my name: ask, and ye shall receive, that your joy may be full.*
>
> **John 16:23-24**

Through that Name you can ask for any resource that you require for doing the works that Jesus did and God ***will give*** it to you. Any resource that you may need you can ask for it and it shall be given to you if you ask in that Name of Jesus. Similarly whenever you actually want to do any of the works that Jesus did such as healing the sick and casting out devils, you can also ask or command that the work be done in the Name of Jesus and Jesus Christ who is the miracle worker ***will do*** it for you. The Father ***will give*** whatever you ask for and Jesus ***will do*** whatever you ask to be done.

Living a supernatural life (Volume 3)

No mountain, enemy or adversary can stand before that Name and not bow to that Name. When you are under the attack of the enemy the Name is a strong tower, which if you run into you will always be saved. That is what we are told in Proverbs 18:10.

> *The name of the Lord is a strong tower: the righteous runneth into it, and is safe.*
> **Proverbs 18:10**

The Name of Jesus and faith in that Name has miracle working power. That is the essence of what Jesus told His disciples in Mark 16:15-18. That Name and your faith in the Name will heal the sick, make the sick whole and cast out devils. The Name will even raise the dead. The Name and faith in the Name performs miracles, signs and wonders. That is what Peter also made us to see by what He said in Acts 3:16.

> *And he said unto them, Go ye into all the world, and preach the gospel to every creature.*
>
> *He that believeth and is baptized shall be saved; but he that believeth not shall be damned.*
>
> *And these signs shall follow them that believe; In my name shall they cast out devils; they shall speak with new tongues;*
>
> *They shall take up serpents; and if they drink any deadly thing, it shall not hurt them; they shall lay hands on the sick, and they shall recover.*
> **Mark 16:15-18**

And his name through faith in his name hath made this man strong, whom ye see and know: yea, the faith which is by him hath given him this perfect soundness in the presence of you all.

Acts 3:16

The power that is in that Name and how to use the Name are discussed respectively in **Chapters 3 and 4** of the **Volume 2** of this *"Living a Supernatural life"* book series. We also discussed in that volume the rights that you have to claim that Name to be yours to use to make requests from God.

That Name now belongs to you for your use; therefore use it with authority and confidence.

YOU HAVE BETTER PROMISES

You have better promises from God than the ones which He made to Abraham and the children of Israel. This is so because you belong to Christ who has mediated a New Covenant with God for man. This New Covenant that He mediated for man is based on better promises than the promises of the Old Covenant of God with the children of Israel. That is what we are made to see in Hebrews 8:6.

> *But now hath he obtained a more excellent ministry, by how much also he is the mediator of a better covenant, which was established upon better promises.*
>
> **Hebrews 8:6**

This is further supported by what Jesus said which is written in Matthew 11:11 when He said that of all the people born of a woman under the Old Covenant of God with man John the Baptist was the greatest; but that the least man born and living under the New Covenant of God for man is greater than John the Baptist.

> *Verily I say unto you, Among them that are born of women there hath not risen a greater than John the Baptist: notwithstanding he that is least in the Kingdom of Heaven is greater than he.*
> **Matthew 11:11**

It follows therefore that because you are born under this New Covenant of God for man you have the potential to be able to do more miracles than Elijah or Elisha, than Moses, than Joshua and than any of the Old Covenant saint. Anything that any of the Old Covenant saints could do you have the potential to do even greater. Jesus confirmed this by what He said as written in Matthew 10:1, Luke 9:1 and in Mark 16:15-18.

> *And when he had called unto him his twelve disciples, he gave them power against unclean spirits, to cast them out, and to heal all manner of sickness and all manner of disease.*
> **Matthew 10:1**

> *Then he called his twelve disciples together, and gave them power and authority over all devils, and to cure diseases.*
> **Luke 9:1**

And he said unto them, Go ye into all the world, and preach the gospel to every creature.

He that believeth and is baptized shall be saved; but he that believeth not shall be damned.

And these signs shall follow them that believe; In my name shall they cast out devils; they shall speak with new tongues;

They shall take up serpents; and if they drink any deadly thing, it shall not hurt them; they shall lay hands on the sick, and they shall recover.
Mark 16:15-18

Not only do you have more potential for working miracles, signs and wonders than any Old Covenant saint but you also have the potential to be wiser than any Old Covenant saint. We can infer this from what Jesus Christ said in Matthew 12:41-42 where He said that He was greater than Solomon. Remember that we are told in Luke 1:31-33 that He was sent to be great.

The men of Nineveh shall rise in judgment with this generation, and shall condemn it: because they repented at the preaching of Jonas; and, behold, a greater than Jonas is here.

Living a supernatural life (Volume 3)

> *The queen of the south shall rise up in the judgment with this generation, and shall condemn it: for she came from the uttermost parts of the earth to hear the wisdom of Solomon; and, behold, a greater than Solomon is here.*
> **Matthew 12:41-42**

> *And, behold, thou shalt conceive in thy womb, and bring forth a son, and shalt call his name JESUS.*

> *He shall be great, and shall be called the Son of the Highest: and the Lord God shall give unto him the throne of his father David:*

> *And he shall reign over the house of Jacob for ever; and of his kingdom there shall be no end.*
> **Luke 1:31-33**

If He was sent to be great and He was wiser than Solomon was and He says in John 20:21 that He has sent you as He was sent it follows that you are also sent to be great and you also have the potential to be richer and wiser than Solomon was. This is true because according to 1 Corinthians 1:24,30 from what Paul the Apostle wrote the Christ that now lives in you is the wisdom of God and the power of God. With the power of God and the wisdom of God now resident in you it follows that you have the potential to be wiser than Solomon.

What you have in Christ

Then said Jesus to them again, Peace be unto you: as my Father hath sent me, even so send I you.
John 20:21

But unto them which are called, both Jews and Greeks, Christ the power of God, and the wisdom of God.

But of him are ye in Christ Jesus, who of God is made unto us wisdom, and righteousness, and sanctification, and redemption:
1 Corinthians 1:24,30

Surely you cannot have the power of God living in you and be a weakling. Neither can you have the wisdom of God living in you and be foolish. It is obvious therefore that your power potential is infinite and your wisdom potential is also infinite. You are now seen by God in a class of a god to the situations and circumstances that you come across. That was why Jesus said as written in John 10:34-35 that you are actually a god. God is now your ability. God has given you everything that you need to have dominion and reign over all the circumstances and situations that you can come across in life. There ought not to be any situation that can constitute a problem for you.

Jesus answered them, Is it not written in your law, I said, Ye are gods?

If he called them gods, unto whom the word of God came, and the scripture cannot be broken;
John 10:34-35

No wonder Jesus was able to say in John 14:12 that whoever believes in Him will do the works that He did and will even do greater works than He did. One of the promises that you have as a New Covenant saint is the promise of the Holy Ghost.

> *Verily, verily, I say unto you, He that believeth on me, the works that I do shall he do also; and greater works than these shall he do; because I go unto my Father.*
> **John 14:12**

God promised that the Holy Ghost will abide with you forever to comfort you, to teach you, to guide you and to make known to you all things, even the deep secret things of God. That is the promise that Jesus made to us in John 14:16-18 and in John 14:26. This is different from the Old Covenant saints because the Holy Spirit did not live in them. He only comes upon them from time to time but He did not abide with them.

> *And I will pray the Father, and he shall give you another Comforter, that he may abide with you for ever;*
>
> *Even the Spirit of truth; whom the world cannot receive, because it seeth him not, neither knoweth him: but ye know him; for he dwelleth with you, and shall be in you.*
>
> *I will not leave you comfortless: I will come to you.*
> **John 14:16-18**

What you have in Christ

But the Comforter, which is the Holy Ghost, whom the Father will send in my name, he shall teach you all things, and bring all things to your remembrance, whatsoever I have said unto you.

John 14:26

He said that the Comforter that the Father will send will actually abide with you. Jesus also promised in Acts 1:8 before He left this earth that after this Comforter, the Holy Ghost has come upon you then you will receive power. You know from the Scriptures that the Holy Ghost came on the day of Pentecost as written below in Acts 2:1-4 and He is now living in you. With the Holy Spirit of God living in you as well as the power of God and the wisdom of God you can see that God's ability, God's wisdom and God's power are now available to you because they are now resident inside you. What you need is to know how to let the Holy Spirit make use of you to manifest His power and wisdom through you.

But ye shall receive power, after that the Holy Ghost is come upon you: and ye shall be witnesses unto me both in Jerusalem, and in all Judaea, and in Samaria, and unto the uttermost part of the earth.

Acts 1:8

And when the day of Pentecost was fully come, they were all with one accord in one place.

And suddenly there came a sound from heaven as of a rushing mighty wind, and it filled all the house where they were sitting.

Living a supernatural life (Volume 3)

And there appeared unto them cloven tongues like as of fire, and it sat upon each of them.

And they were all filled with the Holy Ghost, and began to speak with other tongues, as the Spirit gave them utterance.
Acts 2:1-4

The abiding Holy Spirit that lives permanently in the believer was not promised to the people of the Old Covenant. The Spirit comes upon them to use them and leaves. But the promise for us in this New Covenant is that the Spirit will abide with us permanently living inside the believer. He will not only abide in the believers but He will be oozing out of the New Covenant believer. That was what Jesus referred to in John 7:38 when He said that the rivers of living water will be oozing out of the belly of whoever believes in Him.

He that believeth on me, as the scripture hath said, out of his belly shall flow rivers of living water.
John 7:38

The rivers of living water that Jesus referred to above are actually the unction or anointing from the Holy Spirit. The flow is supposed to be out of the belly of the New Covenant believer. The rivers of living water has healing power because as we have shown earlier we can see from what is written in Mark 5:30, Luke 6:19 and Luke 8:46 the rivers of living water and the virtue that came out of Jesus to heal the sick are the same.

And Jesus, immediately knowing in himself that virtue had gone out of him, turned him about in the press, and said, Who touched my clothes?
Mark 5:30

And the whole multitude sought to touch him: for there went virtue out of him, and healed them all.
Luke 6:19

And Jesus said, Somebody hath touched me: for I perceive that virtue is gone out of me.
Luke 8:46

That was why Paul said in Romans 8:11 that when anyone has the Spirit in him He is supposed to be quickening or healing the mortal body of such a person. The mortal body that God is talking about is your physical human body.

But if the Spirit of him that raised up Jesus from the dead dwell in you, he that raised up Christ from the dead shall also quicken your mortal bodies by his Spirit that dwelleth in you.
Romans 8:11

Whatever God had promised to the people of the Old Covenant no matter how good it may be you know that you are entitled to and you can have something even better than that. This should always be your mental attitude. You must believe that you have a far greater potential than any person born under the Old Covenant.

Living a supernatural life (Volume 3)

That should be your mindset. That should be the Scriptural image that you have in your mind of yourself. You are born again to reign, to rule and to be a winner. Your belief should be this. God promised the Old Covenant Saints health so you know you are entitled to even better health. In fact you are entitled to divine health. God promised the Saints of the Old Covenant divine protection therefore you know that you are entitled to even better protection. God promised them of the Old Covenant prosperity and wealth therefore you know that you are entitled to even greater wealth and prosperity.

This then is a summary of what you have in Christ. This is what God says that you have in Christ. Do you believe that you have these capabilities and attributes that God says that you have in Christ? If you do, then start using what you have in Christ to get what you want from Christ from today on. Start using these characteristics that are yours in your day to day life and start confessing as follows: You should confess what you have and say as follows on the next fourteen pages:

THESE ARE WHAT I HAVE IN CHRIST

"I bear in my body the marks of Jesus Christ. No man should trouble me anymore because I have the mark of Jesus Christ. I have a building of God, a house not made with hands, which is eternal and is in the heavens.

I have life. I have eternal life. I have everlasting life because I believe on the Son, Jesus Christ who is my life. I have the Name of Jesus and through that Name I can ask for any resources that I require for doing the works that Jesus did. I can also use the Name to get Jesus Himself to actually do any of the works.

I have the keys of the Kingdom of Heaven with which I can bind or loose anything. With the keys anything I bind on earth would be bound in Heaven and anything I loose on earth would be loosed in Heaven. Therefore I have the power to effect changes in the spiritual realm right from here on earth.

I have a Comforter, the Holy Spirit, the Spirit of truth who abides with me and who teaches me all things and brings all things that Jesus has said to my remembrance. He guides me into all truths and shows me the things to come. He shows me the things that are of God. He is with me all the time as my Helper and Advocate to give me help and advice especially when I need to defend myself against the wiles and trials from the enemy. When I am delivered for trial either by accusation or through a burden, an ordeal or an adversity I don't have to think of what to say.

Living a supernatural life (Volume 3)

What I will say will be given to me that same hour because I am not the one really speaking. This Spirit of my Father in me is the One that will speak through me.

I have freedom from the law of sin and death. The law of the Spirit of life in Christ has made me free from the law of sin and death. I no longer walk after the flesh but after the Spirit. I therefore live and walk in the Spirit. Therefore I now have peace with God through our Lord Jesus Christ.

I have God's protection. ANYBODY or anything that defiles my body would be destroyed by God. That is absolute protection. So that my protection can be sure I have the laws of God in my heart. God has written them in my mind and He no longer remembers my sins. That is the new Covenant that He has with man. My delight is now in the law of God.

I have regeneration, which is for the glory of God. I have been saved by the washing of regeneration and the renewing of the Holy Spirit, which is a total rebirth of my spirit. This means that I have been *re-gene-rated*. My *genes* are now *re-rated*. I now have super divine genes that cannot be subject to any genetic disorder or malfunction because of the purifying work of the Holy Spirit. With this regeneration a new life was commenced in me. I have been delivered from the bondage of corruption into a glorious liberty. My past sins have been cleansed by the washing of this regeneration and the renewing of the Holy Spirit has changed my old nature. I now partake of the divine nature. I now have the spiritual life with which I can do God's will.

By this regeneration my soul which was dead has been replaced with a new one, which is given eternal life by God. This has given me a new life power of divine origin. I have the divine nature because I am now a partaker of the divine nature of God. God's own nature has been imparted to me. Therefore the words that I speak are spirit and they are life just like Christ said of His Words. When I speak words out now the words as they come out of my mouth can become fire that can destroy any enemy that is intransigent, stubborn and intractable. The power of God is now living in me. I have also escaped the corruption that is in this world through lust. With the divine nature of God that I now have, God's ability was imparted to me. Therefore there is no problem that is too much for me to solve. There is no enemy that is too powerful for me to overcome.

I have an inheritance in the Lord. My inheritance in Christ is sure, incorruptible and cannot fade away. The Lord is my inheritance. I have a goodly heritage. I cannot inherit any bad thing such as diseases and malfunctioning genes.

This also means that I cannot have any genetically based problem because as a result of my regeneration *(re-gene-rated)* my **genes** have now been **re-rated.** I now have divine genes. I have all things that pertain unto life and godliness through the knowledge of Christ *(the Word of God).* I have been called unto glory and virtue not to shame and reproach therefore excellence is my portion in anything that I lay my hands on. All things are mine now and I am Christ's. I have all things. This is the Scriptural picture that I have of myself.

Living a supernatural life (Volume 3)

I have absolute security in Christ. As long as I walk in the truth as given by the Word of God, Satan can no longer harm me. No body can harm me. I am absolutely secured in Christ. Anything that attempts to harm my body God will destroy it because my body is God's habitation. I am of God therefore Satan cannot touch me anymore. He can make the attempt but he can no longer win against me. I am now preserved from Satan's devices. This is my mindset.

I have victory. I have overcome the world. I can stand up to any challenge now and I will always win. Defeats and failures are no longer my portion. I have the faith that can overcome the world. Nothing can overcome me now. This is not a victory being expected. No! It is a victory that I already have.

I am in Christ Jesus and I no longer walk after the flesh but after the Spirit, therefore there is no more condemnation for me anymore. I have been cleansed from all sins by the Blood of Jesus Christ, the Son of God.

I have absolute freedom because I am free from all accusations. I am free. I have my liberty now. Because I have believed the work of redemption that Christ did I have entered into rest. Therefore I now have rest. Nothing can disturb me anymore. I am absolutely complete in Christ. Nothing can mock or reproach me anymore. Reproaches are not my portion in Christ. My portion now is glory and virtue because I have the mind of Christ, the greatest of all minds.

What you have in Christ

I have the mind of Christ. That is the mind that created all things, without which there was nothing created. With that mind I have the potential for more wisdom inside me than Solomon had inside him. I have the potential for more great ideas inside me than any earthly person can dream. I am a genius waiting to explode with great inventions. I have the capability to create things.

I have a mouth and a wisdom which no adversary can resist. Therefore I have the ability to speak rightly all the time so that nobody can resist what I say. It follows therefore that my success is sure. No enemy can stop or overcome me. My commands must be obeyed as long as I stayed in-Christ.

I have the measure of faith, which God has given to all believers. I have even developed my measure further so that I now walk by faith and not by sight. I do not follow what I see, hear, smell, taste or feel. I walk by faith in what the Word of God says. I look not at things which are seen because I know that what I can see, hear, taste, feel or smell is temporal. That which I cannot see, hear, taste, feel or smell is eternal and it is that, which is more real to me. I have the necessary measure of faith to walk with so that I don't have to walk by sight.

I have reconciliation with God because I have been reconciled to God by Jesus Christ. All obstacles between me and God have been removed. I have the assurance that my sins will be forgiven me by God if I confess them.

He will also cleanse me from all unrighteousness. I have complete freedom from darkness into complete light. Jesus was raised from the dead because of my justification. I now have justification because I believe in the work of redemption that Jesus did and I have faith in Him. My justification has nothing to do with any works of the law, which I have done. Because I believe in Jesus I now claim my justification through faith in Him even though I have no works of the law. Justification is freely given to me by God's grace.

My justification is by the Blood of Christ that was shed on the Cross. As a result of that justification given to me, God has freely given me righteousness and I am therefore counted as righteous with the righteousness of Christ imputed to me. I have freedom from the Curse of the law because I am not under the curse anymore therefore every one of the curses in the Curse of the Law no longer applies to me. This is so because I am justified by faith in the redemption which Christ did.

Christ has redeemed me from the Curse of the Law. I am dead to the law so that I may live unto God. Therefore I no longer live in the Law. I live by faith because I have been justified by the faith of Jesus Christ. I have eternal redemption which Christ has obtained for me with His blood.

I have the righteousness of God because I have been given the righteousness of Christ as a gift and I have received it by faith. Therefore I am made the righteousness of God in Christ. It follows therefore that I am righteous.

What you have in Christ

Before God I am just as righteous as Christ because I am now united with Christ such that God now sees me in Christ and reckons Christ's righteousness to me. I have been redeemed from all iniquity and purified unto Christ as a peculiar person who is zealous of good works. I am given righteousness by imputation and I am also empowered to live a righteous, upright and holy life through sanctification.

I have what I will eat and drink. I have the assurance that these will be provided. I don't have to worry myself about these. I have an abundant provision for life. I have the unsearchable riches of Christ. I have been freely given all things. I have divine supplies because God is my supplier. He supplies all my needs according to His riches in glory by Christ Jesus. I have been blessed with every spiritual blessing in heavenly places. Therefore I cannot be poor. I cannot suffer any lack because I have been given all spiritual blessings in heavenly places. I know that all things are first spiritual before they manifest physically therefore spiritual things are more real to me. Every thing I want in this physical realm God has already given them to me in the spiritual realm.

I have God dwelling in me and walking in me. I have God the Father, the Son and the Holy Ghost dwelling in me because I am not in the flesh but in the Spirit. I have the Lord with me always, even unto the end of the world. So wherever I go the Lord Jesus Christ is with me at any time and always. Jesus Christ who is the Lord of Heaven and earth has been given absolute and total authority over every spirit being in Heaven, on earth and under the earth.

Living a supernatural life (Volume 3)

Jesus has given me the proxy use of the authority which He has over all powers both in Heaven and on earth and even under the earth and over any power that wants to oppose me while carrying out His order to evangelize the world. He has not only given me the right to use His authority but He is with me always to support me in its use even unto the end of this age.

Because I have Christ the Son of God living in me I also have life and eternal life. Since Christ who is the wisdom of God and the power of God is living in me I have the power of God and the wisdom of God right inside me. I am also in Christ Jesus and He is my wisdom, my righteousness, my sanctification and my redemption. I also have glory because Jesus Christ has given me the glory that God gave to Him so that I can be one with other believers in Christ. So I have this glory when I am one with the others.

I have the Holy Spirit and He abides in me and teaches me all things and as He teaches me, I abide in Him. I am being changed on a continuous basis into the same image as the Lord Jesus Christ from glory to glory by this Spirit of the Lord that now lives in me. I am also enriched by Christ in all utterances and in all knowledge. I have unction from God that can make all things known to me. There is nothing secret to me that the Spirit cannot find out and reveal to me.

Jesus has sent me to this world as the Father sent Him therefore I have available to me now everything that He had for support when He was here on earth. Since I am sent as Jesus was sent,

He was great therefore I shall be great. Jesus was very prosperous; it follows therefore that I shall be prosperous. Jesus was a star. He was a bright and morning star. Therefore I am destined to be a shining star here on earth.

I have divine healing because I have been healed by the stripes that Jesus Christ took on the Cross. Therefore I cannot be sick and I cannot be asking for healing in prayer since I have been healed. I just take my healing, which is already done, by faith. If I pray to God asking Him to heal me then I make Him a liar. As a faithful ambassador of Christ I have divine health because I am health personified. I have the rivers of living water, which has healing virtue flowing out of my belly and these quicken my mortal flesh all the time on a continuous basis. I have been made perfect. I have been perfected for ever. I have great confidence and my confidence has great recompense of reward. I have sufficiency not of myself, but my sufficiency is of God.

Because God is love and I am a son of God, I have love in me. I have the love of God shed abroad in my heart by the Holy Ghost, which has been given to me. Therefore I cannot hate anybody because I have no hate in me. What I have in me is the perfect love of God. I have complete liberty because I have the Spirit of the Lord in me. I have light in my heart because God has commanded His light to shine out of darkness into my heart, to give me the light of the knowledge of the glory of God in the face of Jesus Christ. I hear God's Words because I am of God. Those who are not of God cannot hear His Words.

Living a supernatural life (Volume 3)

I have the great exceeding power of God available to me. I have been given the power to become a son of God. So I am not just a son of God, I have been empowered to become one so that I can act as one. I now have God working in me to do His will. I don't have to rely on my own strength to do His will. The power of life of the Christ that is living in me is leading me to glory. I have no time for reproaches. Reproaches are a thing of the past for me. With the power of God that is now working in me, I can get God to do exceeding and abundantly above all that I ask or think. Using this power of God that is now living in me I can cast out unclean spirits and heal all manner of sicknesses and diseases.

I now have power over ALL the powers of my enemies. Nothing can hurt me anymore. I have unlimited power in God. Nothing is impossible to me now. I have and can exercise power over all devils. I have the power to do the works that Jesus Christ did and to do even greater works than He did. I have the Name of Jesus with which to do the works that Jesus did. Whatever I ask to be done in the Name of Jesus He will do it. Through the Name of Jesus I can control the elements and cast out devils and do all types of miracles. I have the capability and the potential to do these in the Name of Jesus.

I have the angels of God ministering to me. As of right because I am sent as Jesus was sent I can ask the Father God to send as many as twelve legions of angels, seventy two thousand angels to come to my aid at any particular time if the need arises.

What you have in Christ

I have weapons of warfare that are not carnal but mighty through God to the pulling down of strongholds. With the weapons I can cast down every imagination or high thing that exalts itself against the knowledge of God or that exalts itself against the knowledge of what the Word of God says. I can also force and bring into captivity every thought to the obedience of Christ, which means to the obedience of what the Word of God says since Christ is the Word of God.

I have overcome the wicked. I am strong and the Word of God abideth in me. I already have victory. I have a High Priest, Jesus Christ who is set on the right hand of God in the heavens pleading my case.

I have the power of God working in me. I have been baptized into Christ therefore I have put on Christ it follows therefore that I have the Spirit of power, of love and of a sound mind. I no longer have the spirit of fear or the spirit of bondage to fear. I now have the Spirit of adoption as a son of God. Actually I was predestinated into adoption as a child of God by Jesus Christ to Himself. This Spirit that I now have is also the Spirit of faith. I therefore speak out whatever I believe.

This Spirit of God that I have is quickening and making alive my mortal body. Therefore sickness can no longer put me in bondage. As a son of God I am led by this Spirit of God and this has given me divine boldness in Christ. I have access with confidence to God by the faith of Christ. Jesus has blotted out and taken out of the way all things that are against me and contrary to me and He has nailed them to the Cross.

Living a supernatural life (Volume 3)

Because I am now of God and I have victory over the world. I have overcome the world as well as every spirit that is not of God because the One in me is greater than the one in the world. My faith gets this victory that overcomes the world, which Christ has already obtained for me because I now have Christ the greater One than is the world living in me. The power of God towards me is exceedingly great and mighty and there are great riches of glory in the inheritance that I now have in Christ. Among these are the power of immunity from poison and the power to control wild beasts and devils, which I now have. I have an anointing, which is potentially greater than that of any old Covenant saint. Therefore I have the potential to work more miracles than Elijah or Elisha did, to have more wisdom and riches than Solomon had and to exhibit more power than Samson did. I have more power and miracles inside me than Elijah or Elisha had inside them. Potentially I have more wisdom inside me than Solomon had inside him. This is so because I now have Jesus Christ who is the wisdom of God and power of God living in me and He has been made wisdom to me. He has also been made sanctification unto me.

I have sanctification because I have been sanctified and set apart for God. I am sanctified by God the Father and I am preserved in Jesus. I am sanctified through the Blood of Jesus Christ and in the truth of the Word of God. As I have mentioned earlier I have also been justified in the Name of our Lord Jesus Christ and by the Spirit of our God. Because I have been sanctified Jesus Christ has perfected me forever by the one offering, which He made of Himself for my sins.

Because of this I have been totally sanctified and separated from the guilt of sin. Therefore my standing before God as guiltless is now established. Since Jesus Christ sanctified me, I am now one with Him and He is not ashamed to call me a brother. Because I am sanctified I know that I am now separated from sin and made pure in heart to be holy unto God and sin is no longer my problem, therefore I know that I shall see the Lord. Because I have been sanctified by having faith in Christ Jesus, I have inheritance among the saints who are sanctified through the faith that I have in Christ Jesus. This makes me an heir of God and a joint-heir with Jesus Christ. My sanctification is being perfected daily as I separate myself from all filthiness of the flesh and the spirit.

I have life. Because Jesus lives, I also live. Jesus Christ is made unto me wisdom, righteousness, redemption and sanctification. I am capable of, and have the potential to use God's wisdom and God's righteousness through Jesus Christ.

I have the love of God and nothing can separate me from that love of God; not death, not life, not angels, not principalities, not powers, not present things, not things to come, not height, not depth, not any other creature can separate me from that love of God.

I have better promises from God than the ones which He made to Abraham and the physical children of Israel. This is so because I belong to Christ who has mediated a New Covenant with God for man.

This new Covenant that He mediated for man is based on better promises than the promises of the Old Covenant of God with the children of Israel. It follows therefore that whatever God had promised to the people of the Old Covenant no matter how good it is, I know that I am entitled to something even better than that.

I have a priestly ministry because I am of the Royal Priesthood. I belong to the elect race of the Holy nation of God that is meant to proclaim the praises of God. I have been given a ministry of reconciliation to reconcile sinners back to God."

CHAPTER 5

WHAT YOU CAN DO IN CHRIST

YOU CAN NOW HONESTLY SERVE GOD

As you become born-again and you are regenerated the Blood of Jesus purges your conscience from dead works so that you can now serve the Living God. That is what God has made us to see from what He said through Paul in Hebrews 9:14.

> *How much more shall the blood of Christ, who through the eternal Spirit offered himself without spot to God, purge your conscience from dead works to serve the living God?*
> **Hebrews 9:14**

Your spirit has been set free to worship God. You can now serve God with a clean conscience and not with a guilt conscience. You are now free from all guilt conscience. This is because according to Romans 8:1 there is now no more condemnation for you because you are in Christ if you walk after the Spirit.

Living a supernatural life (Volume 3)

There is therefore now no condemnation to them which are in Christ Jesus, who walk not after the flesh, but after the Spirit.
Romans 8:1

But the truth is that many Christians who are supposed to be in Christ are not walking after the Spirit so they still go about with the guilt-conscience feeling condemned and therefore unable to approach God with boldness.

From what God said in 2 Corinthians 5:21 through Paul, the righteousness of God has been credited and imputed to you and you are now declared righteous. Jesus has taken your guilt and all your iniquities and diseases have been laid on Him. Isaiah prophesied this in Isaiah 53:5-6 and Peter confirmed that this prophecy had been fulfilled from what He said in 1 Peter 2:24. Jesus Christ took your guilt so that you can receive His righteousness.

For he hath made him to be sin for us, who knew no sin; that we might be made the righteousness of God in him.
2 Corinthians 5:21

But he was wounded for our transgressions, he was bruised for our iniquities: the chastisement of our peace was upon him; and with his stripes we are healed.

All we like sheep have gone astray; we have turned every one to his own way; and the LORD hath laid on him the iniquity of us all.
Isaiah 53:5-6

What you can do in Christ

Who his own self bare our sins in his own body on the tree, that we, being dead to sins, should live unto righteousness: by whose stripes ye were healed.
1 Peter 2:24

As we are told in Roman 5:17 God has given you the gift of righteousness. With this gift of righteousness given to you God also started the process of sanctifying you so that you can be empowered to live a righteous life. It is only with this righteousness of God that you can approach God.

For if by one man's offence death reigned by one; much more they which receive abundance of grace and of the gift of righteousness shall reign in life by one, Jesus Christ.
Romans 5:17

With that empowerment your being righteous is not only a matter of declaration but you are also actually empowered to do the works of righteousness. In that case your heart no longer condemns you and if your heart no longer condemns you then you will have confidence when you approach God. You can now approach God with no guilt-complex and with nothing acting as a barrier or gulf between you and God. According to Paul in Romans 5:9 and Roman 8:33 God has justified you and He no longer holds anything against you and since God has justified you no body can lay any charge against you.

Much more then, being now justified by his blood, we shall be saved from wrath through him.

Romans 5:9

Who shall lay any thing to the charge of God's elect? It is God that justifieth.

Romans 8:33

You should also note that because you are now born of God you are no longer subject to the law of sin and death. You no longer have a carnal mind, but the mind of Christ, which is now subject to the law of God and you can now please God. That is what we now know from what is written in Romans 8:7-8.

Because the carnal mind is enmity against God: for it is not subject to the law of God, neither indeed can be.

So then they that are in the flesh cannot please God.

Romans 8:7-8

Since you are born of God you now have God as your Father. Therefore you can now approach Him as a son would approach his father not as a slave to his master. You can now talk directly with God in the most intimate manner. You don't have to use any human being as your go-between to talk to Him. The only mediator that you have between you and the Father is the man Christ Jesus who is the Word of God and who is God according to 2 Timothy 2:15 and John 1:1-3,14.

What you can do in Christ

Study to shew thyself approved unto God, a workman that needeth not to be ashamed, rightly dividing the word of truth.
2 Timothy 2:15

In the beginning was the Word, and the Word was with God, and the Word was God.

The same was in the beginning with God.

All things were made by him; and without him was not any thing made that was made.

And the Word was made flesh, and dwelt among us, and we beheld his glory, the glory as of the only begotten of the Father, full of grace and truth.
John 1:1-3,14

God is now your Father, you are His son and He loves you very much. So your approach to Him should be that of a son to a Father. This is why I feel so perplexed when I see Christians who are supposed to be sons of God making loud, riotous and vociferous noise crying like Baal's prophets blaring at God and shouting at Him all in the name of prayer as if God is deaf and far away from them; something they will not do to their earthly fathers.

Why don't you try and approach God as a Father for a change? You can now live as a son of God because according to John 1:12 God has empowered you to become a son of God.

Living a supernatural life (Volume 3)

> *But as many as received him, to them gave he power to become the sons of God, even to them that believe on his name:*
>
> **John 1:12**

Apart from the fact that He has adopted you to be His son as written in Ephesians 1:5 and Galatians 4:5, He has also sent forth the Spirit of His Son into your heart and therefore empowered you to become His son according to what is written in Galatians 4:6 written below and in John 1:12 written above.

> *Having predestinated us unto the adoption of children by Jesus Christ to himself, according to the good pleasure of his will,*
>
> **Ephesians 1:5**

> *To redeem them that were under the law, that we might receive the adoption of sons.*
>
> **Galatians 4:5**

> *And because ye are sons, God hath sent forth the Spirit of his Son into your hearts, crying, Abba, Father.*
>
> **Galatians 4:6**

To make sure that you can see yourself as His son and no longer a slave so that you can act and think like His son He has also made you His heir through Christ Jesus. This should give you absolute confidence to serve God now as your Father without any inhibition. It should also give you the confidence that God is a Father who is near to you, who you can approach and talk to and not a strange God that you don't know whom you are not sure will hear you when you talk to him.

What you can do in Christ

As we have explained in an earlier Chapter, according to what is written in 2 Corinthians 5:17, you are now a new creature, all things have become new for you. The new creature that you are now partakes of the divine nature of God. That is what we are told by Apostle Peter in 2 Peter 1:4.

> *Therefore if any man be in Christ, he is a new creature: old things are passed away; behold, all things are become new.*
> **2 Corinthians 5:17**

> *Whereby are given unto us exceeding great and precious promises: that by these ye might be partakers of the divine nature, having escaped the corruption that is in the world through lust.*
> **2 Peter 1:4**

Therefore you can now know God intimately since you now have His nature. What this means is that you can now serve God with peace of mind. All anxiety, worry, fear and guilt-conscience that do not allow you to worship God with all your heart no longer have any power over you because Christ has now given you His peace. Your heart should be at peace with God. That is what Jesus made us to see in John 14:27.

> *Peace I leave with you, my peace I give unto you: not as the world giveth, give I unto you. Let not your heart be troubled, neither let it be afraid.*
> **John 14:27**

Living a supernatural life (Volume 3)

Because you are now justified by God, you now have absolute peace with Him through the Lord Jesus Christ. That is what God said through Paul in Romans 5:1. You have now been completely reconciled to God through the death of His Son Jesus Christ. That is what God said through Apostle Paul in Romans 5:10. Therefore you have been restored to true fellowship with God.

> *Therefore being justified by faith, we have peace with God through our Lord Jesus Christ:*
>
> **Romans 5:1**

> *For if, when we were enemies, we were reconciled to God by the death of his Son, much more, being reconciled, we shall be saved by his life.*
>
> **Romans 5:10**

Because you have been restored to true fellowship with the Father and with His Son Jesus Christ, it follows from what is written in 1 John 1:3 that you can now serve God as you are meant or created to do in all honesty. The obstacle of unbelief has been overcome by you.

> *That which we have seen and heard declare we unto you, that ye also may have fellowship with us: and truly our fellowship is with the Father, and with his Son Jesus Christ.*
>
> **1 John 1:3**

What you can do in Christ

Therefore you now know and you should be convinced that you can talk to God and that when you do so ***He hears you.*** That is the confidence that you should now have in Him according to 1 John 5:14. You also know that God talks to you and when He does so you hear Him. That is what Jesus said in John 10:27. You therefore have no problem communicating with Him. ***You hear Him.*** There is no need for you to shout at Him before He hears you because He is very near to you.

> *And this is the confidence that we have in him, that, if we ask any thing according to his will, he heareth us:*
> **1 John 5:14**

> *My sheep hear my voice, and I know them, and they follow me:*
> **John 10:27**

YOU CAN OPEN PEOPLE'S SPIRITUAL EYES

You are free from the power of Satan so that you can open the eyes of the people and turn them from darkness unto light and from the power of Satan unto God that they may receive forgiveness of sins and inheritance among them which are sanctified by the faith that is in Christ Jesus. That is what God made us to see by what is written in Acts 26:18.

Living a supernatural life (Volume 3)

> *To open their eyes, and to turn them from darkness to light, and from the power of Satan unto God, that they may receive forgiveness of sins, and inheritance among them which are sanctified by faith that is in me.*
>
> **Acts 26:18**

It is because you can now do this that made Jesus to give you the command in Matthew 28:19-20 that you should go into the whole world and teach all nations the Gospel of Christ

> *Go ye therefore, and teach all nations, baptizing them in the name of the Father, and of the Son, and of the Holy Ghost:*
>
> *Teaching them to observe all things whatsoever I have commanded you: and, lo, I am with you alway, even unto the end of the world. Amen.*
>
> **Matthew 28:19-20**

He has empowered you to do this because He now has all power in Heaven and in earth according to what He said after His resurrection in Matthew 28:18. He has delegated His power to you as you can see in Matthew 10:1 and Luke 9:1 as well as Luke 10:19 so that as you demonstrate this power of God that you now have you can open the eyes of the people and get them to change. Through the demonstration of this power you can get people to change.

> *And Jesus came and spake unto them, saying, All power is given unto me in heaven and in earth.*
>
> **Matthew 28:18**

What you can do in Christ

And when he had called unto him his twelve disciples, he gave them power against unclean spirits, to cast them out, and to heal all manner of sickness and all manner of disease.
Matthew 10:1

Then he called his twelve disciples together, and gave them power and authority over all devils, and to cure diseases.
Luke 9:1

Behold, I give unto you power to tread on serpents and scorpions, and over all the power of the enemy: and nothing shall by any means hurt you.
Luke 10:19

When people see the supernatural power that God has now vested in you at work they will quickly believe. The reason why there is so much doubt these days about the deity of Jesus Christ and why many are now working against the Christian way of life is because the Christians of today have not been able to demonstrate the awesome power of God that is now vested in them. Jesus Himself said in John 4:48 that unless the people see signs and wonders they will not believe. Most of the Christians of today are no longer preaching the Kingdom of God, which according to what Apostle Paul said in 1 Corinthians 4:20 is not in words but in power. They now preach prosperity, deliverance and healing, etc. but these should not be your main focus.

Living a supernatural life (Volume 3)

> *Then said Jesus unto him, Except ye see signs and wonders, ye will not believe.*
> **John 4:48**

> *For the Kingdom of God is not in word, but in power.*
> **1 Corinthians 4:20**

Your main focus should be the preaching of the good news and letting people know the truth that Kingdom of God is here with us already by demonstrating the Power of God. That will open the spiritual eyes of the people.

You should let people know that when they receive Christ into their hearts they are not joining a religion but the family of God. They are actually becoming a citizen of the Kingdom of God. That is what we are made to see in Ephesians 2:19.

> *Now therefore ye are no more strangers and foreigners, but fellowcitizens with the saints, and of the household of God;*
> **Ephesians 2:19**

You should also let them know that as citizens of that Kingdom of God they are entitled to certain privileges and benefits that they can immediately start to enjoy. Among such benefits are prosperity, deliverance, success, healing and victory etc. These are benefits that should come with their citizenship. You must also show them that if they are to enjoy these benefits then there are laws and rules that they must follow as citizens of the Kingdom of God.

What you can do in Christ

The major rule that citizens of that Kingdom must follow is that they must walk by faith and not by sight and they must live by faith and they must walk in love. That is what we are made to see in 2 Corinthians 5:7, in Romans 1:17 and also from what Jesus said which is written in Mark 12:30-31.

For we walk by faith, not by sight:
2 Corinthians 5:7

For therein is the righteousness of God revealed from faith to faith: as it is written, The just shall live by faith.
Romans 1:17

And thou shalt love the Lord thy God with all thy heart, and with all thy soul, and with all thy mind, and with all thy strength: this is the first commandment.

And the second is like, namely this, Thou shalt love thy neighbour as thyself. There is none other commandment greater than these.
Mark 12:30-31

An addendum to this rule is that the citizens of that Kingdom are not supposed to look at things which are seen but at the things which are not seen. For the things which are seen are temporary but the things which are not seen are eternal. This means that spiritual things should be more real to them than physical things. That is what we can see in 2 Corinthians 4:18.

> *While we look not at the things which are seen, but at the things which are not seen: for the things which are seen are temporal; but the things which are not seen are eternal.*
> **2 Corinthians 4:18**

The most important rule of all that the citizens of that Kingdom of God must follow was given by Jesus in Matthew 6:33. That is they must seek first the things of the Kingdom of God and His righteousness and all other things will be added unto them.

> *But seek ye first the Kingdom of God, and his righteousness; and all these things shall be added unto you.*
> **Matthew 6:33**

YOU CAN DO ALL THINGS

You can do all things through Christ who strengthens you. This is a very wide statement. You may think that this is far-fetched but I did not say it. That is what God made us to see through Paul in Philippians 4:13. Because God is now for you nobody can stand against you and win anymore. That is what we can infer from what is written in Romans 8:31.

> *I can do all things through Christ which strengtheneth me.*
> **Philippians 4:13**

> *What shall we then say to these things? If God be for us, who can be against us?*
> **Romans 8:31**

What you can do in Christ

Therefore whatever you want to do, nobody can stop you from doing it. Nothing can overcome you any longer. You should now know and have the mentality that you can do all things because whatever you ask of God His ability to do it is unlimited and His ability has now become your ability because He is the One that is now working in you according to Philippians 2:13. This should be your mental attitude.

For it is God which worketh in you both to will and to do of his good pleasure.
Philippians 2:13

God can do far and exceeding abundantly above anything that you can ask or think. He can do infinitely beyond anything that you can hope or dream.

That is what God made us to see in Ephesians 3:20. Since you now have His ability and He is the One that is now working in you it follows that you can now do exceeding abundantly above anything that you can think or imagine. You can do infinitely beyond anything that you can hope for or even dream. Anything you can imagine you can do.

Now unto him that is able to do exceeding abundantly above all that we ask or think, according to the power that worketh in us,
Ephesians 3:20

There is no limitation with your God. Whatever you can think or dream God can do it. He can even do much more because there are no impossibilities with Him.

Living a supernatural life (Volume 3)

Whatever you can ask, your God can give you and you should take it that He has given you because according to the Scriptures in Romans 8:32, He has freely given you all things. Not only that, he has said through Paul in 1 Corinthians 3:21-22 that all things are yours.

> *He that spared not his own Son, but delivered him up for us all, how shall he not with him also freely give us all things?*
> **Romans 8:32**

> *Therefore let no man glory in men. For all things are yours;*

> *Whether Paul, or Apollos, or Cephas, or the world, or life, or death, or things present, or things to come; all are yours;*
> **1 Corinthians 3:21-22**

Potentially all things are yours now. This may sound too far-fetched but it is true. Therefore there is nothing that you cannot do and there is nothing that you cannot have. Just have faith.

You only need to ask Him and allow Him to work through you. Jesus has said in John 14:13-14 and also in John 16:23 that whatever you ask the Father in His Name the Father will give to you and whatever you ask to be done in His Name, He Jesus will do it for you. The only proviso for you is that you must make sure that He hears you because once you are sure that He hears you then you know that you have gotten what you asked of Him.

What you can do in Christ

And whatsoever ye shall ask in my name, that will I do, that the Father may be glorified in the Son.

If ye shall ask any thing in my name, I will do it.

John 14:13-14

And in that day ye shall ask me nothing. Verily, verily, I say unto you, Whatsoever ye shall ask the Father in my name, he will give it you.

John 16:23

But according to what we are told by God through Apostle John in 1 John 5:14 when you ask for these according to His will then you know that He hears you. All you have to do therefore is to make sure that you asked for whatever you want according to the will of God

And this is the confidence that we have in him, that, if we ask any thing according to his will, he heareth us:

1 John 5:14

We can conclude that you can do all things now because from what Jesus said in Mark 11:22-23 nothing shall be impossible unto you any longer when you tackle it with the active living faith of God the measure of which has already been given to you according to what is written in Romans 12:3.

And Jesus answering saith unto them, Have faith in God.

For verily I say unto you, That whosoever shall say unto this mountain, Be thou removed, and be thou cast into the sea; and shall not doubt in his heart, but shall believe that those things which he saith shall come to pass; he shall have whatsoever he saith.
Mark 11:22-23

For I say, through the grace given unto me, to every man that is among you, not to think of himself more highly than he ought to think; but to think soberly, according as God hath dealt to every man the measure of faith.
Romans 12:3

The key to doing all things and living a blessed and triumphant life is obedience of God's Word and it can work mightily for you. As written in Psalm 84:11 if you walk uprightly, God will not withhold anything from you.

For the L<small>ORD</small> *God is a sun and shield: the* L<small>ORD</small> *will give grace and glory: no good thing will he withhold from them that walk uprightly.*
Psalm 84:11

From what Jesus said in Matthew 21:21-22, you should know that you can exercise unlimited authority in this life in Christ. Therefore you should no longer be afraid of the circumstances that you come across.

What you can do in Christ

Jesus answered and said unto them, Verily I say unto you, If ye have faith, and doubt not, ye shall not only do this which is done to the fig tree, but also if ye shall say unto this mountain, Be thou removed, and be thou cast into the sea; it shall be done.

And all things, whatsoever ye shall ask in prayer, believing, ye shall receive.
Matthew 21:21-22

You know from what God said through Apostle John in 1 John 4:4 that the greater One than is in the world now lives in you therefore you can do anything. The One in you is greater than anything that you can ever come across or ever want to do. So no matter what may be happening to you or you may be going through know that the One in you is greater than it. You should therefore feel confident to face it.

Ye are of God, little children, and have overcome them: because greater is he that is in you, than he that is in the world.
1 John 4:4

The Jesus that lives in you has already overcome the world. That is what He said in John 16:33. Therefore you have overcome the world because His victory is your victory. It is therefore not surprising that John confirmed in 1 John 4:4 above and in 1 John 5:4 below that you have already overcome the world because the greater One than the one in the world is living in you. Therefore nothing can stop you.

Living a supernatural life (Volume 3)

> *These things I have spoken unto you, that in me ye might have peace. In the world ye shall have tribulation: but be of good cheer; I have overcome the world.*
> **John 16:33**

> *For whatsoever is born of God overcometh the world: and this is the victory that overcometh the world, even our faith.*
> **1 John 5:4**

The Jesus that is living in you now has all power in Heaven and in earth according to what He Himself said in Matthew 28:18 and you have the authority and power of Jesus Christ to use that power. Therefore you don't have to fear anything anymore. The devil can no longer harass you and get away with it. The devil should be very cautious around you. But if the devil knows that you are not sure of the authority that you now have he will try to force you to accept that he has authority over you.

> *And Jesus came and spake unto them, saying, All power is given unto me in heaven and in earth.*
> **Matthew 28:18**

As written by Paul in Romans 5:17 the righteousness of God has been given to you therefore you are now established in righteousness. If that is the case then you are now far from oppression because you will not fear since according to what is written in 2 Timothy 1:7, you no longer have the spirit of fear and from what God says through Isaiah in Isaiah 54:14 if you do not fear you will be far from oppression and from terror.

For if by one man's offence death reigned by one; much more they which receive abundance of grace and of the gift of righteousness shall reign in life by one, Jesus Christ.
Romans 5:17

For God hath not given us the spirit of fear; but of power, and of love, and of a sound mind.
2 Timothy 1:7

In righteousness shalt thou be established: thou shalt be far from oppression; for thou shalt not fear: and from terror; for it shall not come near thee.
Isaiah 54:14

This is so because it is fear that brings oppression. You will also be far from terror because it will not come near you. There is nothing therefore that can stop you from doing whatever you want to do.

You have the power of God in you therefore nothing can be daunting to you anymore. Not even a mountain!

YOU CAN MOVE ANY MOUNTAIN

You can command any mountain to move from one place to another and if you do not doubt in your heart, it will move. **NOTHING** is impossible for you. That is what Jesus said in Matthew 17:20. Therefore faith is the ultimate power made available to you because with that kind of power nothing can stand as an obstacle or mountain to you any longer.

Living a supernatural life (Volume 3)

> *And Jesus said unto them, Because of your unbelief: for verily I say unto you, If ye have faith as a grain of mustard seed, ye shall say unto this mountain, Remove hence to yonder place; and it shall remove; and nothing shall be impossible unto you.*
> **Matthew 17:20**

From what we can see below in Romans 12:3, you have been given the measure of faith with which to move any mountain. He says **the measure** and not **a measure** therefore you have the same as everybody else. Anything that stands as a mountain or wall before you whether lack, failure syndrome, sickness, barrenness, any stubborn affliction or enemy, no matter how high and big it may be, you are far above it and you can move it. That is what we can see from the combination of what is written in Ephesians 1:19-23 and what is written in Ephesians 2:6. From the combination of these verses of the Scripture you can see that where you are now you are far above all principalities, all powers, all dominion, all might and everything that has a name. So you can command any mountain to move be it physical or spiritual.

> *For I say, through the grace given unto me, to every man that is among you, not to think of himself more highly than he ought to think; but to think soberly, according as God hath dealt to every man the measure of faith.*
> **Romans 12:3**

What you can do in Christ

And what is the exceeding greatness of his power to us-ward who believe, according to the working of his mighty power,

Which he wrought in Christ, when he raised him from the dead, and set him at his own right hand in the heavenly places,

Far above all principality, and power, and might, and dominion, and every name that is named, not only in this world, but also in that which is to come:

And hath put all things under his feet, and gave him to be the head over all things to the church,

Which is his body, the fulness of him that filleth all in all.
Ephesians 1:19-23

And hath raised us up together, and made us sit together in heavenly places in Christ Jesus:
Ephesians 2:6

Whatever the mountain may be whether physical or spiritual, when you command it to move it has no option but to move once your faith is in place.

You can now have and demonstrate power above any power that anything that constitutes itself as a mountain or enemy in your life can demonstrate. That is what Jesus promised you in Luke 10:19.

Living a supernatural life (Volume 3)

> *Behold, I give unto you power to tread on serpents and scorpions, and over all the power of the enemy: and nothing shall by any means hurt you.*
>
> Luke 10:19

It is not just that you have power above its power no matter what it may be and no matter the amount of power it pretends to demonstrate you have actually overcome it. That is what we can see from what God said through John in 1 John 4:4.

> *Ye are of God, little children, and have overcome them: because greater is he that is in you, than he that is in the world.*
>
> 1 John 4:4

You have been given a mouth and wisdom, which no adversary can resist if you command it and that includes anything that constitutes itself as a mountain in your life. That is what Jesus promised you as written in Luke 21:15. No matter how high or big the mountain may be, when you command it, your command must be obeyed. It cannot resist your command.

> *For I will give you a mouth and wisdom, which all your adversaries shall not be able to gainsay nor resist.*
>
> Luke 21:15

Whatever you command will be established by God. That is what God made us to know from what He said through Job in Job 28:28. Therefore your commands cannot be resisted.

What you can do in Christ

And unto man he said, Behold, the fear of the Lord, that is wisdom; and to depart from evil is understanding.
Job 28:28

From what God revealed to John in Revelation 5:10, He said that you have been made a king and a priest unto God and you are supposed to reign here on earth and that means subduing all the circumstances and mountains around you.

And hast made us unto our God kings and priests: and we shall reign on the earth.
Revelation 5:10

As a king you have authority over the mountains that you come across. Anything that stands before you as a mountain must bow to you when you command it to do so. This is so because when God created you He created you in His image and after His likeness to have dominion over the fish of the sea, over the fowl of the air, over the cattle and over all the earth and over every creeping thing that creeps upon the earth. That is what God said in Genesis 1:26. So you are created to have dominion. You also created to act like God, in the image of God. This means that you are supposed to be like a carbon copy of God.

And God said, Let us make man in our image, after our likeness: and let them have dominion over the fish of the sea, and over the fowl of the air, and over the cattle, and over all the earth, and over every creeping thing that creepeth upon the earth.
Genesis 1:26

Living a supernatural life (Volume 3)

But because of man's sins, man lost this dominion over the earth. However Jesus Christ came to die for you and me so as to take this dominion back for man. Therefore if you are truly a believer in Christ you can exercise once again your authority over the earth.

That is why God said through John in Revelation 5:10 above that you have been made a king and you are supposed to exercise dominion and reign here on earth. That God has given you dominion means that you have authority, command, control and mastery over those things that you have been given dominion over. It means that you are to rule over them and establish your power and supremacy over them and these include anything that stands as a mountain in your life. Therefore you can speak to your mountains and say what God said to the mountain before Zerubbabel in Zechariah 4:6-7.

> *And hast made us unto our God kings and priests: and we shall reign on the earth.*
> **Revelation 5:10**

> *Then he answered and spake unto me, saying, This is the word of the LORD unto Zerubbabel, saying, Not by might, nor by power, but by my spirit, saith the LORD of hosts.*

> *Who art thou, O great mountain? before Zerubbabel thou shalt become a plain: and he shall bring forth the headstone thereof with shoutings, crying, Grace, grace unto it.*
> **Zechariah 4:6-7**

What you can do in Christ

You can say to your mountain, *"Not by my might, nor by my power but by the Spirit of the Lord that lives in me. Who are you O great mountain? Before me you will become a plain."*

YOU CAN DO SIGNS AND WONDERS

You can do signs and wonders because miracles signs and wonders are now supposed to be following you. You can cast out devils in the Name of Jesus. You can speak with new tongues. You can lay hand on the sick in the Name of Jesus and they shall recover. You can take up serpents. If you drink any poison it will not hurt you. You can do all these in the Name of Jesus. That is what Jesus Himself said in Mark 16:15-18

> *And he said unto them, Go ye into all the world, and preach the gospel to every creature.*
>
> *He that believeth and is baptized shall be saved; but he that believeth not shall be damned.*
>
> *And these signs shall follow them that believe; In my name shall they cast out devils; they shall speak with new tongues;*
>
> *They shall take up serpents; and if they drink any deadly thing, it shall not hurt them; they shall lay hands on the sick, and they shall recover.*
>
> **Mark 16:15-18**

Living a supernatural life (Volume 3)

The signs and wonders follow you as you obey the commands of Jesus to preach the good news of salvation because Jesus who is the miracle worker will be doing the signs and wonders to confirm the words that you speak out. That is what happened to the disciples as we are told in Mark 16:20. That is what will happen in your case too whenever you preach the Gospel of Christ. He will be there to confirm your words. When you preach Christ as the divine supplier he will supply your needs.

> *And they went forth, and preached every where, the Lord working with them, and confirming the word with signs following. Amen.*
> **Mark 16:20**

When you preach Christ as a deliverer He will deliver. When you preach Him as a healer He will heal. When you preach Him as a Saviour He will save. When you preach Christ as a miracle worker He will do miracles, signs and wonders. This is because the signs and wonders are meant to confirm the words of the Gospel of Christ that you speak out. God Himself said through Prophet Isaiah in Isaiah 44:24-26 that He is committed to confirm the words of His servants and perform the counsel of His messengers.

> *Thus saith the LORD, thy redeemer, and he that formed thee from the womb, I am the LORD that maketh all things; that stretcheth forth the heavens alone; that spreadeth abroad the earth by myself;*

> *That frustrateth the tokens of the liars, and maketh diviners mad; that turneth wise men backward, and maketh their knowledge foolish;*
>
> *That confirmeth the word of his servant, and performeth the counsel of his messengers; that saith to Jerusalem, Thou shalt be inhabited; and to the cities of Judah, Ye shall be built, and I will raise up the decayed places thereof:*
> **Isaiah 44:24-26**

You are His messenger because He has sent you to go and preach the Gospel throughout the world therefore whatever you ask for will be performed by Him. If He will confirm the words of His servant how much more so will He do for you who is His son? It is obvious that He will confirm your words also.

YOU CAN LIVE IN PERPETUAL VICTORY

The Scriptures say in Hebrews 13:8 that Jesus Christ is the same yesterday, today and forever. The Scriptures also say in Malachi 3:6 that the Lord changes not. Therefore there is no variableness with God. That is what we are made to see by God from what He said through James in James 1:17.

> *Jesus Christ the same yesterday, and to day, and for ever.*
> **Hebrews 13:8**

Living a supernatural life (Volume 3)

> *For I am the* L<small>ORD</small>*, I change not; therefore ye sons of Jacob are not consumed.*
> **Malachi 3:6**

> *Every good gift and every perfect gift is from above, and cometh down from the Father of lights, with whom is no variableness, neither shadow of turning.*
> **James 1:17**

Since there is no variableness with God it means that if God is living in victory then He must be constantly living in victory. It also follows that the love, holiness, righteousness and wisdom of God are constant and perpetual.

But according to Ephesians 1:13, you are now sealed in Christ through the Holy Ghost. Therefore you are now united with Christ. You are one with Christ and you are therefore a partaker of this constancy of God.

> *In whom ye also trusted, after that ye heard the word of truth, the gospel of your salvation: in whom also after that ye believed, ye were sealed with that Holy Spirit of promise,*
> **Ephesians 1:13**

God is constantly living in victory and since He never changes there can be no defeat in God. Since you are united with Him and you are now a partaker of His divine nature as we are told by Peter in 2 Peter 1:4 written below it follows that you should also be a partaker of His constancy because this is part of His divine nature.

What you can do in Christ

> *Whereby are given unto us exceeding great and precious promises: that by these ye might be partakers of the divine nature, having escaped the corruption that is in the world through lust.*
>
> **2 Peter 1:4**

Therefore if you stay *in Christ* since He is constantly living a victorious life it follows then you are also supposed to be constantly living a victorious life. You should therefore never submit to defeat or failure because if you stand against them they will flee and you will come out victorious in the end.

This is true because God always causes you to triumph *in Christ*. That is what He made us to see from what He said through Apostle Paul in 2 Corinthians 2:14. Have this mindset in you.

> *Now thanks be unto God, which always causeth us to triumph in Christ, and maketh manifest the savour of his knowledge by us in every place.*
>
> **2 Corinthians 2:14**

According to 1 John 4:4 and 1 John 5:4-5, your victory is already confirmed in the spiritual realm therefore you can always claim your victory and make it to manifest in the physical realm.

> *Ye are of God, little children, and have overcome them: because greater is he that is in you, than he that is in the world.*
>
> **1 John 4:4**

> *For whatsoever is born of God overcometh the world: and this is the victory that overcometh the world, even our faith.*
>
> *Who is he that overcometh the world, but he that believeth that Jesus is the Son of God?*
>
> **1 John 5:4-5**

Remember that all things first manifest in the spiritual realm before they manifest in the physical realm and as we are told in 2 Corinthians 4:18 the spiritual things are more real than the physical things. That is the reason why God said that you have already overcome. It is your faith that will bring out the victory which you already have in the spiritual realm to manifest in the physical realm.

> *While we look not at the things which are seen, but at the things which are not seen: for the things which are seen are temporal; but the things which are not seen are eternal.*
>
> **2 Corinthians 4:18**

Jesus Christ can never fail and since you are in Him and sealed with Him it follows that you can never fail. You should be conscious of this truth all the time. That should be your mindset.

Therefore no matter what circumstances you may be going through since you know that Jesus Christ is still the same you should not be disturbed because it is quite sure that victory will be yours and you will come out victorious in the end.

What you can do in Christ

That is why the Scriptures say in Proverbs 4:18 that your path is as a shining light that shineth more and more unto the perfect day. This means that you are sure that every day of your life will be better than the previous day. No matter what you may be going through your mindset should be that every day of your life must be better than the previous day and that you are continuously moving towards perfection.

> *But the path of the just is as the shining light, that shineth more and more unto the perfect day.*
>
> **Proverbs 4:18**

YOU CAN DO ANYTHING THAT YOU CAN THINK

When God created man as we discussed in ***Chapter 1*** of ***Volume 1*** of the *"Living a supernatural life"* book series, He created man a spirit-being living in a body and having a soul. We explained that the soul of man is basically made up of the mind, the emotion and the will of man. We also showed that the mind of man is the decision taker for the whole man. Hence we have the statement written in Proverbs 23:7 that whatever a man thinks in his mind is what determines what he is and what he becomes.

> *For as he thinketh in his heart, so is he: Eat and drink, saith he to thee; but his heart is not with thee.*
>
> **Proverbs 23:7**

Living a supernatural life (Volume 3)

We also looked at what God said in Genesis 11:6 that whatever a man can imagine in his heart he can achieve.

> *And the LORD said, Behold, the people is one, and they have all one language; and this they begin to do: and now nothing will be restrained from them, which they have imagined to do.*
> **Genesis 11:6**

We can then concluded from these that the thinking and the imagination functions of the soul are the keys to determining what a man can do and what a man becomes. Anything you can think you can become and anything you can imagine you can do. This is because it is God that works in you to will and to do His good pleasure.

You can see this from Philippians 2:13. The God in you can do anything that you can think and even above anything that you can think. He can even do exceedingly, abundantly above anything you can ask or think. That is what is written in Ephesians 3:20.

> *For it is God which worketh in you both to will and to do of his good pleasure.*
> **Philippians 2:13**

> *Now unto him that is able to do exceeding abundantly above all that we ask or think, according to the power that worketh in us,*
> **Ephesians 3:20**

What you can do in Christ

With the Lord God in you, it becomes easy for you to walk upon your high places and the high places of your enemies and it is the God in you that will make you to do so because the Lord God is your strength according to Habakkuk 3:19. According to Ephesians 1:19, the divine power of God, which is the power that raised Jesus Christ from the dead, is exceedingly great towards you because you believe.

> *The LORD God is my strength, and he will make my feet like hinds' feet, and he will make me to walk upon mine high places.*
> **Habakkuk 3:19**

> *And what is the exceeding greatness of his power to us-ward who believe, according to the working of his mighty power,*
> **Ephesians 1:19**

Even God Himself said in Genesis 11:6 as we have noted in the previous page that nothing will be restrained from you which you can imagine. This means that whatever you can imagine you have the capability to achieve. Once you can build the picture of what you want in your mind, if you keep that picture long enough in your mind it will gradually start to become real to you. The image will eventually manifest physically if you keep thinking and meditating upon it.

Therefore you should take to heart these words of advice written by an anonymous author.

Living a supernatural life (Volume 3)

"Watch your thoughts and imaginations, they become your words. Watch your words, they become your actions. Watch your actions, they become your habits. Watch your habits, they become your character. Watch your character, it determines your destiny."

The role that your imagination plays in making sure that what you confess with your mouth eventually manifest physically in your life was discussed in **Chapter 8** of **Volume 1** of this **"Living a Supernatural Life"** book series. It is further discussed in **Chapter 8** of this **Volume 3**.

YOU CAN BIND AND LOOSE ANYTHING

You can bind anything on earth and it will be bound in Heaven. You can loose anything on earth and it will be loosed in Heaven. This means that you have the power to effect changes in the spiritual realm right from here on earth. This is an awesome power that you now have through Christ. Jesus Himself said so in Matthew 16:19. With that kind of power available to you how can you fear under any situation when you have the power to bind or loose the controlling power over that situation using these keys of the kingdom?

> *And I will give unto thee the keys of the Kingdom of Heaven: and whatsoever thou shalt bind on earth shall be bound in heaven: and whatsoever thou shalt loose on earth shall be loosed in heaven.*
>
> **Matthew 16:19**

What you can do in Christ

Remember that we have been told in Philippians 2:9-11 that God has given Jesus a Name to which every knee must bow when called? Whether in Heaven, on earth or under the earth all must bow at the call of that Name. This Name Jesus is one of the keys of the Kingdom that Jesus was talking about in the Scripture written above. When you command in that Name that anything be bound it must be bound and when you command in that Name that anything be loosed it must be loosed.

> *Wherefore God also hath highly exalted him, and given him a name which is above every name:*
>
> *That at the name of Jesus every knee should bow, of things in heaven, and things in earth, and things under the earth;*
>
> *And that every tongue should confess that Jesus Christ is Lord, to the glory of God the Father.*
>
> **Philippians 2:9-11**

Every affliction that comes your way, no matter what form it takes has a spirit, which is the controlling power or the strong man behind it. This strong man is seating pretty, feeling comfortable trying to turn your body or your life into a profitable business enterprise for himself by eating away your body, your finances or even your life itself. Once you can bind this strong man or controlling power behind the affliction, you can spoil his goods and whatever he has built in your body or life to perpetuate his stay there.

Living a supernatural life (Volume 3)

It is then that you can get rid of the affliction. That is what Jesus said which is written in Matthew 12:29.

> *Or else how can one enter into a strong man's house, and spoil his goods, except he first bind the strong man? and then he will spoil his house.*
> **Matthew 12:29**

For example when a disease has turned your body into its house and is ravaging your body if you can get the strong man behind that disease bound then it becomes easy to cast out or get rid of the disease. Such a strong man will probably make use of a germ, bacteria, virus or some other living thing, which the spirit can inhabit for the attack on your body. Since they are living things it means that they have life in them. Therefore if you can get rid of the life sustaining the disease then you can get rid of the disease. God has said in Psalm 102:20 that He wants to loose those things that are appointed to death. But He also said that whatever you loose on earth is what He will loose in heaven. Therefore it is you who will first loose those people that are appointed to death before God looses them.

> *To hear the groaning of the prisoner; to loose those that are appointed to death;*
> **Psalm 102:20**

Jesus in His teachings made us to understand that most infirmities are actually a form of bondage by a spirit. That was what Jesus called it in the case of the woman that He met in the synagogue on a Sabbath discussed in Luke 13:10-16.

What you can do in Christ

And he was teaching in one of the synagogues on the sabbath.

And, behold, there was a woman which had a spirit of infirmity eighteen years, and was bowed together, and could in no wise lift up herself.

And when Jesus saw her, he called her to him, and said unto her, Woman, thou art loosed from thine infirmity.

And he laid his hands on her: and immediately she was made straight, and glorified God.

And the ruler of the synagogue answered with indignation, because that Jesus had healed on the sabbath day, and said unto the people, There are six days in which men ought to work: in them therefore come and be healed, and not on the sabbath day.

The Lord then answered him, and said, Thou hypocrite, doth not each one of you on the sabbath loose his ox or his ass from the stall, and lead him away to watering?

And ought not this woman, being a daughter of Abraham, whom Satan hath bound, lo, these eighteen years, be loosed from this bond on the sabbath day?
Luke 13:10-16

Living a supernatural life (Volume 3)

The woman was set loose by Jesus Christ. You too now have the power to set people loose from the spirit of infirmity or from any form of bondage.

Once you give the command to set anyone loose from any form of infirmity here on earth, the command will be confirmed in Heaven. When someone is deaf you can command his ears to be loosed or opened to hear. When someone is dumb you can command his tongue loosed to speak. That was what Jesus did as written in Mark 7:31-37 in the case of the deaf and dumb man that he healed.

> *And again, departing from the coasts of Tyre and Sidon, he came unto the sea of Galilee, through the midst of the coasts of Decapolis.*
>
> *And they bring unto him one that was deaf, and had an impediment in his speech; and they beseech him to put his hand upon him.*
>
> *And he took him aside from the multitude, and put his fingers into his ears, and he spit, and touched his tongue;*
>
> *And looking up to heaven, he sighed, and saith unto him, Ephphatha, that is, Be opened.*
>
> *And straightway his ears were opened, and the string of his tongue was loosed, and he spake plain.*
>
> *And he charged them that they should tell no man: but the more he charged them, so much the more a great deal they published it;*

What you can do in Christ

And were beyond measure astonished, saying, He hath done all things well: he maketh both the deaf to hear, and the dumb to speak.
Mark 7:31-37

Similarly when someone is blind you can command that his eyes be loosed to see as Jesus did in Mark 10:51-52. Even death can be treated similarly because when the cold hands of death decides to take someone and you don't want it so you can command that that person be loosed from the hands of death and if you do not doubt in your heart your command will be confirmed in heaven. What you can bind or loose will depend on the level of insight of the Word of God that you have.

And Jesus answered and said unto him, What wilt thou that I should do unto thee? The blind man said unto him, Lord, that I might receive my sight.

And Jesus said unto him, Go thy way; thy faith hath made thee whole. And immediately he received his sight, and followed Jesus in the way.
Mark 10:51-52

Possession by spirits is also a form of bondage and when you come across anyone possessed of devils you can set him loose here on earth by asking the devils to leave and he will be confirmed loosed in heaven and the devils will leave him. You can see an example of this in Matthew 8:28-32 from what Jesus did when He healed the two men possessed with devils.

Living a supernatural life (Volume 3)

> *And when he was come to the other side into the country of the Gergesenes, there met him two possessed with devils, coming out of the tombs, exceeding fierce, so that no man might pass by that way.*
>
> *And, behold, they cried out, saying, What have we to do with thee, Jesus, thou Son of God? art thou come hither to torment us before the time?*
>
> *And there was a good way off from them an herd of many swine feeding.*
>
> *So the devils besought him, saying, If thou cast us out, suffer us to go away into the herd of swine.*
>
> *And he said unto them, Go. And when they were come out, they went into the herd of swine: and, behold, the whole herd of swine ran violently down a steep place into the sea, and perished in the waters.*
>
> **Matthew 8:28-32**

You can similarly treat debts, poverty and lack as a form of financial bondage and you can therefore set people loose from financial debts, poverty and lack. With this type of power now available to you it is obvious that God will not expect you to just be looking at the storms of life that you come across. God expects you to do something about them because He has given you the power and the authority to deal with them. You can bind all the storms of life that come your way and command them to be still and calm. That was what Jesus did in Luke 8:22-25.

What you can do in Christ

Now it came to pass on a certain day, that he went into a ship with his disciples: and he said unto them, Let us go over unto the other side of the lake. And they launched forth.

But as they sailed he fell asleep: and there came down a storm of wind on the lake; and they were filled with water, and were in jeopardy.

And they came to him, and awoke him, saying, Master, master, we perish. Then he arose, and rebuked the wind and the raging of the water: and they ceased, and there was a calm.

And he said unto them, Where is your faith? And they being afraid wondered, saying one to another, What manner of man is this! for he commandeth even the winds and water, and they obey him.
Luke 8:22-25

You can even take the command that Jesus gave the fig tree in Mark 11:14 saying, "No man eat fruit of thee hereafter for ever" as a command binding the fig tree.

And Jesus answered and said unto it, No man eat fruit of thee hereafter for ever. And his disciples heard it.
Mark 11:14

Once the command was pronounced here on earth it was confirmed in heaven and the consequence was that the tree eventually withered and died.

The power that we now have through these keys given to us by Jesus is limitless. Use the keys! How much power you get out or exhibit using these keys of the Kingdom will depend on the insight that you have of the keys and the Word and the faith that you can exercise in their use.

YOU CAN DO GREATER WORKS THAN ANY OLD COVENANT SAINT

You have the potential for a greater anointing than any Old Covenant saint. That is what we can infer from what Jesus said in Matthew 11:11. As a believer under the New Covenant you have the power to and can do greater miracles than any Old Covenant saint. The power to do so actually lives in you. You have the potential. It is one thing to have the potential it is another thing entirely to exercise and demonstrate that power.

> *Verily I say unto you, Among them that are born of women there hath not risen a greater than John the Baptist: notwithstanding he that is least in the Kingdom of Heaven is greater than he.*
> **Matthew 11:11**

This means that you have the potential to be wiser than Solomon. This is not surprising because we do know that the seat of wisdom is the mind of man and as a regenerated Christian you now have the mind of Christ.

What you can do in Christ

That is what we are told in 1 Corinthians 2:16. This means, according to what we have referred to several times in this book which is written by John the Apostle in John 1:1-3,14 that this mind that you now have made all things and without it was not anything made that was made.

> *For who hath known the mind of the Lord, that he may instruct him? But we have the mind of Christ.*
> **1 Corinthians 2:16**

> *In the beginning was the Word, and the Word was with God, and the Word was God.*

> *The same was in the beginning with God.*

> *All things were made by him; and without him was not any thing made that was made.*

> *And the Word was made flesh, and dwelt among us, and we beheld his glory, the glory as of the only begotten of the Father, full of grace and truth.*
> **John 1:1-3,14**

This mind of Christ, which you now have, is also the custodian of the wisdom of God as we are told by Paul in 1 Corinthians 1:24. From what we are told by the same Paul in 1 Corinthians 1:30 this wisdom of God is now made available to you. You cannot be foolish.

Living a supernatural life (Volume 3)

> *But unto them which are called, both Jews and Greeks, Christ the power of God, and the wisdom of God.*
> **1 Corinthians 1:24**

> *But of him are ye in Christ Jesus, who of God is made unto us wisdom, and righteousness, and sanctification, and redemption:*
> **1 Corinthians 1:30**

What this means is that potentially you can be wiser than Solomon. It also means is that there are potentially more miracles inside you than there was in Elijah, in Elisha, in Moses, in Joshua or in any other Old Covenant saints. You can do what they did and you can even do greater miracles than they did. Potentially there is more power in you than any Old Covenant saint. Potentially there is more wisdom in you than any Old Covenant saint. This is not surprising because you now have the Wisdom of God and the Power of God living in you.

No wonder Jesus said in John 14:12 that you will do the works that He did and even greater works than He did. If that is the case then it follows that you can do greater works than any Old Covenant saint. This should not surprise you because the Holy Spirit that lives permanently in us today was merely dropping in on them in the old Covenant days.

> *Verily, verily, I say unto you, He that believeth on me, the works that I do shall he do also; and greater works than these shall he do; because I go unto my Father.*
> **John 14:12**

YOU CAN DO THE WORKS THAT JESUS DID

You can do the works that Jesus did. You can even do greater works than He did. You may say that is blasphemy but I did not say it. Jesus was the One who said so in John 14:12 as we have seen written in the last section. What this means is that you can cast out devils, you can heal the sick, you can raise the dead, you can control the elements and do all kinds of miracles. To do the works that Jesus did you will need to have the power that He had. But you can only have this power after the Holy Ghost has come upon you. That is what Jesus Himself promised us in Acts 1:8.

> *But ye shall receive power, after that the Holy Ghost is come upon you: and ye shall be witnesses unto me both in Jerusalem, and in all Judaea, and in Samaria, and unto the uttermost part of the earth.*
>
> **Acts 1:8**

Once you receive this power then you can be a witness of Jesus Christ to preach the good news of the Gospel of Christ, which is the major work that Christ did. The other works such as miracles, signs and wonders that He did were just meant to support the main work of preaching the Gospel. He has also given you the charge in Mark 16:15 to preach the good news of the Gospel as your main work.

> *And he said unto them, Go ye into all the world, and preach the gospel to every creature.*
>
> **Mark 16:15**

Living a supernatural life (Volume 3)

As you preach the Gospel miracles, signs and wonders will be following you because whoever believes will cast out devils in Jesus' Name, will speak with new tongues, will take up serpents, will not be hurt if they drink any deadly thing, will lay hands on the sick and they will recover. But as you will see later this power is only for them that believe not for all.

All these will happen so that Jesus can confirm the words of the Gospel that you speak out and He confirmed it in the case of the Apostles. That is what we can see in Mark 16:16-20.

> *He that believeth and is baptized shall be saved; but he that believeth not shall be damned.*
>
> *And these signs shall follow them that believe; In my name shall they cast out devils; they shall speak with new tongues;*
>
> *They shall take up serpents; and if they drink any deadly thing, it shall not hurt them; they shall lay hands on the sick, and they shall recover.*
>
> *So then after the Lord had spoken unto them, he was received up into heaven, and sat on the right hand of God.*
>
> *And they went forth, and preached every where, the Lord working with them, and confirming the word with signs following. Amen.*
>
> **Mark 16:16-20**

What you can do in Christ

As we have said earlier these will be possible for you only after you have obtained the full baptism of the Holy Spirit that Peter talked about in Acts 2:38-39 as written below.

> *Then Peter said unto them, Repent, and be baptized every one of you in the name of Jesus Christ for the remission of sins, and ye shall receive the gift of the Holy Ghost.*
>
> *For the promise is unto you, and to your children, and to all that are afar off, even as many as the Lord our God shall call.*
> **Acts 2:38-39**

To do the works that Jesus did you will need to believe, receive and make use of all the gifts of the Holy Spirit that are listed by Paul in 1 Corinthians 12:7.

> *But the manifestation of the Spirit is given to every man to profit withal.*
> **1 Corinthians 12:7**

If you don't have any of these spiritual gifts Jesus made us to know that if you ask for them God will not deny you of the gifts. That is what Jesus Christ promised to give us in Luke 11:13. God also speaking through Apostle Paul in 1 Corinthians 12:31 instructed and advised us that we should earnestly desire these gifts of the Spirit.

Living a supernatural life (Volume 3)

> *If ye then, being evil, know how to give good gifts unto your children: how much more shall your heavenly Father give the Holy Spirit to them that ask him?*
> **Luke 11:13**

> *But covet earnestly the best gifts: and yet shew I unto you a more excellent way.*
> **1 Corinthians 12:31**

You will also need and make sure that you have all the fruit of the Holy Spirit that are listed by Paul in Galatians 5:22-24. This fruit and gifts of the Spirit belong to the Spirit. They are not the property of any one. It is an evidence that whoever has them has the Holy Spirit in him. You will not only receive the gifts of the Spirit but as part of the works that Jesus did, which you are now also supposed to do, you can impart these gifts to others. Peter and the Apostles did just this as we are told by God through Luke in Acts 8:14-17.

> *But the fruit of the Spirit is love, joy, peace, longsuffering, gentleness, goodness, faith, Meekness, temperance: against such there is no law.*
>
> *And they that are Christ's have crucified the flesh with the affections and lusts.*
> **Galatians 5:22-24**

> *Now when the apostles which were at Jerusalem heard that Samaria had received the word of God, they sent unto them Peter and John:*

Who, when they were come down, prayed for them, that they might receive the Holy Ghost:

For as yet he was fallen upon none of them: only they were baptized in the name of the Lord Jesus.

Then laid they their hands on them, and they received the Holy Ghost.
Acts 8:14-17

YOU CAN IMPART THE GIFTS OF THE HOLY SPIRIT TO OTHERS

You should note that just as you can have the gifts of the Holy Spirit you can also impart these gifts of the Holy Spirit to others. That was why Paul said that he would love to do that for the Romans in Romans 1:11. Jesus said in John 14:12 that you will do the works that He did. But the works that He did included imparting the gift of the Holy Spirit to others.

For I long to see you, that I may impart unto you some spiritual gift, to the end ye may be established;
Romans 1:11

Verily, verily, I say unto you, He that believeth on me, the works that I do shall he do also; and greater works than these shall he do; because I go unto my Father.
John 14:12

Living a supernatural life (Volume 3)

It follows therefore that you can also impart the full baptism of the Holy Spirit to others since that is one of the works that He did as we can see from what is written in John 20:22. This impartation of the Holy Spirit to others is usually done through the laying on of hands.

> *And when he had said this, he breathed on them, and saith unto them, Receive ye the Holy Ghost:*
>
> **John 20:22**

Jesus Himself said that you are supposed to do the works that He did and one of the major work that He did according to what is written in Matthew 3:11 and John 1:33 was that He baptized people with the Holy Ghost. Therefore you can also impart the baptism of the Holy Ghost to other people. Jesus Himself is the baptizer but He can use you as the medium to impart the baptism to others.

> *I indeed baptize you with water unto repentance: but he that cometh after me is mightier than I, whose shoes I am not worthy to bear: he shall baptize you with the Holy Ghost, and with fire:*
>
> **Matthew 3:11**

> *And I knew him not: but he that sent me to baptize with water, the same said unto me, Upon whom thou shalt see the Spirit descending, and remaining on him, the same is he which baptizeth with the Holy Ghost.*
>
> **John 1:33**

YOU CAN SAY NO TO DEATH

Death has no more power over you. You do not have to go when death comes. You can say no to death. In fact, you can choose when to go. This may sound strange to you but it is the truth. That is what we can see from what God said through Paul in Philippians 1:23-25.

> *For I am in a strait betwixt two, having a desire to depart, and to be with Christ; which is far better:*
>
> *Nevertheless to abide in the flesh is more needful for you.*
>
> *And having this confidence, I know that I shall abide and continue with you all for your furtherance and joy of faith;*
> **Philippians 1:23-25**

Your leaving is between you and God, The devil has no say in it. This is so because the devil no longer has the keys of hell and of death. That is what we can see from what is written in Hebrews 2:14. Jesus Christ who lives in you now has the keys. That is what He Himself said in Revelation 1:18.

> *Forasmuch then as the children are partakers of flesh and blood, he also himself likewise took part of the same; that through death he might destroy him that had the power of death, that is, the devil;*
> **Hebrews 2:14**

Living a supernatural life (Volume 3)

> *I am he that liveth, and was dead; and, behold, I am alive for evermore, Amen; and have the keys of hell and of death.*
> **Revelation 1:18**

Therefore you can say just like Paul said as written by Paul the Apostle in 1 Corinthians 15:55, *"O death where is thy sting? O grave where is thy victory?"* You can say no to death. But many Christians don't know that death no longer has any power over them. They are so afraid of death that they almost give up even before death comes. Their fear enslaves them to death. But when death comes if you speak life to it death will run away unless the time set by God for you has come.

> *O death, where is thy sting? O grave, where is thy victory?*
> **1 Corinthians 15:55**

Jesus Christ died so that you can live. That is what we are told in John 3:36. According to Paul in Romans 6:4, you were buried with Christ unto death. But according to Paul in Galatians 3:12-13 God who raised Jesus Christ up from the dead has quickened you together with Him.

> *He that believeth on the Son hath everlasting life: and he that believeth not the Son shall not see life; but the wrath of God abideth on him.*
> **John 3:36**

What you can do in Christ

Therefore we are buried with him by baptism into death: that like as Christ was raised up from the dead by the glory of the Father, even so we also should walk in newness of life.
Romans 6:4

And the law is not of faith: but, The man that doeth them shall live in them.

Christ hath redeemed us from the curse of the law, being made a curse for us: for it is written, Cursed is every one that hangeth on a tree:
Galatians 3:12-13

You are raised with Christ and Christ is now your life. That is what God says in Colossians 3:1,4. According to what is written in Colossians 2:13, Ephesians 2:5-6 and Galatians 2:20 you have actually been made alive with Christ. Therefore death can no longer harass you. You can say no to death when it comes because death no longer has any power over you.

If ye then be risen with Christ, seek those things which are above, where Christ sitteth on the right hand of God.

When Christ, who is our life, shall appear, then shall ye also appear with him in glory.
Colossians 3:1,4

Living a supernatural life (Volume 3)

> *And you, being dead in your sins and the uncircumcision of your flesh, hath he quickened together with him, having forgiven you all trespasses;*
> **Colossians 2:13**

> *Even when we were dead in sins, hath quickened us together with Christ, by grace ye are saved;*

> *And hath raised us up together, and made us sit together in heavenly places in Christ Jesus:*
> **Ephesians 2:5-6**

> *I am crucified with Christ: nevertheless I live; yet not I, but Christ liveth in me: and the life which I now live in the flesh I live by the faith of the Son of God, who loved me, and gave himself for me.*
> **Galatians 2:20**

It is not surprising that John said in 1 John 5:11-13 that you now have life and you have eternal life because according to Peter in 1 Peter 1:3-4, you have been given all things that pertain unto life and godliness and you now partake of the divine nature of God.

> *And this is the record, that God hath given to us eternal life, and this life is in his Son.*

> *He that hath the Son hath life; and he that hath not the Son of God hath not life.*

What you can do in Christ

These things have I written unto you that believe on the name of the Son of God; that ye may know that ye have eternal life, and that ye may believe on the name of the Son of God.
1 John 5:11-13

Blessed be the God and Father of our Lord Jesus Christ, which according to his abundant mercy hath begotten us again unto a lively hope by the resurrection of Jesus Christ from the dead,

To an inheritance incorruptible, and undefiled, and that fadeth not away, reserved in heaven for you,
1 Peter 1:3-4

If you have all things that pertain unto life then it follows that you have life itself. One of the most prominent attributes of God's nature is eternal life. Since you now partake of His divine nature it follows that you now share in this eternal life of Christ.

This eternal life is in Christ Jesus. Therefore when you have Christ in your life and you believe on the Name of Jesus Christ then this eternal life becomes yours. You are then no longer under the Law of sin and death. So they have no control over you.

Living a supernatural life (Volume 3)
YOU CAN KEEP SIN UNDER SUBJECTION

According to Romans 6:11-14 you are now supposed to be dead to sin and alive to God. Sin therefore should no longer reign in your body. You can now keep sin under subjection. You don't have to allow the lusts of sin to rule over you. Sin has no more dominion over you because you are no longer under the law of sin but grace. If you sin now, it is because you choose to sin not because sin has any power over you. So there is no excuse for you to sin. Many times we give excuses for sin but most of these excuses we know are really not tenable or even acceptable to God. Sometimes we call sin by another name to cover it up. Call it what it is! Call it by its name!

> *Likewise reckon ye also yourselves to be dead indeed unto sin, but alive unto God through Jesus Christ our Lord.*
>
> *Let not sin therefore reign in your mortal body, that ye should obey it in the lusts thereof.*
>
> *Neither yield ye your members as instruments of unrighteousness unto sin: but yield yourselves unto God, as those that are alive from the dead, and your members as instruments of righteousness unto God.*
>
> *For sin shall not have dominion over you: for ye are not under the law, but under grace.*
>   **Romans 6:11-14**

What you can do in Christ

As a born-again Christian you should mind mainly the things of the Spirit and walk after the Spirit. If you do so then from Romans 8:5, it is obvious that your thoughts, your affections and your purposes and actions will be directed and set upon the things of the Spirit. Once you can do that you will be able to overcome any temptation. Therefore there is no temptation that can overcome you now unless you agree to be defeated. For any temptation that comes, according to what is written by Paul in 1 Corinthians 10:13 God will not allow you to be tempted above what you can cope with and He has also made a way of escape for you from any temptation if it becomes unbearable. How can you have such a promise from God and not feel confident that you can keep any temptation under control? However despite this promise of God most Christians still fear and yield to temptations because they see the temptations as being too daunting and formidable for them to cope with. They fear because they are not willing to face the temptation squarely.

> *For they that are after the flesh do mind the things of the flesh; but they that are after the Spirit the things of the Spirit.*
> **Romans 8:5**

> *There hath no temptation taken you but such as is common to man: but God is faithful, who will not suffer you to be tempted above that ye are able; but will with the temptation also make a way to escape, that ye may be able to bear it.*
> **1 Corinthians 10:13**

Living a supernatural life (Volume 3)

Throughout the time that Jesus Christ was on earth He was tried and tested just as you are now being tested, yet He was without sin. That is what the Scriptures made us to see in Hebrews 4:15 and 1 Peter 2:22. He came to be tried and tested so that you too can have power over sin, so that sin can no longer be a problem to you. You are now sent as He was sent. That is what He said in John 20:21. Therefore whatever He can overcome you too can now overcome. Whatever was not able to overcome Him when He came should not be able to overcome you now.

> *For we have not an high priest which cannot be touched with the feeling of our infirmities; but was in all points tempted like as we are, yet without sin.*
> **Hebrews 4:15**

> *Who did no sin, neither was guile found in his mouth:*
> **1 Peter 2:22**

> *Then said Jesus to them again, Peace be unto you: as my Father hath sent me, even so send I you.*
> **John 20:21**

But we know from Isaiah's prophecy in Isaiah 7:14-15 concerning the way Jesus was sent that He was sent to know how to refuse the evil and choose the good, which meant that sin would not be His choice. He was capable of knowing all of sin's antics. Therefore sin had no power over Him.

What you can do in Christ

Therefore the Lord himself shall give you a sign; Behold, a virgin shall conceive, and bear a son, and shall call his name Immanuel.

Butter and honey shall he eat, that he may know to refuse the evil, and choose the good.
Isaiah 7:14-15

Since you are now sent as He was sent it follows that sin should no longer be your problem too for you now also know how to refuse the evil and choose the good. You too can see that sin has no more power over you. You now have the freedom to choose. Therefore nothing can stop you from living a triumphant life over sin because God is with you and He is the one upholding you with the right hand of His righteousness. That is what we are made to know from what Prophet Isaiah said in Isaiah 41:10. You can overcome all sins and bad habits.

Fear thou not; for I am with thee: be not dismayed; for I am thy God: I will strengthen thee; yea, I will help thee; yea, I will uphold thee with the right hand of my righteousness.
Isaiah 41:10

You have the power to overcome bad habits because according to 1 John 5:4-5 the victorious life of God, which overcomes the world, is in you and you know that sin is of the world.

For whatsoever is born of God overcometh the world: and this is the victory that overcometh the world, even our faith.

Living a supernatural life (Volume 3)

> *Who is he that overcometh the world, but he that believeth that Jesus is the Son of God?*
>
> **1 John 5:4-5**

You cannot commit sin as a habit anymore since you are born of God and His seed remains in you because we know that sin is of the devil. It is part of the works of the devil and we know that Jesus the Son of God has destroyed the works of the devil so that they should no longer have any power over you. That is what God told us through John in 1 John 3:8-9.

> *He that committeth sin is of the devil; for the devil sinneth from the beginning. For this purpose the Son of God was manifested, that he might destroy the works of the devil.*
>
> *Whosoever is born of God doth not commit sin; for his seed remaineth in him: and he cannot sin, because he is born of God.*
>
> **1 John 3:8-9**

The life of Jesus Christ, which is a sinless life, can be made to manifest in your body, which is also being preserved by Him. That is what God said through Paul in 2 Corinthians 4:11. That is what we should be struggling to attain daily in our Christian walk with God.

> *For we which live are alway delivered unto death for Jesus' sake, that the life also of Jesus might be made manifest in our mortal flesh.*
>
> **2 Corinthians 4:11**

What you can do in Christ

Once you submit yourself to God, you can resist the devil and whenever you do resist him, he must run away from you. He cannot stand before you when you resist him in faith. That is what God said through James in James 4:7.

> *Submit yourselves therefore to God. Resist the devil, and he will flee from you.*
>
> **James 4:7**

YOU CAN HAVE KNOWLEDGE OF THE TRUTH

The Spirit of God, which lives in you, searches all things, even the deep things of God. That is what we are made to know from what God said through Paul in 1 Corinthians 2:10. The Spirit of God in you will search all things and bring all things to your remembrance that Jesus Has said. That is one of the functions of the Holy Spirit that Jesus Himself mentioned in John 14:26. What a wonderful thing for you to know that nothing is really hidden from you any longer?

> *But God hath revealed them unto us by his Spirit: for the Spirit searcheth all things, yea, the deep things of God.*
>
> **1 Corinthians 2:10**

> *But the Comforter, which is the Holy Ghost, whom the Father will send in my name, he shall teach you all things, and bring all things to your remembrance, whatsoever I have said unto you.*
>
> **John 14:26**

Living a supernatural life (Volume 3)

Whatever you desire to know you can know because the Spirit of God in you can make it known to you if you will only give Him the room to operate freely in your life. This is so because you can desire those gifts of the Holy Spirit useful for this purpose such as the gift of the word of knowledge and the gift of the word of wisdom as well as the gift for discernment. When you have these gifts of the Spirit whatever secret thing you desire to know God can make it known to you through His Spirit that is living in you. This is even more so now that Christ who is the Living Word of God lives in you according to what is written in John 14:20.

At that day ye shall know that I am in my Father, and ye in me, and I in you.
John 14:20

This Word of God in you is quick and powerful and sharper than any two-edged sword, piercing even to dividing asunder of soul and spirit, and of the joints and marrow and it is a discerner of the thoughts and intents of the heart. There is no creature that is not manifest in His sight. All things are naked and opened unto His eyes. That is what the Word that is living in you can do as we are told in Hebrews 4:12-13. Therefore as you can see that nothing is hidden from you any longer. Whatever you need to know Christ who now lives in you will make it known to you through His Spirit that now lives in you. After all He has said in John 16:13-14 that the Spirit will receive from Him and will show it to you. He also said that the Spirit will guide you into all truth and show you things to come. So with the Spirit in you there is nothing that can be hidden from you.

What you can do in Christ

For the word of God is quick, and powerful, and sharper than any twoedged sword, piercing even to the dividing asunder of soul and spirit, and of the joints and marrow, and is a discerner of the thoughts and intents of the heart.

Neither is there any creature that is not manifest in his sight: but all things are naked and opened unto the eyes of him with whom we have to do.
Hebrews 4:12-13

Howbeit when he, the Spirit of truth, is come, he will guide you into all truth: for he shall not speak of himself; but whatsoever he shall hear, that shall he speak: and he will shew you things to come.

He shall glorify me: for he shall receive of mine, and shall shew it unto you.
John 16:13-14

As you continue in the Words of Jesus Christ, you will have the knowledge of the truth beyond all doubt. That is what we are told in John 8:31-32 and the knowing of the truth will make you free.

Then said Jesus to those Jews which believed on him, If ye continue in my word, then are ye my disciples indeed;

And ye shall know the truth, and the truth shall make you free.
John 8:31-32

Living a supernatural life (Volume 3)

From what Jesus said in John 14:16-17 the Holy Spirit who is the Spirit of truth now lives in you. This Spirit of truth that lives in you now gives you the access to all truth. Among such truths that you can now have access to are the truths about your true nature in Christ, which we have discussed in *Chapters 2-6* of this book. It is through the revelation given by the Holy Spirit that you can understand these truths. Also without such revelation through the Holy Spirit you cannot know the truths about those things that exist in the spiritual realm, which you cannot see with the physical eyes but which you can see with your inner spiritual eyes and this brings me to the next point. Even in this physical realm you know that your eyes has a limitation as to what it can see. It is that limitation that makes it impossible for human eyes to to see the entire range of the spectrum of light

> *And I will pray the Father, and he shall give you another Comforter, that he may abide with you for ever;*
>
> *Even the Spirit of truth; whom the world cannot receive, because it seeth him not, neither knoweth him: but ye know him; for he dwelleth with you, and shall be in you.*
>
> **John 14:16-17**

YOU CAN SEE THE INVISIBLE

Since you are instructed in 2 Corinthians 4:18 not to look at things, which are seen physically but to look at the things which are not seen physically, it follows that it is possible for you to see the invisible things and you can see such things, which are not seen physically.

What you can do in Christ

While we look not at the things which are seen, but at the things which are not seen: for the things which are seen are temporal; but the things which are not seen are eternal.
2 Corinthians 4:18

Therefore as you are instructed, you should not fix your sight on things which are seen for they are temporary. You should fix your sight to look at spiritual things, which are not seen for they are eternal and should be more real to you. If God says that you can see things which are not seen then you better believe that you can do so.

What God is telling you here is that you should not base your judgments on what your natural senses, which dictate what you can physically see, taste, smell, hear or feel say to you. This is because you should know that what they say are not conclusive evidences about any situation. You should base your decisions about any situation on what the Word of God says about the situation. To you, *seeing is not believing anymore*. You don't have to see before you believe. Instead, you know now that *whatever you believe you will eventually see therefore believing is seeing.* You can recognize the evidences of your senses but you should not base your decisions on them.

You can see by faith beyond what your senses can see. That is why you can call things, which be not as though they were and cause them to appear. This is so because as we are instructed by God through Paul the Apostle in 2 Corinthians 5:7 and also in Romans 1:17, you should live by faith.

Living a supernatural life (Volume 3)

For we walk by faith, not by sight:
2 Corinthians 5:7

For therein is the righteousness of God revealed from faith to faith: as it is written, The just shall live by faith.
Romans 1:17

This means that you should base your decision on whatever the Word of God says concerning any situation. You should not look at symptoms to pass judgment about any situation. You should base your judgment about any situation on whatever the Word of God says about the situation. You should not allow the evidences of your senses to dictate to you or rule you. Note what Jesus said in Mark 11:24 that whatever you ask for in prayer if you believe that you receive it when you pray you will surely get it. Therefore whatever you want to see believe that you see it and you will surely see it. That is what seeing or living by faith is all about.

Therefore I say unto you, What things soever ye desire, when ye pray, believe that ye receive them, and ye shall have them.
Mark 11:24

YOU CAN HEAR GOD'S VOICE

You are the one that Christ refers to as His sheep in John 10:27 therefore you can hear God's voice.

My sheep hear my voice, and I know them, and they follow me:
John 10:27

What you can do in Christ

As you hear Him you follow Him and He knows you. As you listen to God and obey the instructions that He passes on to you, then you can start to live His life in you and you can start to follow the instructions that come from the Holy Spirit who is living within you rather than follow the instructions that come from without through your senses. This will lead you to the type of fellowshipping with the Holy Spirit, which Paul referred to in Philippians 2:1-2.

If there be therefore any consolation in Christ, if any comfort of love, if any fellowship of the Spirit, if any bowels and mercies,

Fulfil ye my joy, that ye be likeminded, having the same love, being of one accord, of one mind.

Philippians 2:1-2

YOU CAN MAKE REQUESTS IN JESUS' NAME

Jesus gave us the instruction in John 14:13-14 that whenever we want to do the works that He did we can ask for anything to be done in His Name and He will do it for us if it will glorify the Father. Therefore anytime *you want to do the works* that Jesus did you can make your request that such works be done in Jesus' Name. Then *Jesus will do it* so that the Father may be glorified in the Son.

Living a supernatural life (Volume 3)

> *And whatsoever ye shall ask in my name, that will I do, that the Father may be glorified in the Son.*
>
> *If ye shall ask any thing in my name, I will do it.*
>
> John 14:13-14

Jesus also gave us another instruction in John 16:23 where He said that whenever we are in need of anything especially if it is something that we need in order to be able to do the works that He did, we can ask the Father for it in His Name and the Father ***will give*** it to us. Whatever we ask for He promised that we shall receive them in order that our joy may be full. It is very important to differentiate these two instructions of Jesus to know what the ***Father will give*** and what ***Jesus will do*** for us. There is a difference between ***giving*** and ***doing***. To be sure that you can get whatever you ask for you must make sure that your request is according to the will of God.

> *And in that day ye shall ask me nothing. Verily, verily, I say unto you, Whatsoever ye shall ask the Father in my name, he will give it you.*
>
> John 16:23

God said in 1 John 5:14-15 that if you ask for anything according to His will He hears you and once you know that He heard you when you asked then you know that you have gotten what you asked of Him.

And this is the confidence that we have in him, that, if we ask any thing according to his will, he heareth us:

And if we know that he hear us, whatsoever we ask, we know that we have the petitions that we desired of him.
1 John 5:14-15

It is obvious that whatever He has commanded, promised or foretold must be His will and you can ask Him for them. You have the assurance that He will give you what you asked for. We have discussed in detail in **Chapter 3** and **Chapter 4** of the **Volume 2** of this *"Living a supernatural life"* book series the use of the Name of Jesus to get things from the Father. We also discussed the use of the Name to do the works that Jesus did. You will do well to read this exposition on the Name of Jesus if you want to know the power that is in that Name, your rights to the use of the Name and how to successfully use the Name to get what you want from God.

YOU CAN LIVE IN DIVINE HEALTH

From what God told us through John in 3 John 2 it is obvious that it is God's wish that we live in divine health and prosperity. That is what God wants for us.

Beloved, I wish above all things that thou mayest prosper and be in health, even as thy soul prospereth.
3 John 2

Living a supernatural life (Volume 3)

If that is God's wish for you it means that it is possible for you to do so. Therefore you can live in divine health and prosperity. But the condition according to God is that your soul, which is basically your mind, must be conditioned to do so.

Once your soul prospers it follows that your entire self, spirit, soul and body will prosper because that is what God wants for you. You can live in divine health because according to Romans 8:11 the Spirit of God in you is supposed to be quickening your mortal body. Your physical body is the part of you that is mortal. The quickening that God is talking about here is therefore for your physical body, which means continuous healing for your body.

But if the Spirit of him that raised up Jesus from the dead dwell in you, he that raised up Christ from the dead shall also quicken your mortal bodies by his Spirit that dwelleth in you.
Romans 8:11

Christ came to destroy the works of the devil and He actually did so. That is what we are made to see from what John wrote in 1 John 3:8. Therefore since sickness is one of the works of the devil, it follows that it no longer has any power over you. You can live a life, which is above sickness and diseases. After all from what God told us through Peter in 1 Peter 2:24, you **have been healed** not *(will be healed)* of all your diseases by the stripes that Jesus took on the Cross. Therefore diseases have no business hanging on your body anymore.

What you can do in Christ

He that committeth sin is of the devil; for the devil sinneth from the beginning. For this purpose the Son of God was manifested, that he might destroy the works of the devil.

1 John 3:8

Who his own self bare our sins in his own body on the tree, that we, being dead to sins, should live unto righteousness: by whose stripes ye were healed.

1 Peter 2:24

According to Psalm 103:3 God who is the God that you are serving is the One that heals all your diseases. If you are serving Him, since He has promised as written in Exodus 23:25-26 that He will take sickness away from you then it is obvious that sickness should no longer be your problem.

Who forgiveth all thine iniquities; who healeth all thy diseases;

Psalm 103:3

And ye shall serve the Lord your God, and he shall bless thy bread, and thy water; and I will take sickness away from the midst of thee.

There shall nothing cast their young, nor be barren, in thy land: the number of thy days I will fulfil.

Exodus 23:25-26

Living a supernatural life (Volume 3)

Not only can you obtain divine healing you can actually live in divine health. In His Covenant promises to you God also said that your young ones will not be attacked by diseases or die prematurely. He said that you will not suffer barrenness and you will not die young. It is obvious therefore that you have an all-round protection from diseases and sicknesses, which if you are ready to claim and make yours will mean that you can live in divine health.

But the problem with many Christians is that they have been made to believe some wrong things about their health. Their minds have been conditioned over time to believe that they must be sick at one time or the other in their lives. Therefore they have prepared their minds to receive sickness whenever it comes to them instead of violently rejecting it.

SICKNESS IS NOT THE AFFLICTION THAT GOD SAYS YOU WILL HAVE

There are some that believe when sickness comes that God has ordained the sickness to come upon them and they quote such Scriptures as Psalm 34:19, which says, *"Many are the afflictions of the righteous but God delivers him out of them all."* So they believe that diseases must come not even once but many times. But the afflictions that God is talking about here are not diseases. They are trials, persecutions and temptations. After all from what is written in Matthew 8:17 Jesus Christ has taken all our infirmities and carried our sicknesses. If He has done so it means that we don't have to carry them any longer. But He said Himself in John 15:20 that we shall suffer persecution.

Many are the afflictions of the righteous: but the LORD delivereth him out of them all.
Psalm 34:19

That it might be fulfilled which was spoken by Esaias the prophet, saying, Himself took our infirmities, and bare our sicknesses.
Matthew 8:17

Remember the word that I said unto you, The servant is not greater than his lord. If they have persecuted me, they will also persecute you; if they have kept my saying, they will keep yours also.
John 15:20

Therefore He did not carry our trials and persecutions. He only took or carried our infirmities and sicknesses. Note that there are differences between on the one part the trials and persecutions that He was talking about and on the other part the infirmities and sicknesses that He carried. The persecution that He is talking about has nothing to do with sicknesses and diseases or infirmities. If Jesus has carried your diseases and infirmities, why must you have to carry it again? If He has carried them then you don't have to carry them also.

SICKNESS IS NOT THE PERSECUTION THAT GOD SAYS YOU WILL HAVE

Another Scripture that leads many Christians to conclude that they should be carrying sicknesses and diseases is James 5:14 where God asked the question *"Is any sick among you?"*

Living a supernatural life (Volume 3)

> *Is any sick among you? let him call for the elders of the church; and let them pray over him, anointing him with oil in the name of the Lord:*
>
> **James 5:14**

We have explained the use and misuse of this Scripture by Christians on **Pages 192-208** of the **Volume 2** of this *"Living a supernatural life"* book series.

You will do well to read this so as to know that you don't have to carry diseases. We showed that the Christian does not have to carry diseases and sicknesses. Trials and persecution are what Jesus said we shall have to carry. We cannot pray our trials and persecutions away. What we need to do is to learn to fight and overcome them because the trials of our faith must come. He said **when afflictions shall come** in Mark 4:17 not *if afflictions shall come*. Therefore we know that it is a sure thing that afflictions will surely come. What Jesus is talking about here is not sickness. He cannot say that He has carried our sickness and still be saying when sickness shall come. Therefore the afflictions, trials and tribulations that Jesus was talking about have nothing to do with sickness. But such afflictions, trials and tribulations shall surely come and you should realize that it is when you go through such afflictions, trials and tribulations that the works of patience are being perfected in you. That is what Paul said in Romans 5:3. You should not see your trials and persecutions as *problems* but as mere *challenges*.

And have no root in themselves, and so endure but for a time: afterward, when affliction or persecution ariseth for the word's sake, immediately they are offended.

Mark 4:17

And not only so, but we glory in tribulations also: knowing that tribulation worketh patience;

Romans 5:3

SICKNESS IS NOT A CHASTENING OF THE LORD

Yet another reason why many Christians believe that they must be sick is that they wrongly see sickness as a chastening of the Lord wrongly going by what is written in Hebrews 12:6-8.

For whom the Lord loveth he chasteneth, and scourgeth every son whom he receiveth.

If ye endure chastening, God dealeth with you as with sons; for what son is he whom the father chasteneth not?

But if ye be without chastisement, whereof all are partakers, then are ye bastards, and not sons.

Hebrews 12:6-8

They are therefore virtually in agreement with the sickness because they wrongly believe that it is of the Lord. They believe that the Lord is using sickness to chasten them because He loves them. Because of that they are in agreement or concur with the sickness or disease and it will definitely stay with them since the Scripture says in Amos 3:3 that two cannot walk together except they are agreed.

> *Can two walk together, except they be agreed?*
> **Amos 3:3**

If you agree and consent with the sickness in your mind it will surely stay with you. But if you violently oppose it in your mind then it will find it difficult to stick to you. God cannot chasten you with sickness or disease. Chastening means *to train*. Are we then saying therefore that God uses sickness or disease as a means of training the Christian?

Why then will God say that if any Christian is sick he should go the elders to pray for him? God cannot be chastening you and at the same time tell you to go and pray the chastening away. As long as you believe that you have to carry sicknesses and diseases you will continue to carry them. But the day you get the truth that Christ has carried your sicknesses and diseases and you no longer have to carry them revealed to you and you believe this truth is the day that you will begin to get your absolute freedom from and control over sicknesses and diseases. From that day on you will realize that you have authority and control over sicknesses and diseases.

What you can do in Christ
CHRIST CARRIED YOUR DISEASES YOU DON'T HAVE TO CARRY THEM ALL OVER AGAIN

Jesus Christ said in John 8:32 that when you know the truth the truth will make you free or liberate you. Immediately you know the truth that ***Christ carried and took your sicknesses and diseases*** as written in Matthew 8:17 and that ***you were healed by the stripes that Jesus took*** according to what is written by Peter in 1 Peter 2:24, you will no longer tolerate any sickness or disease hanging around your body. It must leave you because the Scripture says in Amos 3:3 as written on the previous page that two cannot walk together except they are agreed.

> *And ye shall know the truth, and the truth shall make you free.*
> **John 8:32**

> *That it might be fulfilled which was spoken by Esaias the prophet, saying, Himself took our infirmities, and bare our sicknesses.*
> **Matthew 8:17**

> *Who his own self bare our sins in his own body on the tree, that we, being dead to sins, should live unto righteousness: by whose stripes ye were healed.*
> **1 Peter 2:24**

Therefore since you no longer agree with it there is no option for it but to leave your body. You are in Christ and Christ has already carried your diseases.

Therefore when you still carry your own sicknesses and diseases you are like someone who enters a bus and still carry his luggage on his head in the bus instead of dropping his luggage in the luggage hold of the bus.

JESUS' DEATH SOLVED THE SIN AND THE SICKNESS PROBLEM

Jesus came to deliver you from both sin and sickness. The Scripture says that He bore our sins and healed us. Therefore He has freed us from the power that sin and sickness had over us. They no longer have any power over us. But the pity is that many Christians believe that they are free from the power of sins and believe that whenever sin comes they can always ask God for forgiveness and be forgiven.

But despite the truth that salvation covers freedom from both sins and sicknesses they do not believe that they are freed from sickness so that when sickness comes they can also ask for healing and get it. One of the consequences of sin is sickness. It came as a result of sin. But salvation was meant to deliver us from sin and all its consequences and sickness is one of the consequences of sin.

Therefore salvation covers healing as well. Sin is a form of spiritual sickness while diseases are a form of physical sickness of the body. But your redemption covers healing for both the spiritual and physical sicknesses and you have been redeemed from both.

What you can do in Christ

This is further confirmed by what David said which is written in Psalm 103:1-2, where he said that God forgives all our sins and also heals all our diseases. This means that God's salvation covers the healing of our sins and the healing of our diseases. It is unfortunate that most Christians accept the one and just ignore or reject the other not seeing it as part of their benefits.

Bless the LORD, O my soul: and all that is within me, bless his holy name.

Bless the LORD, O my soul, and forget not all his benefits:
Psalm 103:1-2

The problem with most Christians is that they want to reap what they have not sowed. God said through Apostle Paul in Galatians 6:7 that whatever a man sows is what he will reap.

Be not deceived; God is not mocked: for whatsoever a man soweth, that shall he also reap.
Galatians 6:7

Most Christians when they are sick sow the seeds of doubt and fear in their mind, yet they expect to reap healing fruits from these. That cannot be because God will not contradict His own laws. You cannot sow doubt and reap healing. Whatever you sow is what you are bound to reap. Doctors and the symptoms are telling you that what you have is a terminal disease and that you will soon die.

Living a supernatural life (Volume 3)

But the Word of God is saying that you have been healed therefore arise and walk. But because you have not seen the healing you will rather believe the testimonies of doctors and the symptoms. Though you have not seen the healing faith is your evidence that it is there because faith is the evidence of things not seen. According to Hebrews 11:1, faith is what will give substance to your healing which is unseen.

> *Now faith is the substance of things hoped for, the evidence of things not seen.*
> **Hebrews 11:1**

If you have evidence that point to your healing why don't you look towards that evidence rather than the symptoms and reports that point to the sickness? In Proverbs 4:20-22 the Scriptures say that you should fix your eyes on the Word of God and not let them depart from your eyes. Why are you fixing your eyes on the symptoms of diseases and doctor's reports? Fix your eyes on the ***truth*** of the Word of God rather than the ***facts*** of the symptoms that you see, taste, smell, hear or feel in your natural situations. You should make it a habit to fix your eyes on the Word of God because that is what will give you the faith and faith, which comes from hearing the Word, is the evidence that you need. Face the truth of the Word of God and not the facts that your senses are throwing at you.

> *My son, attend to my words; incline thine ear unto my sayings.*
>
> *Let them not depart from thine eyes; keep them in the midst of thine heart.*

For they are life unto those that find them, and health to all their flesh.

Proverbs 4:20-22

You don't need to beg God to heal you. It is His wish that you be in divine health. That is what we can see in 3 John 2 which is written below. He said so through Apostle John. He said,

"Beloved, I wish above all things that thou mayest prosper and be in health, even as thy soul prospereth."

3 John 2

You are waiting for God to heal you but God is waiting for you to accept the healing that He has already provided for you. Sickness and disease should not be able to overcome you because you now have power over them. They no longer have any power over you. Therefore you can shake yourself completely away from the unscriptural belief that binds you to sickness. You can live in divine health. But the truth is that it is as you think in your heart that you will be.

That is what God made us to know through King Solomon in Proverbs 23:7.

For as he thinketh in his heart, so is he: Eat and drink, saith he to thee; but his heart is not with thee.

Proverbs 23:7

Living a supernatural life (Volume 3)

So if you think that sickness can make your body a home then it will surely come and do so. But if you think in your heart and believe that no sickness has any power to stay in your body then no sickness will be able to make your body a home.

With your faith in the redemption work that Jesus did in place, you don't have to carry any disease or sickness one minute longer than now. You have the power and the authority to command it out of your body. Use them!

Practice is the main objective here. Without practicing the use of this power that you now have you will never know the extent of the power that you have and what you can do with it.

You must practice the use of that power. That was the advice that God gave to Moses in Exodus 4:21 when He sent him to Pharaoh. God knew that it was possible for Moses to have all that power in his hand and not demonstrate it before Pharaoh. That was why God emphasized this to him to make sure that he showed or exhibited the power that He had given him before Pharaoh.

> *And the LORD said unto Moses, When thou goest to return into Egypt, see that thou do all those wonders before Pharaoh, which I have put in thine hand: but I will harden his heart, that he shall not let the people go.*
> **Exodus 4:21**

What you can do in Christ

You now have the power to and you can overcome all sins and every temptation that the enemy may bring to you. You have the power to do and you can do miracles. You can cast out devils and demons. You can heal the sick and you can even raise the dead. You now have the rivers of living waters flowing out of you and with these you can get the sick healed. You can now bind and loose anything. You can bind those things that you don't want and you can loose those things that you do want.

This then is a summary of some of the things that you can do in Christ. These are some of what God says that you can do in Christ. Do you believe that you can do what God says that you can do in Christ? If you do, then start doing what God says that you can do in Christ from today on and you will be surprised. Start using these characteristics that are yours in your day to day life, personalize them and start confessing them. Start confessing what you can now do in Christ as follows on the next five pages:

Living a supernatural life (Volume 3)
THESE ARE WHAT I CAN NOW DO IN CHRIST

"The Blood of Jesus has purged my conscience from dead works so that I can now serve the Living God. Because I am born of God I am no longer subject to the law of sin and death. I can now please God. I can now overcome every bad habit.

I am free from the power of Satan so that I can open the eyes of the people and turn them from darkness unto light and from the power of Satan unto God that they may receive forgiveness of sins and also receive inheritance among them which are sanctified by the faith that is in Christ Jesus. Christ came to destroy the works of the devil and He actually did so. Since sickness is one of the works of the devil, it follows that it no longer has any power over me.

I can do ALL things through Christ who strengthens me. Nothing shall be impossible unto me anymore when I tackle it with the active living faith of God which has been given to me. I can exercise unlimited authority in this life in Christ. I can command a mountain to move from one place to another and if I do not doubt in my heart, it will move. NOTHING is impossible for me.

The divine power of God, the power that raised Jesus Christ from the dead is exceedingly great towards me because I believe. Therefore signs and miracles are following me. I can cast out devils. I can speak with new tongues. I can lay hand on the sick to get them to recover. I can take up serpents.

What you can do in Christ

If I drink poison I will not be hurt. I can do all these in the Name of Jesus. I can do all these because I am not the one really doing them. It is God that works in me to will and to do His good pleasure. The God in me can do anything that I can think and even above anything that I can think. He can even do exceedingly, abundantly above anything I can ask or think. With the Lord God in me, I can walk upon my high places and the high places of my enemies and it is the God in me that will make me to do so because the Lord God is my strength.

I can bind anything here on earth and it will be bound in Heaven. I can loose anything here on earth and it will be loosed in Heaven. This means that I have the power to effect things in the spiritual realm right from here on earth. Through Christ I have this awesome power. I have the potential for a greater anointing than any Old Covenant saint. As a believer under the New Covenant I have been given the power to do and can do greater miracles than any Old Covenant saint and the power to do so actually lives in me and flows out of me.

I can do the works that Jesus did. I can even do greater works than He did. So I can cast out devils, I can heal the sick, I can raise the dead, I can control the elements and do all kinds of miracles. It is the Jesus living in me who does the works.

Death has no more power over me. I do not have to go when death comes. I can choose myself when to go. My going is between me and God, The devil has no say in it. This is so because the devil no longer has the keys of hell and of death. Jesus Christ who lives in me now has the keys.

Living a supernatural life (Volume 3)

I mind the things of the Spirit. My thoughts, my affections and my purposes and actions are directed and set upon the things of the Spirit. Therefore I can keep sin under subjection. Sin has no dominion over me anymore. I can now overcome any temptation. No temptation can overcome me now unless I agree to be defeated. For any temptation that comes, God will not allow me to be tempted above what I can cope with. So I know that I can handle and keep any temptation under control. Where any temptation seems to be getting out of control God has also made a way of escape from such a temptation for me.

I can overcome all sins and bad habits. I have the power to do so. The victorious life of God, which overcomes the world, is in me. I cannot commit sin as a habit anymore since I am born of God and His seed remains in me because Jesus the Son of God has destroyed the works of the devil. The life of Jesus Christ can be made to manifest in my body, which is also being preserved by Him. I can have all the gifts of the Holy Spirit. I can have the fruit of the Holy Spirit. I can and do impart the gifts of the Holy Spirit to others. I can and have obtained the full baptism of the Holy Spirit. I can and do impart the full baptism of the Holy Spirit to others.

As I continue in the Words of Jesus Christ, I can have the knowledge of the truth beyond all doubt. Knowing the truth has made me free. The Spirit of God, which lives in me, searches all things, even the deep things of God. Therefore I can see and do see things, which are not physically visible. Consequently I do not fix my sight on things which are seen for they are temporary.

__What you can do in Christ__

I look at the things, which are not seen for they are eternal and more real to me. I do not base my judgments on what I can see, taste, smell, hear or feel physically. No! I base my judgments on what the Word of God says. I live by faith in whatever the Word of God says concerning any situation.

I can and do hear God's voice and I follow Him and He knows me. Once I submit myself to God, I can and do resist the devil and whenever I do resist him, he must run away from me. He cannot stand before me when I resist him in faith.

In order to do the works Jesus did, I can ask for anything to be done in the Name of Jesus and He will do it for me if it will glorify the Father. I can also ask the Father in the Name of Jesus Christ for anything that I need to do the works that Jesus did and the Father will give it to me. I can ask for anything from God and I can get everything that I pray for. If I ask according to His will He hears me and if I know that He heard me then I know that I have gotten whatever I asked of Him. Whatever He has commanded, promised or foretold, I know that they are His will and I can ask Him for them.

I can live in divine health and prosperity as long as my soul/mind prospers because that is what God wants for me. I can live in divine health because the Spirit of God in me is quickening my mortal body on a continuous basis. Whatever the divinity of God can surmount, overcome or defeat I can now surmount, overcome or defeat also. This is so because I am a partaker of the divine nature. The divine nature that I now have carries greatness, victory and success with it.

Living a supernatural life (Volume 3)

Before God formed me in the belly He already knew me. Before I came forth out of the womb He sanctified me and set me apart. He ordained me a Prophet to the nations. God separated me right from my mother's womb and called me by His grace. God's plans and purpose in my life cannot be stopped or frustrated by anything or anybody. His plans will be realized. Because God the uncreated One is for me, no created thing can harm me or separate me from Him. My security in Him is totally and absolutely assured.

I am kept by the power of God through faith. Therefore nothing can attack me and win against me. Anybody that troubles me God will find it justifiable to recompense tribulation to him. I have been quickened together with Christ and forgiven all my sins. Therefore I can now live free of guilt-conscience. The Spirit of God that raised up Jesus from the dead now lives in me and it is by that same Spirit that God quickens my mortal body on a continuous basis.

I have been chosen and ordained by God so that I can go and bring forth fruit so that my fruit should remain. Whatever resources I ask of the Father in the Name of Jesus Christ the Father will give it to me so that I can bear fruit and whatever work I ask to be done in the Name of Jesus, Jesus will do it so that the Father may be glorified in the Son.

I am renewed in knowledge and in likeness to God because I now have a heart to know that God He is the Lord. I am enriched by Christ in all utterance and knowledge. I can now achieve my full potential in Christ."

CHAPTER 6

WHERE YOU ARE IN CHRIST

YOU ARE IN THE KINGDOM OF GOD

You have been delivered from the power of darkness and you have been translated into the Kingdom of God's dear Son. That is what we are made to see in Colossians 1:13.

> *Who hath delivered us from the power of darkness, and hath translated us into the kingdom of his dear Son:*
> **Colossians 1:13**

He said **hath translated** NOT *will translate* into the Kingdom of God's dear Son; it is obvious therefore that your spiritual translation and relocation to that Kingdom of God in Heaven is already done. You are not going to heaven. No! You are already there in Heaven. You are already translated spiritually to the Kingdom of God and you are already living in Heaven. That is why you are told in Ephesians 2:5-6 that you have been quickened together with Christ, raised up together with Him and made to sit together in heavenly places in Christ Jesus.

Living a supernatural life (Volume 3)

> *Even when we were dead in sins, hath quickened us together with Christ, by grace ye are saved;*
>
> *And hath raised us up together, and made us sit together in heavenly places in Christ Jesus:*
> **Ephesians 2:5-6**

This may sound strange and far-fetched to you but it is the truth. Since you are already translated to Heaven it follows therefore that you are now a citizen of the Kingdom of God in Heaven and that is what God made us to see through Paul the Apostle in Ephesians 2:19.

> *Now therefore ye are no more strangers and foreigners, but fellowcitizens with the saints, and of the household of God;*
> **Ephesians 2:19**

That is why you are called an ambassador of that Kingdom here on earth as written again by Apostle Paul in 2 Corinthians 5:20.

> *Now then we are ambassadors for Christ, as though God did beseech you by us: we pray you in Christ's stead, be ye reconciled to God.*
> **2 Corinthians 5:20**

You are now an ambassador of your Kingdom here on earth. You cannot be an ambassador of a kingdom that you are not a citizen of. The main problem with many Christians is that they are not willing to take God at His Word.

Where you are in Christ

They believe that God must mean something else from what He said in the Scriptures because to them it cannot be as simple as the Scripture is making it to look or sound. They don't believe that God means what He says or that He says what He means. They try to find some other meanings or explanation to whatever God says. But God has warned us in 2 Corinthians 11:3 not to be corrupted by the simplicity that is in the Gospel of Christ. You should not think that this is too simple to be true. Who says that it must be difficult anyway?

> ***But I fear, lest by any means, as the serpent beguiled Eve through his subtilty, so your minds should be corrupted from the simplicity that is in Christ.***
> **2 Corinthians 11:3**

There are certain truths that are now applicable to you as a citizen of the Kingdom of God, which may sound strange to you unless you have a Kingdom mentality. For example in that Kingdom you can no longer be defeated by any adversary who attacks you. Your victory is already assured even before the fight starts. You are destined to win in every battle of life that you come across. This is so because He that lives in you is greater than anybody or anything that you can come across in the world. That is what we see in 1 John 4:4.

> ***Ye are of God, little children, and have overcome them: because greater is he that is in you, than he that is in the world.***
> **1 John 4:4**

Living a supernatural life (Volume 3)

In that Kingdom of God where you are, you can only know of victory, divine health, divine prosperity, absolute and fail-proof protection, good success and fruitfulness. Sickness, lack, poverty, defeat, barrenness and failure have no place in that Kingdom.

These are properties of the kingdom of darkness of this world and they cannot enter into that Kingdom. Therefore you are completely and permanently parted and separated from them provided you stay where God has now put you, which is in Christ. In that Kingdom where you have now been put, according to what is written by Apostle Paul in Romans 8:2,9 you live under the law of the Spirit of life in Christ which has made you free from the law of sin and death.

> *For the law of the Spirit of life in Christ Jesus hath made me free from the law of sin and death.*
>
> *But ye are not in the flesh, but in the Spirit, if so be that the Spirit of God dwell in you. Now if any man have not the Spirit of Christ, he is none of his.*
>
> **Romans 8:2,9**

Therefore sin and death have no more power over you. This is the case now because the power of death, which used to be with Satan in his kingdom, is no longer with him. This is because the keys of hell and death had been taken away from Satan by Jesus Christ who is the first begotten in the Kingdom of God. Therefore the keys are now with Jesus Christ. This truth becomes apparent when one combines what the Scriptures say in both Hebrews 2:14 and Revelation 1:18.

Forasmuch then as the children are partakers of flesh and blood, he also himself likewise took part of the same; that through death he might destroy him that had the power of death, that is, the devil;
Hebrews 2:14

I am he that liveth, and was dead; and, behold, I am alive for evermore, Amen; and have the keys of hell and of death.
Revelation 1:18

You are therefore totally free from the influence of death. Death has no dominion over you anymore. You can tell death where to go whenever it comes to if you are not ready to go.

Your translation to Heaven was a spiritual one and this has made it very difficult for people to see it but they can see the effect of it. That is the essence of what Jesus Himself wanted us to know by what He said in John 3:8 concerning any person that is born of the Spirit. You are now born of God. That is what we know from what is written in John 1:13. But God is a Spirit. That is what we are told in John 4:24. Therefore we can say that you are born of the Spirit. Therefore what Jesus is saying here is that it is impossible for people to know or tell your movements or your whereabouts as a spiritual being. They will only be able to see the effects. This means that the devil and his forces or anybody for that matter, can no longer discern your ways. Hence you should no longer worry yourself or exercise any fear that anybody or evil forces whether physical or spiritual can manipulate your destiny.

> *The wind bloweth where it listeth, and thou hearest the sound thereof, but canst not tell whence it cometh, and whither it goeth: so is every one that is born of the Spirit.*
>
> **John 3:8**

> *Which were born, not of blood, nor of the will of the flesh, nor of the will of man, but of God.*
>
> **John 1:13**

> *God is a Spirit: and they that worship him must worship him in spirit and in truth.*
>
> **John 4:24**

That is why it is impossible for people to know that you are already translated to Heaven because they cannot see your translation. The only things they can see are the effects of your translation because according to Romans 8:9 above you are no longer in the flesh; you are now in the Spirit and the Spirit of God dwells in you. Therefore you should no longer have any fear that somebody or some devil can manipulate your destiny as is the case with most people in this world. This is one major truth that most Christians seem not to take cognizance of. They just do not know where they now are in Christ. They are still afraid that the devil can tamper with their destiny. In their prayers you hear them talking of some evil forces that are changing or manipulating their destiny. They believe that their movements can be monitored by such evil forces of darkness.

Where you are in Christ

But ye are not in the flesh, but in the Spirit, if so be that the Spirit of God dwell in you. Now if any man have not the Spirit of Christ, he is none of his.
Romans 8:9

You see, most people are expecting that this translation to the Kingdom of God in Heaven would be a physical one that they can see. Yes! You will have a physical translation eventually, which you generally refer to as the rapture but that is yet to happen. That one will take place sometimes in the future. On the other hand according to what Jesus said in Luke 17:20-21 this Kingdom of God that we are talking about here cometh not by observation so it is not a physical Kingdom that you can see or observe with your physical eyes or senses.

And when he was demanded of the Pharisees, when the Kingdom of God should come, he answered them and said, The Kingdom of God cometh not with observation:

Neither shall they say, Lo here! or, lo there! for, behold, the Kingdom of God is within you.
Luke 17:20-21

You cannot see it because according to Jesus that Kingdom is right within you if you are truly born-again. You are already enjoying the Kingdom benefits within you. I know that many Christians are waiting to die so that they can go into the Kingdom of God.

But as for you if you are truly born again you are not waiting to die before you go into the Kingdom of God because the Kingdom of God is already in you.

However from what God made us to see through Paul in 2 Corinthians 4:18 this unseen spiritual translation, which you have already passed through is much more real than the physical translation to Heaven that you call the rapture, which you will be able to see, but which is yet to come.

> *While we look not at the things which are seen, but at the things which are not seen: for the things which are seen are temporal; but the things which are not seen are eternal.*
> **2 Corinthians 4:18**

What God is telling us through Paul in the above passage of the Scripture is that this unseen translation should be more real to you than the rapture that you will be able to see but which is yet to come. This is so because even though you cannot see your translation you are already living in the Kingdom of God and you are already experiencing and enjoying the benefits of that Kingdom. Why do I say this? I say this because God told us through Paul in Romans 14:17 that this Kingdom of God is righteousness and peace and joy in the Holy Ghost. You already have and you are already enjoying these three. To confirm this let us now look at each one of them.

> *For the Kingdom of God is not meat and drink; but righteousness, and peace, and joy in the Holy Ghost.*
> **Romans 14:17**

Where you are in Christ

As for righteousness, you are now the righteousness of God in Jesus Christ. That is what we are made to see by Paul the Apostle in 2 Corinthians 5:21. Not only that, according to the same Paul in 1 Corinthians 1:30, Jesus Christ who according to what is written by the same Paul in 1 Corinthians 1:24 is the righteousness of God has now been made righteousness unto you therefore you now have the righteousness of Jesus Christ imputed to you.

> *For he hath made him to be sin for us, who knew no sin; that we might be made the righteousness of God in him.*
> **2 Corinthians 5:21**

> *But of him are ye in Christ Jesus, who of God is made unto us wisdom, and righteousness, and sanctification, and redemption:*
> **1 Corinthians 1:30**

> *But unto them which are called, both Jews and Greeks, Christ the power of God, and the wisdom of God.*
> **1 Corinthians 1:24**

You are enjoying this righteousness of Christ right now because you have received the gift of this righteousness and with it you are supposed to be reigning in life by Christ. This is confirmed by what Paul wrote in Romans 5:17 through the inspiration of the Holy Spirit. You received this through the abundance of grace from God. This means that you are not using your own righteousness anymore but that of Christ.

Living a supernatural life (Volume 3)

> *For if by one man's offence death reigned by one; much more they which receive abundance of grace and of the gift of righteousness shall reign in life by one, Jesus Christ.*
>
> **Romans 5:17**

This Christ's righteousness, which you have, means that no body is more righteous than you are before God when you are clothed with this righteousness of Christ.

As for peace, you now have peace with God through our Lord Jesus Christ. You can know this from your heart and it is confirmed by what God said through Paul in Romans 5:1. You can also see from what Jesus said in John 14:27 that Jesus Christ has left His peace with you and given you His peace. Therefore you are also enjoying peace with God right now. This is the mark of a true Christian. That is, a true Christian is at peace with himself, with God and is in a state of rest within. That is what will show him to be someone who puts his trust in God completely believing that whatever may come his way God is there to fight his battles and therefore he can never be defeated.

> *Therefore being justified by faith, we have peace with God through our Lord Jesus Christ:*
>
> **Romans 5:1**

> *Peace I leave with you, my peace I give unto you: not as the world giveth, give I unto you. Let not your heart be troubled, neither let it be afraid.*
>
> **John 14:27**

As for joy, you also have joy because according to what Jesus said in John 15:11, He spoke His Words to you so that His joy may remain in you and consequently so that your joy may be full.

> *These things have I spoken unto you, that my joy might remain in you, and that your joy might be full.*
> **John 15:11**

So His joy is already in you. As you continue to ask from God and receive from Him your joy gets fuller every day. That is what we can see from what Jesus said in John 16:24. According to the Scriptures in Nehemiah 8:10, the fuller your joy becomes the more the strength that you have also becomes because the joy of the Lord is your strength.

> *Hitherto have ye asked nothing in my name: ask, and ye shall receive, that your joy may be full.*
> **John 16:24**

> *Then he said unto them, Go your way, eat the fat, and drink the sweet, and send portions unto them for whom nothing is prepared: for this day is holy unto our Lord: neither be ye sorry; for the joy of the LORD is your strength.*
> **Nehemiah 8:10**

The more your joy gets fuller the more of the benefits of your salvation that you can draw out of the well of salvation. That in essence is what Prophet Isaiah is saying in Isaiah 12:3.

Living a supernatural life (Volume 3)

Therefore with joy shall ye draw water out of the wells of salvation.
                                    Isaiah 12:3

Therefore as you can see you have righteousness, you have peace, you have joy and you are already enjoying these. Consequently you can say that the Kingdom of God is already in you. Since Christ who is the ruler of this Kingdom of God lives in you, it follows therefore that the directions and instructions to you should come from within you and not from any outside forces, situations, symptoms or circumstances as is common with the people of this world who are still under the rule of the kingdom of darkness. What I am saying here is that you should not base your decisions on what your physical senses are telling you and definitely not on any symptoms that you can see, smell, taste, hear or feel. Rather you should base your decisions concerning any situation on what the Spirit of God that is living in you tells you and this cannot be any different from what the Word of God says about the situation. If you are one of the many Christians who are ***still expecting*** to go to Heaven because they are born-again Christians then you must look at what I am saying here carefully. Remember that you are a spirit-being and look at what I am saying in that light.

What I am telling you here is that you are already spiritually seated there in Heaven. This is true because you have been raised up spiritually together with Christ and you are already seated in heavenly places with Him. That is what we know from what Paul the Apostle wrote in Ephesians 2:6.

Where you are in Christ

And hath raised us up together, and made us sit together in heavenly places in Christ Jesus:
Ephesians 2:6

That is why God also said through the same Paul in Ephesians 2:19 that you are no longer a stranger or a foreigner to Him but you are now a fellow citizen with the saints and you are now of the household of God.

Now therefore ye are no more strangers and foreigners, but fellowcitizens with the saints, and of the household of God;
Ephesians 2:19

You are already translated spiritually to Heaven and have become a citizen of Heaven even though you are still living here on earth in the physical. That is why you have been made an ambassador here on earth where you are now a stranger representing the Kingdom of God to which you now belong. That is what we are made to see from what God said through Apostle Paul in 2 Corinthians 5:20.

Now then we are ambassadors for Christ, as though God did beseech you by us: we pray you in Christ's stead, be ye reconciled to God.
2 Corinthians 5:20

The truth is that many born again Christians are still struggling to go to Heaven but you are already living there.

Living a supernatural life (Volume 3)

Many also believe that they have already taken and are on the flight to Heaven but they are yet to arrive there. But in your own case, you have already arrived there and you are already living there. That is the way you should see yourself. Believe this truth and start to live your life in the light of that truth.

When you do that you will find that you will then be able to see beyond this earthly realm. To make matters worse many Christians even believe that they are yet to catch the flight and therefore they are still expecting to catch the flight to Heaven. They are praying and struggling so as not to miss the flight. You see! They are trying to get to God but in your case you have the privilege of talking with God every day because you have already landed there in Heaven. In fact you not only talk to Him every day, He is always with you as He had promised you in Matthew 28:20. He is in you and you are in Him. You are together all the time. Because you are now of His Kingdom you can hear Him whenever He talks to you. That is what He said in John 8:47. So you have no problem hearing Him.

> *Teaching them to observe all things whatsoever I have commanded you: and, lo, I am with you alway, even unto the end of the world. Amen.*
> **Matthew 28:20**

> *He that is of God heareth God's words: ye therefore hear them not, because ye are not of God.*
> **John 8:47**

Where you are in Christ

Many of my Christian friends are still hoping and struggling to use their faith to believe that sometimes very soon; someday they will really land in Heaven. Of course because they are hoping, they need their faith to uphold their hope since according to what God said in Hebrews 11:1, it is faith that gives substance to things hoped for. Therefore they need faith to turn their hope into reality. But as for you since you are not hoping anymore to go to Heaven because you are already there it follows that you do not need any faith for that.

Now faith is the substance of things hoped for, the evidence of things not seen.
Hebrews 11:1

You do not need any faith for something that you already know that is a reality. In fact you have been made a king and a priest and you are supposed to be reigning now here on earth. It is a Kingdom in which all its citizens are kings. That is what God made us to see by what He said in Revelation 5:10 and that is why Christ who is our King is called the King of kings since all the citizens that He reigns over are also kings. Therefore no situation or circumstance can put you under its control or domination any longer. You are supposed to be reigning and have dominion over every situation or circumstance of life that comes your way now. You have control over every situation by the Spirit of God. Even though you are still in this world you are no longer of this world; you belong to the Kingdom of God.

Living a supernatural life (Volume 3)

And hast made us unto our God kings and priests: and we shall reign on the earth.
Revelation 5:10

Even though you cannot see that Kingdom with your natural eyes, but because you are born of the Spirit you can see, enjoy and partake of the Kingdom spiritually and it should be very real to you.

It is only when one is born of the Spirit that he can see this Kingdom as confirmed by Jesus in John 3:3.

Jesus answered and said unto him, Verily, verily, I say unto thee, Except a man be born again, he cannot see the Kingdom of God.
John 3:3

This Kingdom of God to which you now belong, which is within you is an everlasting Kingdom. Your membership of the Kingdom is supposed to bring you glory because God has called you into His Kingdom unto glory not unto shame. That is what He made us to see from what He said in 1 Thessalonians 2:12. It is obvious therefore that you have an honourable calling.

Where you are now therefore, nothing shameful can hang around you. Any move of the devil to put you in shame will be turned to give you glory instead.

That ye would walk worthy of God, who hath called you unto his kingdom and glory.
1 Thessalonians 2:12

Where you are in Christ
YOU DWELL IN CHRIST

You dwell IN CHRIST. He lives in you and you live by Him because He has given you His Spirit. That is what we are made to see in John 6:56-57. This is also confirmed by what John said in 1 John 4:13.

He that eateth my flesh, and drinketh my blood, dwelleth in me, and I in him.

As the living Father hath sent me, and I live by the Father: so he that eateth me, even he shall live by me.
John 6:56-57

Hereby know we that we dwell in him, and he in us, because he hath given us of his Spirit.
1 John 4:13

Because you abide in Christ and you have the Word of God abiding in you it follows that whatever you ask of the Father is done for you. That is what Jesus said in John 15:7.

If ye abide in me, and my words abide in you, ye shall ask what ye will, and it shall be done unto you.
John 15:7

You are not just living in Christ; you have been sealed in Christ with the Holy Spirit of promise.

Living a supernatural life (Volume 3)

That is what we are made to see from what God said through Paul in Ephesians 1:13. You are not only living in Him, you live and move and have your being **IN CHRIST**. That is what we can understand from what God said through Paul in Acts 17:28.

> *In whom ye also trusted, after that ye heard the word of truth, the gospel of your salvation: in whom also after that ye believed, ye were sealed with that holy Spirit of promise,*
> **Ephesians 1:13**

> *For in him we live, and move, and have our being; as certain also of your own poets have said, For we are also his offspring.*
> **Acts 17:28**

In fact, the truth of the matter is that your life is now hidden with Christ in God. You know this because that is what you are told in Colossians 3:3. Therefore NOTHING evil can attack you anymore and win against you. You are insulated from all evil. They can attack you but they cannot win against you.

> *For ye are dead, and your life is hid with Christ in God.*
> **Colossians 3:3**

Whatever wants to attack you must first attack God and win. If it can attack God and get away with it then it must also attack Jesus Christ who has all power in heaven and in earth and get away with it before it can get to you.

Where you are in Christ

Since no evil can touch God at all not to talk of attacking Him and getting away with it, it means that no evil can touch you if you stay where you are supposed to be **IN CHRIST**. You are now insulated from the attacks of the enemy. Not that attempts will not be made to attack you but such attempts will always end in your victory. That you dwell in Christ is not a hypothetical proposition at all. It is real because you are not only in Him, your flesh is part of His flesh and your bones are part of His bones. That is what we know from what is written in Ephesians 5:30.

For we are members of his body, of his flesh, and of his bones.
Ephesians 5:30

Since your flesh is part of His flesh and your bones are parts of His bones, it follows therefore that your eyes have become His eyes. Your hands have become His hands. Your feet have become His feet. Your mind has become His mind especially since you now have the mind of Christ as written in 1 Corinthians 2:16.

For who hath known the mind of the Lord, that he may instruct him? But we have the mind of Christ.
1 Corinthians 2:16

Your thoughts have therefore become His thoughts. It follows therefore that your actions have become His actions and His Name has become your name. Therefore His Name now belongs to you.

Living a supernatural life (Volume 3)

That is the reason why Apostle Peter said in Acts 3:6 that the Name of Jesus belonged to him. His Name now belongs to you also since you have become a part of Him.

> *Then Peter said, Silver and gold have I none; but such as I have give I thee: In the name of Jesus Christ of Nazareth rise up and walk.*
>
> **Acts 3:6**

According to Philippians 2:9-11, this Name of Jesus, which now belongs to you and is available for you to use, is far above every other name. At the call of that Name every knee must bow whether in Heaven or in earth or under the earth. That is a great weapon in your hand to make every knee bow before you. You have been given the authority to use the Name to ask for anything from God and to get anything done. That is the authority that Jesus gave you in His promises in John 14:13-14 as well as in John 16:23. He has said that whatever you ask for in that Name shall be given to you by the Father and whatever you ask to be done in that Name, He Jesus shall do it for you. What more do you need? What can God not do? We know that with God all things are possible. Therefore you only need to know how to ask as well as have the faith with which to get what you want.

> *Wherefore God also hath highly exalted him, and given him a name which is above every name:*

That at the name of Jesus every knee should bow, of things in heaven, and things in earth, and things under the earth;

And that every tongue should confess that Jesus Christ is Lord, to the glory of God the Father.
Philippians 2:9-11

And whatsoever ye shall ask in my name, that will I do, that the Father may be glorified in the Son.

If ye shall ask any thing in my name, I will do it.
John 14:13-14

And in that day ye shall ask me nothing. Verily, verily, I say unto you, Whatsoever ye shall ask the Father in my name, he will give it you.
John 16:23

YOU ARE BURIED WITH CHRIST AND RESURRECTED WITH HIM

You are crucified with Christ, nevertheless you live, yet not you, but Christ liveth in you. The life, which you live now you live by the faith of Christ. That is what you know from what you are told by God through Paul in Galatians 2:20. Since Christ is the Word of God what this means is that you live your life based on faith in the Word of God.

Living a supernatural life (Volume 3)

I am crucified with Christ: nevertheless I live; yet not I, but Christ liveth in me: and the life which I now live in the flesh I live by the faith of the Son of God, who loved me, and gave himself for me.
Galatians 2:20

You do not live your life based on the symptoms that you see all around you. No! You don't live your life based on the circumstances or situations that you find yourself. No! You only live your life based on what the Word of God says. From what God said through Paul in Romans 6:11 you are now dead to sin and alive to God through Jesus Christ our Lord and Saviour.

Likewise reckon ye also yourselves to be dead indeed unto sin, but alive unto God through Jesus Christ our Lord.
Romans 6:11

Therefore your love of sin is now dead as a result of Christ who lives in you. Sin no longer rules over you because it no longer has any power over you. Having being buried with Christ by baptism unto death, you have been quickened, spiritually resurrected and raised up from the dead together with Christ and you have been made to sit on the right hand of God together with Him. Therefore where you are seating now, you are far above all the oppressions of the enemy. That is what Paul made us to see from the combination of what he wrote in Romans 6:4, Ephesians 2:5 and also in Colossians 3:1. These we can say confirm what Jesus said in John 5:24 where He said that because you believe in Him you have passed from death unto life.

Therefore we are buried with him by baptism into death: that like as Christ was raised up from the dead by the glory of the Father, even so we also should walk in newness of life.
Romans 6:4

Even when we were dead in sins, hath quickened us together with Christ, by grace ye are saved;
Ephesians 2:5

If ye then be risen with Christ, seek those things which are above, where Christ sitteth on the right hand of God.
Colossians 3:1

Verily, verily, I say unto you, He that heareth my word, and believeth on him that sent me, hath everlasting life, and shall not come into condemnation; but is passed from death unto life.
John 5:24

You cannot see this physically neither can it be discerned physically but it is true. This is so because it is hard for the carnal mind to visualize this since it can only be discerned spiritually.

YOU ARE SEATING TOGETHER WITH CHRIST

You have been raised up together with Christ and you are seating together with Christ in the heavenly places.

Living a supernatural life (Volume 3)

Therefore you are seated on the right side of God with Him in heavenly places because you are IN CHRIST. You know this is true because that is what God said through Paul in Ephesians 2:6. It is true that you are physically walking about here on earth but spiritually you are sitting in Heaven together with Christ. You must be conscious of this truth at all times.

> *And hath raised us up together, and made us sit together in heavenly places in Christ Jesus:*
> **Ephesians 2:6**

YOU ARE FAR ABOVE ALL THINGS

You are now seating with Christ in the heavenly places as we showed in the last section. However we are told in Ephesians 1:19-23, that where Christ is seating He is far above all principality and power, and might, and dominion and anything that has a name.

> *And what is the exceeding greatness of his power to us-ward who believe, according to the working of his mighty power,*
>
> *Which he wrought in Christ, when he raised him from the dead, and set him at his own right hand in the heavenly places,*
>
> *Far above all principality, and power, and might, and dominion, and every name that is named, not only in this world, but also in that which is to come:*

Where you are in Christ

And hath put all things under his feet, and gave him to be the head over all things to the church,

Which is his body, the fulness of him that filleth all in all.
                                    Ephesians 1:19-23

Everything has been put under His feet. Therefore since you are seating with Him, it follows that you are also far above all principality and power, and might, and dominion and anything that has a name. Since you are in Christ and everything has been put under His feet even if you are in the sole of His feet, it follows that everything is now under your feet also. Therefore you are far above diseases, poverty, failure, barrenness and all afflictions since they have names. They are all under your feet. You are far above all the earthly oppressive forces and mentalities. They are all under your feet.

They have no control over your life because you can put them under control. You should have the mental attitude that you are above all things. What this means is that whatever form a situation that may be attempting to afflict or attack you takes, you take it that you are far above it. This is so because it must definitely have a name and if it has a name then you are far above it. If you are above it then it must obey you when you command it because your being above it means that you have dominion over it. Even if there is no name currently given to it you can call it "No name" and that becomes its name. If that is the case then you are also far above it.

Living a supernatural life (Volume 3)

With your mind focused on this it is obvious that you can no longer be intimidated by any situation that confronts you. Since you are now seating with Christ in heavenly places it follows that you are from above and if you come from above, then from what we are told in John 3:31 it follows that you are above **ALL** things on earth.

> *He that cometh from above is above all: he that is of the earth is earthly, and speaketh of the earth: he that cometh from heaven is above all.*
>
> **John 3:31**

Where you are now, even death has no power over you because you are far above it. You are not only far above death; even the keys that control hell and death have been taken away from the devil that used to have them. Jesus Christ who is the first begotten Son in the Kingdom of Heaven in which you now belong was the One who took the keys from Satan. That is what we can infer from the combination of what God said in the following Scriptures; Hebrews 2:14, Revelation 1:18 and also in Romans 8:2,9. So the keys of hell and death are now in your Kingdom and the control over death is now based in your Kingdom. You are no longer under the law of sin and death. Therefore even death cannot intimidate you anymore.

> *Forasmuch then as the children are partakers of flesh and blood, he also himself likewise took part of the same; that through death he might destroy him that had the power of death, that is, the devil;*
>
> **Hebrews 2:14**

Where you are in Christ

I am he that liveth, and was dead; and, behold, I am alive for evermore, Amen; and have the keys of hell and of death.
Revelation 1:18

For the law of the Spirit of life in Christ Jesus hath made me free from the law of sin and death.

But ye are not in the flesh, but in the Spirit, if so be that the Spirit of God dwell in you. Now if any man have not the Spirit of Christ, he is none of his.
Romans 8:2,9

Where you are now, **ALL** things have been put in subjection under your feet. You are crowned with glory and honour and God has set you over the works of His hands. That is what God is making us to see from what is written in Hebrews 2:5-8.

For unto the angels hath he not put in subjection the world to come, whereof we speak.

But one in a certain place testified, saying, What is man, that thou art mindful of him? or the son of man, that thou visitest him?

Thou madest him a little lower than the angels; thou crownedst him with glory and honour, and didst set him over the works of thy hands:

> *Thou hast put all things in subjection under his feet. For in that he put all in subjection under him, he left nothing that is not put under him. But now we see not yet all things put under him.*
>
> **Hebrews 2:5-8**

YOU ARE IN GOD'S FAMILY

You are now a member of God's family. That is what we are told in Ephesians 3:15. You have been accepted into the family of God's beloved. You know you have been predestinated into the adoption as God's child by Jesus Christ to Himself to the good pleasure of His will and to the praise of the glory of His grace. That is what God said through Paul in Ephesians 1:5-6.

> *Of whom the whole family in heaven and earth is named,*
>
> **Ephesians 3:15**

> *Having predestinated us unto the adoption of children by Jesus Christ to himself, according to the good pleasure of his will,*
>
> *To the praise of the glory of his grace, wherein he hath made us accepted in the beloved.*
>
> **Ephesians 1:5-6**

Since you now belong to God's family Satan can no longer direct what happens in your life because you no longer belong to him or to his family. God is the One who can make plans concerning your life now.

A man cannot be planning the life of another man's children. He can only plan for his own children's life. Therefore since you are no longer in Satan's family, Satan has no right to be planning what happens in your life anymore. But many Christians who claim that they are children of God in God's family are still of the opinion that Satan can somehow manipulate and control their life.

YOU ARE IN THE LIGHT

Since like begets like, God is Light, you are His son therefore you are a child of Light. It follows that you are light also. No wonder therefore that Jesus called you the light of the world in Matthew 5:14.

> *Ye are the light of the world. A city that is set on an hill cannot be hid.*
> **Matthew 5:14**

You have been called out of darkness into His marvelous light. You are of the royal priesthood; you belong to His chosen generation.

You are peculiar. It follows therefore that you are in the light. That is what God made us to see from what He said through Peter in 1 Peter 2:9-10. Since you are light it follows that no works of darkness can hang around you any longer. Therefore such afflictions as sickness, lack, poverty, defeat, failure and barrenness, which are all works of darkness, can no longer hang around you.

> *But ye are a chosen generation, a royal priesthood, an holy nation, a peculiar people; that ye should shew forth the praises of him who hath called you out of darkness into his marvellous light:*
>
> *Which in time past were not a people, but are now the people of God: which had not obtained mercy, but now have obtained mercy.*
> **1 Peter 2:9-10**

This is so because wherever there is light darkness must disappear. You have no cause now to be afraid of any divination, enchantment, curse, juju or works of darkness.

YOU ARE NEAR TO GOD

Before now you were a stranger from the Covenants of promise with no hope, but now in Christ Jesus you have been made near to God through the Blood of Jesus Christ. That is what we know from Ephesians 2:12-13. In actual fact according to what God said through Paul in Ephesians 2:18, where you are now, you have direct access to God through Christ who is the only way to our Father, God. Jesus said so Himself in John 14:6.

> *That at that time ye were without Christ, being aliens from the commonwealth of Israel, and strangers from the covenants of promise, having no hope, and without God in the world:*

But now in Christ Jesus ye who sometimes were far off are made nigh by the blood of Christ.
Ephesians 2:12-13

For through him we both have access by one Spirit unto the Father.
Ephesians 2:18

Jesus saith unto him, I am the way, the truth, and the life: no man cometh unto the Father, but by me.
John 14:6

As we are told in 1 Corinthians 1:9, you have been called unto the fellowship of God's Son Jesus Christ our Lord and you have also been elected.

God is faithful, by whom ye were called unto the fellowship of his Son Jesus Christ our Lord.
1 Corinthians 1:9

You should therefore give diligence to make your calling and election sure, so that you will not fail or fall. Just like it was difficult for people to accept the truth about Jesus' identity, when He came to this earth, it will also be equally difficult for most people to agree with this your new identity in Christ. However, whether people agree with you or not, all these promises of God concerning you are true.

Their agreeing or not agreeing cannot change an iota of these truths. This is so because all the promises of God in Christ are yes and in Him Amen, unto the glory of God by you. That is what we know from what God said in 2 Corinthians 1:20.

> *For all the promises of God in him are yea, and in him Amen, unto the glory of God by us.*
> **2 Corinthians 1:20**

What God says you are, whether people agree with it or not, you are. What God says that you have does not depend on what any other person says or think. Whether people agree with it or not since God says you have it you should be confident that you have it. Whatever God says that you can do, you should be confident that you can do it. It all depends on whether you agree with what God says in your mind or not. As long as your mind and your thoughts are fixed on what God says about your new identity in Christ, nothing can change these truths about you. Agree with God in your mind that you are where God says that you are. It does not matter whether you cannot see it or feel it just believe and agree with God that you are there. Even though human evidence may contradict all these things about your new identity in Christ, nevertheless they are true because the Word of God says so.

YOU ARE FAR FROM OPPRESSION

You have been made the righteousness of God in Christ. That is what we can see from what is written in 2 Corinthians 5:21.

Where you are in Christ

> *For he hath made him to be sin for us, who knew no sin; that we might be made the righteousness of God in him.*
> **2 Corinthians 5:21**

This is because according to what God made us to see through Paul the Apostle in 1 Corinthians 1:30 Christ has been made righteousness unto you.

> *But of him are ye in Christ Jesus, who of God is made unto us wisdom, and righteousness, and sanctification, and redemption:*
> **1 Corinthians 1:30**

Therefore you can say that you have been established in the righteousness of God as God Himself promised in Isaiah 54:14. Because you have now been established in the righteousness of God, it follows that you are far from oppression. This must be true because no oppression can come near the righteousness of God.

> *In righteousness shalt thou be established: thou shalt be far from oppression; for thou shalt not fear: and from terror; for it shall not come near thee.*
> **Isaiah 54:14**

You don't have to fear under any situation now because no oppression can come near you. The righteousness of God has become a hedge around you protecting you from all the oppressions of the enemy. Where you are now because you are born of God and have kept yourself far away from sin, the devil can no longer touch you. That is what God made us to see through what is written in 1 John 5:18.

Living a supernatural life (Volume 3)

> *We know that whosoever is born of God sinneth not; but he that is begotten of God keepeth himself, and that wicked one toucheth him not.*
> **1 John 5:18**

The only way the devil can touch you now is if you refuse to keep your distance from the devil and his antics especially if you refuse to leave sin alone but still indulge in sin. If you really stay where you are supposed to stay which is in-Christ the devil can no longer touch you.

You need not fear any oppression because according to what God said through John in 1 John 4:4 you have already overcome all the oppressions of the devil and his forces. That is the reason why God removed the spirit of fear from you and gave you His Spirit of power and love and of a sound mind as we are told by Apostle Paul in 2 Timothy 1:7. Because you are now in Christ you are very far from oppression. Oppression should now be very afraid of you and should be running away from you.

> *Ye are of God, little children, and have overcome them: because greater is he that is in you, than he that is in the world.*
> **1 John 4:4**

> *For God hath not given us the spirit of fear; but of power, and of love, and of a sound mind.*
> **2 Timothy 1:7**

<u>Where you are in Christ</u>
This then is a summary of where you are in Christ. This is where God says that you are. Do you believe that you are where God says that you are? If you do then start living there. Start making use of the truth that you are there. Start confessing where you are as follows in the next four pages:

Living a supernatural life (Volume 3)
THIS IS WHERE I AM IN CHRIST

"I am born of the Spirit therefore I can now see the Kingdom of God. I now belong to the Kingdom of God. God has called me into His Kingdom and unto glory not unto shame. I have an honourable calling. Where I am now therefore, nothing shameful can hang around me. I have been called out of darkness into His marvelous light. I have been translated into the Kingdom of God's dear Son. I have been delivered from darkness. I am now a citizen of that Kingdom. In that Kingdom I can no longer be defeated by any adversary who attacks me. In that Kingdom, we only know of divine health, divine prosperity, victory, absolute fail-proof protection, fruitfulness and good success. Sickness, lack, poverty, defeat, barrenness and failures have no place in that Kingdom. I am completely and permanently separated from them. I now live under the law of the Spirit of life in Christ which has made me free from the law of sin and death. I am not in the flesh but in the Spirit because the Spirit of God dwells in me. I have been called unto the fellowship of God's Son Jesus Christ our Lord and I have also been elected. Once I give diligence to make my calling and election sure, I cannot fail or fall. I dwell **IN CHRIST**. He lives in me and I live by Him. I abide in Christ and I have the Word of God abiding in me. Because of these, whatever I ask of the Father will be done unto me. I have been sealed in Christ with the Holy Spirit of promise. I live in God and God lives in me. I live and move and have my being **IN CHRIST**. My life is hidden with Christ in God. Therefore **NOTHING** evil can touch me anymore. I am insulated from all evil. Whatever wants to touch me must first touch God, then touch Christ before it can get to me.

Where you are in Christ

Since no evil can touch God, it means that no evil can touch me if I stay where I am supposed to be **IN CHRIST**. Because I am **IN CHRIST**, I am part of the **BODY** of Christ. I am part of His flesh and part of His bones. Therefore I also have His Name, which is far above every other name. I have therefore been given the authority to use His Name. At the call of that Name every knee must bow whether in Heaven or in earth or under the earth. He has given me the authority to use that Name and the Name now belongs to me because I am a member of His Body-the Body of Christ. I am of the royal priesthood; I belong to His chosen generation. I am peculiar. I am crucified with Christ, nevertheless I live, yet not I, but Christ liveth in me. I am therefore dead to sin and alive to God through Jesus Christ my Lord and Saviour. My love of sin is now dead as a result of Christ who lives in me. Having being buried with Christ by baptism unto death, I have been quickened, spiritually resurrected and raised up from the dead together with Christ and I have been made to sit on the right hand of God together with Him. Therefore where I am seating now, I am far above all oppressions of the enemy. I have been raised up together with Christ and I am seating together with Christ in the heavenly places. Therefore I am seated on the right side of God with Him in heavenly places because I am **IN CHRIST**.

Because I am seating with Christ I am far above all principality and power, and might, and dominion and anything that has a name. Everything is under my feet. Therefore I am far above diseases, poverty, failure, barrenness and all afflictions. I am far above all the earthly oppressive mentalities.

Living a supernatural life (Volume 3)

Because I come from above, I am above **ALL** things on earth. Where I am now even death has no power over me because the first begotten Son in our Kingdom has taken the keys of hell and death from the devil who used to have them. So the keys are now in our Kingdom and we have control over death. We are no longer under the law of sin and death. Therefore death cannot intimidate me anymore. I am a member of God's family. I have been accepted into the family of His beloved. I am made near to God through the Blood of Jesus Christ. Where I am now, I have direct access to God through Christ who is the only way to our Father, God. Where I am now, **ALL** things have been put in subjection under my feet. I am crowned with glory and honour and God has set me over the works of His hands.

I have passed from death unto life. Whether people agree with me or not, all these promises of God concerning me are true. Their agreeing or not agreeing cannot change an iota of these truths. This is so because all the promises of God in Christ are yes and in Him Amen, unto the glory of God by me. What God says I am, whether people agree with it or not, I am.

Whatever God says that I have does not depend on what any other person says or think I have it. What God says I can do, I can do. They all only depend on whether I agree with what God says in my mind. As long as my mind and my thoughts are fixed on what God says about my new identity in Christ, nothing can change these truths about me."

CHAPTER 7

WHAT WILL YOU DO ABOUT THESE?

Are you truly a born-again Christian? Are you? If you are then it follows that all the statements discussed in these last five Chapters are already real for you in the spiritual realm. But you need to make them manifest for you in the physical realm if you are to actually take hold of them and physically make use of them so as to be able to enjoy the benefits that accrue to you through them. ***Now that you know these truths what will you do about them?*** Many of these characteristics look too far-fetched to be true but they are true. They are true because the Scriptures say so and if we agree that the Scriptures is a true record of the Word of God and that the Scriptures cannot be broken then we must agree that they are true. Grace has made them all available to you now but it is your faith that will draw them out for you. That is what we are made to see in Ephesians 2:8. They are the benefits of your salvation but you must note however that it is with joy that you can only draw them out. That is what we can see in Isaiah 12:3.

Living a supernatural life (Volume 3)

For by grace are ye saved through faith; and that not of yourselves: it is the gift of God:
Ephesians 2:8

Therefore with joy shall ye draw water out of the wells of salvation.
Isaiah 12:3

This means that you cannot draw the benefits out murmuring, complaining, brooding and worrying or by feeling sorry for yourself. If you want them to become real to you in the physical realm, then you must be cheerful, change your current mindset, believe these statements and start to confess them on a continuous basis and use your faith to make them to manifest physically in your life.

Supernatural living involves the release of these statements of **TRUTHS** of your new invisible nature in Christ into the **FACTS** of your visible human nature. You must practice these at all times. This means that you must superimpose the truths of your invisible nature in Christ that you now have over the facts of your visible human nature.

The law of the spirit says that if you believe these statements then as you continue to speak these out and confess them, they will become established and they will become a reality and manifest physically in your life. When you start to make these confessions, they will look strange and not real to you. But as you continue to make the confessions, they will become real and tangible to you. You must take hold of them and make them yours.

What will you do about these?

Keep meditating on them and keep thinking about them in your heart and as you do so, they will manifest physically in your body and your life. That was what God wanted us to see through what Solomon wrote in Proverbs 23:7 when he said that it is as you think in your heart that you will be.

> *For as he thinketh in his heart, so is he: Eat and drink, saith he to thee; but his heart is not with thee.*
> **Proverbs 23:7**

This means that it is your mindset that determines what you become in life. You cannot be thinking poverty and expect to be rich. You cannot be thinking sickness and expect to be in health. You cannot be thinking the thoughts of a barren and infertile woman and expect to be fruitful. You cannot be thinking weakness and expect to be strong. You cannot be thinking like a slave and expect to live like a king.

It is what you have in your mind that determines your size in life and what you have in your mind is determined by the knowledge that is available to you. If you have read these previous five chapters then you now have the knowledge of who you are, what you are, what you have, what you can do and where you are. If you have imbibed these truths, they should start to change your thinking about who you really are. The knowledge that you have is what will determine how you react to every situation and how your attitude will be in every situation that you come across in life.

Living a supernatural life (Volume 3)

For you to be able to enjoy the status that you now have and all the benefits that should accrue to you it is imperative that you will have to reprogram your mindset in order that you may be able to appropriate these truths for yourself.

If you believe them then you must think about them all the time and meditate on them day and night and confess them. They will then become real to you. It is only when they are real to you that they can do you any good. Remember that it is the thoughts that you have in your mind that lead to the actions that you take on the outside. Similarly it is the actions that you take that lead to your habits and these in turn decide your character or image. Finally it is your character or attitude to life as well as your image that decides your destiny. Therefore it all starts from thoughts in your mind. If you must personally appropriate these truths concerning your new invisible divine nature in Christ for yourself then you must continually think and meditate on them. The change has to start from your mind. You have to plant these in your mind. You must personally appropriate these truths concerning your new divine nature in Christ for yourself before you can put them to work in your life. It is only then that they will benefit your life and your profiting will become apparent to all. Many Christians pray for these attributes but God has already made them available to them. They are praying to be what God says that they already are. They are praying to have what God says that they already have. They are praying to be where God says they are already.

What will you do about these?

They are praying to be able to do what God says that they can do. This is because they don't know that all these things already belong to them as their heritage in Christ. So they are praying to have the power that is already theirs.

YOU ARE AN EMBODIMENT OF POWER

From what you have read in the previous five chapters you can see that the day that you received Christ as your Saviour, you were automatically and immediately transformed into a carrier of God's power. You became on that day an embodiment of power. Every other claim to power that is not of God whether they are witches, wizards, voodoos, fairies, juju, magic, occult, and all others of the kingdom of darkness are all automatically put under you. You are far above them and they are all under your feet. They should no longer manifest themselves with any authority whatsoever wherever you are and get away with it. You can tell them to shut up if they attempt to manifest around you and they must obey you. That is your heritage now in the Lord Jesus Christ and that is what you should program your mind to believe now. All things have been made available to you and you will only get them through the knowledge of the Word (CHRIST). But I want you to know that life will not give you what you deserve it will only give you what you demand.

You have been given power. You have been given riches. You have been given wisdom. You have been given strength. You have been given honour.

Living a supernatural life (Volume 3)

You have been given glory. You have been given blessing. Jesus Christ has taken all these. That is what we are told in Revelation 5:12. But He took these so that you and I can have them. You can see this from what He said in John 17:22 where He said that the glory that the Father had given Him, He has given to us.

> *Saying with a loud voice, Worthy is the Lamb that was slain to receive power, and riches, and wisdom, and strength, and honour, and glory, and blessing.*
> **Revelation 5:12**

> *And the glory which thou gavest me I have given them; that they may be one, even as we are one:*
> **John 17:22**

However, you must realize that Satan will not allow you to have these on a platter of gold. He will contend every one of them with you all the way throughout your life. Therefore you must be ready to contend with Satan for your heritage in Christ.

You know who you are now but Satan will contend this with you. Just like he asked Jesus to prove that He was the Son of God as written in Matthew 4:3, he will also ask you to prove that you are who God says that you are.

> *And when the tempter came to him, he said, If thou be the Son of God, command that these stones be made bread.*
> **Matthew 4:3**

He will ask you to prove that you are what God says that you are; that you have what God says that you have; that you can do what God says that you can do and that you are where God says that you are. That is the essence of the temptation that he brought into the mind of Jesus when he came to tempt Him. You must be ready to contend for all of those things that are now yours as a result of your redemption with Satan.

YOU MUST CONTEND FOR YOUR RIGHTS

Even though God has given you power, riches, wisdom, strength, honour, glory and all the characteristics that we discussed in the last five Chapters you will have to contend with Satan for each one of them. He will come with all kinds of thoughts to make you believe that these truths about you are not as sure as you are making them. He will contend all of them with you to convince you that they are not true. However, you must remember once again that it is grace that has made all of these available to you. But it is your faith that will draw them out and make them to manifest physically in your life. Therefore if you are not willing to contend with Satan in faith for these you will not be able to enjoy them. Because of its importance, I repeat here what God told the children of Israel as written in Deuteronomy 2:24. He said that He has given them the king and the land of the Amorites but that they must go in and contend with the king in battle to take the land.

Living a supernatural life (Volume 3)

> *Rise ye up, take your journey, and pass over the river Arnon: behold, I have given into thine hand Sihon the Amorite, king of Heshbon, and his land: begin to possess it, and contend with him in battle.*
>
> **Deuteronomy 2:24**

As you can see from the Scripture above, even though God has given them the land He still expected them to go and contend or fight for it.

That is exactly the same thing that God wants you to do. He has already given you the inheritances that you now have in Christ. They are already true for you in the spiritual realm but you will have to contend with Satan for them if you want them to manifest and be true for you in the physical realm. That Satan will contend these with you is not a matter of *"if"*. It is a sure thing. That is why God said through Isaiah in Isaiah 59:19 that *"when"* the enemy shall come in like a flood and not *"if"* the enemy shall come in like a flood.

> *So shall they fear the name of the Lord from the west, and his glory from the rising of the sun. When the enemy shall come in like a flood, the Spirit of the Lord shall lift up a standard against him.*
>
> **Isaiah 59:19**

Therefore you must be prepared for the contest with Satan in order to wrest your inheritances from him. Whether you like it or not Satan will contend every one of God's promises concerning your new identity in Christ with you.

What will you do about these?

God wants you to contend with Satan for every one of them. They are already yours but you still have to contend with Satan for them. That is why God told you in James 4:7 to resist the devil and when you resist him he will flee from you.

> *Submit yourselves therefore to God. Resist the devil, and he will flee from you.*
> **James 4:7**

The way to resist him is to first submit yourself to God then fight the good fight of faith against him by making sure you stand in faith on every one of those inheritances that you now have as a result of your being in Christ. That is the advice that God has given us through Paul in 1 Timothy 6:12. Fighting the good fight of faith means that you will not follow your senses, symptoms or allow what is happening around you to shake your faith in the truth that all those characteristics listed are true of you.

> *Fight the good fight of faith, lay hold on eternal life, whereunto thou art also called, and hast professed a good profession before many witnesses.*
> **1 Timothy 6:12**

If you can contend with Satan and fight the good fight of faith to the end then like Apostle Paul said which is written in 2 Timothy 4:7-8, apart from the truth that you will be able to enjoy the benefits of your new birth inheritances in Christ here on earth there will also be a crown of righteousness waiting for you in Heaven.

> *I have fought a good fight, I have finished my course, I have kept the faith:*
>
> *Henceforth there is laid up for me a crown of righteousness, which the Lord, the righteous judge, shall give me at that day: and not to me only, but unto all them also that love his appearing.*
>
> **2 Timothy 4:7-8**

But you will not enjoy these benefits of your new birth inheritances if you are not willing to contend with the devil for your rights. Furthermore when you look at some of those truths concerning you as written in the previous Chapters, then you can infer so many other truths from the Scriptures that you can use in your fight against the enemy. You should personalize all such truths for your own use because they are now true of you. For example, the Scriptures say that you are now righteous; therefore everything said of the righteous is now true of you.

FOLLOW THE FOOTSTEPS OF CHRIST

God has said through Jeremiah in Jeremiah 1:12 that He would hasten His Words to perform.

> *Then said the LORD unto me, Thou hast well seen: for I will hasten my word to perform it.*
>
> **Jeremiah 1:12**

What will you do about these?

Concerning these promises of God about your new identity in Christ God is also saying what He said to Jeremiah above to you. He is saying that He will hasten His Words concerning you to perform. So when you proclaim them and speak them out boldly God will make sure that they are fulfilled in your life. He will hasten them to perform. You must start speaking out these statements concerning your new identity in Christ. That was what Jesus did when He came to this earth. Christ started speaking out the truth about His identity right from His childhood days. You have to learn to do the same thing about your new identity in Christ.

That is why you are so advised in Philippians 2:5 by God through Apostle Paul that you should let the mind that was in Christ Jesus be in you also.

> *Let this mind be in you, which was also in Christ Jesus:*
> **Philippians 2:5**

You know from 1 Corinthians 2:16 that you now have the mind of Christ. Therefore what God is telling you above is that you should allow the mind of Christ that you now have to determine your decisions and attitude. Once you do this you will see that you will have the same attitude as Jesus Christ.

> *For who hath known the mind of the Lord, that he may instruct him? But we have the mind of Christ.*
> **1 Corinthians 2:16**

Living a supernatural life (Volume 3)

A major thing to note concerning the attitude of Jesus is that He was always speaking out boldly the truths concerning His life, His mission, His authority and His eventual destination. In Ephesians 5:1 we are also advised by God through Apostle Paul to be followers of God as dear children.

> *Be ye therefore followers of God, as dear children;*
> **Ephesians 5:1**

Children normally follow the footsteps of their Fathers. As a child of God you should follow the footsteps of God who is your Father.

One of the things that God does, which you should also learn to do is that He speaks whatever He wants into existence. You are therefore supposed to also speak those things that you want in your life into existence. This is imperative because that is the way God operates and you should learn to operate in the same way.

You must learn to operate the way God operates. If you want to know how God speaks things into existence then you should note what God revealed to us through Apostle Paul in Romans 4:17.

> *As it is written, I have made thee a father of many nations, before him whom he believed, even God, who quickeneth the dead, and calleth those things which be not as though they were.*
> **Romans 4:17**

What will you do about these?

So God calls those things that *are not* as though *they were*. When you believe what God has called or said about you as though they were then the things He called or said about you will appear or manifest. That is the way you are supposed to operate.

Even though most of the things that God said concerning your new nature in Christ are not presently visible you should call and proclaim them as if they are physically visible already and they will eventually become visible. That is what the fight of faith is all about. The fight of faith is the only fight that God commanded you to fight.

I know that some of these statements will look strange to you and may even look stupid but remember that people also considered the statements that Jesus made as strange and even sometimes stupid. In any case you should remember what God said through Apostle Paul in 1 Corinthians 1:27-28. He said that God's method is that He chooses the foolish things of the world to confound the wise and the weak things of the world to confound the things which are mighty. He chooses the base things of the world, the things which are despised and the things which are not to bring to nought the things that are.

> ***But God hath chosen the foolish things of the world to confound the wise; and God hath chosen the weak things of the world to confound the things which are mighty;***

Living a supernatural life (Volume 3)

> *And base things of the world, and things which are despised, hath God chosen, yea, and things which are not, to bring to nought things that are:*
>
> **1 Corinthians 1:27-28**

Therefore let nobody intimidate you by making you feel that you are nobody or inconsequential. It is in that state that God's glory can best be shown through you because the weaker you are the stronger in God you really are. You should not border yourself about what people will think or say about you. If you can proclaim this your new identity by confessing these and live accordingly then I can assure you that if you believe what you have proclaimed and treat them as though they already exist.

Then those things that you have proclaimed will appear or manifest physically in your life. This is because God created you in His image so that you can do what He does. This means that you are created to be a creator. As a born-again Christian you must know that those things that you can see are insignificant compared to those things that you cannot see. That is why you are advised by God in 2 Corinthians 4:18 through Paul not to fix your sight on the things which you can see but you should fix your sight on the things which you cannot see.

> *While we look not at the things which are seen, but at the things which are not seen: for the things which are seen are temporal; but the things which are not seen are eternal.*
>
> **2 Corinthians 4:18**

What will you do about these?

For example, you know that the air around you in the house where you are currently reading this book contains thousands of different sound waves, pictures and data that you cannot hear or see. Yet they are there. The fact that you cannot hear the sounds, see the pictures or the data does not mean that they are not there. There are all types of sound waves in the air and all types of picture waves floating around all over the place. The fact that you cannot hear or see them does not mean that they are not there. Just put the right radio for receiving sound waves and the right television and satellite dish receiver with the appropriate decoder for receiving pictures or data in place and you can receive thousands of sound waves as well as thousands of transmitted pictures or data originating from different countries all over the world and even from outer space. You cannot possibly see all the things that exist in your surrounding but your not seeing them does not mean that they do not exist.

Your radio receiver or satellite dish did not create the sound waves or pictures that you receive with them. Before you installed them the sound waves or the picture waves had been there. All that your television, satellite dish, decoder and radio receivers did was to collect the waves and process them in such a way that you can receive them and therefore hear the sounds and see the pictures. They have been there all along but you could not see them. Such are the things of the spirit too. Because you cannot see them does not mean that they do not exist. In fact their existence is more real than the existence of the things that you can see.

Living a supernatural life (Volume 3)

The spiritual things should be more real to you as a Christian than the physical things. That is the essence of what God said through Paul in 2 Corinthians 4:18, which we have previously written above.

This should help you to be able to visualize that even though you cannot see all those things that God has told you concerning who you now are, what you now are, what you now have, what you can now do and where you now are in Christ it does not mean that they are not true. They are not only true they are very real. You will note also that the sound waves, pictures and data that you can receive depend on the direction that your receiving antenna is facing or aligned to as well as the type of receiving antenna that you have.

Aligning yourself with Christ, speaking them out in faith and acting them are the equivalence of your having the right receiver and decoder that are properly aligned to receive your inheritances in Christ and make them to become real and manifest physically in your life.

Therefore as a born-again Christian you must begin to make statements that confirm your new nature in Christ. It is because you do not know who you really are that has made you to allow yourself to be pushed around and put in any form of bondage by the devil. How can you the son of the King of kings who is also a king allow yourself to be treated like a nobody being pushed around like a ship without a rudder and without respect by the forces of darkness?

What will you do about these?

If you can only grasp the importance of whom you now are and use the authority that you now have over the forces of darkness then sickness, poverty, barrenness, failure and all such tools that the enemy uses for the oppression of the people will begin to show great respect for you especially when they know that you really know who you are **IN CHRIST**.

When your enemies know that you are aware of the authority that you now have over them and they know that you are ready to enforce your authority over them they will not come near you. They will start to show a lot of respect for you. You must begin to realize that you no longer belong to this earthly kingdom. You are a citizen of a Kingdom of God and you should have the Kingdom mentality. If you have the Kingdom mentality you will know that you come from above therefore you are above everything in this earthly realm.

The Bible says He that comes from above is above all. That is what the Scripture says in John 3:31.

> *He that cometh from above is above all: he that is of the earth is earthly, and speaketh of the earth: he that cometh from heaven is above all.*
>
> **John 3:31**

As a citizen of the Kingdom of God you have power far above what any enemy can demonstrate here on earth. In the Kingdom of God where you now belong sickness, barrenness, poverty, failure and all such oppressive tools of the devil have no *loci standi* there.

Living a supernatural life (Volume 3)

I will now show in the next few chapters how you can use these Scriptural images that you now have of who you are, what you are, what you have, what you can do and where you are to build up an image of yourself in your mind and develop the Kingdom mentality. When you build up such an image in your mind, it will build up your confidence and help you to fight and drive off every attack of the devil in every critical situation that you may come across in life. This will help you to bring such situations under cheap control. Once you can do this it will provoke you to face whatever the enemy brings your way squarely.

Now that you have the right Scriptural image of yourself you should be able to stand firm in every situation that you come across. You must precondition your mind and continue to renew it with the Word of God that He has spoken about you.

By doing so, you will be transforming yourself into what God said that you are as we are told by Paul in Romans 12:2. Without the renewing of your mind with the Word there can be no transformation for you. Therefore start nurturing your mind on a daily basis with these thoughts of your new identity in Christ because you will never go higher than the height that you believe in your mind that you can achieve.

> *And be not conformed to this world: but be ye transformed by the renewing of your mind, that ye may prove what is that good, and acceptable, and perfect, will of God.*
> **Romans 12:2**

What will you do about these?

You can never rise any higher than your thoughts. They are your limiting factors. In the next chapter we shall discuss how you can develop a positive Scriptural image of yourself and in the next five chapters after that we shall look at how you can use the Scriptural image that you now have of yourself, which you have now formed in your mind to develop the type of reasoning and attitude that will give you the victory mindset in all the situations that you come across in life. We shall consider five practical situations as examples. We have written out how your mind should react to develop a positive response to each situation. You must realize that the attitude you develop towards a situation and your reaction to that situation will determine whether that situation will overwhelm you or you will subdue the situation. *How should you react or think?* The five cases we shall look at and consider are listed below.

1. **When sickness comes or you are struggling with an inherited disease. It may be that they have even told you that what you have is a terminal disease. How should you react?**

2. **When tormented by afflictions and you are under the heavy burden of the affliction. How do you react?**

3. **When struggling with sin and you are finding it difficult to leave the sin. How do you react?**

4. **When you have prayed and prayed but you are not sure of answer to your prayer. How do you react?**

5. **When faced with what looks to you like an impossible situation; a situation that seems daunting to you. How should you react?**

In the next Chapter we shall discuss the importance of building the correct Scriptural image of oneself. Each of the above situations will then be treated in the following five Chapters respectively. In each case we shall look at the way that you can use the Scriptural image of yourself based on the different characteristics that you now have to develop a mindset and the right attitude with which to tackle each situation. In each situation you should be able to bring back to your mind a picture of who you are in Christ, what you are in Christ, what you have in Christ, what you can do in Christ and where you are in Christ. Once you can bring these pictures of your true identity in Christ into your mind you can consider the problem solved.

That should help you to develop a Kingdom mentality, manifest the victory that you already have over any situation and live the Kingdom life that is already yours right here on earth. You will then know how to react to the situations mentioned above. It is then that the questions that we have asked for each situation will have meanings to you. You must have a Kingdom mentality if you are to live above these situations.

CHAPTER 8

BUILDING A SOUND SCRIPTURAL IMAGE

The way you see yourself determines what you will achieve and what you can become in life. Forget what other people think of you. It is the image that you have of yourself that matters most because you can never rise above whatever image you have of yourself. As your creator God knows what He has put inside you. So whatever God says that you are, that you have or that you can do you better listen carefully to Him. What God sees you to be is what you really are not what others see you to be. Therefore you must catch and build a good Scriptural image of yourself based on who the Scripture, which is God's Word says that you are, what He says that you are, what He says that you can do, what He says that you have and where He says that you are. Whatever picture you so develop should then be brought into your mind so that the imagination function of your mind can continue to process the image and play back the picture from time to time. This is required because your imagination function has been so designed by God in such a way that whatsoever you can imagine you can achieve. That is what God confirmed by what He said in Genesis 11:6.

Living a supernatural life (Volume 3)

> *And the LORD said, Behold, the people is one, and they have all one language; and this they begin to do: and now nothing will be restrained from them, which they have imagined to do.*
>
> **Genesis 11:6**

God created man and He knows the capabilities that He built into man at creation. Therefore if God says that whatever man can imagine man can achieve then we better believe God and therefore act accordingly knowing that we are capable of achieving whatever we can imagine.

GOD USES OUR IMAGINATION

You will note that whenever God wants to bless a man He first tries to get the picture of that blessing into the man's imagination. That was what He did as we are told in Genesis 13:14-17 with Abram who later became Abraham. He asked Abram to look with the eyes of his imagination to see what He is proposing to give him or make him.

> *And the LORD said unto Abram, after that Lot was separated from him, Lift up now thine eyes, and look from the place where thou art northward, and southward, and eastward, and westward:*
>
> *For all the land which thou seest, to thee will I give it, and to thy seed for ever.*

Building a sound Scriptural image

And I will make thy seed as the dust of the earth: so that if a man can number the dust of the earth, then shall thy seed also be numbered.

Arise, walk through the land in the length of it and in the breadth of it; for I will give it unto thee.
Genesis 13:14-17

Obviously you can see from the verses written above that God was not telling Abram to look with his physical eyes. This is so because the land that will be big enough to hold his seed, which God said would be great in number (as the dust of the earth) could not have been limited to what he could see with his physical eyes.

It was obvious to Abram that God was telling him to look with his spiritual eyes, that is through the eyes of his imagination so that a picture of the area that God had given him could be built up in his mind. It would then be possible for his imagination function machine to bring this picture into his mind for processing from time to time until the picture virtually became a reality to him.

The reason for this was because God knew that whatever we are imagining in our hearts is what we shall eventually bring forth in our lives. That was what Jesus also made us to see by what He said as written in Matthew 12:35. David had also said the same thing in Proverbs 23:7.

Living a supernatural life (Volume 3)

A good man out of the good treasure of the heart bringeth forth good things: and an evil man out of the evil treasure bringeth forth evil things.
Matthew 12:35

For as he thinketh in his heart, so is he: Eat and drink, saith he to thee; but his heart is not with thee.
Proverbs 23:7

It is what you imagine or think in your heart that you will eventually bring forth physically in your life. Therefore if you are imagining sickness, poverty, barrenness, failure or any of such negative things in your mind then that is exactly what you will bring out in your life and that is what you will be. Therefore we should be careful and watch on a continuous basis what we allow into our mind to be processed by the imagination function machine in our mind. That is why we are so advised by Apostle Peter in 1 Peter 1:13 to gird up the loins of our mind.

Wherefore gird up the loins of your mind, be sober, and hope to the end for the grace that is to be brought unto you at the revelation of Jesus Christ;
1 Peter 1:13

God told Abram to use his spiritual eyes to look and create an image or picture in his mind of what He intended to give him or make him so that the imagination function engine in his mind can process the image from time to time.

Building a sound Scriptural image

This is so that he can keep this image in focus at all times until it becomes a physical reality in his life. It is the same with us. God is also telling us to use our imagination to look into the Scriptures and see with our spiritual eyes what He has made us or given us. That was why God gave us the directive through Prophet Isaiah in Isaiah 51:2 where He said that we should look unto Abraham so that we can see him as an example for us to follow. God is telling us that we will have to do what Abraham did, which was to look with the eyes of imagination.

Look unto Abraham your father, and unto Sarah that bare you: for I called him alone, and blessed him, and increased him.
Isaiah 51:2

You must get the Scriptural picture of what God is saying that you are well rooted in your mind and well focused upon by your imagination so that the imagination function machine of your mind can process the picture from time to time. This is necessary because whatever picture from the Scripture you can focus upon in your imagination can always be turned into a reality in your life, especially since it is also fertilized by the words that you speak out when such words agree with the picture.

One of Satan's tactics against the Christian is to try to blur this Scriptural picture in the mind of the Christian so that he cannot see it clearly thereby creating doubt in the mind of such a Christian. He will therefore not be able to get that picture established in his life.

Living a supernatural life (Volume 3)

God told Abram to lift up his eyes and look from the place where he was northwards, southwards, eastwards, and westward so as to get the picture to plant in his mind for his imagination function machine to process. God was telling him that whatever image or picture he could catch from what he could see was his to claim. Whatever he could see then was his to claim.

If you are truly a born-again Christian then just as God told Abram what He had made him so is He telling you to look into the Scriptures to see what He has made you and what He has given you. It is in the Scriptures that you will find a picture of what God has made you and what God is telling you is that whatever picture of yourself you can find in the Scriptures is yours to claim. If you talk and walk in the consciousness of the picture it will manifest and become a reality in your life.

WHAT YOU SEE IS WHAT YOU GET

You should start to see the Scriptural image of yourself as painted by the Word. You know water can act as a mirror because when you face water and look into the water you will see an image, which is a reflection of your face. That was what God wanted us to know by what He said through Solomon in Proverbs 27:19 when He said face answers to face in water. But He went a stage further by saying that just as in water face answers to face so the heart of man answers to man.

> *As in water face answereth to face, so the heart of man to man.*
>
> **Proverbs 27:19**

Building a sound Scriptural image

This means that the picture you can see in your heart is what you will be. Just as water act as and is likened to a mirror through which you can see your image so is the Word of God likened to water as expressed by God through Apostle Paul in Ephesians 5:26. You can therefore also use the Scriptures as a mirror. Therefore when you set your face and look into the Scriptures you are bound to see a Scriptural picture of yourself. But the image you get will depend on what you choose to see in the Scriptures. Therefore make sure you see the positive pictures painted of you in the Word.

> *That he might sanctify and cleanse it with the washing of water by the word,*
> **Ephesians 5:26**

You know some Christians believe that being poor is a necessity to get to Heaven. They believe that if you are rich you cannot make Heaven. Many believe this because of what Jesus said in Matthew 19:23-24. That is how many see this.

> *Then said Jesus unto his disciples, Verily I say unto you, That a rich man shall hardly enter into the kingdom of heaven.*
>
> *And again I say unto you, It is easier for a camel to go through the eye of a needle, than for a rich man to enter into the kingdom of God.*
> **Matthew 19:23-24**

But as you can see Jesus did not say that a rich man cannot enter the Kingdom of Heaven; it is only going to be more difficult for him than for a poor man and the reason why can be seen from what preceded these statements of Jesus. It was the case of a rich young man who came to Jesus wanting to go to Heaven. When Jesus asked him about the Law it was obvious that the young man had kept the Law. Here was a young man who fulfilled the Law not because he was born-again or redeemed but by a choice of his will. If such a man can keep the Law by a choice of his will then it is obvious that you who have been redeemed and who now have the help of the Holy Spirit should have no problem keeping the Law. But when Jesus told the young man to go and sell all that he had and give them to the poor. That was just too much for the young man. You can see therefore that what led Jesus into making the statements written in the verses above was that most rich people will love their riches more than they love God and in that position they cannot make Heaven. But you have a choice.

IT IS A CHOICE

Many if not most rich people will not go to Heaven. Not because they are rich but because they love their riches more than they love God. They centre their hearts on their riches. But the *love of money* is the root of all evil, not money itself. Similarly not all poor people will go to Heaven. As you can see in the Scriptures, Lazarus was poor and he went to Heaven. But Abraham was rich and he also went to Heaven. So you can be rich and go to Heaven and you can be poor and go to Heaven.

Building a sound Scriptural image

It is a choice. It all depends on the type of image you choose to put in your heart from the Scriptures because whatever you have in your heart is what you will bring forth in your life. You can choose to be rich and you can choose to be poor. But whichever one you choose of the two, poverty or riches, your love for God must be first and foremost in your heart if you want to go to Heaven. You must also keep His commandments and be a doer and not just a hearer of His Word. That is what we can infer from what Jesus Himself said as written in John 14:21,23 and John 15:10. He said,

He that hath my commandments, and keepeth them, he it is that loveth me: and he that loveth me shall be loved of my Father, and I will love him, and will manifest myself to him.

Jesus answered and said unto him, If a man love me, he will keep my words: and my Father will love him, and we will come unto him, and make our abode with him.
John 14:21,23

If ye keep my commandments, ye shall abide in my love; even as I have kept my Father's commandments, and abide in his love.
John 15:10

You should begin to imbibe every positive Scriptural truth that you can discover and build up a picture of that truth in your mind. If you believe in the reality of this imagined picture, which you have built up in your mind and start to walk in the consciousness of the truth of the Scripture then the picture will physically manifest.

Living a supernatural life (Volume 3)

The picture will then become a reality in your life. This is so because the Word has embedded in it the power to fulfill. In every Word of God that you speak out the power to fulfill is embedded inside it.

THE WORD HAS THE POWER TO FULFILL

Any picture that you can get from the Scriptures can be made to become a physical reality in your life. This is because as Jesus said in John 6:63 when the Word enters into you it will quicken your spirit because the Word is spirit and it is life.

> *It is the spirit that quickeneth; the flesh profiteth nothing: the words that I speak unto you, they are spirit, and they are life.*
> **John 6:63**

Therefore whenever you can get a Scriptural picture from the Word the Spirit behind that Word will enter into you. It is the Spirit behind that Word that will establish the reality of that Scripture physically in your life thereby enabling you to walk in the reality of that Scriptural picture or image that you have in your mind. This was what the Prophet Ezekiel was getting across to us in Ezekiel 2:2 when he said that when God spoke to him the Spirit entered into him. It was the Spirit behind that Word of God that entered into him. It was not just the hearing of the Word that Ezekiel was talking about here but hearing and receiving the Spirit of the Word. Therefore whenever you go beyond the realm of just hearing the Word into the realm of receiving the Spirit behind the Word then this Spirit will make the Word to perform what He says in your life.

Building a sound Scriptural image

And the spirit entered into me when he spake unto me, and set me upon my feet, that I heard him that spake unto me.

Ezekiel 2:2

Now let us look at some examples of the type of Scriptural pictures that you should be trying to build up in your mind that can help you to get over the common situations that you will come across in life. I will give examples here of typical situations that I have come across in my own life and which I believe are common to most Christians.

1. REGAINING ONE'S CAPTIVITIES

One common situation is one in which you have been deprived of something that belongs to you or your entitlements by someone who is in a position of authority over you or who is stronger than you and it looks as if you have lost what should have been yours. Such a person may be using his strength, his smartness or his authority over you and depriving you of what should have been yours. Get into the Word and get a Scriptural image of what Isaiah 49:24-26 says. Meditate on this until the picture becomes very clear in your mind and you can start to use the imagination function of your mind to process it. What that Scripture says is this. No matter how strong or powerful that one who has taken your portion captive may be it will be taken away from him and given back to you. Even if such an adversary has a legal or lawful right to take it away from you, God is saying that He will contend with him to take it back from him.

Living a supernatural life (Volume 3)

Shall the prey be taken from the mighty, or the lawful captive delivered?

But thus saith the LORD, Even the captives of the mighty shall be taken away, and the prey of the terrible shall be delivered: for I will contend with him that contendeth with thee, and I will save thy children.

And I will feed them that oppress thee with their own flesh; and they shall be drunken with their own blood, as with sweet wine: and all flesh shall know that I the LORD am thy Saviour and thy Redeemer, the mighty One of Jacob.

Isaiah 49:24-26

God is saying here that no matter who that your adversary may be and whatever reason he may have for taking your goods captive He will contend with such a person and retrieve your captivity from him. Look at what God said below. If you can allow the Spirit of this Word of God to enter into you to reveal the Word to you and you allow it to be processed long enough by the imagination function of your mind the power to fulfill this Word of God will enter into you and make sure that what the Word says is fulfilled in your life.

2. REVIVING DEAD DESTINIES

For some Christians most things that they lay their hands upon seem to just die.

Building a sound Scriptural image

And their lives have become a struggle. They have been involved in projects, businesses, and all sorts of ideas but somehow these get to a point where progress just stops and they get the impression that whatever they lay their hands upon dies.

If you are in that kind of situation you need to get into the Word and find the right Scriptural picture. First try and get the picture of what Jesus said in Luke 21:15 and get the image of you having the necessary wisdom to get whatever you want. Also get a picture of having an irresistible mouth with which to command the situations of your life. Then get the image of what Jesus said in Matthew 16:19 fixed in your imagination and let the Spirit of that Scripture enter into you. Once that is done then you know that you can loose the bounds on those dead projects or businesses and bring them back to life again because you now have the capability to command anything bound or loosed and your commands must be obeyed.

> *For I will give you a mouth and wisdom, which all your adversaries shall not be able to gainsay nor resist.*
> **Luke 21:15**

> *And I will give unto thee the keys of the kingdom of heaven: and whatsoever thou shalt bind on earth shall be bound in heaven: and whatsoever thou shalt loose on earth shall be loosed in heaven.*
> **Matthew 16:19**

Living a supernatural life (Volume 3)
To really bring this into reality you can get into the Scriptures in Ezekiel 36:1-11 and Ezekiel 37:1-14 and read these over and over, meditating on them day and night, imagining them and seeing yourself doing likewise until the Spirit of the Scriptures enters into you. Once the Spirit of the Scripture enters into you then you can start to prophecy life to those dead projects, businesses and marriage relationships that you want to bring back to life. Catch the image of these Scriptures and you can bring all those dead things back to life.

> *Also, thou son of man, prophesy unto the mountains of Israel, and say, Ye mountains of Israel, hear the word of the LORD:*
>
> *Thus saith the Lord GOD; Because the enemy hath said against you, Aha, even the ancient high places are ours in possession:*
>
> *Therefore prophesy and say, Thus saith the Lord GOD; Because they have made you desolate, and swallowed you up on every side, that ye might be a possession unto the residue of the heathen, and ye are taken up in the lips of talkers, and are an infamy of the people:*
>
> *Therefore, ye mountains of Israel, hear the word of the Lord GOD; Thus saith the Lord GOD to the mountains, and to the hills, to the rivers, and to the valleys, to the desolate wastes, and to the cities that are forsaken, which became a prey and derision to the residue of the heathen that are round about;*

Building a sound Scriptural image

Therefore thus saith the Lord GOD; Surely in the fire of my jealousy have I spoken against the residue of the heathen, and against all Idumea, which have appointed my land into their possession with the joy of all their heart, with despiteful minds, to cast it out for a prey.

Prophesy therefore concerning the land of Israel, and say unto the mountains, and to the hills, to the rivers, and to the valleys, Thus saith the Lord GOD; Behold, I have spoken in my jealousy and in my fury, because ye have borne the shame of the heathen:

Therefore thus saith the Lord GOD; I have lifted up mine hand, Surely the heathen that are about you, they shall bear their shame.

But ye, O mountains of Israel, ye shall shoot forth your branches, and yield your fruit to my people of Israel; for they are at hand to come.

For, behold, I am for you, and I will turn unto you, and ye shall be tilled and sown:

And I will multiply men upon you, all the house of Israel, even all of it: and the cities shall be inhabited, and the wastes shall be builded:

Living a supernatural life (Volume 3)

And I will multiply upon you man and beast; and they shall increase and bring fruit: and I will settle you after your old estates, and will do better unto you than at your beginnings: and ye shall know that I am the LORD.

Ezekiel 36:1-11

The hand of the LORD was upon me, and carried me out in the spirit of the LORD, and set me down in the midst of the valley which was full of bones,

And caused me to pass by them round about: and, behold, there were very many in the open valley; and, lo, they were very dry.

And he said unto me, Son of man, can these bones live? And I answered, O Lord GOD, thou knowest.

Again he said unto me, Prophesy upon these bones, and say unto them, O ye dry bones, hear the word of the LORD.

Thus saith the Lord GOD unto these bones; Behold, I will cause breath to enter into you, and ye shall live:

And I will lay sinews upon you, and will bring up flesh upon you, and cover you with skin, and put breath in you, and ye shall live; and ye shall know that I am the LORD.

So I prophesied as I was commanded: and as I prophesied, there was a noise, and behold a shaking, and the bones came together, bone to his bone.

And when I beheld, lo, the sinews and the flesh came up upon them, and the skin covered them above: but there was no breath in them.

Then said he unto me, Prophesy unto the wind, prophesy, son of man, and say to the wind, Thus saith the Lord GOD; Come from the four winds, O breath, and breathe upon these slain, that they may live.

So I prophesied as he commanded me, and the breath came into them, and they lived, and stood up upon their feet, an exceeding great army.

Then he said unto me, Son of man, these bones are the whole house of Israel: behold, they say, Our bones are dried, and our hope is lost: we are cut off for our parts.

Therefore prophesy and say unto them, Thus saith the Lord GOD; Behold, O my people, I will open your graves, and cause you to come up out of your graves, and bring you into the land of Israel.

And ye shall know that I am the LORD, when I have opened your graves, O my people, and brought you up out of your graves,

And shall put my spirit in you, and ye shall live, and I shall place you in your own land: then shall ye know that I the LORD have spoken it, and performed it, saith the LORD.
Ezekiel 37:1-14

Get these Scriptural truths well established in your mind and allow your imagination machine to start processing them then you will soon start to see yourself prophesying to the dead businesses and projects in your life. Once you start to do these you will find that the Spirit of these Scripture will inject life into the Scriptures and empower them to perform according to what is written. You will then see that whatever comes out of your mouth will be empowered to fulfill whatever you say. Whatever you then prophecy will surely be established.

3. HEALING THE SICK

This is one Scriptural picture that most Christians find very difficult to build an image of in their minds. They just cannot see the truth of the Word as given in the Scriptures. The Scriptures made us to understand from what God said through Peter in 1 Peter 2:24 that we **have been** healed. But the picture that most Christians have in their mind is that they ***will be*** healed. If you have been healed you need not pray for healing.

> *Who his own self bare our sins in his own body on the tree, that we, being dead to sins, should live unto righteousness: by whose stripes ye were healed.*
> **1 Peter 2:24**

Building a sound Scriptural image

Most Christians can just not get in their hearts the picture of this healing, which God has already done because they keep looking at the symptoms that they can see in the physical. They still see themselves sick and oppressed by sicknesses and diseases. But their healing was done more than two thousand years ago by the stripes which Jesus took on His body. That is what God said through Peter in the Scripture above. Because Christians cannot paint a picture of this healing in their hearts or mind they still go ahead asking God to come and heal them. But God has already healed them. God has already done every thing that He has to do about their healing. It is the Christian who now has to get the healing image or picture in his mind. Once they can get the healing in their hearts then the healing can be brought forth in their lives because according to Jesus in Matthew 12:35 it is from the treasures of our hearts that we bring forth the things that appear in our lives. How to deal with sickness is covered in detail in the next Chapter.

A good man out of the good treasure of the heart bringeth forth good things: and an evil man out of the evil treasure bringeth forth evil things.

Matthew 12:35

Therefore when a Christian is sick, rather than pray to God asking God to come and heal him what he should pray for is that God should help him to get the knowledge that will give him the picture of healing in his heart. His effort should be directed at changing the picture that he has built in his heart so that he can get the healing picture in his heart.

Living a supernatural life (Volume 3)

This is necessary because as Jesus has told us in the previous Scripture it is what a man has in his heart that he will bring out in his life. Therefore if one can get healing into his heart that is exactly what he will bring out. When a Christian feels that he needs healing what he should do then is to try to get in his heart the picture of the healing that God has done so that it can manifest physically in his life. Therefore when such a Christian asks God to help him to get the healing picture in his heart then God will work on his heart to change what he has in his heart to healing. He can then bring forth healing from his heart. The healing will then flow out into his life from his heart. This is confirmed further by what Jesus told us in John 7:38.

> *He that believeth on me, as the scripture hath said, out of his belly shall flow rivers of living water.*
>
> **John 7:38**

What Jesus said here showed that the rivers of living water should be flowing out of our belly. The rivers of living water that Jesus was talking about here was what He also referred to as the virtue that came out of Him to heal the lady with the issue of blood disease as written in Luke 8:43-48.

> *And a woman having an issue of blood twelve years, which had spent all her living upon physicians, neither could be healed of any,*
>
> *Came behind him, and touched the border of his garment: and immediately her issue of blood stanched.*

Building a sound Scriptural image

And Jesus said, Who touched me? When all denied, Peter and they that were with him said, Master, the multitude throng thee and press thee, and sayest thou, Who touched me?

And Jesus said, Somebody hath touched me: for I perceive that virtue is gone out of me.

And when the woman saw that she was not hid, she came trembling, and falling down before him, she declared unto him before all the people for what cause she had touched him, and how she was healed immediately.

And he said unto her, Daughter, be of good comfort: thy faith hath made thee whole; go in peace.

Luke 8:43-48

It is obvious therefore that when we pray healing down we are not doing the right thing. We are supposed to pray healing out from within us not down from above. The healing virtue is already resident inside us so once we can get the picture of the healing Scripture into our heart we can then bring the healing out from within us. This is further established by what God said through Apostle Paul in Romans 8:11 where He said that the Holy Spirit that is now living in us is supposed to be quickening our mortal body just like He raised Jesus from the dead. To quicken means to heal, to revitalize, to refresh, to revive, to rejuvenate, to renew, invigorate or regenerate.

Living a supernatural life (Volume 3)

> *But if the Spirit of him that raised up Jesus from the dead dwell in you, he that raised up Christ from the dead shall also quicken your mortal bodies by his Spirit that dwelleth in you.*
> **Romans 8:11**

The mortal body to be quickened is our physical body. He is therefore saying that our body should be receiving healing, renewal and rejuvenation through the ministry of the Holy Spirit who lives in us.

IGNORANCE IS SATAN'S WEAPON

If you can get healing into your heart then you will be able to bring forth healing from your heart. What Scriptural picture of yourself do you have in your heart? It is very important that you know this because the Spirit of whatever picture you have will enter into you and give you the enablement to be able to walk in the reality of that picture. You must start to think the way God says that you are as you can see from the Scriptures. Knowledge is what will determine whether you will win against Satan in his effort to take control of your mind and consequently control your destiny. The main weapon that Satan uses against the Christian is ignorance and his antics of trying to battle man in the reasoning arena where he can then bring a distorted view of what the Scripture says or even blatant lies into the mind of man for man to reason out. That was what he did with Adam and Eve at the beginning.

Building a sound Scriptural image

He used the ignorance of Eve who was not there when God talked to Adam to bring a distorted view of what God told Adam to her for her to ponder in her mind. He is still doing the same thing even today with man. For example God said,

1. You were healed **(1Peter 2:24)** But you still feel the pain. You still feel sick.
2. You are strong **(Joel 3:10)** But you still feel weak.
3. You have power **(Luke 10:19)** But you still feel beaten.
4. You are blessed **(Ephesians 1:3, 2 Peter 1:3)** But you still feel poor and suffer lack.

You don't have to reason these with Satan. Just believe what the Scripture says and act it. Unless you have the correct Scriptural picture of these well rooted in your mind Satan will seek to distort these pictures in your mind so that you will not be able to stand on these Scriptural truths. Don't let Satan create doubts in your mind about anything that God has spoken in His Word. You must be conscious of Satan's methods of asking questions such as: *"Did God really say this?" "Are you sure?" "Can it be that simple?" "Do you think so?"etc*. If you are not totally sure of what the Word of God says in your mind Satan will confuse you like he did to Eve.

Let me paint a Scriptural picture of you as we have discovered in the earlier Chapters of this book.

Living a supernatural life (Volume 3)

1. ***You are a spirit-being*** and as a spirit-being your ways cannot be sabotaged by anybody because they cannot discern your ways anymore. Nobody can subvert your destiny any longer. **(John 3:6 and John 3:8)**

2. ***You are a son of God.*** You are not only a son of God you are a god. Just like God made Moses a god unto Pharaoh so has he made you a god to all your enemies. You now partake of the divine nature of God. He gave you His divine nature so that you can act like a god and be a god to all your adversaries. **(John 1:12, and John 10:34, Exodus 7:1, Luke 21:15, Ecclesiastes 8:4, and 2 Peter 1:4)**

3. ***You have the mind of Christ.*** This is the mind that made all things. Therefore nothing can be daunting to you anymore. You have the potential to come up with great earth-moving ideas that can change the world. They say that ideas rule the world and you now have the greatest mind of all minds therefore with the mind that you now have you now have the capability to bring out the best of ideas. You are a genius in waiting.**(1 Corinthians 2:16, and John 1:1-3, 14)**

4. ***You are a citizen of the Kingdom of Heaven.*** You have been translated into the Kingdom of Heaven. But you are now an ambassador of Heaven here on earth. As an ambassador of Heaven here on earth you are health personified.

Building a sound Scriptural image

Therefore sickness can no longer inhabit your body as of right. As an ambassador of Heaven here on earth you can no longer lack whatever you need. Your home Kingdom of Heaven will provide all your needs. **(Colossians 1:13, 2 Corinthians 5:20, Philippians 4:19, and also in Proverbs 13:17 and Matthew 6:33)**

5. *You are sent by Jesus as He was sent* by the Father therefore you are entitled to all the facilities that He was entitled to. Whatever Jesus can do you now have the potential to do. Whatever supported Him when He was on earth is now supporting you. Wherever He tapped power from when He was on earth you too can now tap power from. **(John 20:21, John 14:12)**

6. *You have the potential for a higher anointing than any old Covenant saint.* You can do whatever Jesus did. You can even do greater things than Jesus did. In actual fact you can do all things through Christ who strengthens you. You are more than a conqueror. Whatever Moses, Elijah, Elisha, David, Solomon and any other Old Covenant saint was able to do you have the potential to do even greater things now. Whatever wisdom they exhibited you have the potential to exhibit even greater wisdom now. **(Matthew 11:11, Philippians 4:13, John 14:12 Philippians 2:13, 1 Corinthians 2:16)**

Living a supernatural life (Volume 3)

    7. *You are a king* and you are supposed to be reigning here on earth. As a king you reign by your words and by your wisdom. God has given you a mouth and a wisdom so that when you speak no adversary can resist whatever you say. **(Revelation 5:10, Luke 21:15 as well as in Proverbs 8:12-16 and Ecclesiastes 8:4)**

Keep these pictures firmly in your mind for your imagination function to process. The imagination function of the mind and how to use this positively to receive revelation knowledge **RHEMA** Word from God has been discussed in much detail in the *Volume 1* of this *"Living a Supernatural Life"* book series.

In the following five Chapters we show in detail how your mind should reason so as to develop the right Scriptural image whenever you are challenged by any situation, sickness, disease, affliction or sin that we have mentioned earlier in the last *Chapter.* In the five typical situations that we considered we looked at the type of questions that should be coming to your mind and the way your mind should be reasoning if you want to subdue the situation.

CHAPTER 9

ARE YOU SICK?

DO YOU NOT KNOW THAT HEALING IS PACKAGED WITH YOUR SALVATION?

Probably the worst situation is that you have been sick for years, and you have gone to the doctors and they have told you that what you have is a terminal disease that they can do nothing about. They have done the usual tests, examined you thoroughly, and have come to the conclusion that you should just be expecting to die soon. They are telling you that you will not be able to recover your health, because for one reason or the other, they have found from the tests that they conducted on you that there is no hope for you. But cheer up because if you are a born again Christian, I want you to know that sickness or any disease cannot put you under bondage. And even if you already have the symptoms, I want you to know that as a result of your new birth healing is now automatically yours. Don't take what the doctors or the symptoms say as the final word on your situation. You should take note of the things discussed in this Chapter and the healing privileges that are yours as a result of your salvation because your healing is already packaged with your salvation.

Living a supernatural life (Volume 3)

That healing is already packaged with your salvation can be seen from the commission that God gave to Jesus Christ when He came to the world, which is clearly stated in Luke 4:18-19 read by Jesus Himself and written below.

The Spirit of the Lord is upon me, because he hath anointed me to preach the gospel to the poor; he hath sent me to heal the brokenhearted, to preach deliverance to the captives, and recovering of sight to the blind, to set at liberty them that are bruised,

To preach the acceptable year of the Lord.
Luke 4:18-19

From what Jesus read in these verses we can see clearly that the commission that God gave to Jesus, which was what Jesus came to do on earth, was in two parts. On the one part, He was anointed to do something. On the other part, He was sent to do certain other things.

He was anointed to   Preach the gospel to the poor.

He was sent to   Heal the brokenhearted.

Preach deliverance to the captives.

Preach recovery of sight to the blind.

Set at liberty them that are bruised.

Preach the acceptable year of the Lord.

Are you sick?

From the above, you can see that practically everything that He was sent to do has to do with healing. Healing the broken-hearted is healing; deliverance is also a form of healing; the recovery of sight is a form of healing and setting people at liberty also involves healing them. Therefore we can say that He was anointed to save the people, but He was also sent to heal the people. So Jesus was sent not only to save the people, but He was also sent to give them Divine health and where they have failed to take hold of divine health, then divine healing, which is different from divine health. The first part of His commission is dedicated to salvation, but the second part is dedicated mainly to divine healing. This healing covers not just physical body healing, but the healing of such things as businesses, healing of marriages and also spiritual healings.

Jesus was anointed to preach salvation, but He was sent to heal the people. Generally most people are agreed that Jesus fulfilled the first part of His Commission that He was anointed to do by His death on the Cross. If we know that He also fulfilled what He was sent to do, which is the second part of His commission then we can conclude that healing is our inheritance in Christ.

Did Jesus fulfill the tasks that He was sent to do? God spoke to us concerning this through those who were with Him when He was here physically on earth.

For example, through Luke God told us in Acts.10:38 that, ***(Jesus healed all that were oppressed of the devil)***

Living a supernatural life (Volume 3)

> *How God anointed Jesus of Nazareth with the Holy Ghost and with power: who went about doing good, and healing all that were oppressed of the devil; for God was with him.*
> **Acts 10:38**

And through Matthew He said the following in Matthew12:15 and Matthew14:14. *(Jesus healed them all)*

> *But when Jesus knew it, he withdrew himself from thence: and great multitudes followed him, and he healed them all;*
> **Matthew 12:15**

> *And Jesus went forth, and saw a great multitude, and was moved with compassion toward them, and he healed their sick.*
> **Matthew 14:14**

Therefore from what God said through Luke and Matthew above we can conclude that Jesus also fulfilled the second part of His commission. Hence we can conclude that healing is already packaged with our salvation. What this means is that when you get saved and accept Jesus Christ as your Saviour, then apart from being saved you are also healed and entitled to live in divine health from that point on. Both had been purchased for you by Jesus since He died on the Cross. However it is when you realize this, believe it, and accept that it has been done for you, that you can then enjoy the full privileges and the benefits of the healing that are now yours through that work of redemption that Jesus did.

Are you sick?

It is one thing to be entitled to divine health; it is another thing to actually live in divine health. The power to actually live this comes as a result of the level of revelation and knowledge and insight that you have of your entitlements.

For instance, we know that Christ died to save all people, but it is only those who believe this truth and accept Jesus Christ as their Saviour that will enjoy the privileges and benefits that go with their salvation. If you believe that you have been saved, but do not believe that you have been given divine health, then you cannot enjoy the health part of the privileges and benefits that comes with your salvation and which you are now entitled to. Both salvation and divine health had been purchased for you, but it is for you to accept them. Many people are aware of their salvation, which they obtained through the redemption work of Jesus Christ, but they are not aware of the divine health and healing, which they are also supposed to have received through the same redemption work of Christ. Therefore they keep struggling under the burden of diseases and all types of sicknesses. They are told by doctors that they are sick and they just accept it not knowing that they have been freed from such afflictions through the work of redemption that Christ did on the Cross. They are the type of people that God referred to as being destroyed because they lack knowledge. That what you get from your salvation depends on the knowledge that you have is well illustrated by the Parable of freed slaves written below which is taken from the book series titled, *"You are a New Creature" Volumes 1,2,3 and 4* written by the same author,

A PARABLE OF FREED SLAVES

The Kingdom of Heaven can be likened to a far country into which millions of slaves have been taken, and in which the practice of slavery had been the order of the day. Many families in the country own and keep slaves that have been brought to that country from lands that are far away.

The slaves have no rights of their own. They work for and live with their owners and masters. They are being used for the most menial and dirty jobs in the land. Then one day the government of that country made a proclamation, which was passed into law, declaring that from the date of the announcement or proclamation of the law, all slaves in the land are to be freed by their owners. The proclamation was supposed to be issued and published in all the newspapers in the country.

All slaves from that date are to become free citizens of the country, entitled to the country's passport, and all the rights and privileges that every free citizen of that country has. They were to collect their passports from the nearest government office to where they are residing. But each slave was supposed to physically collect these in person. They cannot be collected by a proxy for any slave. To help the freed slaves to be able to establish themselves, the government also decided that each of the freed slaves would be given a piece of land and a house in which to live. They are not only given these, the government also decided that each slave would be given a lump sum of money with which to start life as a free citizen.

Are you sick?

The amount of money that each slave is to be given will depend on his age, his marital status and the size of his family.

Summarizing, we have the following as the entitlement of every slave starting from the date of proclamation of the law to free them. Each slave will be entitled to the following:

1. His or her freedom.
2. Free citizenship and passport of the country with all the rights and privileges of a citizen.
3. Land and house in which to live.
4. A lump sum of money with which to start life as a free citizen.

But as is usual in most situations of this type, for various reasons, not all the slaves became free or had all their rights and privileges restored to them on the day of that proclamation. Among the many cases recorded were the following categories.

Some slaves, who heard the proclamation on that date went straight to their masters, demanded their freedom and they were promptly freed on that day. They went to the government offices nearest to them to collect their passports, the land, the house and the sum of money that the government had promised them. And they were also promptly given all these. We can say that they were the luckiest of the slaves because they had the appropriate knowledge and they took the right actions.

Living a supernatural life (Volume 3)

Some slaves heard the proclamation and demanded their freedom from their masters, but their masters refused to give them their freedom. So they ran away and took their freedom by force.

Some slaves heard the proclamation and their masters freed them. However, they could not see themselves as free citizens. Their mental attitude was not that of a free man. They still had the mentality of, and behaved like, a slave. They therefore could not pursue their other benefits.

Some slaves heard the proclamation and demanded their freedom from their masters. But their masters refused to give them the freedom. So they obeyed their masters, stayed put and struggled no further for their freedom.

Some slaves heard the proclamation but did not demand for their freedom from their masters. They still preferred to be slaves because they were not sure that they could stand on their own. Therefore they were afraid to leave their masters and they stayed put with their masters.

Some slaves did not hear or know of this proclamation until about a year after it was made. Their masters tried to hide the information from them. But when they eventually heard, they demanded their freedom from their masters, and their masters promptly freed them.

Are you sick?

Some slaves heard of the proclamation of their freedom, but did not believe that it was true. Therefore they did not even attempt to obtain their freedom.

Some slaves heard of the proclamation that they had been freed demanded their freedom from their masters and they were promptly freed. But they did not know or hear of the fact that they were citizens of the country, so they did not go to collect their passports. Neither did they hear of the offer of land, house and money, so they did not collect any of these.

Some slaves heard of the proclamation, demanded their freedom and were promptly freed by their masters. They also heard that they were entitled to the country's citizenship and passport, applied for this and they were promptly given. But they did not hear or know of the land and house offer, and they also did not hear of the money offer. Therefore they did not apply for any of these.

Some slaves heard of the proclamation, demanded their freedom and their masters promptly freed them. They also heard of their entitlement to the country's passport and citizenship, as well as the land and house that they had been offered. They applied for all the three, and were promptly given all. But they did not hear or know of the offer of money; therefore they did not apply for this. They only applied for what they had knowledge of and they were promptly given. However, there were some things that they did not know about.

Living a supernatural life (Volume 3)

Some slaves heard of the proclamation of their freedom, and they promptly applied for their freedom and were given their freedom by their masters. But even though they heard of all the other privileges and rights offered them, they did not believe these. Therefore they did not apply for the citizenship; neither did they apply for the land and house nor the money.

Some slaves did not hear of the proclamation of their freedom. However, on their own, they have been perfecting all kinds of schemes to get themselves freed.

Some slaves heard of the proclamation of their freedom, but they thought that it was all tricks, and so did not believe it. They therefore on their own started to develop all sorts of plans and schemes to get themselves freed.

Some slaves heard of the proclamation of their freedom, applied for it and were promptly freed by their masters. But after tasting freedom for sometimes, they decided to go back to their masters and be slaves again because they could not stand on their own.

The Kingdom of Heaven is similar to these. They have many things in common, but we shall only look at a few of these cases.

Are you sick?

The first thing I want us to consider is this question. When were the slaves set free? You will agree with me that they were all set free on the day of proclamation of their freedom. But not all of them became free on that day. They only became free when they heard of the proclamation and took the necessary actions. We should also ask the question, when were they given the citizenship of that country? So it is with salvation. All people were saved two thousand years ago as a result of the redemption work that Jesus Christ did on the Cross on Calvary. But it is only when you know, accept the offer and take the necessary action to accept Jesus Christ as your Saviour that it becomes a reality to you and you can then enjoy all the rights and privileges that goes with your acceptance of Christ as your Saviour.

The second thing to note is this. The fact that some slaves did not hear or know about the proclamation freeing them did not mean that they had not been freed. They had been freed, only they did not know. And as long as they did not know, their suffering as a slave continued. So it is with the Kingdom of Heaven, the fact that some people have not heard of the work of salvation that Christ did on the Cross on Calvary did not mean that they have not been saved. They have been saved, and set free from everything that is caused by sin, such as poverty, curses, sickness and disease. A provision has been made for their freedom two thousand years ago, but they are still being subjected to these things because of their lack of knowledge. They have been saved all right but it is the day that they actually come to accept Christ into their lives as their Saviour that their salvation becomes a reality.

Living a supernatural life (Volume 3)

And only then can they enjoy the privileges that go with the salvation. That was why God said through Hosea in Hosea 4:6 that His people are destroyed because of their lack of knowledge, and through Prophet Isaiah in Isaiah 5:13 that His people are gone into captivity because they had no knowledge. Lack of knowledge is a destiny destroyer. Many people have lived and died not achieving their destiny on earth because they lacked knowledge.

> *My people are destroyed for lack of knowledge: because thou hast rejected knowledge, I will also reject thee, that thou shalt be no priest to me: seeing thou hast forgotten the law of thy God, I will also forget thy children.*
> **Hosea 4:6**

> *Therefore my people are gone into captivity, because they have no knowledge: and their honourable men are famished, and their multitude dried up with thirst.*
> **Isaiah 5:13**

The third thing to note is this. Some of the slaves heard of the proclamation of freedom for them, they took the offer and they gained their freedom. But either because they did not hear of, or heard but did not believe, the fact that they are also citizens of the country, entitled to a passport and a house of their own, they did not pursue these. Therefore they had no passport; neither did they have a land or house of their own.

Are you sick?

They were therefore unable to take advantage of the fact that they are citizens of the country, since they did not know that they were. So is the Kingdom of Heaven. Many heard of, and believed the work of salvation that Jesus Christ did on the Cross on Calvary. But they are either not aware of the fact that the work include the physical healing of their body, or they are aware of it but did not believe it. Therefore they are still groaning under the oppression of sickness and diseases.

Just like the slaves that did not know that they are entitled to the citizenship of the country, they too are not aware that they are now citizens of the Kingdom of God, and entitled to all kinds of rights and privileges that should accrue to them as a citizen of the Kingdom of God. They are missing all the things that they should be enjoying right here on earth such as divine health, success and victories, which are benefits that they should derive from their salvation. Therefore what gains you get from your redemption, depends on the level of knowledge and insight that you have of what your redemption covers.

Whatever you do not know belongs to you; it is obvious that you will not expect to have it as of right. If you want it you will have to beg for it instead of demand for it as of right. But if you know that it belongs to you then you will demand for it from whoever is holding it because you will believe that it is yours as of right. Therefore having knowledge empowers you.

Living a supernatural life (Volume 3)

Let us consider this last case. Some slaves did not hear of the proclamation of their freedom, and some heard but did not believe. Meanwhile they are running around looking for ways of escape from their masters and slavery. They have devised all types of plans and schemes to free themselves.

So is the Kingdom of Heaven. Many people are not aware of the salvation work that Jesus Christ did on the Cross at Calvary, and many are aware but do not believe it. So they have gone to devise their own schemes and methods for reaching God, or for going to Heaven. These are those who practice all sorts of religions that they believe will lead them to God. But they are mistaken because there is only one route to God, and that is through Jesus Christ. Jesus Himself said in John 14:6 that He is the way, the truth and the life: and no man can come to the Father except through Him.

> *Jesus saith unto him, I am the way, the truth, and the life: no man cometh unto the Father, but by me.*
> **John 14:6**

Note again that He did not say that Christ *will redeem* you from the Curse of the Law. No! He said that Christ *has redeemed* you from the Curse of the Law. So it is something, which is already done. You are not going to be redeemed from the Curse of the Law; you have already been redeemed from it. What is the Curse of the Law?

Are you sick?

If you look at the book of Moses called Deuteronomy in Deuteronomy 28:15-68, you will see all the various curses that God pronounced there. These basically are most of what forms the Curse of the Law. As you can see if you read this, you will find that most of the curses that form the Curse of the Law are mainly the afflictions and oppressions that Satan uses against you including diseases and sicknesses. If there is any sickness or disease, which is not included in the curses that God listed in the above Scripture then what God said in Deuteronomy 28:61, (Verse Sixty-One) which is written below has made sure that it is also included in the Curse of the Law.

Also every sickness, and every plague, which is not written in the book of this law, them will the LORD bring upon thee, until thou be destroyed.
Deuteronomy 28:61

You have been healed already of the disease that you are carrying about. This means that when you continue to pray for healing, then you have got it all wrong. Why should you be praying for something that God has said that He has already done for you, and He has already given to you? I know that you will ask the question, "Since God said that I am already healed, why am I sick then? Why have I not received my healing?"

The author has also written a book titled, *"Why Healing Delays"* which specifically deals with the answers to these questions.

Living a supernatural life (Volume 3)

You have been healed already of the disease that you are carrying about. This means that when you continue to pray for healing, then you have got it all wrong. Why should you be praying for something that God has said that He has already done for you, and He has already given to you? I know that you will ask the question, "Since God said that I am already healed, why am I sick then? Why have I not received my healing?" The author has also written a book, which specifically deals with the answers to these questions.

If you want to know the answers to these questions then read the book titled, *"Why Healing Delays"* which is written by the same author. But suffice to say here now that if you are sick and you have not seen your healing manifest physically, it is because you lack the knowledge to get you out of it or the knowledge to keep you away from diseases.

You need to have knowledge in order to have a good understanding of why you are still being harassed by diseases, despite the fact that God said that you have been healed. God through Paul in Galatians 3:13-14 puts this healing which Christ has given you in another way. He said there that Christ has redeemed you from the curse of the law.

> *Christ hath redeemed us from the curse of the law, being made a curse for us: for it is written, Cursed is every one that hangeth on a tree:*

Are you sick?

> *That the blessing of Abraham might come on the Gentiles through Jesus Christ; that we might receive the promise of the Spirit through faith.*
>
> **Galatians 3:13-14**

Therefore if a disease is not covered by all the curses given in verses fifteen to sixty, then this verse sixty-one brings it under the Curse of the Law. We can therefore conclude that every disease is part of the Curse of the Law. Of course, the Curse of the Law covers more than diseases. It covers practically every affliction or oppressions that you may find yourself going through. Therefore being redeemed from the Curse of the Law is of wider application than being healed of diseases.

If you want to know in detail the things that you now have in Christ as a result of your redemption then I strongly advise you to read the books titled, *"You are a New Creature" Volumes 1,2,3 and 4* written by the same author. When you read these books the perception that you now have of the gains of your salvation and what you are capable of will definitely receive a great and permanent transformation. God wishes His people well. He desires Divine health for His people. That is what He told us through John in 3 John 2.

> *Beloved, I wish above all things that thou mayest prosper and be in health, even as thy soul prospereth.*
>
> **3 John 2**

Living a supernatural life (Volume 3)

You cannot say that someone who is not fruitful is prosperous neither can you say that someone who is not fruitful is in health. God wants health for your spirit, for your soul, and for your body. God wants you to swim in Divine health with ease. However it is only as much as your soul (i.e. your mind) prospereth that you will enjoy this. You must have prosperity in your mind if you want to enjoy prosperity. If you do not believe and have prosperity and health in your mind then it will not be possible for you to prosper and be in health physically. Therefore as you can see from what God is saying here, your mind holds the key to your prospering and being in health. If you want to know the roles that your mind plays in determining what you get out of your redemption then you should read **Chapter 1** of **Volume 1** of this **"Living a Supernatural life"** book series written by the same author. You must note that, when we talk of Divine health, we are not talking of the health that you receive by going to doctors for treatment, or for prescriptions. Divine health is different from that kind of health, which you receive by taking drugs or medication. Divine health is health at the Celestial level. It is health that comes directly from God. The health that you enjoy by visiting doctors and taking drugs or medication is health at the Terrestrial level. Such health is obtained by trial and error. On the other hand, Divine health is guaranteed health. There is no trial and error about divine health. You will know that where you are now, no disease, not even barrenness can hang upon you to put you in any bondage.

You will know that even when they do come God will heal you as written in Exodus 15:26 because God is the Saviour and Healer of His people.

Are you sick?

> *And said, If thou wilt diligently hearken to the voice of the LORD thy God, and wilt do that which is right in his sight, and wilt give ear to his commandments, and keep all his statutes, I will put none of these diseases upon thee, which I have brought upon the Egyptians: for I am the LORD that healeth thee.*
>
> **Exodus 15:26**

This is also a Covenant promise of divine health that God made with His people. In this Covenant, God has given four conditions that we must satisfy in order that we can live in divine health. Note that this is not only a Covenant of divine healing. It is actually a Covenant of divine health because divine healing is different from divine health. Once you satisfy the conditions that God listed above you don't even have to pray for divine health. God will make sure that you live in divine health. The four conditions that you must satisfy to enjoy divine health are the following.

1. You must diligently hearken to the voice of the Lord your God.
2. You must do that which is right in God's sight. (Not necessarily right in your own sight.)
3. You must give ear to God's commandments.
4. You must keep all of God's statutes.

So it is God's wish that you live in absolute divine health, but if you must do so then you must fulfill the above four conditions.

Living a supernatural life (Volume 3)

Obviously you cannot be said to be living in divine health if you are suffering under the bondage of any disease. But the truth is that most Christians do not believe that they can live in absolute divine health. They believe that they can be sick from time to time and then have divine healing. That is the limit that the faith of most Christians will take them. But God's wish for you is that you live in absolute divine health. If you have the necessary faith for divine health and fulfill the four conditions that God has set down for you above then you can live in absolute divine health in which case such things as barrenness and diseases will be a thing of the past for you. As a born again Christian your salvation also entitles you to this Covenant of divine health.

GOD'S BLESSING COVERS BOTH WEALTH AND HEALTH

When God blesses you, He does not expect you to spend the blessing from Him on paying for your health, because He has already packaged health with your salvation. That has always been the way God works. Any blessing from God cannot be accompanied with trouble, grief or sorrows.

Whenever God has moved to save His people, the *salvation* has always been accompanied with *healing*. That was why David was able to write the following words in Psalm 118:25.

> *Save now, I beseech thee, O LORD: O LORD, I beseech thee, send now prosperity.*
> **Psalm 118:25**

Are you sick?

He said, "Save now I beseech thee O Lord"
That is the salvation package.

He said, "O Lord, I beseech thee, send now prosperity"
That is the health and wealth package.

Prosperity and blessing from God always covers both wealth and health, therefore you can see why the second sentence above is called the healing package. David was saying there that God should save now, and send wealth and health, because each time that there is salvation, prosperity in wealth and health should accompany it. To show you that whenever salvation is expected, divine wealth and health are expected to accompany it, look at what king David said again in Psalm 28:9.

> *Save thy people, and bless thine inheritance: feed them also, and lift them up for ever.*
> **Psalm 28:9**

He said, "Save thy people"
That is the salvation package.

He said, "Bless thine inheritance"
That is the health and wealth package
This is because God's blessing covers both health and wealth.

God wants you to be wholly prosperous, body, soul and spirit. That is what He made us to know through Apostle Paul which is written in 1 Thessalonians 5:23.

Living a supernatural life (Volume 3)

> *And the very God of peace sanctify you wholly; and I pray God your whole spirit and soul and body be preserved blameless unto the coming of our Lord Jesus Christ.*
> **1 Thessalonians 5:23**

This means that God wants your spirit to be prosperous. He wants your soul to be prosperous and He wants your body to be prosperous. God wants you whole. You cannot be said to be whole if you are under the bondage of sickness.

Therefore what God is saying here is that it is not His wish that you should be suffering from diseases. Finally, so that you will know that it is God's wish that you should be prosperous, look at what He made us to know through David in Psalm 35:27.

> *Let them shout for joy, and be glad, that favour my righteous cause: yea, let them say continually, Let the LORD be magnified, which hath pleasure in the prosperity of his servant.*
> **Psalm 35:27**

This shows that God delights in your being prosperous. If we take into consideration the truth that God's prosperity covers both wealth and health it follows then that what God is telling you through David here is that He takes pleasure in your being wealthy and also in your being in good health. God wants His people to enjoy prosperity in its fullest not a hypothetical prosperity but one that is real.

Are you sick?
YOU HAVE BEEN HEALED ALREADY

If you know this and you are still sick then you should proclaim your freedom from sickness because you are now a member of the Body of Christ. How can the Body of Christ be sick? Christ was never sick when He was here on earth. Your mentality should be this; how can you be sick when you have been healed of any disease that can ever attack you by the stripes that Jesus Christ took on His body on the Cross? That should be your understanding of what 1 Peter 2:24 says.

> *Who his own self bare our sins in his own body on the tree, that we, being dead to sins, should live unto righteousness: by whose stripes ye were healed.*
> **1 Peter 2:24**

The redemption work that Jesus Christ did was a two-part deliverance work. On the one part it covered the deliverance, spiritual healing and cleansing of your heart and soul from sins by His blood of Jesus that He shed. On the other part it covered the deliverance, physical healing and cleansing of your body from diseases by the stripes that He took on His body. The unfortunate thing however is that while most Christians know and claim the spiritual healing from sins they just do not know about the physical healing for their body. Healing is not only packaged with your salvation you have actually been healed already. We have noted earlier that you do not really need to pray for healing, because healing is already packaged with the salvation that Jesus Christ brought you through His death and resurrection.

Living a supernatural life (Volume 3)

In this Chapter we are going to elaborate on this, so that there will be no doubt in your mind after going through the Chapter, that healing is already yours. You have already been healed, so you don't have to be sick anymore. It is something that is already done therefore snap out of that disease that is worrying you. You have been healed from whatever they have told you that is causing you to be under the bondage of disease. You don't have to stand that sickness one moment longer. You don't have to stand it anymore. You can say goodbye to it.

Say it with a total conviction in your mind because you are already healed. Jesus Christ has finished the work of healing you two thousand years ago. Let me repeat here what God told us through Apostle Peter in 1 Peter 2:24. It is very important that you note what God said through Apostle Peter here. God said, *"Ye **were healed"***. This means that you **have been healed**, NOT you **will be healed**. It is past tense.

> *Who his own self bare our sins in his own body on the tree, that we, being dead to sins, should live unto righteousness: by whose stripes ye were healed.*
>
> **1 Peter 2:24**

This is the truth, but as you know what happens to you depends on what you decide to believe in your mind. If you believe that you have been healed and focused your mind on that, then your healing will eventually manifest. The healing is already yours in the spiritual realm but it is your stand in faith in your mind that will make it to manifest in the physical realm in your body.

Are you sick?

What God said in Proverbs 23:7 through Solomon is very important. He said that it is as one thinks in his heart that he is. You are as you think in your mind.

> *For as he thinketh in his heart, so is he: Eat and drink, saith he to thee; but his heart is not with thee.*
>
> **Proverbs 23:7**

Therefore if you think that you are healed of whatever disease is trying to put you in bondage, then you are. If on the other hand, you think that you are not healed of it, then you are not. Your mind has to do with what you are. It all has to do with what your mind accepts. It is the thought in your mind that determines what you become and what happens to you. It is what your mind accepts that you become. We have discussed in detail the way the mind of man works in *Chapter 1* of *Volume 1* of this *"Living a Supernatural life"* book series

YOU DON'T EVEN NEED TO PRAY FOR HEALING

You have been healed. That is what God said through Peter in 1 Peter 2:24 above. You are not supposed to be praying for healing. How can you be praying to be healed when you are already healed? If you are praying for healing, then it means that you do not believe that you are already healed and you are still expecting your healing which means that you are making God a liar. You are supposed to be in good health because you have been healed. If you are not in good health, you are supposed to claim your good health back from the devil who is stealing your health.

Living a supernatural life (Volume 3)

You should exercise your authority over Satan or any of his agents who may be stealing your health. Jesus told us in John 10:10 that Satan is the thief who comes to steal, to kill and to destroy your health.

> *The thief cometh not, but for to steal, and to kill, and to destroy: I am come that they might have life, and that they might have it more abundantly.*
> **John 10:10**

We are also made to know by God in Acts 10:38 that sickness is an oppression of the devil. Therefore we know that the thief of our health is the devil.

> *How God anointed Jesus of Nazareth with the Holy Ghost and with power: who went about doing good, and healing all that were oppressed of the devil; for God was with him.*
> **Acts 10:38**

The thief of your health is the devil. You have to know this. Not only that, you also have to know that the devil cannot win against the power that you now have in Christ therefore he is very weak compared to you now. As a born again Christian, you have authority over the devil now. That you have been healed is sure but to see it depends on the amount of insight and understanding that you have of this Word of God. To get the healing then depends on your mind accepting it. You should not allow the devil to dictate what happens in your life. Do not allow them to have the last say.

Are you sick?

You have to be sure of yourself here, because it is only when you find out a thief that he will restore to you what he has stolen. He will restore what he has stolen even seven-fold. If he is not found out, he will keep what he has stolen, and the oppression will continue. That is what God made us to see in Proverbs 6:30-31.

> *Men do not despise a thief, if he steal to satisfy his soul when he is hungry;*
>
> *But if he be found, he shall restore sevenfold; he shall give all the substance of his house.*
> **Proverbs 6:30-31**

Therefore, until Satan knows that you know that he is the thief of your health, the oppression continues and the struggle continues. But now you know the devil is the thief of your health. You also know now that you are stronger than he is because the greater One now lives in you as revealed to you through Apostle John in 1 John 4:4. Therefore you should let Satan know that you have the knowledge of these truths and by using this knowledge you can exercise your authority over him.

> *Ye are of God, little children, and have overcome them: because greater is he that is in you, than he that is in the world.*
> **1 John 4:4**

You should give Satan no room at all to manipulate your thoughts and therefore your life. Take a good look at what Jesus said in Luke 11:21-22, which is written below. He said,

Living a supernatural life (Volume 3)

"When a strong man armed keepeth his palace, his goods are in peace:

But when a stronger than he shall come upon him, and overcome him, he taketh from him all his armour wherein he trusted, and divideth his spoils."

Luke 11:21-22

Therefore, all you need do is exercise your authority. You are the stronger man now. You can take anything that the devil has stolen from you back from him. If he steals your health you can take it back. You don't have to carry any sickness one moment longer than now.

When you exercise your authority, your body will be at peace. You must have and exhibit a superiority complex over Satan and all his oppressing spirits because you are far above them and their cohorts. If you don't enforce your authority over them they will seek to enforce their own authority over you.

YOU ARE FAR ABOVE ANY DISEASE

You have been raised up with Christ and Christ is seating in heavenly places far above all principality and power and might and dominion and every name that is named not only in this world but also in that which is to come and that is where you are now. That is what God made us to know from what He said in Ephesians 2:6 and Ephesians 1:19-21 through Apostle Paul as written below.

Are you sick?

> *And hath raised us up together, and made us sit together in heavenly places in Christ Jesus:*
> **Ephesians 2:6**
>
> *And what is the exceeding greatness of his power to us-ward who believe, according to the working of his mighty power,*
>
> *Which he wrought in Christ, when he raised him from the dead, and set him at his own right hand in the heavenly places,*
>
> *Far above all principality, and power, and might, and dominion, and every name that is named, not only in this world, but also in that which is to come:*
> **Ephesians 1:19-21**

It follows that you are now seated far above all the oppressing spirits. You have been healed. You don't need to pray for healing. You have been redeemed from every Curse of the Law and every sickness is a part of the Curse of the Law. You have been healed from every sickness that you can ever imagine.

You don't have to allow Satan to plant any sickness on you. You have the power to reject whatever Satan brings to you. But the truth is that many Christian will still continue to be sick and tossed about by Satan because they are just not aware of the privileges that they now have as a result of their redemption. Let me illustrate your situation with the following parable.

Living a supernatural life (Volume 3)

A PARABLE OF THE MORTGAGED HOUSE

The Kingdom of Heaven can be likened to a certain man who had a house, which he mortgaged to purchase a loan from a bank, leaving all the documents relating to the house with the bank. When it was time to pay back the loan he could not pay, therefore the bank took possession of his property and leased the house to some tenants of the bank. A rich friend of this man now came and paid the bank fully all that he owed the bank because the rich friend loved his friend and decided to repurchase the house for his friend. This rich friend then collected all the documents deposited with the bank, and gave them all back to his friend, the original owner of the house.

Some months after the man had repossessed his house, through the loving kindness of his rich friend, he found that the bank was still sending tenants into his house, and taking rents from them. The bank was still claiming some authority over the house. He ran back to his rich friend begging him to come and help him to evict the tenants in his house.

I want you to put yourself in the place of this man. If you find yourself in that kind of situation, what will you do? Before taking your decision, I want you to remember that your house has been fully repossessed for you, and that you now have all the documents relating to the house with you. What will you do? **Will you:**

Are you sick?

1. Go to your rich friend that helped you to repurchase your house, and ask him to come and help you to evict the tenants that the bank sent into the house?

2. Speak to the tenants directly and order them to go off your property?

3. Go to the bank and tell them to come and remove the tenants that they have allowed into your property?

Which of the three options above will you take?

Ttaking the first option, which was the one taken by the man is foolish. That is obvious. This is so because all the documents with which you want to prosecute and evict the tenants are already with you. Your friend that helped you to repurchase your house has handed them all back to you. Therefore you only need your friend now as a witness. You have all that you need to exercise full authority over your house now.

The second option whereby you go to the tenants and command them to leave your property is a good one and is feasible. But the tenants will only leave if they are sure that you have the authority that you claim over the house because they already believe that the bank has the authority over the house.

You have to establish your authority over them, and you must let them know unequivocally that you have absolute authority over your house. Remember that they derive the authority from the bank.

Living a supernatural life (Volume 3)

The third option whereby you command the bank to come and evict the tenants that they have put in your property, is also a good one and it is feasible. Better still, you can attack the problem from the two angles using options two and three.

The story is a very good illustration of what your relationship should be with diseases, Satan, and Jesus. You are the man who owns the house in question. The house in that story is your body. The bank manager is Satan. The tenants sent in by the bank into the house are the diseases, sicknesses and all the other afflictions such as barrenness that come into your body. The rich friend of yours that helped you to repossess the house is Jesus. When Satan attacks your body with a disease and you pray to God to come and heal you of the disease, you are taking the first option above and you are behaving exactly as the man in this parable did. You do not need to take that option.

You don't have to ask Jesus to come and help you to drive out diseases. You only need Jesus Christ as a witness to the truth that your house has been repossessed for you. And surely He is, because the Bible refers to Him as a true witness in Revelation 3:14, and refers to Him as a faithful witness as written in Revelation 1:5.

> *And unto the angel of the church of the Laodiceans write; These things saith the Amen, the faithful and true witness, the beginning of the creation of God;*
> **Revelation 3:14**

Are you sick?

> *And from Jesus Christ, who is the faithful witness, and the first begotten of the dead, and the prince of the kings of the earth. Unto him that loved us, and washed us from our sins in his own blood,*
>
> **Revelation 1:5**

When you speak directly to the diseases that attack your body, you are taking the second option above, and you have every right to do so. In fact that is what God expects you to do. That is why He said you should speak to your mountains. When you challenge Satan and tell him to remove his diseases from your body, you are taking the third option, and you also have every right to do so. You have authority, not only over the diseases, but also over Satan who brings them.

God has healed you. Jesus Christ has purchased your healing. If Satan now sends his demons and spirits to live in your body, and cause all kinds of infirmities that lead to such things as barrenness and diseases then it is Satan and his demons that you must face to evict them. You do not need to pray to God to evict them for you. God has already done His part. He has purchased your healing for you and He gave you authority over Satan. You now have power, which is over and far above Satan's power. That is what Jesus promised you in Luke 10:19.

> *Behold, I give unto you power to tread on serpents and scorpions, and over all the power of the enemy: and nothing shall by any means hurt you.*
>
> **Luke 10:19**

Living a supernatural life (Volume 3)

You are now loaded with so much power and authority that you must now be a no-go area to any enemy. No disease should be able to have a permanent resting-place in your body. Sicknesses and diseases should no longer have any hold on you. You must enforce your authority over Satan and all his agents using the information and knowledge now at your disposal. The knowledge at your disposal are the statements of God on this issue. You have been given the power and strength to achieve whatever destiny that God has purposed for you. Nothing can intimidate you anymore unless you permit it to do so either through your ignorance concerning the power that you now have or through your laziness and fear to use the power. Just like God said to the children of Israel through Zephaniah in Zephaniah 3:13, nothing should make you afraid anymore.

> *The remnant of Israel shall not do iniquity, nor speak lies; neither shall a deceitful tongue be found in their mouth: for they shall feed and lie down, and none shall make them afraid.*
>
> **Zephaniah 3:13**

You must note that the statement in 1 Peter 2:24 explained previously on Page 570 is not a promise of healing by God. God did not say, "I will heal you by the stripes that Jesus took". NO! God said you have been healed by the stripes that Jesus took. This is a statement of an accomplished fact. The statement is that you have been healed by the stripes that Jesus took on the Cross on Calvary. All you need to do is to now ask yourself the following questions. Is the Word of God true?

If it is true, then ask yourself this question. Did Jesus take the stripes? If you are convinced that He did, then you know that you have been healed. You have been healed of every disease or sickness that has attacked you and caused you to be under bondage. It is already done by God. You don't even need to pray for your healing, just believe it, and start confessing it so as to claim it. Then start living in the reality of it by making sure that you do those things that the sickness or disease has attempted to stop you from doing. Take actions that show your faith in this truth.

For example, a woman that is sure that she has been healed of all diseases causing her to be barren will be certain in her mind that there will be no menstrual blood flow during her next menstrual period. Therefore such a woman will not go to the chemist to buy a ***ladies sanitary pad*** or ***tampax*** to use for her next menstruation. If she goes to purchase these in readiness for her menstruation it means that she does not believe that she has already received her healing. It means that she is still hoping that she will be healed. To show that she believes that she has been healed, what she should be doing is to purchase the necessary baby clothes and the other items required for looking after the baby in readiness for the baby that she is expecting.

WHY THEN ARE PEOPLE STILL PRAYING FOR HEALING?

You will ask me, "Why should we not pray for healing? What about the prayer of faith that James said that we should pray for the sick in James 5:14-16, which is written below?"

Living a supernatural life (Volume 3)

> *Is any sick among you? let him call for the elders of the church; and let them pray over him, anointing him with oil in the name of the Lord:*
>
> *And the prayer of faith shall save the sick, and the Lord shall raise him up; and if he have committed sins, they shall be forgiven him.*
>
> *Confess your faults one to another, and pray one for another, that ye may be healed. The effectual fervent prayer of a righteous man availeth much.*
>
> **James 5:14-16**

Doesn't that contradict my saying that you do not need to pray for healing when you are sick? No, it doesn't contradict what we are saying here. You will do well to read this and confirm this yourself. We have proved this in an earlier volume on **Page 192-207** of **Volume 2** of this **"Living a Supernatural life"** book series.

YOU ARE AN AMBASSADOR FOR CHRIST

Do you not know that since you became born-again you have also been made an ambassador of the Kingdom of God for Christ here on earth? That is what God made us to see through Apostle Paul in 1 Corinthians 5:20. Your mentality should therefore be that you are no longer of this kingdom of darkness ruled by the devil but you are now representing your Kingdom here on earth. If you are an ambassador then you should take cognizance of what God said through Solomon in Proverbs 13:17. He said that a faithful ambassador is health.

Are you sick?

Now then we are ambassadors for Christ, as though God did beseech you by us: we pray you in Christ's stead, be ye reconciled to God.
2 Corinthians 5:20

A wicked messenger falleth into mischief: but a faithful ambassador is health.
Proverbs 13:17

Don't you know what this means? This means that if you are faithful as an ambassador of your Kingdom here on earth, then you are **health personified**. How can health be sick? How can health be looking for healing? Your mentality now should be that you cannot be sick because you are health personified if you are faithful as an ambassador of Christ. Therefore any disease trying to attach itself to your body is a pretender who will leave you as soon as it knows that you know your rights and authority over it and you can see through its actions.

DO YOU KNOW THAT THE RIVERS OF LIVING WATER SHOULD BE FLOWING OUT OF YOU?

How can you be entertaining any sickness when Jesus said in John 7:38 that you are supposed to have the rivers of living water flowing out of you that should be quickening your body?

He that believeth on me, as the scripture hath said, out of his belly shall flow rivers of living water.
John 7:38

Living a supernatural life (Volume 3)

WHAT ARE THESE RIVERS OF LIVING WATER?

What are these rivers of living water that should be flowing out of you? For a clue to the answer to that question take a look at what God told us through Jeremiah in Jeremiah 17:13.

> *O LORD, the hope of Israel, all that forsake thee shall be ashamed, and they that depart from me shall be written in the earth, because they have forsaken the LORD, the fountain of living waters.*
> **Jeremiah 17:13**

The Lord is the fountain of living waters. This means that when you believe on Christ, and you accept Him as your Saviour, the Holy Spirit that is in you will then become the fountain and the source of this living water. The living water comes from the Holy Spirit that is now resident in you. To bring this home to you and show you that the healing power is already resident inside you, look at what God said through the Apostle Paul in Romans 8:11. He said there that the Holy Spirit, which is now living in you, would quicken your mortal body.

> *But if the Spirit of him that raised up Jesus from the dead dwell in you, he that raised up Christ from the dead shall also quicken your mortal bodies by his Spirit that dwelleth in you.*
> **Romans 8:11**

Are you sick?

Your ***mortal body*** that God is talking about here is this present physical body that you are currently residing in. It is the only body that you will ever have, which is mortal. The word mortal means "subject to death" or "perishable". Therefore God is talking here of the body that you have which is subject to death or which is perishable. It is this physical body that you presently live in that is subject to death and perishable. It is obvious therefore that the quickening of the body that God is talking about in that verse is healing for this your physical body. And this covers fruitfulness also. This means therefore that the Spirit of God that is living in you is supposed to be healing your physical body of all the diseases that attempt to hang on you. He pours out the river of living waters to clean out any contamination in your body.

HEALING POWER SHOULD FLOW OUT OF YOU

You therefore need to be very sensitive to the Holy Spirit that is living inside of you because it is He, the Holy Spirit, who gives the power through which the supernatural can be effected in your life. When Jesus came physically to this earth, we are told in Luke 6:19 that as He went about, virtue went out of Him and healed all people that came into contact with Him wherever the faith to be healed was present.

> *And the whole multitude sought to touch him: for there went virtue out of him, and healed them all.*
>
> **Luke 6:19**

Living a supernatural life (Volume 3)

There was the case of the woman with the issue of blood. Jesus Himself said that He knew that somebody had touched Him because He knew that virtue had gone out of Him. He said this even though many people must have probably touched Him because there was a multitude of people thronging Him. But He knew that somebody had touched Him with the purpose of specifically drawing out the virtue for healing from Him. That story is recorded for us in Luke 8:43-48.

And a woman having an issue of blood twelve years, which had spent all her living upon physicians, neither could be healed of any,

Came behind him, and touched the border of his garment: and immediately her issue of blood stanched.

And Jesus said, Who touched me? When all denied, Peter and they that were with him said, Master, the multitude throng thee and press thee, and sayest thou, Who touched me?

And Jesus said, Somebody hath touched me: for I perceive that virtue is gone out of me.

And when the woman saw that she was not hid, she came trembling, and falling down before him, she declared unto him before all the people for what cause she had touched him, and how she was healed immediately.

Are you sick?

> *And he said unto her, Daughter, be of good comfort: thy faith hath made thee whole; go in peace.*
> **Luke 8:43-48**

The healing virtue carried by Jesus was the Holy Spirit. But now the same Holy Spirit lives in you and should also flow out of you to do healing because you are now a temple of the Holy Spirit. That is what God made us to see in 1 Corinthians 3:16.

> *Know ye not that ye are the temple of God, and that the Spirit of God dwelleth in you?*
> **1 Corinthians 3:16**

Not only does the Holy Spirit lives in you but we now know that Jesus Christ Himself who is the carrier of this virtue also lives in you and the life, which you now live, you live by His faith. That is what we are made to understand by God through Paul in Galatians 2:20. Most Christians attempt to *pray the healing down* and they fail. No! You *preach healing out.*

> *I am crucified with Christ: nevertheless I live; yet not I, but Christ liveth in me: and the life which I now live in the flesh I live by the faith of the Son of God, who loved me, and gave himself for me.*
> **Galatians 2:20**

Christ Himself said that once you believe in Him, then He will come and live in you and you will live by Him. That is the essence of what He said in John 14:23, in John 6:56-57 and also in John 15:4-5.

Living a supernatural life (Volume 3)

> *Jesus answered and said unto him, If a man love me, he will keep my words: and my Father will love him, and we will come unto him, and make our abode with him.*
>
> John 14:23

> *He that eateth my flesh, and drinketh my blood, dwelleth in me, and I in him.*
>
> *As the living Father hath sent me, and I live by the Father: so he that eateth me, even he shall live by me.*
>
> John 6:56-57

> *Abide in me, and I in you. As the branch cannot bear fruit of itself, except it abide in the vine; no more can ye, except ye abide in me.*
>
> *I am the vine, ye are the branches: He that abideth in me, and I in him, the same bringeth forth much fruit: for without me ye can do nothing.*
>
> John 15:4-5

You must realize that Christ is now dwelling in you and you are dwelling in Him. He is in you and you are in Him. Obviously you must be saying to yourself, "How can Christ be living in me?" But this is a spiritual thing and you cannot comprehend spiritual things with your physical senses. We have said earlier that these rivers of living water were what Jesus had in Him, which He called virtue that flowed out of Him to heal the lady with the issue of blood.

Are you sick?

If you are aware of this then what is that sickness doing in your body? Why is it still there? If there is a sickness in your body it is there because you allowed it since you have the virtue with which to deal with it if you choose to do so. Let the virtue flow out of you. The story is also stated in Mark 5:28-30 written below.

> *For she said, If I may touch but his clothes, I shall be whole.*
>
> *And straightway the fountain of her blood was dried up; and she felt in her body that she was healed of that plague.*
>
> *And Jesus, immediately knowing in himself that virtue had gone out of him, turned him about in the press, and said, Who touched my clothes?*
>
> **Mark 5:28-30**

Do you not know that the rivers of living water that you have in you is the Holy Spirit, the same Spirit that raised Jesus Christ up from the dead and that the Spirit should have a quickening effect on your mortal body? So He should be quickening your mortal body. That is what we are made to see in Romans 8:11. Obviously you are not aware of this because if you are you would have made use of these rivers of living water, which should be oozing out of you to quicken your mortal body such that no sickness can be any problem to you.

> *But if the Spirit of him that raised up Jesus from the dead dwell in you, he that raised up Christ from the dead shall also quicken your mortal bodies by his Spirit that dwelleth in you.*
>
> **Romans 8:11**

Living a supernatural life (Volume 3)

The truth that Christ lives in you should make you to expect and hope that glory will also manifest in your life. That is what we are made to understand by God through Apostle Paul in Colossians 1:27. *"Christ in you, the hope of glory."*

> *To whom God would make known what is the riches of the glory of this mystery among the Gentiles; which is Christ in you, the hope of glory:*
> **Colossians 1:27**

That Jesus Christ lives in you now is a truth that you must accept by faith. That is what God told us through Apostle Paul in Ephesians 3:17. It is by faith that you must accept this truth.

> *That Christ may dwell in your hearts by faith; that ye, being rooted and grounded in love,*
> **Ephesians 3:17**

We can conclude then that if the Spirit of Jesus Christ who carried the virtue that was doing those supernatural acts recorded in the Bible now lives in you, then the virtue should now be coming out of you as well. That was what Jesus confirmed by the statement that He made in John 7:38, which we repeat here below.

> *He that believeth on me, as the scripture hath said, out of his belly shall flow rivers of living water.*
> **John 7:38**

Are you sick?

This means that the supernatural power that you require for the healing of not only your body but even other people's body is right on the inside of you.

That power should be flowing out of you. Here then is the reason why most Christians fail to experience this supernatural healing here on earth. They expect God to send the healing power down to them. They keep praying asking God to come and heal them or heal the sick that they come across but the answers refuse to come. They expect God to send down to them the power that would heal them of diseases and barrenness. But God is saying here that this power is already resident inside you if you are a believer in Christ. It is from the inside of you that this power will flow out. The power that will heal you and even heal other people is already inside of you. It is you that have to allow it to flow out of you. ***You cannot pray the power down. You have to command or preach the power out of you.***

Let us look at this from another dimension. If Jesus Christ lives in you then the power of God lives in you because we know that Jesus Christ is the power of God. That is what God told us in 1 Corinthians 1:24 through Apostle Paul. Therefore the power of God with which you are supposed to be healed of diseases and barrenness and also heal others is already resident in you. It is you who will have to make up your mind that you want this power to flow out of you to do the healing work that you require. Having decided to do so, you must give the Spirit that is now resident inside of you the opportunity to fully express Himself through you.

> *But unto them which are called, both Jews and Greeks, Christ the power of God, and the wisdom of God.*
>
> **1 Corinthians 1:24**

YOU MUST FOCUS YOUR MIND ON THIS

You already have the measure of faith you need to obtain your healing from sicknesses and diseases. All you need to do is know that you have a Covenant of good health and fruitfulness with God and that the Spirit of God lives inside of you. You must also know that this Spirit of God is supposed to be continuously healing your body by quickening it. But the things that you treasure in your heart, which are the things that you occupy your mind with, have a lot to do with this. For it is out of your heart that you will bring forth whatever will manifest in your life. That is what Jesus Himself said in Luke 6:45. Therefore if you want healing then it is from your heart that you will bring the healing out.

> *A good man out of the good treasure of his heart bringeth forth that which is good; and an evil man out of the evil treasure of his heart bringeth forth that which is evil: for of the abundance of the heart his mouth speaketh.*
>
> **Luke 6:45**

If what you are always thinking of in your mind is sickness, then that is the treasure that you have in your heart, and that is what you will bring out of your heart.

It is obvious then that the rivers of living water will not be able to flow out. But if what you are always thinking of in your mind is good health then that is what you will have as a treasure in your heart and that is what you will bring out of your heart. The Holy Spirit that is inside of you is supposed to quicken your body, by pouring out the rivers of living water to flow out and do the healing of your body. If there is no healing in your heart, there is no way that you can bring forth healing from it. Therefore you must be very careful as to what things you allow to stay in your heart or your mind.

YOUR BODY IS A HABITATION OF GOD

Because your body is supposed to be the temple of the Holy Spirit of God, He will protect it from anything that attempts to defile it. That is what we are made to see by God through Paul in 1 Corinthians 3:16-17. God will destroy such a thing.

> *Know ye not that ye are the temple of God, and that the Spirit of God dwelleth in you?*
>
> *If any man defile the temple of God, him shall God destroy; for the temple of God is holy, which temple ye are.*
> **1 Corinthians 3:16-17**

Do you not know that any disease that may be trying to inhabit your body, which is a temple of God, is defiling it? Therefore such a disease is a candidate for destruction by God. You have a right to demand for its destruction.

THE MORE INTENSE THE SICKNESS THE BETTER

When the sickness seems to be overwhelming you and putting so many parts of your body under pressure and pain you should remember two things. The first is that such sickness cannot be your friend; it can only be your enemy. Therefore you must take your stand against it. The second is that your body that is being put under such strain is the abode of the Holy Spirit. You must have the consciousness of the truth that you have the Holy Spirit living in your body. Now the Scripture says in Isaiah 59:19 that when the enemy shall come in like a flood, the Holy Spirit of the Lord shall lift up a standard against him.

> *So shall they fear the name of the Lord from the west, and his glory from the rising of the sun. When the enemy shall come in like a flood, the Spirit of the Lord shall lift up a standard against him.*
>
> **Isaiah 59:19**

Sickness comes as an enemy attacking the abode of the Holy Spirit in you. Therefore you can expect the Holy Spirit to lift up the standard and fight back against the enemy as promised.

YOUR HEALING IS ALREADY INSIDE YOU

May be you are one of those citizens of the Kingdom of God currently living on earth who believe that their healing will have to come from above.

Are you sick?

The truth is that you have already been healed and no further healing will come from above. You were healed over two thousand years ago by the stripes that Jesus took. The earlier you believe this truth the better for you.

Your healing is already done. This needs to be emphasized again. Note that what God said which is written in 1 Peter 2:24 is, ***"Ye were healed"*** not ***"Ye will be healed"*** The healing was done by the stripes that Jesus took over two thousand years ago. The healing is already done therefore no further healing is coming down from anywhere. Your healing is already in you. You just have to get this point because it will make the difference as to whether you will receive that healing or not. Look at this once again below. It is you who must now make the healing, which is already effected in the spiritual realm to manifest in this physical realm by having and holding on in patience to your faith in what the Word of God says. It is then that you can inherit this Word of God to you. That is what we are made to see in Hebrews 6:12. It is with faith and patience that you will inherit the healing that God has put in place for you.

> ***Who his own self bare our sins in his own body on the tree, that we, being dead to sins, should live unto righteousness: by whose stripes ye were healed.***
> **1 Peter 2:24**

> ***That ye be not slothful, but followers of them who through faith and patience inherit the promises.***
> **Hebrews 6:12**

It is your faith that will trigger the rivers of living water in you to ooze out and effect the quickening of your mortal body so that your healing can manifest physically for all to see.

IS YOUR DISEASE GENETICALLY INHERITED?

Are you suffering from what doctors' say could be an inherited disease? Doctors might have told you that what you have is an inherited disease, a genetic disease or a genetic abnormality. Even in that situation you have nothing to worry about. I have good news for you.

YOU CANNOT INHERIT A DISEASE

You are now born into a Kingdom where you cannot inherit a disease. This is so because as part of your being born again into that Kingdom you were saved by the washing of regeneration and the renewing of the Holy Spirit. That is what we are made to understand from the Scriptures in Titus 3:5.

> *Not by works of righteousness which we have done, but according to his mercy he saved us, by the washing of regeneration, and renewing of the Holy Ghost;*
>
> **Titus 3:5**

Therefore what you have is a total rebirth known as regeneration into the Kingdom of God's dear Son. You are now a son of God, a new creature with new *divine genes*. That is what being *re-gene-rated* means. This means in effect that your *genes* are now *re-rated*.

Are you sick?

The rating for your new genes now is such that no earthly disease can attack them and overcome or change them because they are **divine genes**. Your genes are **super divine genes.** Therefore your genes can no longer be subject to any genetic disorder or abnormalities. They cannot malfunction because they are divine genes, which have been made so by the purifying work of the Holy Spirit. With this regeneration a totally new life is commenced in you. Therefore let nobody intimidate you by telling you that you have a genetically derived disease. Similarly in this Kingdom of God into which you have now been born, you cannot inherit diseases or any bad thing because in that kingdom you can only have a goodly heritage. That is what the Scripture says in Psalm 16:6. Your inheritance now is in the Lord. The Lord Himself is your inheritance. That is what you can see in Psalm 16:5. How can the Lord be your inheritance as well as malfunctioning genes?

> *The lines are fallen unto me in pleasant places; yea, I have a goodly heritage.*
> **Psalm 16:6**

> *The LORD is the portion of mine inheritance and of my cup: thou maintainest my lot.*
> **Psalm 16:5**

Therefore where you now are, diseases, afflictions and malfunctioning or abnormal genes can no longer be your inheritance. They are no longer your portion. There is nothing goodly about them. You can no longer have any genetically-based problem.

Living a supernatural life (Volume 3)

That should be your mentality. That should be what is occupying your mind now because as we are told in Proverbs 23:7 it is as you think in your mind that you will be. If you believe in your heart that you can no longer have a genetically-based disease that is how it will be. But if you think that you have or can still have a genetically derived disease then that is how it will be also.

> *For as he thinketh in his heart, so is he: Eat and drink, saith he to thee; but his heart is not with thee.*
> **Proverbs 23:7**

In this Kingdom of God where you are nothing can reproach you anymore because your calling into that kingdom is to glory and virtue. There is no glory or virtue in diseases.

EVEN DEATH HAS NO POWER OVER YOU

You can rest assured as a righteous man knowing that even death cannot do anything to you unless it is time for you to die, because righteousness will deliver you even from death. That is what God said through Solomon in Proverbs 10:2. Remember that you have been given the gift of righteousness. As a man given the gift of righteousness by God whatever you do will lead you to life, not to death because you will be doing only right things. That is what God made us to know through Solomon in Proverbs 10:16.

Are you sick?

> *Treasures of wickedness profit nothing: but righteousness delivereth from death.*
> **Proverbs 10:2**

> *The labour of the righteous tendeth to life: the fruit of the wicked to sin.*
> **Proverbs 10:16**

That is not all. Now that Christ is in you, the Holy Spirit in you is life because of that righteousness that you have.

That is what God made us to understand from what He said through Apostle Paul in Romans 8:10. Therefore death cannot come near you unless of course your time has come or you give him the permission to do so. Therefore if sickness attacks you, you can rest assured that you cannot die of the disease. From what God said through Solomon in Proverbs 10:3, since He has now considered you to be righteous He will not allow your soul to famish.

> *And if Christ be in you, the body is dead because of sin; but the Spirit is life because of righteousness.*
> **Romans 8:10**

> *The LORD will not suffer the soul of the righteous to famish: but he casteth away the substance of the wicked.*
> **Proverbs 10:3**

Living a supernatural life (Volume 3)
YOU ALREADY HAVE WHAT YOU ARE PRAYING FOR

Most of the things that you are praying for are already supplied, even your health. That is the way God sees it. You just need to know how to key in to get them. You are now on the supply side of Heaven, not on the demand side.

As long as you are a representative of Heaven here on earth and faithful to your calling, your needs are supplied even before you asked for them because the will of God in Heaven will be carried out here on earth in your life. You only need to be faithful to the terms of the Covenant. You are already blessed with all things. Including divine health and healing. That is what we can see in Ephesians 1:3 and also in 2 Peter1:2-3.

> *Blessed be the God and Father of our Lord Jesus Christ, who hath blessed us with all spiritual blessings in heavenly places in Christ:*
> **Ephesians 1:3**

> *Grace and peace be multiplied unto you through the knowledge of God, and of Jesus our Lord,*

> *According as his divine power hath given unto us all things that pertain unto life and godliness, through the knowledge of him that hath called us to glory and virtue:*
> **2 Peter 1:2-3**

Are you sick?

Note that God is saying in these verses that *you have been* blessed, not that *you will be* blessed. God is telling you through Paul and Peter here that you have already been blessed with all spiritual blessings in heavenly places in Christ. It is obvious therefore that you have already been given most of the things that you are praying for and asking God to bless you with. God confirmed this through Peter that you have been given all things that pertain unto life and godliness.

But you will only get them through the knowledge of Christ, which means through the knowledge of the Word of God. Definitely we know that health pertain unto life, because if you are sick, you can loose your life in the process. In fact sickness is known as the beginning of death. But for you your sickness can no longer be unto death, because health is one of the things that you have been given since it pertains unto life. Most of the things that you are asking for in prayer are already yours if they pertain unto life and godliness. If there is anything that you need, which you have not got then one reason why you have not got it is because you need the appropriate knowledge of Christ, which means that you need the appropriate knowledge of the Word of God that you require to get it. When you are praying for health, you are praying for something that is already yours, which you have already been given. This will become clear to you by the time you finish reading this Chapter

You may think that because God said spiritual blessings these are not tangible blessings that you can really enjoy now.

Living a supernatural life (Volume 3)

But I want you to know that these cover all things because all things are first spiritual before they manifest physically. Even the house that you are living in was first a spiritual object when it was still a thought or an idea in your mind or in the architect's mind. It was after the thought or idea was implemented that it became a physical thing that you can now see and enjoy today. So when God says spiritual blessings, He is actually talking of all blessings. It is you who now have to convert the spiritual blessings to physical blessings with the knowledge and application of the appropriate Word of God through your confessions and actions.

In that verse God also states that you have been called unto glory and virtue. Definitely, there is nothing glorious or virtuous about diseases and sicknesses. Therefore you have not been called to diseases and sicknesses. If you are sick of any disease, you have every right to command the disease to leave your body because it is not supposed to be there. We have discussed the particular case of cancer diseases in *Volume 1* of this *"Living a Supernatural Life"* book series and we showed there that cancer is the result of cells of the body that have rebelled against the law of God laid down for the growth of cells. Because they are in rebellion God has passed and pronounced the judgment on such cells. It is for us to enforce the judgement of God by voicing them out and commanding such cells to order. You have the authority to command them. Any disease that hangs on to your body is exalting itself above the knowledge of Christ, who is the Word, who says that you have been called unto glory and virtue, and that you have been healed by His stripes.

Are you sick?

But you should remember that God said through Paul in 2 Corinthians 10:4-6 that you can cast down any imagination that exalts itself against the knowledge of God (the Word) through the weapons that you now have. And you can bring any such thought that exalts itself against the knowledge of the Word of God captive and in obedience to the Word of God (Christ). But note that your own obedience of the Word of God must first be fulfilled.

> *For the weapons of our warfare are not carnal, but mighty through God to the pulling down of strong holds;*
>
> *Casting down imaginations, and every high thing that exalteth itself against the knowledge of God, and bringing into captivity every thought to the obedience of Christ;*
>
> *And having in a readiness to revenge all disobedience, when your obedience is fulfilled.*
> **2 Corinthians 10:4-6**

Therefore the diseases that hang on your body contrary to the Word of God, which says that you have been healed, can be brought in subjection to what the Word says. You don't have to pray for healing to come down from God to you. You already have it. Praying for healing to come down from God is a waste of time for any Christian. As a born again Christian the Holy Spirit is already living inside you. He doesn't have to come from above. He is already in you.

Living a supernatural life (Volume 3)

The power that you require for your healing is already inside of you if you are a Christian. God does not have to bring it down to you. That is what we have seen earlier from what Jesus said in John 7:38. He said,

> *"He that believeth on me, as the scripture hath said, out of his belly shall flow rivers of living water."*
>
> **John 7:38**

The living water, which is the power that you require is already in you and has to flow out of you. It doesn't have to come down to you or flow into you from God. It is already resident inside you. You just have to make it flow out of you. It is from your heart that the living water will flow out.

Most Christians when they pray try to pray the power to heal down instead of commanding the power out. No!

You don't pray the power down; you command the power out because the power for healing is already living in you.

WHY ASK FOR WHAT YOU ALREADY HAVE?

Do you believe that the Bible is the Word of God? Do you also believe that God cannot lie and the Word of God cannot change or be broken? If you do why then do you pray asking God to bless you when as we have explained before He has said that you have been blessed with all spiritual blessings in heavenly places in Christ?

Are you sick?

That is what God's Word said in Ephesians 1:3. So when you pray that kind of prayer asking God to bless you then you are either saying that the Word of God is not true or that you don't believe that God will keep His Word. God said that you have been blessed *with all* spiritual blessings yet you are still praying to God asking him to bless you. By so doing, aren't you saying that what God said in that verse is not true? If the blessings are not manifesting physically in your life, then you need to look at what Jesus said which is written in Matthew 6:33.

Blessed be the God and Father of our Lord Jesus Christ, who hath blessed us with all spiritual blessings in heavenly places in Christ:
Ephesians 1:3

But seek ye first the Kingdom of God, and his righteousness; and all these things shall be added unto you.
Matthew 6:33

You should seek first the Kingdom of Heaven and its righteousness then all other things will be added unto you. All the other things that you are praying for are therefore just add-ons, extras and appendices. Therefore set your priorities right. Most Christians act as if some parts of the Bible are true, and some parts are not true? God said you have been *blessed with all things.* Which one is left that you have not got, that you are asking for? *He has already blessed you with all spiritual blessings.* Get the mindset that you are already blessed with all things and that is what will manifest in your life.

Living a supernatural life (Volume 3)

We have explained earlier that all blessings are first spiritual before they manifest as physical blessings and He said that you have been blessed with *ALL OF THEM*. I did not say it. God said it. He said it through Paul. *You have been blessed with all blessings*, not some of them. If you have been blessed with all blessings why are you still praying to be blessed? You don't need to pray asking for blessings, for health and even for fruitfulness. Just fulfill the terms of the Covenant of God and these things will manifest physically in your life. If God says that you have been blessed with all spiritual blessings and you are not getting all those blessings, then what you need to do is to search to see the conditions for your getting the blessings to manifest physically in your life and fulfill those conditions.

That will show you why you are not getting them. If you do not fulfill those conditions, even if you pray day and night, the blessings will not come. But if you fulfill the conditions then you don't need prayers to get the blessings to manifest physically in your life. Some people will say "But God also told us through Paul to be careful for nothing but in everything by prayer and supplication with thanksgiving let our requests be made known unto Him" Yes, that is what God said through Paul in Philippians 4:6.

> *Be careful for nothing; but in every thing by prayer and supplication with thanksgiving let your requests be made known unto God.*
> **Philippians 4:6**

Are you sick?

Now what God said you should pray and bring forward here are your requests. Should your requests include what God has told you that He has already given you? If you have a child and you told him that you have bought him a gift say a car. But because he has not seen the car he keeps coming to you telling you to buy him a car. Won't you think that he is making you a liar? He does not need to ask you to buy him a car anymore. What he needs to do is to be reminding you that he has not gotten the car yet. To bring this home to you let me further illustrate this with a parable just like Jesus used to illustrate the Kingdom of God using parables.

A PARABLE OF THE RICH MAN AND HIS SON

The Kingdom of Heaven can be likened to a very rich man who had a son.

He gave his son a large sum of money, which he paid into a coded account. He gave his son the code and the checkbook, which he is to use to draw money out of the account. But instead of the son using the code and writing the check to withdraw money, he keeps going back to the father and asking him for money. What will you think of that son? That is exactly what you look like to God when you pray to God asking Him to bless you, to heal you or give you a child. Should you be requesting from God what He has told you that He has already given you? The answer to that question is **NO**.

Living a supernatural life (Volume 3)

What God is asking you to request from Him here are those things that you want, which he has not already given you. There are many of these. They include such request as asking for an unsaved friend to be touched by God, so that he can give his life to God. But when it comes to those things that God has told you that He has already given you, then your prayer should be a prayer of thanksgiving. You only need to fulfill the terms required to obtain these. What you need to say to God in such a situation is *"Thank you Father, for giving me--------------."*

That was exactly what Jesus did when He was here on earth. Remember His Prayer in John 11:41 when He was at Lazarus' grave? *"Father I thank thee that thou hast heard me"* He knew from the promises of God that whenever He prays to God He the assurance that He hears Him. Therefore all He needed to do was to thank God. Remember that He told us in 1 John 5:15 that once we know that He hears us then we have the assurance that we have gotten what we asked for?

> *Then they took away the stone from the place where the dead was laid. And Jesus lifted up his eyes, and said, Father, I thank thee that thou hast heard me.*
> **John 11:41**
>
> *And if we know that he hear us, whatsoever we ask, we know that we have the petitions that we desired of him.*
> **1 John 5:15**

Are you sick?
Think about this question seriously.. How can you,

1. Have God living inside of you as stated by Apostle John in **1 John 4:4 and 1 John 4:13;**
2. Be hidden with Christ in God as stated by Apostle Paul in **Colossians 3:3-4;**
3. Become one with God, sealed together with God and inseparable from His love as written in **Colossians 1:18, Ephesians 1:13 as well as Romans 8:38-39;**
4. Have the divine nature of God as we are told by Apostle Peter in **2 Peter 1:4;**
5. Have the rivers of living water flowing out of your belly as we are told by Jesus Himself in **John 7:38;**
6. Be blessed with all spiritual blessings in the heavenly places as we are told by Paul in **Ephesians 1:3;**
7. Be given all things that pertain unto life and godliness as stated by Peter in **2 Peter 1:3;**

And still have diseases ravaging your body and reigning over you? Is that really possible? Definitely NOT! Unless you do not know these truth about you.

If you have all these characteristics and attributes that we have discussed in this book, diseases can no longer be your portion unless of course you have not gotten the revelation of these Scriptures in your heart and you don't know that you have these characteristics. If you have not done so read the Scriptures below again and meditate on them until you get this revelation.

Living a supernatural life (Volume 3)

Ye are of God, little children, and have overcome them: because greater is he that is in you, than he that is in the world.
1 John 4:4

Hereby know we that we dwell in him, and he in us, because he hath given us of his Spirit.
1 John 4:13

For ye are dead, and your life is hid with Christ in God.

When Christ, who is our life, shall appear, then shall ye also appear with him in glory.
Colossians 3:3-4

And he is the head of the body, the church: who is the beginning, the firstborn from the dead; that in all things he might have the preeminence.
Colossians 1:18

In whom ye also trusted, after that ye heard the word of truth, the gospel of your salvation: in whom also after that ye believed, ye were sealed with that Holy Spirit of promise,
Ephesians 1:13

For I am persuaded, that neither death, nor life, nor angels, nor principalities, nor powers, nor things present, nor things to come,

Are you sick?

Nor height, nor depth, nor any other creature, shall be able to separate us from the love of God, which is in Christ Jesus our Lord.
Romans 8:38-39

Whereby are given unto us exceeding great and precious promises: that by these ye might be partakers of the divine nature, having escaped the corruption that is in the world through lust.
2 Peter 1:4

He that believeth on me, as the scripture hath said, out of his belly shall flow rivers of living water.
John 7:38

Blessed be the God and Father of our Lord Jesus Christ, who hath blessed us with all spiritual blessings in heavenly places in Christ:
Ephesians 1:3

According as his divine power hath given unto us all things that pertain unto life and godliness, through the knowledge of him that hath called us to glory and virtue:
2 Peter 1:3

How can all these be true of you and you are still harassed by sicknesses and diseases? If you are sick, it must be as a result of a lack of awareness of the true and new divine nature that you now have. Therefore, you have to be conscious of your true divine nature that you now have in Christ. ***You must have the correct Scriptural image of yourself.*** God can never lie.

Living a supernatural life (Volume 3)

You now partake of the same divine nature with God. So you should not be held bondage by any disease. Believe this and be conscious of this truth that you can no longer be held bondage by any disease and speak it out loud. Get this revelation and you will have your freedom.

Always speak out this statement boldly to the hearing of others. ***"I have the divine nature of God, therefore I cannot be held in bondage by any disease."*** Have this superiority mentality. See yourself above sicknesses and diseases. If you can confess this your new nature genuinely with boldness and firm belief without doubting in your mind, diseases may come near you but they will no longer be able to make your body their abode. You don't have to be harassed and buffeted by diseases any longer but it all depends on the level of insight that you have of the Word of God.

CHAPTER 10

TORMENTED BY AFFLICTIONS?

If you are tormented by any affliction it means that you don't really know the power and authority that you now have as a born-again Christian in-Christ. With all the power that is now available to you as a Christian afflictions should not be your problem. By the time you go through this Chapter whatever affliction that may be tormenting you will no longer mean much to you because you will realize that you are far above any affliction. Let me just review here some aspects of the true Scriptural picture of who you really are now. If you can see this picture of yourself then your worries will be over. The first thing you must know and note is that you are now a citizen of the Kingdom of God.

YOU ARE A CITIZEN OF THE KINGDOM OF GOD

We have shown in Chapter 6 that you are now a citizen of the Kingdom of God. That is what you are told in Colossians 1:13. You have been translated into the Kingdom and you now belong to that Kingdom.

Living a supernatural life (Volume 3)

> *Who hath delivered us from the power of darkness, and hath translated us into the Kingdom of his dear Son:*
> **Colossians 1:13**

You must realize that you are now a citizen of that Kingdom. You should therefore know those things that you are entitled to as a citizen of that Kingdom. One of your entitlements as a citizen of that Kingdom is that afflictions should no longer be capable of tormenting you.

If you are tormented by any affliction it means that you do not know yet what authority and power you have in the Kingdom of God to which you now belong. This is so because in that Kingdom you have not only been made but empowered to become a son of God. That is what we are told in John 1:12

> *But as many as received him, to them gave he power to become the sons of God, even to them that believe on his name:*
> **John 1:12**

A son of God is a little god on his own and should not see himself as someone that can just be treated with impunity without respect by the enemy or by any affliction. If you realize that you are a son of God the enemy is bound to have respect for you. But you must know this and be conscious of it yourself before you can earn the respect of others. A son of God that knows that he is a son of God cannot be tormented by any affliction unless he does not realize who he is.

Tormented by afflictions?
YOU ARE A TEMPLE OF GOD

As a citizen of the Kingdom of God you have been given a new Spirit, the Spirit of God and this Spirit, who is God, now lives in you, therefore your body is a temple of God where God lives. That is what you are told in 1 Corinthians 3:16. Your body is a temple of God and He has said that He would destroy anything that defiles His temple. That is what we can understand by what He said in 1 Corinthians 3:17.

> *Know ye not that ye are the temple of God, and that the Spirit of God dwelleth in you?*
> **1 Corinthians 3:16**

> *If any man defile the temple of God, him shall God destroy; for the temple of God is holy, which temple ye are.*
> **1 Corinthians 3:17**

Any affliction that comes to torment you regardless of what form it takes is defiling your body, which is God's temple and God has promised to destroy whoever defiles His temple. So you don't even have to struggle with the affliction. Let God take care of it. God will destroy it.

You cannot now be tormented by any affliction unless you are ignorant of your present position in Christ and the promises of God to you. But should in case you have not really seen your position let me further show you just who you are now in Christ.

Living a supernatural life (Volume 3)

YOU ARE ANOINTED OF GOD

As a member of the Heavenly Kingdom, you are anointed by God and therefore you have become God's anointed. That is what we can infer from what is written in 2 Corinthians 1:21. Now I want you to note what God made us to understand through David concerning His anointed in 1 Samuel 26:9. He said nobody can stretch forth his hands against God's anointed and be guiltless. Therefore as God's anointed no affliction can stretch forth its hand against you and be guiltless. Therefore if any affliction stretches forth its hands against you, such an affliction is guilty before God and it is disobeying God's order. Therefore it will incur the wrath of God. This should be your mindset at all times.

> *Now he which stablisheth us with you in Christ, and hath anointed us, is God;*
> **2 Corinthians 1:21**

> *And David said to Abishai, Destroy him not: for who can stretch forth his hand against the LORD'S anointed, and be guiltless?*
> **1 Samuel 26:9**

Because you are God's anointed, He has decreed that nothing should touch you for evil nor harm you. Even though you may not know it, God's protective decree is resting upon you. That is the meaning of God's pronouncement as is written down by King David in Psalm 105:14-15. Look at it below.

> *He suffered no man to do them wrong: yea, he reproved kings for their sakes;*

Tormented by afflictions?

> *Saying, Touch not mine anointed, and do my prophets no harm.*
>
> **Psalm 105:14-15**

Therefore God will not allow anybody or any affliction to do you any harm. Any affliction that comes your way you can rest assured that it cannot harm you because God is your defender now and God will deal with it. We are told that God built a protective hedge around Job, around his house and around all that he had on every side as we are told in Job 1:10.

> *Hast not thou made an hedge about him, and about his house, and about all that he hath on every side? thou hast blessed the work of his hands, and his substance is increased in the land.*
>
> *Job 1:10*

Similarly God has also made such a protective hedge around you. Even though you may not see it you can rest assured that there is such a hedge around you. But if you do not know that there is such a hedge of protection around you like Job you may be feeling afraid and frightened. If you know this truth however you will be as bold as a lion and you will not be worried about any affliction that may come your way. Remember that it was the hedge of protection around Job that Satan gave as one reason why he could not touch Job. One other thing that will make you bold is that as a citizen of the Kingdom of God you are no longer seen as a stranger by God. That is what we shall discuss in the following section.

YOU ARE NO LONGER A STRANGER TO GOD

As a citizen of the Heavenly Kingdom you are no longer a stranger or a foreigner to God. You are now a fellowcitizen of the household of God with the saints. That is what you can see from Ephesians 2:19 as written below.

> *Now therefore ye are no more strangers and foreigners, but fellowcitizens with the saints, and of the household of God;*
> **Ephesians 2:19**

You are not only a fellowcitizen; you are now a beloved of the Lord. We can see this from what is written by John in 1 John 4:11. You are one of those citizens that God is talking about here. As a beloved of the Lord therefore, from what is written in Deuteronomy 33:12 He has said that you will dwell in safety. Nothing can harm you. Definitely if an affliction is tormenting you and putting your life in danger it cannot be said of you that you are dwelling in safety. Therefore no affliction can harm you.

> *Beloved, if God so loved us, we ought also to love one another.*
> **1 John 4:11**

> *And of Benjamin he said, The beloved of the LORD shall dwell in safety by him; and the LORD shall cover him all the day long, and he shall dwell between his shoulders.*
> **Deuteronomy 33:12**

Tormented by afflictions?

You should be confident and know that you are safe. You don't have to be tormented by any affliction if you know your rights as a born-again Christian and God's promises to you as a beloved of the Lord. You can always hold God to His Words because His Words never fails. Whatever He says that He will do He will surely do because His Word cannot be broken.

YOU ARE A LIGHT IN THIS WORLD

Every citizen of this Heavenly Kingdom where you now belong is supposed to be a light in this world and he is supposed to be shining. That is what Jesus Himself said in Matthew 5:14. Definitely you cannot be under the torment of any affliction and be said to be shining. Therefore have the mindset that afflictions cannot torment you. When Jesus, the first begotten of that Kingdom came to this world, He was the light of the world as long as He was around. That is what He said in John 9:5. But now that He has left the world every person born into that Heavenly Kingdom living here on earth becomes a light to this world. You are a light and you are supposed to be shining. This should be your mindset.

> *Ye are the light of the world. A city that is set on an hill cannot be hid.*
> **Matthew 5:14**

> *As long as I am in the world, I am the light of the world.*
> **John 9:5**

Living a supernatural life (Volume 3)
YOU ARE SUPPOSED TO BE SHINING

As a light in this world you are supposed to shine. You are supposed to shine so much that people will glorify God for your sake. Obviously you cannot be shining if you have an affliction bugging you and people will definitely not glorify God for that therefore God does not expect any affliction to suppress your shining. You are set to shine.

Wherever you are all forces of darkness must bow because you are now light and darkness cannot stand before light. Any affliction that is not allowing you to shine is exalting itself against the knowledge of the Word of God that says that you are supposed to be light and you are supposed to be shining. Such an affliction is disobeying the Word of God and as written by Paul in 2 Corinthians 10:4-6, you can bring it into subjection to submit to the Word of God.

> *For the weapons of our warfare are not carnal, but mighty through God to the pulling down of strong holds;*
>
> *Casting down imaginations, and every high thing that exalteth itself against the knowledge of God, and bringing into captivity every thought to the obedience of Christ;*
>
> *And having in a readiness to revenge all disobedience, when your obedience is fulfilled.*
> **2 Corinthians 10:4-6**

Tormented by afflictions?
YOU ARE TO SHINE MORE AND MORE

In fact because you have been justified as is written by Paul in 1 Corinthians 6:11 you are now **the just** therefore as the just you are not only supposed to shine, your path is supposed to be shining more and more everyday unto the perfect day. That is what is written in Proverbs 4:18. What this means is that you must shine today more than you shone yesterday and you will shine tomorrow more than you are shining today. You are supposed to be shining increasingly every day of your life. How can you say that a person being tormented by an affliction is shining? If you are being tormented by an affliction that can be considered a reproach it cannot be said that you are shining. Get this picture in your mind and you will be able to repel all afflictions

> *And such were some of you: but ye are washed, but ye are sanctified, but ye are justified in the name of the Lord Jesus, and by the Spirit of our God.*
> **1 Corinthians 6:11**

> *But the path of the just is as the shining light, that shineth more and more unto the perfect day.*
> **Proverbs 4:18**

YOU HAVE THE POWER OF GOD

If you are not convinced yet that no affliction can torment you let me give you another dimension to the spirit being that you now are.

Living a supernatural life (Volume 3)

It is that you should know that now that you are born of God your ways can no longer be discerned by any enemy. That is the essence of what Jesus is telling us as written by Apostle John in John 3:8. It is obvious therefore from this verse that you should no longer be an easy prey for any affliction. Afflictions will come and if you do not know your rights they will want to stay glued to you. As a born-again Christian who knows his rights and authority however, no affliction can stay put to your body or to your life because you now have **the great exceeding power of God** available to you. That is what the Scriptures say in Ephesians 1:19, which is written below.

> *The wind bloweth where it listeth, and thou hearest the sound thereof, but canst not tell whence it cometh, and whither it goeth: so is every one that is born of the Spirit.*
> **John 3:8**

> *And what is the exceeding greatness of his power to us-ward who believe, according to the working of his mighty power,*
> **Ephesians 1:19**

That great exceeding power of God is now living in you because Jesus Christ who is the power of God as we are told by Paul the Apostle in 1 Corinthians 1:24 is now living in you.

> *But unto them which are called, both Jews and Greeks, Christ the power of God, and the wisdom of God.*
> **1 Corinthians 1:24**

That is what the Scriptures say in John 14:23. In fact it is the power of God that is now working in you.

> *Jesus answered and said unto him, If a man love me, he will keep my words: and my Father will love him, and we will come unto him, and make our abode with him.*
> **John 14:23**

YOU NOW HAVE GOD WORKING IN YOU

Now Jesus Christ who is the power of God that is now living in you is the One working in you. That is what we are made to understand by what God said through Paul in Philippians 2:13.

> *For it is God which worketh in you both to will and to do of his good pleasure.*
> **Philippians 2:13**

It is obvious therefore that you don't have to face any affliction with your own strength. You don't have to be tormented by any affliction. With the power of God that is now working in you it is possible for God to do exceeding and abundantly above all that you can ask of Him or even think. That is what God made us to understand through Apostle Paul as written in Ephesians 3:20, which is written below. If God can do above what you can ask or even think how can you still have any apprehension about any affliction tormenting you? You can definitely leave all your afflictions for God to handle.

Now unto him that is able to do exceeding abundantly above all that we ask or think, according to the power that worketh in us,
                                         Ephesians 3:20

There is no affliction that you can come across that God cannot handle. After all God has made a Covenant with you that covers your protection, your health, your fruitfulness, your deliverance from all the snares of the enemy. It also guarantees your victory over the enemy in every encounter with the enemy. Your success in everything that you lay your hand upon and your prosperity in life are also guaranteed.

YOU HAVE POWER ABOVE YOUR ENEMIES

God has said that He has given you power above that of your enemies and that includes any enemy that you can come across in any situation that you may find yourself. That is what Jesus Himself told us in Luke 10:19. Therefore have the mindset that you have power over and above whatever power your enemy can demonstrate. But any affliction that comes your way is an enemy and must be treated that way.

Behold, I give unto you power to tread on serpents and scorpions, and over all the power of the enemy: and nothing shall by any means hurt you.
                                         Luke 10:19

Tormented by afflictions?

If the power that you have now been given as a citizen of the Heavenly Kingdom is far above all the powers of your enemies it follows that the power that you now have is far above any power that any affliction can demonstrate. Therefore you don't have to worry yourself about any affliction that may attempt to torment you. You have the power to deal with it. Nothing can hurt you anymore that you cannot subdue. You don't need to worry yourself about any affliction. Even if the affliction originates from a devil you have the power to cast the devil out.

YOU HAVE THE POWER TO CAST OUT DEVILS

You have now been given unlimited power in God. Nothing is impossible to you anymore. That is what God made us to see in Mark 9:23. You have and can exercise power over all devils. That is what God said through Luke in Luke 9:1. Even if the affliction originates from a demon or is a demonic oppression you still have nothing to worry about because you have also been given the power to deal with demons. You have been given the power to cast out demons. That is what we are told in Matthew 10:1.

> *Jesus said unto him, If thou canst believe, all things are possible to him that believeth.*
> **Mark 9:23**

> *Then he called his twelve disciples together, and gave them power and authority over all devils, and to cure diseases.*
> **Luke 9:1**

Living a supernatural life (Volume 3)

And when he had called unto him his twelve disciples, he gave them power against unclean spirits, to cast them out, and to heal all manner of sickness and all manner of disease.
Matthew 10:1

Therefore if you come across any affliction that has a demonic origin or is demon-powered you have the capacity to cast out whatever demon is behind such an affliction. What you need to do is to learn how to control this power that you now have. Because you believed and became a citizen of this Heavenly Kingdom you have been given the power to cast out devils and to control the elements. That is basically what Jesus Himself said in Mark 16:17.

And these signs shall follow them that believe; In my name shall they cast out devils; they shall speak with new tongues;
Mark 16:17

Therefore whatever the affliction may be, it can no longer be a problem to you. You have power over it. Whether it is demonic or not you are in control. If it is demon-controlled you can cast out the demons behind it using the Name of Jesus.

Whatever devils may be behind it you can cast them out in the Name of Jesus. How to use the Name of Jesus to cast out demons and do the works that Jesus did has been thoroughly explained and covered in the ***Volume 2*** of this *"Living a supernatural life"* book series written by the same author.

Tormented by afflictions?

For you as a Christian demonic oppression should no longer be a problem because you have been given the power to cast out demons in the Name of Jesus. They should no longer be in any position to torment you. If you are having problems that are demonic in nature or origin you will do well to read the *Volume 2* of this *"Living a Supernatural Life"* book series.

YOU HAVE THE WEAPONS TO FIGHT WITH

To help you to deal with any attack of the enemy or any affliction using the power that you have now been given you have also been given the weapons with which to invoke this power to fight the enemy. These weapons that you have been given are not carnal but they are mighty through God and can be used to pull down the strong holds of the enemy.

The weapons can be used to cast down every imagination or high thing that exalts itself against the knowledge of what the Word of God says about you. With the weapons you can even bring into captivity every thought that opposes what the Word of God says about you and force them to obey what the Word of God says. That is what God made us to see by what He said through Apostle Paul in 2 Corinthians 10:4-6 as we have seen earlier.

> *For the weapons of our warfare are not carnal, but mighty through God to the pulling down of strong holds;*

> *Casting down imaginations, and every high thing that exalteth itself against the knowledge of God, and bringing into captivity every thought to the obedience of Christ;*
>
> *And having in a readiness to revenge all disobedience, when your obedience is fulfilled.*
>
> **2 Corinthians 10:4-6**

These weapons and how you can use them to pull down the strong holds of the enemy are discussed in ***Volume 2*** of this ***"Living a supernatural life"*** book series written by the same author. With such awesome power and such weapons at your disposal how can you be afraid of any affliction? How can you be tormented by any affliction? The only reason why that will happen is if you are ignorant of the weapons and power that are now available to you or if you are not walking or living by faith because you can only invoke this power by faith.

YOU ARE TO WALK BY FAITH

In this Heavenly Kingdom that you now are a citizen of, its citizens are supposed to walk by faith and live by faith. That is a decree not a choice. It is a directive as written in 2 Corinthians 5:7 and Hebrews 10:38. Faith is the engine that drives the economy of that Kingdom. Without faith there is hardly anything you can get from that Kingdom. Without faith you will just be an onlooker in that Kingdom. Your faith properly focused and directed is what will get you from that Kingdom the things that you need to excel and live above all afflictions here on earth.

Tormented by afflictions?

For we walk by faith, not by sight
2 Corinthian 5:7

Now the just shall live by faith: but if any man draw back, my soul shall have no pleasure in him.
Hebrews 10:38

YOU CAN COMMAND ANY AFFLICTION

Why should you be worried of any affliction? After all we have shown in *Volume 1* of this *"Living a Supernatural Life"* book series that you can curse afflictions and diseases and you can command them. We even showed that most afflictions have spirits behind them and therefore when you command them you are actually commanding the spirits behind them. As long as you walk by faith and live by faith you can command any mountain before you and ask it to move, whether it is a mountain of affliction or any other thing and it must move when you command it to move.

That is what Jesus said as written in Matthew 17:20. You therefore have every right to command that affliction that is tormenting you and tell it to move away from you. But if you refuse to command it your struggle with it will continue. How can you have such authority and power at your disposal and still be tormented by any affliction?

Living a supernatural life (Volume 3)

> *And Jesus said unto them, Because of your unbelief: for verily I say unto you, If ye have faith as a grain of mustard seed, ye shall say unto this mountain, Remove hence to yonder place; and it shall remove; and nothing shall be impossible unto you.*
>
> **Matthew 17:20**

Nothing is impossible for you anymore if you keep to the rule of the Kingdom to walk by faith and live by faith as we are directed to do in the two verses from Paul previously written on page 628, 2 Corinthians 5:7 and Hebrews 10:38. Once you live and walk by faith whatever you command must obey your instructions. Nothing can resist whatever command you give. That is how powerful you are now. Have this mindset.

YOU HAVE A MOUTH AND WISDOM

To help you to establish your authority as a citizen of that Kingdom so that whatever you command will obey you, you are given a mouth and wisdom, which no adversary can resist or gainsay. That is the promise of Jesus to you in Luke 21:15.

> *For I will give you a mouth and wisdom, which all your adversaries shall not be able to gainsay nor resist.*
>
> **Luke 21:15**

What this means is that with the mouth and the wisdom that you have now been given, if you command any thing that stands as a mountain in your life, it cannot resist your command. It must obey you.

Tormented by afflictions?

If it doesn't obey you then it means that you did not give your command in faith believing that you must be obeyed. If you have that kind of mouth and wisdom how can you be tormented by any affliction? If you are it means that you don't really know the power that is available to you with which you can deal with such an affliction. It may also be that you don't know how to use the power.

There is so much power available to you now as a new Covenant saint so much so that no affliction should be able to torment you anymore. In any case you should realize and have the mental attitude that whatever affliction comes your way it is allowed because God knows that you are quite capable of dealing with it. You should also have it in your mind that should you be finding it difficult to cope with it, God has already prepared a way of escape for you. That is what we are made to understand by what God said through Apostle Paul in 1 Corinthians 10:13, which is shown below.

> *There hath no temptation taken you but such as is common to man: but God is faithful, who will not suffer you to be tempted above that ye are able; but will with the temptation also make a way to escape, that ye may be able to bear it.*
> **1 Corinthians 10:13**

Therefore afflictions should not be able to torment you because you know that whatever affliction you may be going through you are quite capable of coping with it.

Living a supernatural life (Volume 3)

As a matter of fact where an affliction is weighing you down you even have the power to demand from God that angels be sent to help you. That is what I want to show you in the following section.

ANGELS CAN BE DISPATCHED TO HELP YOU

Do you know that as a citizen of this Heavenly Kingdom whenever you feel that the battle being waged against you is hot, very intensive and you feel that you cannot cope with it on your own you have the right to send to your heavenly Father and ask Him to dispatch more than twelve legions of angels (that is seventy two thousand angels) to come to your aid? Jesus said that He could do that in Matthew 26:53 and since He said in John 20:21 that He was sending you just as the Father hath sent Him it means that whatever support He had when He came you too can now have. That is the essence of what Jesus was saying in that verse. Therefore you too can call on the Father to send you more than twelve legions of angels (72 thousands) if the need arises.

> *Thinkest thou that I cannot now pray to my Father, and he shall presently give me more than twelve legions of angels?*
> **Matthew 26:53**

> *Then said Jesus to them again, Peace be unto you: as my Father hath sent me, even so send I you.*
> **John 20:21**

Tormented by afflictions?

Angels are invisible beings that are extremely powerful so much so that I can make bold to tell you that whatever problem you maybe having just one angel will be enough to solve the problem. We are told in the Scriptures of one angel that killed one hundred and eighty five thousand people in the camp of the Assyrian army when they came against Israel. That is what we are made to understand from 2 Kings 19:35 which is written below.

> *And it came to pass that night, that the angel of the LORD went out, and smote in the camp of the Assyrians an hundred fourscore and five thousand: and when they arose early in the morning, behold, they were all dead corpses.*
> **2 Kings 19:35**

Surely knowing that one angel is capable of killing one hundred and eighty five thousand soldiers, I doubt if you will ever come across any affliction or situation that will require as many as twelve legions of angels to deal with it and subdue it. However their services are available to you should you ever need them because they are supposed to be ministering spirits that are available to cater for your needs whenever such needs arise since you are now an heir of God through your salvation? That is what we can understand by what is written in Hebrews 1:13-14. What a comfort and an assurance that is to you?

> *But to which of the angels said he at any times, Sit on my right hand, until I make thine enemies thy footstool?*

> *Are they not all ministering spirits, sent forth to minister for them who shall be heirs of salvation?*
>
> **Hebrews 1:13-14**

How can you have access to such awesome power and still be tormented by any affliction? It is obvious that if you know your rights and use what you have available to you no affliction can be in any position to torment you. In fact, I can tell you that the more severe your affliction the easier for you.

THE MORE SEVERE THE BETTER

Let's suppose that the affliction is so hot that you are even being flooded from all directions by the enemy. I tell you even that should not be of much concern to you. This is so because the spirit that now lives in you, who Himself is God, takes over the fight at that point. That is true because it is when the enemies come in like a flood that this Spirit will raise up a standard against them. That is what God told us through Prophet Isaiah in Isaiah 59:19 as written below.

> *So shall they fear the name of the LORD from the west, and his glory from the rising of the sun. When the enemy shall come in like a flood, the Spirit of the LORD shall lift up a standard against him.*
>
> **Isaiah 59:19**

Therefore as you can see, you really do not have to worry yourself about any affliction no matter its intensity.

Tormented by afflictions?

You cannot be tormented by any affliction if you know your rights as a Christian and a later day saint. Afflictions should not be your problem since you have been assured of victory over them.

In fact the hotter they come the better for you for it is then that you will see God's power that is now resident in you in its full manifestation as stated in the verse above. As a Christian you should realize that the enemy will contend with you all the good promises that God has made concerning you. The enemy will like to convince you that those promises cannot be true just like he did to Eve and Adam. But no matter what the enemy may bring if you stay in-Christ where you are supposed to be you are already designated as the winner even before the fight starts. God has declared you not only a conqueror but even more than a conqueror in the struggle against the enemy.

YOU HAVE ALREADY WON THE BATTLE

Do you not know that your victory is already certain even before the fight with any affliction starts? God has declared you the winner in any fight or struggle that you can ever be involved in. You must therefore have the winner mentality because you know that no matter what the affliction is, no matter its intensity you have already won against it because the power of the One that now lives in you is greater than the power of any affliction that you can ever come across in this world. That is what God said through John in 1 John 4:4 and also in 1 John 5:4-5.

> *Ye are of God, little children, and have overcome them: because greater is he that is in you, than he that is in the world.*
> **1 John 4:4**

> *For whatsoever is born of God overcometh the world: and this is the victory that overcometh the world, even our faith.*

> *Who is he that overcometh the world, but he that believeth that Jesus is the Son of God?*
> **1 John 5:4-5**

Therefore you cannot be tormented by any affliction. If any affliction is tormenting you it must mean that you are not making use of the power that is now resident inside you because if you are no affliction will be able to overcome you. **You must have the greater-One mentality** and see yourself in an impregnable position where the enemy cannot hold sway.

God said that you have already overcome through your faith so if you ever loose any battle against any affliction, it is because you have refused to stand in faith refusing to believe in the power that is now living inside you. In the Kingdom of God to which you now belong you are entitled to divine health, healing, divine prosperity, victory, absolute and fail-proof protection, fruitfulness and good success etc. All such afflictions as sicknesses, lack, poverty, defeat, failure and barrenness etc. have no place in that Kingdom.

Tormented by afflictions?

You are completely and permanently insulated and separated from them if you stay IN CHRIST where you are supposed to be and you make use of the power of God that is now resident in you. Therefore you can see that you need not exercise fear or anxiety because of any affliction that may come your way. When you exhibit fear or anxiety about any affliction you are giving the affliction the permission to torment you because what the Scriptures made us to understand in Job 3:25 is that whatever you fear will come upon you and whatever you are afraid of will come unto you. Remember also that when you fear it means that you are not operating in faith.

> *For the thing which I greatly feared is come upon me, and that which I was afraid of is come unto me.*
> **Job 3:25**

No affliction can torment you where you are if you live your life by the rule of your Kingdom, which is by faith. Therefore relax! Get a true Scriptural perspective or image of yourself, imbibe that image, then your struggles with afflictions will end and your worries will be over. Do you remember the story of the prodigal son that Jesus narrated in Luke 15:11-20? It was when the prodigal son *came to himself* and got a true image of himself that his situation changed. Please read the story below.

> *And he said, A certain man had two sons:*

Living a supernatural life (Volume 3)

And the younger of them said to his father, Father, give me the portion of goods that falleth to me. And he divided unto them his living.

And not many days after the younger son gathered all together, and took his journey into a far country, and there wasted his substance with riotous living.

And when he had spent all, there arose a mighty famine in that land; and he began to be in want.

And he went and joined himself to a citizen of that country; and he sent him into his fields to feed swine.

And he would fain have filled his belly with the husks that the swine did eat: and no man gave unto him.

And when he came to himself, he said, How many hired servants of my father's have bread enough and to spare, and I perish with hunger!

I will arise and go to my father, and will say unto him, Father, I have sinned against heaven, and before thee,

And am no more worthy to be called thy son: make me as one of thy hired servants.

Tormented by afflictions?

> *And he arose, and came to his father. But when he was yet a great way off, his father saw him, and had compassion, and ran, and fell on his neck, and kissed him.*
>
> **Luke 15:11-20**

When you get the true Scriptural image of your position in Christ compared to the affliction that you are going through you will also *come to yourself* and your situation will change. You will then realize that you are in an unassailable position.

YOU ARE MORE THAN A CONQUEROR

It is not only that you have won against any affliction that may come your way but you are actually declared to be more than a conqueror. You should not feel tormented by any affliction because with God for you nothing can defeat you anymore. If God be for you nobody can be against you and win unless you allow him either through your ignorance of the power that is now available to you or through your carelessness. That is the essence of what God is telling us in Romans 8:31. How then can any affliction torment you? You are just too much now for any enemy to handle. You are now more than a conqueror. That is what we are told in Romans 8:37.

> *What shall we then say to these things? If God be for us, who can be against us?*
>
> **Romans 8:31**

> *Nay, in all these things we are more than conquerors through him that loved us.*
>
> **Romans 8:37**

That you are more than a conqueror means that you have not only conquered whatever is afflicting you but you have gone beyond the conquering stage into the celebrating stage. You are supposed to be celebrating and demonstrating your victory over all afflictions. That is why God said that you have already overcome them in 1 John 4:4 because no matter how great the affliction that you are going through the power that you now have living in you is much greater than the affliction. If you can only know the power that is now residing in you your problems will be over.

> *Ye are of God, little children, and have overcome them: because greater is he that is in you, than he that is in the world.*
>
> **1 John 4:4**

Get this picture of the power in you because with the power now living inside you even death cannot win against you.

EVEN DEATH CANNOT WIN AGAINST YOU

In **Volume 1** of this *"Living a supernatural life"* book series we showed that the power of death is no longer with Satan. Therefore even if the affliction that you are going through is threatening death you have nothing to fear.

Tormented by afflictions?

This is so because in the Kingdom to which you now belong death has no power over its citizens if they know their rights. Yes! The power of hell and death ***used to be with Satan*** as we are told in Hebrews 2:14 because he had it. But the power of hell and death, which used to belong to the devil, has been taken away from him by the firstborn and first begotten Son of the Kingdom to which you now belong, Jesus Christ. So Satan no longer has it. Christ has defeated the devil and taken the keys of hell and death from him. Jesus Christ now has the keys of hell and death. That is what Jesus Himself said in Revelation 1:18. So the devil cannot frighten you with death any longer. In fact you are the one with the trump card now since the Holy Spirit is living in you.

> *Forasmuch then as the children are partakers of flesh and blood, he also himself likewise took part of the same; that through death he might destroy him that had the power of death, that is, the devil;*
> **Hebrews 2:14**

> *I am he that liveth, and was dead; and, behold, I am alive for evermore, Amen; and have the keys of hell and of death.*
> **Revelation 1:18**

Jesus now has the keys of hell and death therefore Satan and his cohorts cannot threaten the citizens of the Heavenly Kingdom to which you now belong with death because death no longer has any power over them.

When you know that even death cannot win against you how can you be afraid of any other affliction? After all the worst that any affliction can bring is death. Whatever torments any affliction may be threatening to bring to you can be put under control and bound by you. This is so because you have been delivered from all oppressions of the enemy. Therefore relax your mind and set your mind on God.

YOU HAVE BEEN DELIVERED FROM ALL OPPRESSIONS

You have to realize that now that you have been translated into this Kingdom of God's dear Son and have become a citizen of that Kingdom, you have also been totally and absolutely delivered from the kingdom of darkness and from all its weapons and tools of oppression. That is what God made us to see from what He said in Colossians 1:13 through Apostle Paul. They may oppress you but they have no power over you.

> *Who hath delivered us from the power of darkness, and hath translated us into the Kingdom of his dear Son:*
> **Colossians 1:13**

In the Kingdom where you are now, no adversary can attack you and defeat you if you keep yourself where you are supposed to be in-Christ. No affliction or oppression from the kingdom of darkness can harm you anymore. This is because in this Kingdom of God to which you belong,

Tormented by afflictions?

God has already declared you the winner in every battle that you will have to face even before the battle starts. All you have to do is just tackle them with faith and you are sure to end up the winner. God has given you power and authority over every adversary that you can come across. God did not say that adversaries will not come against you but what God said is that when they do come He has provided you with the necessary weapons with which to deal with them.

YOU HAVE THE KEYS OF THE KINGDOM OF HEAVEN

Some of the weapons that God has given you to help you combat any situation that may arise and put it under control are the keys of the Kingdom of Heaven. When you became a citizen of the Heavenly Kingdom, you also became a member of the Body of Christ to whom the keys of the Kingdom of Heaven has now been made available. With these keys whatever you bind on earth God will bind in Heaven and whatever you loose on earth God will loose in Heaven. That is the promise that Jesus gave us in Matthew 16:19. In that promise He said, *"whatsoever* you bind or loose" and that covers everything. You can bind and loose anything.

> *And I will give unto thee the keys of the Kingdom of Heaven: and whatsoever thou shalt bind on earth shall be bound in heaven: and whatsoever thou shalt loose on earth shall be loosed in heaven.*
> **Matthew 16:19**

Living a supernatural life (Volume 3)

So you now have access to these keys of the Kingdom of Heaven. These keys include among others the Word of God, the Name of Jesus and the Blood of Jesus. These are powerful keys with which you can lock and unlock any situation. Once you have the keys you can use them to bind anything here on earth and it will be bound in Heaven. You can also use them to loose anything here on earth and it will be loosed in Heaven. Note that the power to bind and loose anything here on earth is now with you not in Heaven.

You start the loosing and the binding process here on earth then Heaven will seal it. As a citizen of Heaven here on earth, the power and the authority to do these have now been delegated to you. Heaven will only permit whatever you permit here on earth. Since whatever you bind or loose here on earth will be bound or loosed in Heaven it is obvious therefore that you have the power to effect changes also in the spiritual realm from right here on earth. So your power and authority is not limited to this physical realm.

Therefore as you can see, you have the power to bind any force that is bringing affliction into your life. Even if it is a demonic power that you cannot see physically you also have the power to bind it. You have such an awesome power available to you. In fact it is very difficult to fathom or comprehend how awesome the power that is now available to the born-again Christian. Once you invoke that power, Heaven will confirm it. How can you have such power and authority and still be afraid of any affliction?

How can you have such power and authority and still have any affliction tormenting you? Do you not know that once you become a member of that Kingdom of God your life is hidden with Christ in God?

YOUR LIFE IS HID WITH CHRIST IN GOD

You ought to realize that as a citizen of the Heavenly Kingdom, your life is now hidden with Christ in God. That is what we are made to understand by what is written in Colossians 3:3.

> *For ye are dead, and your life is hid with Christ in God.*
> **Colossians 3:3**

You are now secured in Christ and Christ is secured in the Father. Therefore nothing evil can touch you and stick to you anymore unless you permit it. You are now insulated from all evils. Whatever wants to touch you now must first pass God and then pass Christ before it gets to you. Since no evil can pass God, it means that no evil can get to you and stick to you if you stay where you are supposed to be – **IN CHRIST** and you do not break the hedge of God's security around you. With this level of security provided for you how can you still believe that any affliction can torment you? If any affliction is tormenting you it must mean that you do not really know your true position now in Christ or you are not operating by the rule of your Kingdom, faith.. You are far above all afflictions. That should be your mental attitude to any affliction.

Living a supernatural life (Volume 3)

YOU ARE FAR ABOVE ANY AFFLICTION

You are far above any affliction because you have been raised up together with Christ in the spirit realm and you are now seating together with Christ in the Heavenly places on the right side of God. Even though this is a mystery, it is true. That is what the Bible says in Ephesians 2:6. You are now seating together with Christ Jesus. But in Ephesians 1:19-23 we are told that where Jesus Christ is now seating, He is far above all principality and power and might and dominion and every name that is named not only in this world but in the world to come and all things have been put under His feet and that is where you are now. Can you not see where you are now?

And hath raised us up together, and made us sit together in heavenly places in Christ Jesus:
Ephesians 2:6

And what is the exceeding greatness of his power to us-ward who believe, according to the working of his mighty power,

Which he wrought in Christ, when he raised him from the dead, and set him at his own right hand in the heavenly places,

Far above all principality, and power, and might, and dominion, and every name that is named, not only in this world, but also in that which is to come:

Tormented by afflictions?

And hath put all things under his feet, and gave him to be the head over all things to the church,

Which is his body, the fulness of him that filleth all in all.
Ephesians 1:19-23

Because you are now seating with Christ you are also far above all principality and power and might and dominion and anything that has a name. Everything is now under your feet. Doesn't that affliction that is disturbing you have a name? If it does you are far above it. Even if where you are in Christ is the sole of His feet you are still above everything. Everything is now under your feet because God has put them under the feet of Christ and you are in Christ. So they are also under your feet. This should excite you. If you really believe that what the Scripture is saying is true then there can be no cause for you to worry about any affliction at all. Whatever God says is true whether you believe it or not. The problem that you will have if you don't believe it is that even though it is true it will not manifest in your own case. This is because you can only make it to manifest by using your faith. The Word of God cannot be broken. Whatever the Word says stands and nothing can change it. That is what Jesus told us in John 10:35 and also in Matthew 24:35. The Word of God cannot pass away.

If he called them gods, unto whom the word of God came, and the scripture cannot be broken;
John 10:35

Living a supernatural life (Volume 3)

> *Heaven and earth shall pass away, but my words shall not pass away.*
>
> **Matthew 24:35**

From all these you can see that you are far above diseases, poverty, failure, barrenness and all other afflictions. You are far above all the earthly oppressive mentalities that Satan is using as his tools. You are now from above therefore you are above all things in the earthly realm and that includes any affliction. That is what Jesus made us to see in John 3:31.

> *He that cometh from above is above all: he that is of the earth is earthly, and speaketh of the earth: he that cometh from heaven is above all.*
>
> **John 3:31**

Therefore no affliction can torment you if you know your rights. It may attack you but it cannot win against you. You are far above it if you stay where you are supposed to be **IN-CHRIST**. If any affliction is tormenting you it is because you are looking at symptoms and you are allowing them to dictate the confessions that come out of your mouth thereby hindering God's promises of victory over afflictions in your life.

If after all that we have discussed in this Chapter you still have any affliction tormenting you or any affliction that you are still afraid of then you need to read this Chapter over again to get a true Scriptural picture of yourself so that you can come to yourself.

Tormented by afflictions?

You need to *come to yourself* just like the prodigal son did in Luke 15:17 to realize who he really was. You also need to realize who you really are.

> *And when he came to himself, he said, How many hired servants of my father's have bread enough and to spare, and I perish with hunger!*
>
> **Luke 15:17**

Once you can get the right scriptural image of yourself you will know that affliction can no longer torment you. You will know that where you are now seating you are far above all afflictions and no affliction has power over you and therefore no matter what it does you will know that you will win in the end. ***Therefore you should no longer have any torment as a result of any affliction.***

Afflictions are meant to scare you but you are created to scare them. In the position that you are now no affliction should scare you. Actually you should be spoiling to have a showdown with Satan and his hosts everywhere. Wherever you see Satan showing or demonstrating his tricks and pretending to have power either directly or through his agents, you should immediately show your holy anger and command him to stop it.

Once you know your power over Satan you will be eager to go into a combat with him because you know that he will always lose the battle. He will fail and he will continue to fail as long as you are willing to fight him.

Living a supernatural life (Volume 3)

You must behave like David did whenever you come across Satan manifesting and demonstrating his fake power. When David met Goliath boasting he was annoyed and decided to put Goliath in his place. He showed Goliath that the One with him is far greater than whoever was with Goliath.

You must have a superiority complex. No satanic force or agent or even Satan himself should be boasting wherever you are. You should see yourself as superior to any satanic or demonic force. Wherever you are satanic forces there should be totally subdued. They should not be able to manifest.

CHAPTER 11

ARE YOU STRUGGLING WITH SIN?
YOU ARE SANCTIFIED

You cannot be struggling anymore with sin. Sin is the main problem that keeps Christians from living a fulfilled life in Christ. As long as there is sin in a Christian's life such a Christian cannot go to God to ask for anything and have the confidence that he has got it. As a born-again Christian God has given you righteousness as a gift so that you can live a righteous life. But that alone will not make you live a righteous life. Therefore to make sure that you can actually live a righteous life God has also sanctified you.

It is sanctification that gives you the power to turn God's gift of righteousness into the reality of living a righteous life. God said through Apostle Paul as written in 1 Corinthians 6:11 that once you accept Christ as your Saviour and get born-again, then you are washed, you are sanctified and you are justified in the Name of the Lord Jesus, and by the Spirit of God.

> *And such were some of you: but ye are washed, but ye are sanctified, but ye are justified in the name of the Lord Jesus, and by the Spirit of our God*
> **1 Corinthians 6:11**

God even made us to understand in 2 Thessalonians 2:13 through Apostle Paul that He chose to give you salvation through sanctification of the Spirit. Therefore your salvation is actually obtained through sanctification of the Spirit. That should show you just how important sanctification is in your life.

> *But we are bound to give thanks alway to God for you, brethren beloved of the Lord, because God hath from the beginning chosen you to salvation through sanctification of the Spirit and belief of the truth:*
> **2 Thessalonians 2:13**

WHAT DOES IT MEAN TO BE SANCTIFIED?

What does it mean to be sanctified? In order to really get the meaning of what God did by sanctifying you; we need to know what justification means. What happened was that God conferred the righteousness status on you when He justified you. God declared you righteous. It was only the status that justification confers. But before you can actually make that righteousness effective in your life you need to be empowered to live a righteous life.

Are you struggling with sin?

It is one thing to be declared righteous it is another thing to live a righteous life. Sanctification is what empowers you to do righteousness and live a righteous life. Therefore while justification confers the status of righteousness on you, sanctification is what actually empowers you to do righteousness and be righteous. God knows that having declared you righteous, you also need to be empowered to be able to do righteousness, and thus be righteous, so that your righteousness will not just be by declaration alone, but by your actions as well. It is for this purpose of empowering you that God has made sanctification available to you. It is sanctification that empowers you to be able to do righteousness. This is because obedience of the Word of God is only possible after your receiving the sanctification of the Spirit and the sprinkling of the Blood of Jesus Christ. That is what we can see in 1 Peter 1:2.

Elect according to the foreknowledge of God the Father, through sanctification of the Spirit, unto obedience and sprinkling of the blood of Jesus Christ: Grace unto you, and peace, be multiplied.
1 Peter 1:2

Once sanctified, every barrier to your obedience of the Word of God is removed because your conscience is cleansed to be able to reason in agreement with God's Word. Whatever is stopping you from living a sinless life is removed by your sanctification? Once sanctified, you can live a sinless, righteous life here on earth.

Living a supernatural life (Volume 3)

No force in hell can force you to sin anymore. This is because by sanctification, you are supernaturally and divinely enabled to live a sinless and righteous life. Sanctification empowers you to overcome every arrangement of hell to frustrate your living a righteous life because it purges your conscience.

With sanctification, your victory at all times against sin is guaranteed every time it comes. You now have the divine abilities of God to overcome sin and all its consequences, unless of course if you choose not to do so by agreeing to yield to it.

To sanctify means to separate and set apart. You should note however that the sanctification of the believer by God is a two-fold operation involving both the believer's vertical and horizontal relationships. On the one hand, in the believer's vertical relationship with God, by sanctification the believer is **set apart** by God and **separated for God's use**.

That is what God does when He needs to separate and set apart someone or something for His own use. He sanctifies that someone or something. He made us to know this through Moses in Numbers 8:17 and also through Prophet Jeremiah in Jeremiah 1:5.

> *For all the firstborn of the children of Israel are mine, both man and beast: on the day that I smote every firstborn in the land of Egypt I sanctified them for myself.*
> **Numbers 8:17**

> *Before I formed thee in the belly I knew thee; and before thou camest forth out of the womb I sanctified thee, and I ordained thee a prophet unto the nations.*
>
> **Jeremiah 1:5**

On the other hand, we can see that in the believer's horizontal relationship with sin, by sanctification the believer is **set apart** by God and **separated from sin**. That is what God told us through Paul the Apostle as written in 1 Thessalonians 4:3-7.

> *For this is the will of God, even your sanctification, that ye should abstain from fornication:*
>
> *That every one of you should know how to possess his vessel in sanctification and honour;*
>
> *Not in the lust of concupiscence, even as the Gentiles which know not God:*
>
> *That no man go beyond and defraud his brother in any matter: because that the Lord is the avenger of all such, as we also have forewarned you and testified.*
>
> *For God hath not called us unto uncleanness, but unto holiness.*
>
> **1 Thessalonians 4:3-7**

Living a supernatural life (Volume 3)

We are also told virtually the same thing as you can see in Hebrew 9:13-14, which is written below. Therefore as a believer in Christ by sanctification you are set apart and separated for God's use and also set apart and separated from sin.

> *For if the blood of bulls and of goats, and the ashes of an heifer sprinkling the unclean, sanctifieth to the purifying of the flesh:*
>
> *How much more shall the blood of Christ, who through the eternal Spirit offered himself without spot to God, purge your conscience from dead works to serve the living God?*
> **Hebrews 9:13-14**

By sanctification, what God does is to consecrate you, to purify you and set you apart as a vessel of honour. Once you are thus sanctified, grace and peace will be multiplied unto you to be able to obey God and do the work of righteousness. This is possible because when God sanctifies you by the blood of Jesus Christ, the blood actually purges your conscience of every evil work. That is what God said in Hebrews 9:14, which we have written above.

Indirectly it is your conscience that directs your will and therefore your actions. What sanctification does is that it gives you the right conscience to know what is good and what is bad. It also makes you to feel bad about doing what is bad, and to feel good about doing what is good. Once you have the right conscience, you can do that which is right all the time.

Are you struggling with sin?

It is your conscience that speaks to you and convicts you of any action that you want to take which is sinful. Once the Holy Spirit comes into your spirit to live there, your conscience will change in line with God's conscience. Your conscience is what bears witness to you as to whether what you want to do is right or wrong. That is what God said through Apostle Paul in Romans 2:15.

> *Which shew the work of the law written in their hearts, their conscience also bearing witness, and their thoughts the mean while accusing or else excusing one another;*
> **Romans 2:15**

The Holy Spirit will not force His own conscience on you. You will have to accept the Holy Spirit's conscience freely into your spirit. He is there to tell you when you are doing any wrong thing but He will not force you to do what is good.

IT GIVES YOU POWER OVER SIN

Sanctification gives you power over sin and therefore power over all the consequences of sin. Without the sanctification by the Blood of Jesus, you have no power over sin. It is the Blood that cleanses you from all sins and it also gives you power over sin. That is what God said through Apostle John in 1 John 1:7. It is the Blood that purges your conscience of sin.

Living a supernatural life (Volume 3)

> *But if we walk in the light, as he is in the light, we have fellowship one with another, and the blood of Jesus Christ his Son cleanseth us from all sin.*
>
> **1 John 1:7**

When you want to do the will of God, Satan, the enemy is always there to oppose you. You can only defeat Satan by the word of your testimony and by the Blood. You need a combination of both. Your will alone cannot win against Satan. You know that many times you have struggled to overcome the sin nature but it has been difficult. Such things as lies, envy and anger are things many Christians do without even considering that they are not to be seen in a Christian. They do them before they can even think. You need to be sanctified by God through the Blood of Jesus Christ in order to be empowered to live a sinless and obedient life. You need both the word of your testimony and the Blood to overcome Satan. That is what God told us through John in Revelation 12:11.

> *And they overcame him by the blood of the Lamb, and by the word of their testimony; and they loved not their lives unto the death.*
>
> **Revelation 12:11**

Do you remember what Paul said in Romans 7:15? He said that those things that he hates are the things that he sometimes does. Note therefore that on your own and by your will alone you cannot win against sin. Even though you have crucified the natural man he will still want to prove that he is still alive.

Are you struggling with sin?

For that which I do I allow not: for what I would, that do I not; but what I hate, that do I.
Romans 7:15

You need to be sanctified by God through the Blood of Jesus Christ if you must win against sin and be empowered to live a sinless life. Remember what Jesus Christ also said when He was talking about temptation to His disciples to show them just how weak they were against temptation in Matthew 26:41? He said,

"Watch and pray, that ye enter not into temptation: the spirit indeed is willing, but the flesh is weak."
Matthew 26:41

He said that even where your spirit is willing to live a pious life the flesh is weak. The flesh will always let you down. That is why God made sure that your sanctification covers your spirit, your soul and your body. Therefore you need to be sanctified wholly, spirit, soul and body, so that you can live above sin. You can see that your sanctification should cover all the three component parts that you are made of from what God told us through Paul in 1 Thessalonians 5:23.

And the very God of peace sanctify you wholly; and I pray God your whole spirit and soul and body be preserved blameless unto the coming of our Lord Jesus Christ.
1 Thessalonians 5:23

Living a supernatural life (Volume 3)

You need to appropriate your justification by the Blood through faith to be able to have the righteous consciousness. You also need faith to appropriate your sanctification by the Blood to be able to live a sin-free life. Once you have faith in the truth that you have been sanctified and empowered to live a sin-free life you will believe that you now have power over sin and sin will therefore no longer have dominion over you.

Remember that it is as you think in your heart that you will be. That is what we are made to see as written in Proverbs 23:7. It is only through faith that you can appropriate the sanctification that God has given you. That is what God made us to understand through Luke in Acts 26:18.

> *For as he thinketh in his heart, so is he: Eat and drink, saith he to thee; but his heart is not with thee.*
> **Proverbs 23:7**

> *To open their eyes, and to turn them from darkness to light, and from the power of Satan unto God, that they may receive forgiveness of sins, and inheritance among them which are sanctified by faith that is in me.*
> **Acts 26:18**

YOU NEED THE WORD AND THE BLOOD

You need both the Word and the Blood to overcome. That is what we have seen earlier in Revelation 12:11.

Are you struggling with sin?

And they overcame him by the blood of the Lamb, and by the word of their testimony; and they loved not their lives unto the death.
Revelation 12:11

With the Word, you are told what you ought to do, and what you ought not to do. With the Blood, you are empowered to do what you ought to do, and empowered to stay clear of what you ought not to do.

As we have said earlier by sanctification, what God does is to consecrate you, to purify you and set you apart as a vessel of honour thereby empowering you to be able to do righteousness. Sanctification is a moral and spiritual transformation that allows or empowers you to do righteousness. Without sanctification, you will find it difficult on your own and under your own power to do the works of righteousness.

It is sanctification that equips you morally to be able to do righteousness. Justification and sanctification have been described in the following way by some. They say, "With justification, God provided you with the route to righteousness, but with sanctification, He provided you with the vehicle to take you there through that route."

In fact you are justified to be righteous and sanctified to make the possibility of your justification and your righteousness sure. It is so that born-again Christians will have power over sin and therefore the possibility to live pious lives that God has decided to sanctify them.

Living a supernatural life (Volume 3)

As you read and meditate more on the Word of God and bring your life more in line with the Word you will begin to see those aspects of your life that are not in agreement with the Word and you will start to separate yourself from such things. As we have noted earlier in what Paul wrote in 1 Thessalonians 5:23, sanctification covers your whole self, *(spirit, soul and body)* not just your body.

> *And the very God of peace sanctify you wholly; and I pray God your whole spirit and soul and body be preserved blameless unto the coming of our Lord Jesus Christ.*
> **1 Thessalonians 5:23**

Once you are sanctified, you are preserved blameless unto the coming of our Lord Jesus Christ. Without sanctification you cannot be admitted into the family of God. Once you are sanctified, you become one with Him, and you can be counted among the brethren of Jesus Christ. You then become a member of the family of God, and Jesus Christ becomes your brother. That is what God told us in Hebrews 2:11.

> *For both he that sanctifieth and they who are sanctified are all of one: for which cause he is not ashamed to call them brethren,*
> **Hebrews 2:11**

He also said as we have noted earlier in Jude 1:1 that once you are sanctified, then you are preserved in Jesus Christ. It is then that the operation that puts you in Christ becomes a reality in your life.

> *Jude, the servant of Jesus Christ, and brother of James, to them that are sanctified by God the Father, and preserved in Jesus Christ, and called:*
> **Jude 1:1**

It is the sanctification that makes it possible for you to become one with Christ. It is sanctification that gives you the opportunity to have a spiritual union with Christ. Sanctification is very important to you as a believer in Christ because without sanctification you cannot see the Lord. This is so because it is sanctification that allows you to live a holy life. Without holiness, you cannot see the Lord. That is what we are told in Hebrews 12:14.

> *Follow peace with all men, and holiness, without which no man shall see the Lord:*
> **Hebrews 12:14**

There is something interesting about sanctification that I want you to note here. It is this truth that when God sanctifies anything, He puts His Name on that thing forever and His eyes and His heart are perpetually set on that thing. That is the essence of what God told us in 2 Chronicles 7:16.

> *For now have I chosen and sanctified this house, that my name may be there for ever: and mine eyes and mine heart shall be there perpetually.*
> **2 Chronicles 7:16**

Living a supernatural life (Volume 3)

Therefore you are now stamped with God's Name forever and God's eyes and heart are now perpetually set on you. Now think about this! With God's eyes and heart perpetually set on you, there should be no cause for you to make sinning a habit. Knowing this truth should restrain you from sin.

Before you can live the life of righteousness, that is to live above sin, you need to be sanctified by God. It is the sanctification that empowers you to be able to live a pious life. Even Jesus Christ, before the Father sent him into the world, was sanctified. That is what Jesus Himself told us as written down by John in John 10:36.

> *Say ye of him, whom the Father hath sanctified, and sent into the world, Thou blasphemest; because I said, I am the Son of God?*
> **John 10:36**

It was that sanctification which He had that empowered Him to live the righteous sinless life that He lived while here on earth. Jesus did not need to be sanctified before coming into the world, because He is God.

But He came to be an example to us, to show us the way to God, and how to live a righteous sinless life. He sanctified Himself for our sake, so that we too may be sanctified. That is what He Himself said in John 17:19.

> *And for their sakes I sanctify myself, that they also might be sanctified through the truth.*
> **John 17:19**

Are you struggling with sin?

You need to be sanctified if you are to live a successful Christ-like life here on earth. Your sanctification is very important. You can also look at it this way. With justification, God gave you the key to the door of righteousness. But with sanctification, God used the key to open the door of righteousness for you. With justification, God removed from you the guilt and the penalty of sin. But with sanctification, God empowered you to be able to say **"NO"** to sin. That means He gave you the power over sin. What that means is that once sanctified, sin no longer has any power over you. When you start walking in the light of this revelation that you have been sanctified and set apart, all struggling will end in your life. You will no longer have to struggle with sin because you will know that you have power over sin. It is sanctification that gives you power over sin.

You are supposed to be dead to sin but alive to God through Jesus Christ. You now have the power to make sure that sin will no longer have any dominion over you. That is what God said through Apostle Paul in Romans 6:1-3, and Romans 6:11-14.

> *What shall we say then? Shall we continue in sin, that grace may abound?*
>
> *God forbid. How shall we, that are dead to sin, live any longer therein?*
>
> *Know ye not, that so many of us as were baptized into Jesus Christ were baptized into his death?*
>
> **Romans 6:1-3**

Living a supernatural life (Volume 3)

> *Likewise reckon ye also yourselves to be dead indeed unto sin, but alive unto God through Jesus Christ our Lord.*
>
> *Let not sin therefore reign in your mortal body, that ye should obey it in the lusts thereof.*
>
> *Neither yield ye your members as instruments of unrighteousness unto sin: but yield yourselves unto God, as those that are alive from the dead, and your members as instruments of righteousness unto God.*
>
> *For sin shall not have dominion over you: for ye are not under the law, but under grace.*
> **Romans 6:11-14**

All those sins that you want to leave but which you have been unable to leave will become easy for you to leave once you receive your sanctification by faith. As soon as you do that you will have the power and the willingness to say no to sin since sin will no longer have dominion over you.

For example, there may be that adultery partner of yours that you have found very difficult to leave. Even though your spirit and your conscience have been convicting you that what you are doing is wrong, and you are tired of the relationship, you are still struggling with the sin. You are just powerless against the sin. Whenever it comes, no matter how much you have determined in your mind not to fall, you find yourself falling.

Are you struggling with sin?

If you have been sanctified, then you can say goodbye to that sinful relationship. You must believe that you can always say no to the sin. This is so because once sanctified, you are empowered to leave the sin, because you have been made free from the power and dominion of that sin. That is what God told us through Paul in Romans 6:18 and Romans 6:22.

> ***Being then made free from sin, ye became the servants of righteousness.***
> **Romans 6:18**

> ***But now being made free from sin, and become servants to God, ye have your fruit unto holiness, and the end everlasting life.***
> **Romans 6:22**

Because you are now sanctified, that urge and temptation that you have to steal things, the urge to cheat others, you will now be able to overcome. The urge to fight, the urge to gossip about other people, the urge to tell lies, the urge to hate and revenge when offended, and all such temptations to sin, you will now be able to overcome. Every temptation to sin you will now be able to face squarely, suppress and defeat unless of course you choose not to do so. The power to do so is now in your hand. With sanctification, you now have a fence of immunity against sin around you. Sin can no longer intimidate you, or tempt you and win, unless you want it to win. The yoke of sin has been broken in your life. You don't have to sin anymore. If you sin, it is because you choose to do so. If you sin it is because you decided to ignore the little gentle voice of your conscience speaking to you.

Living a supernatural life (Volume 3)

Remember that Jesus Christ said in John 20:21 that He has sent you even as His Father had sent Him.

Then said Jesus to them again, Peace be unto you: as my Father hath sent me, even so send I you.
John 20:21

And we know from Isaiah 7:14-15 that He was sent to know how to refuse the evil and choose the good.

Therefore the Lord himself shall give you a sign; Behold, a virgin shall conceive, and bear a son, and shall call his name Immanuel.

Butter and honey shall he eat, that he may know to refuse the evil, and choose the good.
Isaiah 7:14-15

With sanctification you too have been given the power to know how to choose the good and refuse the evil. Therefore you too have also been sent to know how to refuse the evil and choose the good. It is in order that you may be able to do this that you have been sanctified because it is sanctification that empowers you to do so. That means you now have the freedom to choose between the good and the bad what you will do.

God made this quite clear to us in James 1:13-15 that sin can no longer rule over you. He said that when you sin now you sin because you choose to sin after being drawn away by your own lust and enticed to sin. You cannot blame God or anybody for any temptation that you may have. See what He said below.

Are you struggling with sin?

Let no man say when he is tempted, I am tempted of God: for God cannot be tempted with evil, neither tempteth he any man:

But every man is tempted, when he is drawn away of his own lust, and enticed.

Then when lust hath conceived, it bringeth forth sin: and sin, when it is finished, bringeth forth death.
James 1:13-15

God has given you power over sin. Not only that He has assured you that whatever temptations may come your way; it will not be more than you can bear. He even went further to tell you that He has made a way of escape for you from whatever temptation may come your way. This is an assurance that even if you are being tried you will win in the end. You need not fall. That is what God said through Apostle Paul in 1 Corinthians 10:13.

There hath no temptation taken you but such as is common to man: but God is faithful, who will not suffer you to be tempted above that ye are able; but will with the temptation also make a way to escape, that ye may be able to bear it.
1 Corinthians 10:13

You now have all it takes to live above sin. You have what it takes to rise above any challenges that sin may pose. You have now conquered sin.

Living a supernatural life (Volume 3)

You know that when you have conquered sin and have no sin-complex, your conscience will be clear, and you will have total assurance when you approach God for anything that God will hear you. Yet if you can know and you are sure that He hears you when you pray, then you know that you have got whatever you asked of Him. That is what God said through John the beloved in 1 John 5:14-15.

> *And this is the confidence that we have in him, that, if we ask any thing according to his will, he heareth us:*
>
> *And if we know that he hear us, whatsoever we ask, we know that we have the petitions that we desired of him.*
> **1 John 5:14-15**

When you have been sanctified, then you have conquered the sin problem in your life, and all struggles with sin in your life will end. Whatever makes you feeble against sin has now been taken away from you. The decision to sin is yours and completely yours because like we have said of Jesus previously you now also know how to refuse the evil and choose the good since according to John 20:21, which we have previously written and discussed on pages 135-145, 221, 325-332, 668 as well as on pages 707-709, you are now sent as Jesus was sent.

You cannot put that decision on anybody's doorstep. Nobody can force you to sin. You must take the responsibility for all the decisions of your life. You cannot heap the blame on Satan as most people do.

Are you struggling with sin?

When Satan tempts you God has given you the power to say no to Satan's antics. Neither can you heap the blame for your sin on anybody else. You are totally responsible for your sins. That is the understanding that we have from what God said in James 1:13-16.

> *Let no man say when he is tempted, I am tempted of God: for God cannot be tempted with evil, neither tempteth he any man:*
>
> *But every man is tempted, when he is drawn away of his own lust, and enticed.*
>
> *Then when lust hath conceived, it bringeth forth sin: and sin, when it is finished, bringeth forth death.*
>
> *Do not err, my beloved brethren.*
> **James 1:13-16**

If you have any sin that has blemished your Christian life, and has rendered your Christianity impotent and unproductive, now you know that it ought not to be a problem to you anymore, if you are truly born-again and sanctified. Once you are born-again and sanctified, every area of your life that is crooked as a result of sin can be straightened if you choose to.

Every but in your life, every reproach in your life, every humiliation in your life, every strain in your life, that has come there as a result of sin, you can remove if you are born again and sanctified. You now have the choice. You are on the driver's seat of your life.

Living a supernatural life (Volume 3)

This is the beauty of what God has done for you by sanctifying you. Sanctification has brought you power over sin. While the unbelievers and unsaved people in various other religious organizations all over the world are always attributing power to the devil by claiming that it is the devil that makes them to sin, you as a born-again Christian believer in Christ cannot do the same. You should know better than that. You should know the truth that the devil has no more power over you to make you sin. You should know that the sanctification that God gave you has empowered you to rise above sin and therefore if you sin it is because you made the choice to sin.

Therefore you have no excuse. Since you are now sanctified, you can now have dominion over sin. Whatever makes you feeble against sin has been destroyed. You are free from the slavery of sin. Whatever is contending your obedience of God with you no longer has power over you. Whatever is challenging your determination to be free from sin no longer has any power over you.

You now have a fence of immunity against sin around you, which Satan cannot break unless you allow him. You have the choice. You now have what it takes to rise above any challenges that sin may pose. You should therefore no longer have any sin-complex. When you start to walk in the light of these revelations all struggling will end in your life. You will no longer have to struggle with sin. But remember that as with all the other blessings of God that comes with your redemption, it is by faith that you appropriate this blessing of sanctification.

Are you struggling with sin?

God has imputed the righteousness of Christ to you and declared you righteous. He gave you His righteousness; that is why He had sanctified you so as to empower you to be able to do the works of righteousness. But you get this by faith.

Now you have seen what God has done for you to make sure that when sin comes with its temptations you will have the confidence to know that it can no longer overcome you. Sin will block your way to God's blessings and the fulfillment of all of God's promises to you but you don't have to fear for sin shall not have dominion over you anymore. That is what God made us to see through Paul in Romans 6:14.

> *For sin shall not have dominion over you: for ye are not under the law, but under grace.*
> **Romans 6:14**

There is therefore no need to fear sin anymore for you as a Christian. But if you are to be free from sin then you must guard your thoughts and you should not allow Satan to succeed when he uses his wiles against you. We have shown in *Chapter 2* of the *Volume 1* of this *"Living a supernatural life"* book series by the same author that Satan has no power over you and that all he uses against you as written in Ephesians 6:11 are his wiles, which are just tricks.

> *Put on the whole armour of God, that ye may be able to stand against the wiles of the devil.*
> **Ephesians 6:11**

Living a supernatural life (Volume 3)

If you are not careful Satan will take advantage of you and before you know it you would have fallen. We are warned about this in the Scripture. God told us through Apostle Paul in 2 Corinthians 2:11 that we should not let Satan get any advantage of us for we are no longer ignorant of his devices. You definitely have no cause to be struggling with any sin now

> *Lest Satan should get an advantage of us: for we are not ignorant of his devices.*
> **2 Corinthians 2:11**

CHAPTER 12

NOT SURE OF ANSWER TO YOUR PRAYER?

Many Christians pray but they come out of the prayer not really sure that they have received the answer to their prayer. As a new Covenant Christian you cannot have any doubt that whenever you pray your prayer is answered. You don't even have to think about it. As of right when you pray you know that you have received the answer. Therefore the next time you pray on the same issue it should not be to ask for the same thing but to thank God for giving it. However if you have any doubt as to whether your prayer was answered or not then it means that you are either not a citizen of the Kingdom of God yet or that you are not living by the rules of the Kingdom. We shall look at the various rules of that Kingdom and as we look at each rule it will necessitate your asking yourself certain questions. Such questions will help you to find out if you are really living by the rules of your Kingdom or not. First let us consider the truth that says that as a citizen of that Kingdom you have been justified and therefore you are now *"the just"*. That is what you can see from what God said through Paul in 1 Corinthians 6:11. As *"the just"* however you are supposed to walk and live by faith. That is what God instructed you to do from what He said through Paul in 2 Corinthians 5:7 and in Romans 1:17.

Living a supernatural life (Volume 3)

> *And such were some of you: but ye are washed, but ye are sanctified, but ye are justified in the name of the Lord Jesus, and by the Spirit of our God.*
> **1 Corinthians 6:11**

> *For we walk by faith, not by sight:*
> **2 Corinthians 5:7**

> *For therein is the righteousness of God revealed from faith to faith: as it is written, The just shall live by faith.*
> **Romans 1:17**

Therefore you should ask yourself the question, *"Am I walking and living by faith?"* This is necessary because if you are walking by faith you will not be basing your judgments on what the symptoms or what your senses tell you. Many Christians pray and hope but it is possible to pray and know surely that the prayer is answered.

ARE YOU WALKING BY FAITH?

As *"the just"* in the Kingdom where you now are a citizen you are not supposed to walk or live by sight but you are supposed to walk and live by faith in what the Word of God says. If you are walking or living by faith and not by sight how could you have known that your prayer has not been answered? The only reason that can lead you to claim that your prayer has not been answered is if you walk or live by sight. This is so because it will then be obvious that you are basing your judgment on the symptoms that you can physically see, hear, taste, smell or feel.

Not sure of answer to your prayer?

But in the Kingdom of Heaven where you now belong, its citizens are supposed to walk and live by faith. Therefore once you pray, you know by faith that the prayer has been answered and that is settled. You don't go back to observe the symptoms anymore.

This is so because with faith you can see things which are not physically visible yet; you can feel things which you cannot physically feel yet; you can taste things which you cannot physically taste yet. You can also smell things which you cannot physically smell yet and you can hear things which you cannot physically hear yet. Therefore even though the answer to the prayer is not apparent in the physical, you can see it spiritually before it manifests physically. We have said that whatever you can see spiritually by faith you can make to eventually manifest physically. All things manifest first in the spiritual realm, which is more real before they manifest in the physical realm, which is transient. In fact as a Christian you should fix your sight on those things in the spiritual realm that you cannot see, feel, taste, smell or hear physically. They should be more real to you than those things in the physical realm which you can see, feel, taste, smell or hear. That is what we are made to understand by what God said through Paul the Apostle as written in 2 Corinthians 4:18. How do you see the invisible things? You see the invisible things through the eyes of faith.

> *While we look not at the things which are seen, but at the things which are not seen: for the things which are seen are temporal; but the things which are not seen are eternal.*
> **2 Corinthians 4:18**

Now, the people of this earthly kingdom cannot know or agree that their prayers are answered until they can sense it with their physical senses. This means that until they see it, feel it, taste it, smell it or hear it they will not believe. However you as a citizen of the Kingdom of God should know that your prayer has been answered because you are supposed to walk by faith and see by faith into the invisible. Therefore things in the invisible realm should be more real to you than what you can sense in the visible realm with your physical senses. If you are having doubts as to whether your prayer has been answered then we should ask you this question, ***"Are you focusing your sight on things seen such as symptoms, situations and circumstances?"*** This is what we shall look at in the next section.

ARE YOU NOT LOOKING AT THINGS SEEN?

You are definitely looking at things, which are seen. That is why you believe that your prayer has not been answered. But as a citizen of the Heavenly Kingdom you do not base your judgments on symptoms and situations that you can see, taste, smell, hear or feel in the physical realm. That may be the reason why you believed that your prayer has not been answered or how else could you have known and concluded that your prayer was not answered. You are not supposed to do that as you can see from the instruction given to us in 2 Corinthians 4:18, which we have written in the previous page. You are supposed to base your judgments on faith in what the Word of God says and not on what your senses are saying to you.

Not sure of answer to your prayer?
WHEN YOU ASK YOU WILL RECEIVE

We know that the Word of God says that everyone that asks receives, whoever seeks finds and to whosoever knocks the door shall be opened.

Therefore when you ask you know that you will receive. That is what Jesus said in Matthew 7:7-8. When you ask and you don't receive then you need to go beyond the asking stage to the seeking stage because it may be hidden in which case you have to seek for it. If after seeking for it you still did not find it then you need to go beyond the seeking stage to the knocking stage because it is probably locked up and kept in a strong room in which case you have to knock until the door is opened. But you know that anything you receive from God you can only receive it by faith. So when Jesus said that whosoever asks receives, if you believe that His Word is the truth then you must believe that when you asked you received. If you did not receive then it means that you do not have the faith to receive. You received when you asked but you did not have the faith to take hold of it. Therefore if you say that your prayer was not answered when you prayed it means that you don't believe what Jesus said here. Please take time to read His statement below and meditate upon it. You have asked therefore you must receive. This should be your mindset all the time when you ask God for anything. If you say your prayer has not been answered then you don't believe what Jesus said here.

> *Ask, and it shall be given you; seek, and ye shall find; knock, and it shall be opened unto you:*

> *For every one that asketh receiveth; and he that seeketh findeth; and to him that knocketh it shall be opened.*
>
> **Matthew 7:7-8**

ARE YOU SURE YOUR PRAYER WAS HEARD?

God has said that if you know and you are convinced that He heard you when you prayed then you know that you got whatever you asked of Him. He said this in 1 John 5:14-15.

> *And this is the confidence that we have in him, that, if we ask any thing according to his will, he heareth us:*
>
> *And if we know that he hear us, whatsoever we ask, we know that we have the petitions that we desired of him.*
>
> **1 John 5:14-15**

Therefore your problem boils down to knowing that God heard you when you prayed. Therefore if you believe that your prayer has not been answered then it means that you actually doubt as to whether God heard the prayer in the first place. So your problem then boils down to knowing that God hears you when you pray. To get the answer to your prayer requires only that you know that God heard you when you prayed. You need faith to know that God heard you. To help your faith you need to note what the Word of God says in Psalm 34:15 that for a righteous man the eyes of the Lord are upon him and His ears are open unto his cry.

Not sure of answer to your prayer?
The eyes of the LORD are upon the righteous, and his ears are open unto their cry.
Psalm 34:15

Therefore if you can only be a righteous man then you will know that when you cry the Lord hears you and delivers you out of all your troubles. So to give you an assurance that God heard you when you prayed all you need to do is to know you are righteous. This is not difficult because God has imputed the righteousness of Christ to you as a gift in order to make you righteous before Him.

DO YOU KNOW THAT YOU ARE GIVEN RIGHTEOUSNESS AS A GIFT?

We have seen earlier that as soon as you are truly born again then you become a member of the Kingdom of God and you are given the righteousness of God as a gift, which you are supposed to receive by faith. That is what we are told in Romans 5:17.

For if by one man's offence death reigned by one; much more they which receive abundance of grace and of the gift of righteousness shall reign in life by one, Jesus Christ.
Romans 5:17

If you can get an understanding of this gift of righteousness that you have been given by God, you will no longer doubt your standing before God.

Living a supernatural life (Volume 3)

You will realize that you can always get whatever you ask of Him because you will be receiving it not because of your righteousness but because of the righteousness of God that you have been given with which you are approaching God. Christ who is the Sun of righteousness as we have been made to understand in Malachi 4:2 has been made righteousness unto you as we are told in 1 Corinthians 1:30.

> *But unto you that fear my name shall the Sun of righteousness arise with healing in his wings; and ye shall go forth, and grow up as calves of the stall.*
> **Malachi 4:2**

> *But of him are ye in Christ Jesus, who of God is made unto us wisdom, and righteousness, and sanctification, and redemption:*
> **1 Corinthians 1:30**

God created the moon to rule the night on earth. But the moon has no light of its own. Therefore God aligned the moon to the sun in such a way that it reflects the light of the sun and consequently rules the earth by night as God has ordained for it to do by using the light of the sun. You too, even though you have no righteousness of your own, can now also reflect the righteousness of Jesus Christ who is the Sun of righteousness by aligning yourself to Jesus so that you can reign in life here on earth as stated by Paul in Romans 5:17 written on the previous page. When you receive this gift of righteousness then you are supposed to reign here on earth using this righteousness of Christ. How can you reign if you are not getting what you ask for?

Not sure of answer to your prayer?

Once you receive this gift of the righteousness of Jesus Christ then from that point on it is with this righteousness of Jesus Christ that you approach God to ask for anything in the Name of Jesus Christ. The righteousness of Christ is imputed to you and it is this that the Father sees when you approach Him. So He sees you as righteous now. Paul writing in Romans 4:6 made us to see that it is possible for God to impute righteousness to a man apart from works.

> *Even as David also describeth the blessedness of the man, unto whom God imputeth righteousness without works,*
> **Romans 4:6**

So it is not how pious you are or the amount of the works of righteousness that you have done that makes you righteous before God. He has imputed the righteousness of Christ to you as a gift, which once you accept makes you righteous before Him. Once you know that you are seen as righteous before God you can be bold in your asking from Him and you can be sure that your prayer will be answered because the prayer of a righteous man availeth much. Pray to God with the consciousness that you are approaching Him using the righteousness of Christ and your confidence that your prayer has been answered will soar. It is bound to soar because you know that you are using God's own righteousness to approach God and God therefore considers you to be righteous.

GOD NOW SEES YOU AS RIGHTEOUS

When you approach the Father to ask for anything in the Name of Jesus you are considered righteous before God if you have received the gift.

Living a supernatural life (Volume 3)

The righteousness of Jesus Christ is reckoned to you because Jesus Christ has now been made righteousness to you as we have previously seen above in what we are told by God through Paul in 1 Corinthians 1:30 which we write below. We can therefore deduce that you are taken to be righteous because of the righteousness of Christ, which has been given to you. If you are now righteous then you need to look at what God said through Apostle James in James 5:16 concerning the righteous. He said that the fervent prayer of the righteous avails much.

> *But of him are ye in Christ Jesus, who of God is made unto us wisdom, and righteousness, and sanctification, and redemption:*
> **1 Corinthians 1:30**

> *Confess your faults one to another, and pray one for another, that ye may be healed. The effectual fervent prayer of a righteous man availeth much.*
> **James 5:16**

Therefore since you are now using the righteousness of Jesus Christ and you are now considered righteous before God, it follows therefore that if you are fervent with your prayer and you pray effectually to God it will avail much before God because you are now approaching God not with your own righteousness but with the righteousness of Christ. As far as God is concerned you are now righteous with the righteousness of Christ but you must see yourself as righteous to enjoy these benefits of the righteous.

Not sure of answer to your prayer?

As a matter of fact when you approach God, He sees you through Christ as a sweet savour of Christ whose image you are now conforming to. That is what God made us to understand through Paul the Apostle from what is written in 2 Corinthians 2:15 and Romans 8:29.

> *For we are unto God a sweet savour of Christ, in them that are saved, and in them that perish:*
> **2 Corinthians 2:15**

> *For whom he did foreknow, he also did predestinate to be conformed to the image of his Son, that he might be the firstborn among many brethren.*
> **Romans 8:29**

It is Jesus Christ that God smells in you when you approach Him now for anything. God now sees you through Jesus Christ. If you believe this you cannot have any doubt that your prayer was answered. How can you believe that Christ's righteousness can fail to receive what it wants from God? Therefore stop having the sin-complex before God. Instead approach God with a righteousness-complex and your confidence that your prayer has been answered will soar up. But many Christians don't know this. It is the lack of this knowledge that causes many people to believe that their prayer has not been answered. That was why God told us through Prophet Hosea in Hosea 4:6 and Prophet Isaiah in Isaiah 5:13 that it is the lack of knowledge that leads His people into destruction and captivity.

Living a supernatural life (Volume 3)

> *My people are destroyed for lack of knowledge: because thou hast rejected knowledge, I will also reject thee, that thou shalt be no priest to me: seeing thou hast forgotten the law of thy God, I will also forget thy children.*
>
> **Hosea 4:6**

> *Therefore my people are gone into captivity, because they have no knowledge: and their honourable men are famished, and their multitude dried up with thirst.*
>
> **Isaiah 5:13**

If you don't know that once you are convinced that God heard you when you prayed then you have gotten what you prayed for you will continue to depend on your senses. As long as you cannot see it, feel it, taste it, smell it, hear it or sense it you will not believe that you have got it. You need to know and be convinced that God heard you when you prayed because if you are sure that your prayer was heard when you prayed then you know that you've got what you asked for. But remember that we have said that because you are righteous, whenever you cry unto the Lord He has assured you that He hears you. Therefore, that you are heard when you pray is no longer in contention if you know that you now have the righteousness of Christ. You only have to know that since you are righteous God has heard you and once you know this then you know that you have got the answer to your prayer. This however depends on you asking according to His will. But if you look at this carefully you will see that even that is not an obstacle. You may be saying to yourself,

Not sure of answer to your prayer?

"But He said that it is if I ask according to His will that He hears me so how can I know that I have asked according to His will?" Therefore you also need to be convinced that you asked according to His will. That is what we shall consider in the next section.

DID YOU ASK ACCORDING TO GOD'S WILL?

It is not difficult to know if you asked according to His will in which case you can be sure that He hears you. This is because you know that whatever He has promised you in His Word are His will. Therefore if you ask for whatever He has promised then you can be sure that He hears you because you will then be asking according to His will. God also said in 3 John 1:2 that His wish for you above all things is that you prosper and be in health.

> *Beloved, I wish above all things that thou mayest prosper and be in health, even as thy soul prospereth.*
> **3 John 1:2**

Therefore whatever you ask for that will lead to your prospering and being in health you can rest assured that you are asking according to His will. If you want to be sure that your prayer is according to the will of God then you must follow the following rules.

You must learn to pray in the spirit for the Spirit makes intercession for us according to the will of God. That is what the Scriptures say in Romans 8:26-27

Living a supernatural life (Volume 3)

> *Likewise the Spirit also helpeth our infirmities: for we know not what we should pray for as we ought: but the Spirit itself maketh intercession for us with groanings which cannot be uttered.*
>
> *And he that searcheth the hearts knoweth what is the mind of the Spirit, because he maketh intercession for the saints according to the will of God.*
>
> **Romans 8:26-27**

Your prayer must also be full of thanksgiving for that is the will of God. That is what we are made to see by Paul the Apostle in 1 Thessalonians 5:18.

> *In every thing give thanks: for this is the will of God in Christ Jesus concerning you.*
>
> **1 Thessalonians 5:18**

When you pray for the upliftment and standing of the saints of God that they should stand to the end and not fall; that will lead to the winning of souls for God. Such a prayer is prayed according to the will of God.

That is what we can see from John 6:39-40. When miracles happen people will believe and come and give their lives to the Lord according to what Jesus said in John 4:48.

> *And this is the Father's will which hath sent me, that of all which he hath given me I should lose nothing, but should raise it up again at the last day.*

<u>Not sure of answer to your prayer?</u>
And this is the will of him that sent me, that every one which seeth the Son, and believeth on him, may have everlasting life: and I will raise him up at the last day.
John 6:39-40

Then said Jesus unto him, Except ye see signs and wonders, ye will not believe.
John 4:48

Therefore any prayer prayed to wrought miracles of healings and prosperity is according to the will of God. When people see you prosper and shining it becomes a testimony that can bring others to God, Therefore any prayer you pray to be prosperous and shine here on earth is a prayer prayed according to the will of God. It is God's will that you prosper and be in good health. That is what we are made to see in 3 John 1:2. But you must note that what you are asking for is not to be consumed on your own lust otherwise according to James 4:3 the prayer will not be answered. We shall now look at some things that may lead to unanswered prayers.

Beloved, I wish above all things that thou mayest prosper and be in health, even as thy soul prospereth.
3 John 1:2

Ye ask, and receive not, because ye ask amiss, that ye may consume it upon your lusts.
James 4:3

HAVING INIQUITY IN YOUR HEART?

If you have iniquity in your heart the Lord will not hear you when you call on Him. That is what we are made to understand by what is written in Psalm 66:18

> *If I regard iniquity in my heart, the Lord will not hear me:*
> **Psalm 66:18**

Obviously if the Lord does not hear you there is no way that He can answer your prayer. Therefore it is very important that you do away with iniquity in your life. The fact that you have been imputed with the righteousness of Christ does not mean that you can live in sin and expect God to answer your prayer. No! Your righteousness is given to you by **grace.** But from Romans 6:1-2 we see that you cannot be living in sin and expect grace to abound.

> *What shall we say then? Shall we continue in sin, that grace may abound?*
>
> *God forbid. How shall we, that are dead to sin, live any longer therein?*
> **Romans 6:1-2**

NOT OPENING YOUR MOUTH WIDE?

Many people when they pray do so as if they are afraid to speak out loudly and clearly what they want. They tend to think that there are some forces that can block what they are trying to get from God if such forces can hear them. So they pray quietly or even with their mouths closed.

Not sure of answer to your prayer?

But God wants you to open your mouth wide to say what you want. He has promised you as written in His Word in Psalm 81:10 that if you open your mouth wide He will fill it. He will not only fill it, He said in Psalm 81:14 that He will also subdue your enemies and turn His hand against your adversaries. When you open your mouth wide to ask for what you want with confidence it shows that you have no fear in you and you have trust in God.

> *I am the LORD thy God, which brought thee out of the land of Egypt: open thy mouth wide, and I will fill it.*
> **Psalm 81:10**

> *I should soon have subdued their enemies, and turned my hand against their adversaries.*
> **Psalms 81:14**

Therefore when you open your mouth wide in prayer to God you know that God will fill your mouth with songs of praise because He will answer your prayer. God is asking you to open your mouth wide to speak out what you want. But He said His people will not open their mouth wide. Don't let that be true of you also. He said had they opened their mouth wide He would have dealt serious destructions to their enemies before them. Therefore open your mouth wide and let God deal with your problems. You should have no doubt that God will answer you when you call upon Him because He said in His Word in Psalm 91:14-16 that if you set your love upon Him when you call upon Him He will answer you and that He will be with you in trouble to deliver you and honour you.

> *Because he hath set his love upon me, therefore will I deliver him: I will set him on high, because he hath known my name.*
>
> *He shall call upon me, and I will answer him: I will be with him in trouble; I will deliver him, and honour him.*
>
> *With long life will I satisfy him, and shew him my salvation.*
>
> **Psalm 91:14-16**

Since you have asked you must receive. After all He has said in His Word in Matthew 7:8 that whoever asks receives. But there is the condition that you must ask in faith.

> *For every one that asketh receiveth; and he that seeketh findeth; and to him that knocketh it shall be opened.*
>
> **Matthew 7:8**

DID YOU PRAY IN HOPE AND NOT IN FAITH?

God has promised in so many places in the Scriptures to answer you when you call. In one such promise He said through Prophet Jeremiah in Jeremiah 33:3 that when you call unto Him He will answer you and will show you great and mighty things that you do not know. Jesus Himself gave us the key to praying and receiving. Jesus said in Mark 11:24 that if you **believe that you receive** what you ask for when you pray **then you will have** what you asked for.

Not sure of answer to your prayer?

Call unto me, and I will answer thee, and shew thee great and mighty things, which thou knowest not.
                                    Jeremiah 33:3

Therefore I say unto you, What things soever ye desire, when ye pray, believe that ye receive them, and ye shall have them.
                                    Mark 11:24

Therefore your problem boils down to believing when you pray that you **have received** what you asked for as at the time that you asked for it. Note here that God is not saying that you should believe that you **will receive** at some time in the future what you have asked for. If you do that then you are **praying in hope** and not **praying in faith**. Therefore if you have doubts that your prayer has been answered it may be that you prayed in hope instead of faith. You did not believe that you received what you asked for when you prayed but believed that you will receive it sometimes later.

You have to believe that you received it when you prayed for it. It is only when you do this that you can be said to have prayed in faith and it is when you pray in faith that you can be sure that you received the answer to your prayer when you prayed. That is what walking and living by faith is all about. If you have any doubt concerning the answer to your prayer then check yourself as to whether you actually prayed in faith or you prayed in hope. If you prayed in faith then there is this question that you must consider, **"Faith in what?"**

DID YOU PRAY WITH FAITH IN JESUS' NAME?

Did you pray or ask for what you want in the Name of Jesus? If you prayed in that Name why will your prayer not be answered when you have been given authority to use the Name of Jesus and assured by God that when you use the Name to ask for anything it shall be done for you? Whatever you ask from God in the Name of Jesus God will give it to you. Also whenever you want to do any of the works that Jesus did if you command for it to be done in the Name of Jesus He will do it.

Jesus said these in John 14:12-13 and John 16:23-24 which we have written on the next two pages. Therefore when you are looking for resources ask God for the resources in the Name of Jesus and God will give them to you. But when you want to do any of the works that Jesus did then command that it be done in the Name of Jesus and Jesus will do it. However you should know that it is the Name coupled with having unflinching faith in the Name that will get you what you want. Therefore I ask you, *"Did you have faith in that Name when you prayed?"*

DID YOU USE THAT NAME CORRECTLY?

If your prayer concerns your trying **to do the works that Jesus did** perhaps it was your method of approach that was wrong because in that case you need to command that the work be done in Jesus' Name. The Name of Jesus is the major key with which you unlock the door of the store for the resources of heaven.

Not sure of answer to your prayer?

But when it concerns doing the works that He did Jesus said in John 14:12-13 that what you need to do is to command that the work be done in His Name and He Jesus *will do* it so that the Father can be glorified

> *Verily, verily, I say unto you, He that believeth on me, the works that I do shall he do also; and greater works than these shall he do; because I go unto my Father.*
>
> *And whatsoever ye shall ask in my name, that will I do, that the Father may be glorified in the Son.*
>
> **John 14:12-13**

You do not have to beg the Father to come and do the works that Jesus did. Just command that it be done in the Name of Jesus and it will be done. But if He is to do it when you ask, it must mean that you believe and have faith in the power that is in that Name of Jesus through which you are asking for it to be done. It must also mean that you are not seeking your own glory but the glory of the Father through the Son. He has given you the authority to command in His Name. You must give the command with boldness and absolute faith in the power that is in the Name.

Jesus also gave a promise concerning your prayers when you want *to get the resources that you will require* to yield fruits in order that your joy may be full. He said this as written in John 16:23-24 that you should direct such requests to the Father in His Name and the Father *will give* them to you. Jesus *will do*, the Father *will give*.

> *And in that day ye shall ask me nothing. Verily, verily, I say unto you, Whatsoever ye shall ask the Father in my name, he will give it you.*
>
> *Hitherto have ye asked nothing in my name: ask, and ye shall receive, that your joy may be full.*
>
> **John 16:23-24**

There is a difference between *doing* and *giving* therefore there is a difference in the use of the Name for asking the Father *to give* something and the use of the Name for asking Jesus *to do* something. So I ask you, *"Did you use the Name of Jesus correctly in your prayer?"* We have discussed in detail how to use the Name of Jesus Christ in prayer to God for the resources that we need and in commands to do the works of miracles signs and wonders that Jesus did in *Volume 2* of this *"Living a supernatural life"* book series.

YOU CAN GET EVERYTHING YOU PRAY FOR

Many Christians believe that there are some things that are beyond them in prayer, which they consider that only those who are prayer giants or faith giants can get from God. They see themselves as not strong enough, not consecrated enough, not righteous enough or not deep enough in prayer or faith to get such things from God. But I want you to know that you can actually get everything that you pray for and ask for in the Name of Jesus.

Not sure of answer to your prayer?

The Name of Jesus, which you have been given with which to ask for everything that you want is far above every other Name and at the call of that Name every knee must bow whether in Heaven where angels are or in earth where humans are or under the earth where demons are. That is what we are made to understand from what is written in Philippians 2:9-11.

> *Wherefore God also hath highly exalted him, and given him a name which is above every name:*
>
> *That at the name of Jesus every knee should bow, of things in heaven, and things in earth, and things under the earth;*
>
> *And that every tongue should confess that Jesus Christ is Lord, to the glory of God the Father.*
>
> **Philippians 2:9-11**

This means that angelic and spiritual beings in Heaven, human beings in the earth and demonic beings under the earth must all bow at the call of the Name of Jesus. When you command them in that Name they must obey. That is how awesome that Name is. God has given you the authority to use this all-powerful Name to ask for anything that you want from Him and to command anything and any situation. The Name now belongs to you. It is yours to use. Just like Peter said that the Name of Jesus was his own to use in Acts 3:6 and he used the Name to command the healing of a lame man. So it is with you now. From what Jesus said in Mark 16:17-18 the Name is also yours to use for doing miracles.

Living a supernatural life (Volume 3)

Then Peter said, Silver and gold have I none; but such as I have give I thee: In the name of Jesus Christ of Nazareth rise up and walk.

Acts 3:6

And these signs shall follow them that believe; In my name shall they cast out devils; they shall speak with new tongues;

They shall take up serpents; and if they drink any deadly thing, it shall not hurt them; they shall lay hands on the sick, and they shall recover.

Mark 16:17-18

YOU HAVE THE RIGHTS AND AUTHORITY TO USE THE NAME OF JESUS?

Since Jesus the owner of the Name gave you the authority to use His Name as we can see in John 14:13 and also in John 16:23, which we have previously discussed you now have the Name to use as your own to ask for whatever you want from God just as Peter used it. This authority that Jesus gave to you for the use of His Name has given you a *legal-right* to that Name of Jesus. You must understand how to use the authority that you have been given.

And whatsoever ye shall ask in my name, that will I do, that the Father may be glorified in the Son.

John 14:13

<u>*Not sure of answer to your prayer?*</u>
And in that day ye shall ask me nothing. Verily, verily, I say unto you, Whatsoever ye shall ask the Father in my name, he will give it you.
John 16:23

As a matter of truth you are now born into the family of God. That is what we are made to understand by what is written by the Apostle John in John 1:12-13.

But as many as received him, to them gave he power to become the sons of God, even to them that believe on his name:

Which were born, not of blood, nor of the will of the flesh, nor of the will of man, but of God.
John 1:12-13

This gives you a ***spiritual birth-right*** to that Name of Jesus. It is now your spiritual family Name. We are also made to understand by what Paul wrote in Galatians 3:27 that once you are born-again you are baptized into Christ and once you are baptized into Christ you have put on Christ. Therefore the Name of Jesus has become your spiritual baptismal Name. This gives you a ***spiritual baptismal-right*** to that Name of Jesus.

For as many of you as have been baptized into Christ have put on Christ.
Galatians 3:27

Living a supernatural life (Volume 3)

You are now Christ's ambassador here on earth. That is what we are told in 2 Corinthians 5:20. As Christ's ambassador you have become His representative here on earth. You therefore also have a *proxy-right* to that Name of Jesus.

> *Now then we are ambassadors for Christ, as though God did beseech you by us: we pray you in Christ's stead, be ye reconciled to God.*
> **2 Corinthians 5:20**

Finally, you know that when you become born-again you are not only baptized into Christ but you actually become a member of the Body of Christ. This is not a hypothetical thing because according to Ephesians 5:30 what this means is that your flesh has become member of His flesh and your bones members of His bones. Now every part or member of your body bears your name.

Similarly since you are spiritually a member of the Body of Christ the Name Jesus has now become your *spiritual Name.* It is obvious therefore that you have *a spiritual birthright* to that Name of Jesus.

> *For we are members of his body, of his flesh, and of his bones.*
> **Ephesians 5:30**

If you have doubts as to whether your prayer was answered then you must also check to see if you are abiding in Christ.

Not sure of answer to your prayer?
ARE YOU ABIDING IN CHRIST?

If you are of the Kingdom of Heaven according to what Jesus said in John 14:20 you are supposed to be IN CHRIST. It is when you abide in Him that you can ask whatsoever you will and it will be done for you.

> *At that day ye shall know that I am in my Father, and ye in me, and I in you.*
> **John 14:20**

Jesus has said in John 15:7 that if you abide in Him and His Word abide in you then you can ask for anything and it shall be done for you.

> *If ye abide in me, and my words abide in you, ye shall ask what ye will, and it shall be done unto you.*
> **John 15:7**

Therefore if you prayed and your prayer is not answered then it could boil down to the fact that you are either not in Christ or His Word is not in you. Are you abiding in Him? Is His Word abiding in you? If your answers are affirmative in both cases then you should get whatever you ask for.

WERE YOU FIGHTING SATAN IN THE FAITH ARENA OR IN THE SENSE ARENA?

You must make sure that your prayer battles are fought in the *faith arena* and not in the *sense, sight or symptoms arena*.

Living a supernatural life (Volume 3)

Prayer is a spiritual weapon therefore you don't need to see, hear, smell, taste or feel anything physically before you know that your prayer is answered. If you fall into the trap of having to see, hear, smell, taste or feel physically before you know that your prayer has been answered then you will give Satan a field day to throw his antics at you. His antics include putting questions in your mind such as, ***"Did God really say so?" "Don't you think?" "Can't you see?" "Don't you smell?" "Don't you feel?" "Do you think so?" "Are you sure?" "Can this be so simple?" "Can't you feel the pain?"***

If you give Satan that inroad into your mind then you will fall because Satan is an expert at throwing such thoughts and questions into the mind and building them into strong holds in the mind. That is what he has been doing right from the early days of man since the time of Adam and he has perfected those antics of his. Therefore if you allow him to take you out of the faith arena you will loose the battle against him. As a Christian that belongs to the Kingdom of God you must stand firm in the faith arena.

Always tackle Satan in the faith arena. Never go into the sense or reasoning arena with Him. The only fight that you are asked to fight as a New Covenant Christian is ***the good fight of faith.*** That is the instruction that you are given through Paul in 1 Timothy 6:12.

> *Fight the good fight of faith, lay hold on eternal life, whereunto thou art also called, and hast professed a good profession before many witnesses.*
>
> **1 Timothy 6:12**

Not sure of answer to your prayer?

The people of this earthly kingdom walk by sight therefore they do not agree that they are healed until they can no longer feel the pain. They don't believe that their prayer for prosperity is answered until they can see the money. They don't agree that their prayer for a child has been answered until they can see themselves pregnant.

But that is not supposed to be the case with you as a citizen of the Kingdom of God. With you even though you can still feel the pain you know that you have been healed by the stripes that Jesus took on the Cross as written by Apostle Peter in 1 Peter 2:24 and you must appropriate the healing by faith. You must not walk by sight like the earthly human beings. You are now a heavenly spirit being with the divine nature of God running through your veins.

> *Who his own self bare our sins in his own body on the tree, that we, being dead to sins, should live unto righteousness: by whose stripes ye were healed.*
>
> **1 Peter 2:24**

Even though you cannot see any money you know that you are rich because you know that God will supply all your needs according to His riches in glory by Christ Jesus as written in Philippians 4:19. Therefore all you need to do is to appropriate your needs by faith.

> *But my God shall supply all your need according to his riches in glory by Christ Jesus.*
>
> **Philippians 4:19**

Living a supernatural life (Volume 3)

Even though you cannot see any pregnancy you know that your prayer for a child has been answered and you have been given your child, which you should appropriate by faith because He has said in Exodus 23:26 that none shall be barren in your land.

> *There shall nothing cast their young, nor be barren, in thy land: the number of thy days I will fulfil.*
> **Exodus 23:26**

All you have to do therefore as a new Covenant saint and a citizen of the Kingdom of God is to stand in faith and appropriate these promises of God for you by faith and thank God for them. You may say, "How can I appropriate these by faith when I have no faith?" You cannot say that you do not have faith because God has given each and everyone in that Kingdom the measure of faith, which is the same for everyone. That is what is implied by what He said in Romans 12:3. You have the measure of faith. What you have to do is to grow that measure of faith that you have been given and you grow it by practicing the use of it.
He said *the measure* NOT *a measure* therefore it is the same for all. However, some people have developed their own by frequently exercising it.

> *For I say, through the grace given unto me, to every man that is among you, not to think of himself more highly than he ought to think; but to think soberly, according as God hath dealt to every man the measure of faith.*
> **Romans 12:3**

Not sure of answer to your prayer?
YOU ARE AN HEIR OF GOD

As a citizen of the Kingdom of God do you know that you are also an heir of God? That is what we are made to see from what Paul wrote in Galatians 4:7. You are an heir to all that God is and to all that God has. You are actually a joint-heir of God with Christ. That is what we are told in Romans 8:17.

> *Wherefore thou art no more a servant, but a son; and if a son, then an heir of God through Christ.*
> **Galatians 4:7**

> *And if children, then heirs; heirs of God, and joint-heirs with Christ; if so be that we suffer with him, that we may be also glorified together.*
> **Romans 8:17**

This should at least make you happy and give you confidence that when you ask from God you will get what you ask for. You should not be asking as a beggar. You should be asking as of right as His son and His heir because it is your heritage. You should also know as we are told by David in Psalm 24:1 that the earth and everything in it belongs to God. Therefore there is nothing that you want that you cannot get from God who is now your Father. Your Father owns everything and you can ask for whatsoever you want from Him.

Living a supernatural life (Volume 3)

The earth is the LORD'S, and the fulness thereof; the world, and they that dwell therein.
Psalms 24:1

Being an heir of God has given you the right to ask for whatever you want. According to John in 1 John 5:15, we have confidence that when we ask God, He hears us and once we know that He hears us then we know He will give us what we asked for.

And if we know that he hear us, whatsoever we ask, we know that we have the petitions that we desired of him.
1 John 5:15

You have a birthright to whatever God owns. Since God owns all things and you are now a son of God as we are told by Apostle John in John 1:12-13 you have a birthright to all your Father owns.

But as many as received him, to them gave he power to become the sons of God, even to them that believe on his name:

Which were born, not of blood, nor of the will of the flesh, nor of the will of man, but of God.
John 1:12-13

This means that you have a birthright to all things. With that kind of credentials how can you pray to God who is now your Father and still doubt that He has given you what you asked for?

Not sure of answer to your prayer?
YOU ARE AN AMBASSADOR OF CHRIST

You are supposed to be an ambassador of your Kingdom here on earth. That is what you can see from what Paul the Apostle said in 2 Corinthians 5:20.

> *Now then we are ambassadors for Christ, as though God did beseech you by us: we pray you in Christ's stead, be ye reconciled to God.*
> **2 Corinthians 5:20**

This means that you are Christ's representative, How can you as an ambassador now representing your Kingdom here on earth ask for anything that you need to do your work successfully from your home Kingdom and be denied the thing? These earthly nations do not deny their ambassadors the things they need.

How can your Father God in the Heavenly Kingdom who is rich in all things and just in His actions, deny His own ambassadors of the things that they need? Whatever needs you have can be met from the resources of your home Kingdom the Kingdom of God. Since you are an ambassador of Christ you should try to find out how you have been sent.

Knowing how you have been sent will help you to know what rights and authority you have as an ambassador. It is therefore imperative that you should find out how you have been sent. But thank God Jesus Himself stated how you have been sent before He left this earth. *So how have you been sent?*

Living a supernatural life (Volume 3)
YOU ARE SENT AS JESUS WAS SENT

As an ambassador of the Heavenly Kingdom here on earth you must know that you have been sent to this earth by Jesus just as the Father sent Him when He came to this earth. That is what Jesus Himself made us to know from what He said in John 20:21.

> *Then said Jesus to them again, Peace be unto you: as my Father hath sent me, even so send I you.*
> **John 20:21**

If you really believe that you have been sent as Jesus was sent then you should ask yourself if there was any prayer of Jesus that was not answered when He was here on earth. In fact Jesus claimed that the Father was always hearing Him and He even thanked the Father for that on several occasions. Why then should yours be any different? It should not be different since you have been sent as He was sent. Therefore when you ask you must receive unless you are asking amiss when you pray just to satisfy your own lust. That is one of the reasons that we are given in the Scriptures why we can ask and not get the answer as written in James 4:3.

> *Ye ask, and receive not, because ye ask amiss, that ye may consume it upon your lusts.*
> **James 4:3**

You should realize and be conscious of the truth that since you have been sent as Jesus was sent whatever you ask of the Father in the Name of Jesus the Father will give it to you so that your joy may be full.

_____*Not sure of answer to your prayer?*_____

This is provided that it will bring glory to the Father through the Son. You now belong to the Kingdom of Heaven therefore your paramount desire now as an ambassador of that Kingdom here on earth should be to seek after the things that will enhance the image or picture of that Kingdom here on earth. You have been promised that if you seek after the things of your Kingdom first all your other needs will be met. Jesus said so and it is written in Matthew 6:33. But the problem is that many Christians are seeking these extras first.

> **But seek ye first the Kingdom of God, and his righteousness; and all these things shall be added unto you.**
>
> **Matthew 6:33**

YOU HAVE THE KEYS OF THE KINGDOM OF HEAVEN

Some other weapons that God has given you to use when you pray are the ***keys of the Kingdom of Heaven*** with which you can bind or loose anything here on earth such that whatever you so bind or loose will be confirmed bound or loosed in Heaven as well. That is what we are told in Matthew 16:19.

> **And I will give unto thee the keys of the Kingdom of Heaven: and whatsoever thou shalt bind on earth shall be bound in heaven: and whatsoever thou shalt loose on earth shall be loosed in heaven.**
>
> **Matthew 16:19**

Living a supernatural life (Volume 3)

With such weapons how can you have any problem getting the answer to your prayer? After all if there is any thing getting in the way of the answers to your prayer you can command that thing bound and therefore powerless against your prayer. Similarly you can command the answers to your prayer loosed from every yoke that is tying them down. As you can see the binding or loosing of anything starts with you not with God. You do it first on earth then God confirms it in Heaven.

These are great prayer weapons in your hand if you know how to use them. Most Christians do not take cognizance of the power that is now available to them through these weapons. Look at what Jesus said in Matthew 12:29. He said if you are to enter a strong man's house and spoil his goods then you will have to first bind the strong man and then you can plunder or spoil his house.

> *Or else how can one enter into a strong man's house, and spoil his goods, except he first bind the strong man? and then he will spoil his house.*
> **Matthew 12:29**

You have the keys with which to bind the strong man now. Therefore you can bind whatever strong man is behind any problem that you have. We are made to see in 1 John 3:8 that it was for the purpose of destroying the works of the devil that Jesus Christ the Son of God was manifested.

> *He that committeth sin is of the devil; for the devil sinneth from the beginning. For this purpose the Son of God was manifested, that he might destroy the works of the devil.*
> **1 John 3:8**

Not sure of answer to your prayer?

The possibilities are infinite. For example, you can bind and take captive every negative, destructive, wicked and retrogressive thought concerning your life, your finances, your health and your business. You can bind every word that has been uttered against you or your destiny by any divining powers and render them inactive in your life. You can bind and lock every gate in your life that has been opened to the enemy through which the enemy has been troubling your life. You can bind all prayer-hindering demons operating where you are and render them ineffective against you.

You can bind every principality, power, and spiritual wickedness in high places that is causing poverty, failure and all types of distress in your life. You can bind every devourer in your life or your business. If you are finding it difficult to pursue your projects or ideas to logical conclusions then you can bind that evil spirit that makes it impossible for you to pursue anything to its logical conclusion. You no longer need to fear curses because you have been redeemed from curses. You can bind all demons in charge of things like curses, stagnancy, procrastination, backwardness, misfortune, fear, anxiety, pre-mature birth and barrenness in your life.

You can bind every demon that is operating around you including anti-progress demons and anti-prayer demons. You can also bind the demons in charge of barrenness, the demons in charge of misfortune, the demons in charge of sorrow and the demons in charge of diseases. You can bind every destiny hunting demon that you come across.

Living a supernatural life (Volume 3)

You can also bind the demons in charge of stagnancy, the demons in charge of lack, the demons in charge of failure and the demons in charge of sudden death. You can even bind and render impotent every spiritual communication gadgets that the enemy is using against you.

You can bind every spiritual computer, every spiritual satellite, every spiritual radio and television and every spiritual machine being used by the enemy and the forces of darkness against you. You not only have the weapons with which to bind you also have the weapons with which to loose. For example you can loose yourself from every yoke of the oppressor in your life, from every yoke of poverty and from every spiritual prison house where your things are kept in the spiritual realm. You can set your divinely appointed helpers loose from every yoke of the oppressor so that they can begin to locate you. You can set loose your finances and blessings that are being kept in spiritual prisons. You can set loose blessings to locate you from the east, from the west, from the north and from the south. You can also set loose yourself and your business from every covenant of poverty and unfruitfulness.

You can loose your life, your business and your marriage from the bondage of the devil such as lack, bankruptcy, sorrow, lack, forgetfulness, sickness, disease and curses including generational curses and ancestral curses. You can loose your health from the bondage of disease. You can loose your womb or reproductive organs from the bondage of barrenness. You can lose your marriage from the bondage of troubles. You can loose your finance from the bondage of lack. You can loose your business from the bondage of bankruptcy. You can loose your destiny from the bondage of destiny hunters.

Not sure of answer to your prayer?

You can loose your life from the bondage of witchcraft, spells, charms, curses and jinxes. You can loose your mind from the bondage of fear. You can loose yourself from every curse placed upon your destiny. The possibilities are limitless. They only depend on the level of insight that you have of these keys that God has now put in your hand. If you will only use these keys that God has given you with which you can bind or loose things with wisdom you will find that nothing can put you in bondage or act as an impediment to your prayer any longer.

THE HOLY SPIRIT WILL HELP YOU TO PRAY

God has given you His Spirit to help you to pray for what you want so that you will not pray amiss. This is because He knows that you may sometimes not know what to pray for and how to pray for it. The Spirit speaks the language of the spirit, knows what to ask for and knows the mind of God. If you will therefore allow the Spirit of God in you to pray at such times then He will know what to ask for and how to ask for it. This is the promise of God to you in Romans 8:26.

> *Likewise the Spirit also helpeth our infirmities: for we know not what we should pray for as we ought: but the Spirit itself maketh intercession for us with groanings which cannot be uttered.*
> **Romans 8:26**

With the Spirit making intercession for you it is not possible for you to ask amiss and you will then be sure that your prayer has been heard by God. You will therefore know that it has been answered.

Living a supernatural life (Volume 3)

This is so because the Spirit will only ask what is in the will of God for you. He will not ask anything against the will of God for you. But you know that if you ask for anything according to the will of God then you are sure that God hears you and once you know that He hears you then you know that you have what you asked of Him. That is what God made us to know by what He said through Apostle John in 1 John 5:14-15 as we had shown earlier. Therefore it is obvious that when the Spirit helps you to pray you must get what you prayed for. The Spirit is given to you for you to profit by.

> *And this is the confidence that we have in him, that, if we ask any thing according to his will, he heareth us:*
>
> *And if we know that he hear us, whatsoever we ask, we know that we have the petitions that we desired of him.*
>
> 1 John 5:14-15

As a citizen of the Kingdom of God you now have working in you the great exceeding power of God. That is the essence of what God is telling us in Ephesians 1:19.

> *And what is the exceeding greatness of his power to us-ward who believe, according to the working of his mighty power,*
>
> Ephesians 1:19

With that power of God that is now working in you it is possible for you to get God to do exceeding and abundantly above all that you can ask or even think. That is what we are also told by Paul in Ephesians 3:20.

<u>Not sure of answer to your prayer?</u>
Now unto him that is able to do exceeding abundantly above all that we ask or think, according to the power that worketh in us,
Ephesians 3:20

Therefore whatever you ask for in prayer you should have no doubt that it is done. You should never think that there is anything you ask from God which is beyond what God can give you. God is much more than anything that you can ask.

JESUS IS INTERCEDING FOR YOU

You should also realize that as a citizen of the Kingdom of God you have Jesus Christ as a High Priest who is at the right hand of God in Heaven interceding for you with the Father. That is what we can see from what is written in Romans 8:34.

Who is he that condemneth? It is Christ that died, yea rather, that is risen again, who is even at the right hand of God, who also maketh intercession for us.
Romans 8:34

This means that whatever you ask of God Jesus is there to put in *"a word in edgeways"* for you in support of your case. When Jesus came to this earth there was nothing He asked of the Father, which He did not get. Why will you think that He can now not get what He is asking for you? Definitely He will get whatever He asks of God.

Living a supernatural life (Volume 3)

We have shown earlier that once you know that your prayer was heard by God when you prayed then you know that you received what you asked of Him when you prayed. But since Jesus now acts as your intercessor when you pray and He has said that the Father always hears Him it follows that any time you pray that prayer is heard by God. Jesus Himself said that the Father hears Him always. That is what He said in John 11:42.

> *And I knew that thou hearest me always: but because of the people which stand by I said it, that they may believe that thou hast sent me.*
> **John 11:42**

If the Father always hears Him and He is interceding for you it follows that you will get whatever you asked for. This should be your mental attitude in prayer.

You have the authority to use His Name to ask. At the same time He is there interceding for you. With that kind of support how can you still doubt that your prayers are answered when you pray to God? As you can see therefore Jesus who is the author and finisher of your faith as we are told in Hebrews 12:2 is there to make sure that you get from God whatsoever you ask for in faith using His Name.

> *Looking unto Jesus the author and finisher of our faith; who for the joy that was set before him endured the cross, despising the shame, and is set down at the right hand of the throne of God.*
> **Hebrews 12:2**

Not sure of answer to your prayer?
YOU HAVE A HIGHER ANOINTING THAN ANY OLD COVENANT SAINT

When Elijah was here on earth he got answers to the prayers he made to God. So did Elisha. So did Joshua. So did Moses. Yet these were saints of the Old Covenant. Elijah commanded the strange fire of God to come down on Mount Carmel to consume the sacrifice, wood, stones, dust and even licked the water. Joshua also commanded the sun to stand still upon Gibeon and the moon in the valley of Ajalon.

These are Old Covenant saints. But you as a born-again Christian are a New Covenant saint. As a New Covenant saint you should know that you are capable of a much higher anointing than any Old Covenant saint. That is the implication of what Jesus said in Matthew 11:11.

> *Verily I say unto you, Among them that are born of women there hath not risen a greater than John the Baptist: notwithstanding he that is least in the Kingdom of Heaven is greater than he.*
> **Matthew 11:11**

Therefore if these Old Covenant saints can ask from God in prayer and receive answers to their prayers why will you who has the potential for a much higher anointing now ask and still doubt that you have received answer to your prayer?

Living a supernatural life (Volume 3)

Get the true Scriptural picture of what is happening to your prayers in the spiritual realm. You need to adjust your thinking and your confessions to agree with the truth that your prayer was answered when you prayed. After all that you have read in this Chapter do you still believe that your prayer will not be answered by God or that you can pray to God and not receive an answer? If that is the case obviously you can now know why.

CHAPTER 13

FACED WITH AN IMPOSSIBLE SITUATION?

If you believe that you are facing what looks like an impossible situation and you have any fear about such a situation then you really do not know who you are in Christ or where you now are in Christ. This is so because as a born-again Christian in Christ you are now seen as labourers *together with God*. That is what we are made to know in 1 Corinthians 3:9.

> *For we are labourers together with God: ye are God's husbandry, ye are God's building.*
> **1 Corinthians 3:9**

The truth that you are *together with God* and not alone should give you the confidence to know that when you ask anything of God you are bound to get it. In that case how can any situation be impossible to you? You are now *together with God* and we know that with God all things are possible. That is what Jesus said written in Mark 10:27. God lives in you now therefore you are always with God. It follows therefore that nothing can be impossible for you anymore since you are with God.

Living a supernatural life (Volume 3)

> *And Jesus looking upon them saith, With men it is impossible, but not with God: for with God all things are possible.*
> **Mark 10:27**

You are not only with God you are actually with Christ in God. That is what we are told in Colossians 3:3. God is now living in you as we can see from what Jesus said in John 14:20. This means that you now carry divinity right inside you.

> *For ye are dead, and your life is hid with Christ in God.*
> **Colossians 3:3**

> *At that day ye shall know that I am in my Father, and ye in me, and I in you.*
> **John 14:20**

Do you not know that it is the God that is living in you that is now working in you? That is what we are made to see by God through Apostle Paul in Philippians 2:13.

> *For it is God which worketh in you both to will and to do of his good pleasure.*
> **Philippians 2:13**

You should pause to take in and meditate on the implication and impact of this truth. ***If it is God that works in you and you know this how then can any situation be an impossible one to you?*** If it is impossible to you then it must mean that it is impossible to God who is now the One working in you.

Faced with an impossible situation?

With the attributes that you now have you should not be looking at any situation as an impossible situation. We have discussed these attributes earlier on in **Chapter 2 to Chapter 6** of this book. Therefore there is really no point going over them again. However I will like to highlight some of them here and leave you to go through them, reconsider the situation that you find yourself, do an analysis of the situation and weigh it against all the attributes that you now have and the help that are now available to you. If after this you still believe that any situation is an impossible situation to you then it is obvious that it is because you are not who I think that you are or you just refuse to receive and lay God's Word in your heart. So let us look at a few of these attributes that you now have.

YOU ARE A SON OF GOD

This is so because if you are truly born again then you have been given the power to become a son of God. That is what we are told in John 1:12. You are now a child of the Most High. That is what David also said in Psalm 82:6.

> *But as many as received him, to them gave he power to become the sons of God, even to them that believe on his name:*
> **John 1:12**
>
> *I have said, Ye are gods; and all of you are children of the most High.*
> **Psalms 82:6**

Living a supernatural life (Volume 3)

According to the Scripture above you are a child of the Most High God. How can the Most High God, the all powerful, almighty, omniscient and omnipresent God be your Father and you are still having any apprehension over any situation that you come across in life? As a matter of truth can't you see from above Scripture that as a son of God you are also a god? We know that all things produce after their own kind. The son of a goat is a goat. The son of a lion is a lion. The son of God must be a god. You are a son of God therefore you are a god.

YOU ARE A GOD

God has made you a god to every situation that you come across. When God sent Moses to Pharaoh He made him a god to Pharaoh. That is what God told Moses in Exodus 7:1. This means that God put Pharaoh under the dominion of Moses and whatever Moses says to Pharaoh made Pharaoh to tremble.

> *And the LORD said unto Moses, See, I have made thee a god to Pharaoh: and Aaron thy brother shall be thy prophet.*
> **Exodus 7:1**

Moses gave out commands to Pharaoh, which when not obeyed led to punishment for Pharaoh. If you are a god to something any disobedience on its part to any instruction from you will be punished. Pharaoh had no alternative but to yield to Moses in the end. Every refusal to yield on his part brought punishment upon him and upon his people.

Faced with an impossible situation?

You are not an ordinary human being; you are a god with the divine nature of God running through your veins. You too have now also been made a god to all the situations and circumstances that you come across in life just like God made Moses a god to Pharaoh. Therefore all such situations and circumstances should be under your control. But if you do not know that you are a god to them they will seek to control you and push you around like they will normally do to any man. If you do not know who you are they may even end up killing you. You will then die like an ordinary man or like one of the earthly princes as we are told in the Scriptures in Psalm 82:6-7 concerning the gods who do not live like gods.

> *I have said, Ye are gods; and all of you are children of the most High.*
>
> *But ye shall die like men, and fall like one of the princes.*
> **Psalm 82:6-7**

How can you be a god to the situations and circumstances around you and still have apprehension about any of them being an impossible situation? If you know who you are in-Christ you cannot have such apprehension.

No situation can be impossible to you anymore. You should be in control over every situation that you come across. If you are struggling with any situation then you don't know who you are in-Christ.

YOU HAVE THE DIVINE NATURE

God did not just make you a god He gave you the divine nature by making you a partaker of His divine nature. That is what we are made to see in 2 Peter 1:4.

> *Whereby are given unto us exceeding great and precious promises: that by these ye might be partakers of the divine nature, having escaped the corruption that is in the world through lust.*
>
> **2 Peter 1:4**

Therefore you are not only a god to those situations that you come across; you now have the divine nature of God with which to tackle and rule over all the situations and circumstances that you come across. The divine nature empowers you so that you can actually live like a god to rule and reign over all the situations that you come across.

YOU HAVE THE MIND OF CHRIST

God did not only give you His divine nature He also gave you His mind, the mind of Christ. That is what God made us to know in 1 Corinthians 2:16.

> *For who hath known the mind of the Lord, that he may instruct him? But we have the mind of Christ.*
>
> **1 Corinthians 2:16**

Faced with an impossible situation?

With this mind of Christ you can tackle every situation that you come across since we are told in John 1:1-3 and John 1:14 that this is the mind through whom all things were made and without that mind was not anything made that was made. How can you have such a mind and still find any situation daunting?

In the beginning was the Word, and the Word was with God, and the Word was God.

The same was in the beginning with God.

All things were made by him; and without him was not any thing made that was made.
John 1:1-3

And the Word was made flesh, and dwelt among us, and we beheld his glory, the glory as of the only begotten of the Father, full of grace and truth.
John 1:14

Therefore nothing should be daunting for you anymore. With Christ's mind you have the capacity and ability to comprehend anything now. There is no level of wisdom that this mind of Christ that you now have cannot comprehend and absorb. This is so because as we are told by Paul in 1 Corinthians 1:24 that this mind of Christ is the repository of the wisdom of God.

But unto them which are called, both Jews and Greeks, Christ the power of God, and the wisdom of God.
1 Corinthian 1:24

Living a supernatural life (Volume 3)
YOUR VICTORY IS ALREADY ASSURED

No matter what any situation may bring, your victory over the situation is already assured. You have already overcome the situation because the greater One than is in that situation is in you. This means that the Christ living in you is greater than whatever may be in that impossible situation. That is what you can see from what Apostle John wrote in 1 John 4:4.

> *Ye are of God, little children, and have overcome them: because greater is he that is in you, than he that is in the world.*
> **1 John 4:4**

Therefore you have already overcome any situation that may arise in this world. No matter what may be the situation or circumstance that you come across, no matter how terrible, no matter how mighty you are already a winner. You have already won the fight because as written in Exodus 14:14 the Christ living in you who is God is the One who will fight for you.

> *The LORD shall fight for you, and ye shall hold your peace.*
> **Exodus 14:14**

You will not need to fight for yourself because you no longer need to use the arm of the flesh to do your fighting. It is the Lord God Himself who will fight your battles for you. That is what God said as we are told in 2 Chronicles 20:17. **Can God loose a battle? No!** If you know that God cannot lose a battle then you know that you cannot lose.

> *Faced with an impossible situation?*
> *Ye shall not need to fight in this battle: set yourselves, stand ye still, and see the salvation of the LORD with you, O Judah and Jerusalem: fear not, nor be dismayed; to morrow go out against them: for the LORD will be with you.*
> **2 Chronicles 20:17**

Therefore whatever the situations may bring you can rest assured that victory is already yours in Christ. In any situation or circumstance that you may find yourself just rest assured that you have overcome because you are already declared to be the winner even before the fight starts. You have already conquered. In fact you are more than a conqueror.

YOU ARE MORE THAN A CONQUEROR

Whatever battles you may be going through as a result of the situation that seems impossible, you know that you are much more than a conqueror through Christ. That is what we are made to know from what God said in Romans 8:37.

> *Nay, in all these things we are more than conquerors through him that loved us.*
> **Romans 8:37**

This means that the victory is already won and you are actually now supposed to be enjoying the victory. You obtained the victory through Jesus Christ. Note that you have actually gone past the victory stage. You should now be living the victory.

Living a supernatural life (Volume 3)
NOTHING CAN HOLD YOU IN BONDAGE

You cannot be held bondage to any situation now because you now have the Spirit of the Lord living in you and we know that wherever the Spirit of the Lord is there is liberty. That is what we are told by Paul the Apostle in 2 Corinthians 3:17. Therefore no matter what the situation is that you may be going through it cannot hold you in any bondage. Your liberty is totally assured.

> *Now the Lord is that Spirit: and where the Spirit of the Lord is, there is liberty.*
> **2 Corinthians 3:17**

Whatever you require to do in order to get above the situation and put it under control you know you can do it because you now know that you can do all things through Christ who strengthens you. That is what God made us to understand in Philippians 4:13. How can you have the capacity to do all things and still be apprehensive about any situation?

> *I can do all things through Christ which strengtheneth me.*
> **Philippians 4:13**

Nothing can be impossible for you anymore. This is so because you know as we have shown earlier that it is God that now works in you. Because it is God that works in you, it is obvious therefore that whatever God can do you can now do. That was why Jesus said in John 14:12 that you will do the works that He did and that you will even do greater works than He did.

Faced with an impossible situation?

Verily, verily, I say unto you, He that believeth on me, the works that I do shall he do also; and greater works than these shall he do; because I go unto my Father.
John 14:12

If you are capable of doing the works that Jesus did then it is obvious that you can calm the storm in any situation.

YOU ARE FAR ABOVE THAT SITUATION

Where you are now, you are far above all the circumstances and situations that you can ever come across in this life's journey because you have been translated and raised up together with Christ and made to sit together in Christ in Heavenly places. That is what Apostle Paul made us to see in Ephesians 2:6.

And hath raised us up together, and made us sit together in heavenly places in Christ Jesus:
Ephesians 2:6

From Ephesians 1:19-23 written below you can see that based on where Jesus Christ in whom you are seating is, it follows that you are now far above all principality and power and might and dominion and anything that is named. Therefore no situation should be able to scare or intimidate you anymore.

Living a supernatural life (Volume 3)

And what is the exceeding greatness of his power to us-ward who believe, according to the working of his mighty power,

Which he wrought in Christ, when he raised him from the dead, and set him at his own right hand in the heavenly places,

Far above all principality, and power, and might, and dominion, and every name that is named, not only in this world, but also in that which is to come:

And hath put all things under his feet, and gave him to be the head over all things to the church,

Which is his body, the fulness of him that filleth all in all.
Ephesians 1:19-23

You may say, "But I cannot see or feel this translation." Yes! You cannot see or feel it because it is a spiritual translation. But remember that all things are first in the spiritual realm before they appear in the physical realm. You ought to remember that the spiritual things should be more real to you than the physical things.

That is the essence of what God is telling us through Apostle Paul in 2 Corinthians 4:18. That is one attribute of God that you must learn to imitate if you want to live above every situation that you come across in life. That is the attribute of seeing the invisible.

Faced with an impossible situation?

While we look not at the things which are seen, but at the things which are not seen: for the things which are seen are temporal; but the things which are not seen are eternal.
2 Corinthians 4:18

The Word says that you are now seating in Jesus in the Heavenly places and where Jesus is seating now is far above any name. Therefore where you are now, you are higher than anything that is named not only in this world but also in the world to come. Obviously the circumstances and situations that we are talking about here that you are apprehensive about have names. Therefore it follows that you are far above all the circumstances and situations that you can ever come across because they have names.

If you are far above them they cannot oppress you so how can you be apprehensive about them? If you are apprehensive about them then you don't really know where you are and what power you have living in you. Even where the circumstances and situations that you come across seem to be overwhelming you and you feel that you are being drowned by them it is at such times that you should even relax your mind the more. This is so because you know that the Spirit of the Lord is now living inside you if you are truly a born-again Christian and it is when the enemy comes at you like a flood that this Spirit of the Lord will lift up a standard against him. That is what we are told in Isaiah 59:19. So, the hotter the situation becomes the better for you because it is then that the Spirit of the Lord will take over the fight. If that is the case then no matter what the situation is you are covered.

> *So shall they fear the name of the LORD from the west, and his glory from the rising of the sun. When the enemy shall come in like a flood, the Spirit of the LORD shall lift up a standard against him.*
>
> **Isaiah 59:19**

YOU HAVE THE POWER TO BIND OR LOOSE

Even where all hell is let loosed you have been given the weapons of warfare with which you can fight to make sure that no situation gets out of control for you.

Among such weapons of warfare that you have been given are the keys of the Kingdom of Heaven with which you can bind or loose any situation here on earth. Once you use the keys to bind or loose anything it shall be bound or loosed correspondingly in Heaven. That is what Jesus promised us in Matthew 16:19.

> *And I will give unto thee the keys of the Kingdom of Heaven: and whatsoever thou shalt bind on earth shall be bound in heaven: and whatsoever thou shalt loose on earth shall be loosed in heaven.*
>
> **Matthew 16:19**

This means that when any situation is getting out of hand you can bind it and God will confirm it bound in Heaven.

Faced with an impossible situation?

How can you have that much power over and above the situations that you come across in life and still be apprehensive about any situation? You have the ability to put any situation under control. This makes your position unassailable. Remember that it is you who starts the binding or losing process not God. This is the mistake that most Christians make. They ask God to do the binding and losing for them.

YOU HAVE AN ASSURANCE OF PROTECTION

You are now in Christ. That is what we are made to know in John 14:20. The Christ that you are in is also hidden in God. That is what we are made to know in Colossians 3:3.

> *At that day ye shall know that I am in my Father, and ye in me, and I in you.*
> **John 14:20**

> *For ye are dead, and your life is hid with Christ in God.*
> **Colossians 3:3**

Any situation that wants to swallow you up will therefore first have to contend with God before it can even touch you. Do you think that it can overcome God? If you know that it cannot overcome God then it should be obvious to you that it cannot overcome you.

Therefore your protection from such a situation is certain. If you know for sure that it cannot overcome you and that your protection from it is certain, how can you see it as an impossible situation? If you are anxious about any situation it may lead you to fear. But you no longer have the spirit of fear if you are a born-again Christian in Christ.

YOU NO LONGER HAVE THE SPIRIT OF FEAR

The Spirit that you now have in you is that of power, of love and of a sound mind. That is what we are told by God through Apostle Paul both in 2 Timothy 1:7 and in 1 Corinthians 6:19. If you have such a Spirit how can you fear in any situation?

> *For God hath not given us the spirit of fear; but of power, and of love, and of a sound mind.*
> **2 Timothy 1:7**

> *What? know ye not that your body is the temple of the Holy Ghost which is in you, which ye have of God, and ye are not your own?*
> **1 Corinthians 6:19**

Therefore you need not fear under any situation. Whatever may be the situation that you are going through you don't have to be apprehensive or fear because you know that victory is yours.

Faced with an impossible situation?

You know that you love God therefore you do not have to fear under any circumstance because God has made sure that no matter what you may be going through everything must work out in the end to your good if you love Him. That is what we are made to see by Paul in Romans 8:28. Therefore you know that all things will work together for good to you.

> *And we know that all things work together for good to them that love God, to them who are the called according to his purpose.*
> **Romans 8:28**

Therefore feel contented and know that whatever situation you may be going through everything will eventually work out for your good. There is therefore no reason for you to be apprehensive. You love God but God loves you even more.

GOD LOVES YOU

If you can just fathom how much God loves you and what you now are to God you will realize that nothing can separate you from the love of God unless you want it. That is what we can see from what God used Apostle Paul to say in Romans 8:39.

> *Nor height, nor depth, nor any other creature, shall be able to separate us from the love of God, which is in Christ Jesus our Lord.*
> **Romans 8:39**

Living a supernatural life (Volume 3)

If anything attempts to oppress you God will fight on your behalf. Therefore you can trust God to do the fighting for you and if God fights for you who can come against you and win? No one! You don't even have to beg God to do the fighting for you because God actually considers it a righteous thing to recompense tribulation to them that trouble you. That is what He made us to see from 2 Thessalonians 1:6. Therefore relax. *God is on your side and if God be for you can anyone be against you and win? No!*

> *Seeing it is a righteous thing with God to recompense tribulation to them that trouble you;*
> **2 Thessalonians 1:6**

That is to show you just how much God loves you. To assure you even more let me tell you that when you are deeply troubled about any situation your mind will be kept by the peace of God, which passeth all understanding. That is what God is telling us through Apostle Paul in Philippians 4:7.

> *And the peace of God, which passeth all understanding, shall keep your hearts and minds through Christ Jesus.*
> **Philippians 4:7**

To make sure that you are at peace God has even assured you that no trial will come your way, which is more than you can bear.

Faced with an impossible situation?

That is what He promised as we can see written by Paul in 1 Corinthians 10:13. He not only promised this He even assured you further that should any trial come your way, which you think that is too heavy for you to bear, even though He knows that you can bear it He still will give you a way of escape from it so that your mind can be at peace.

> *There hath no temptation taken you but such as is common to man: but God is faithful, who will not suffer you to be tempted above that ye are able; but will with the temptation also make a way to escape, that ye may be able to bear it.*
> **1 Corinthians 10:13**

Therefore as you can see the Lord has made available for you all that you will need to be able to sail through every situation without any problem. In fact, according to 1 Peter 3:12,

> *For the eyes of the Lord are over the righteous, a nd his ears are open unto their prayers: but the face of the Lord is against them that do evil.*
> **1 Peter 3:12**

He has promised you that He will never leave you or forsake you. His eyes are all over you and His ears are open unto your prayers. If that is the case how can you be apprehensive about any situation? You have God's assurance that you can sail through any situation without being hurt no matter the situation.

Living a supernatural life (Volume 3)

You should never fear no matter what any situation may bring to you. Remember that it is the power of God that is now keeping you through faith. That is what God made us to see from what He said through Apostle Peter in 1 Peter 1:3-5.

> *Blessed be the God and Father of our Lord Jesus Christ, which according to his abundant mercy hath begotten us again unto a lively hope by the resurrection of Jesus Christ from the dead,*
>
> *To an inheritance incorruptible, and undefiled, and that fadeth not away, reserved in heaven for you,*
>
> *Who are kept by the power of God through faith unto salvation ready to be revealed in the last time.*
>
> **1 Peter 1:3-5**

If you know that it is the power of God that is keeping you definitely you will not be apprehensive about any situation that you come across because this power of God that is now keeping you cannot be subdued by any thing. Therefore you should rest assured that no matter what situation you may be going through you have the resources to put it under control.

NOTHING CAN HURT YOU ANYMORE

Come to think of it God has said in Luke 10:19 that He has given you power over all the powers of your enemies. Jesus Himself said this.

Faced with an impossible situation?

Behold, I give unto you power to tread on serpents and scorpions, and over all the power of the enemy: and nothing shall by any means hurt you.

Luke 10:19

Definitely any situation that is making you to worry can be seen as an enemy therefore God has given you situation.

Come on now! If you can dare to use the power that you have been given over the situations that you come across, it is obvious that no situation can put you under any stress to the point where you will become anxious or apprehensive about it.

Even where the situation threatens death you now know that the devil no longer has the power of death. He had it but he no longer has it. That is what we know from Hebrews 2:14. We now know from Revelation 1:18 that Jesus in whom you are now has the keys of hell and death. Therefore Satan no longer has the power to effect his death threats against you. This should give you an assurance that your death is not in the hands of the devil or any of his hosts. They have no authority to take your life unless of course if you give it to them.

Forasmuch then as the children are partakers of flesh and blood, he also himself likewise took part of the same; that through death he might destroy him that had the power of death, that is, the devil;

Hebrews 2:14

> *I am he that liveth, and was dead; and, behold, I am alive for evermore, Amen; and have the keys of hell and of death.*
> Revelation 1:18

YOU ARE SENT TO WALK IN VICTORY

Finally if you realize that as written by Paul the Apostle in 2 Corinthians 5:20 you are now sent as an ambassador of Jesus Christ to this world and from what Jesus Himself said in John 20:21 you have been sent into this world by Him just as the Father had sent He Himself.

> *Now then we are ambassadors for Christ, as though God did beseech you by us: we pray you in Christ's stead, be ye reconciled to God.*
> 2 Corinthians 5:20

> *Then said Jesus to them again, Peace be unto you: as my Father hath sent me, even so send I you.*
> John 20:21

Because you are sent as Jesus was sent it follows that you now have the support that Jesus had when He was here on earth. Therefore you can conclude that whatever cannot touch Jesus should not be touching you. Whatever cannot disturb Jesus should not be able disturb you. Because you are sent as Jesus was sent whatever was sustaining Jesus when He was here on earth is now available for you to tap power from for your own sustenance.

Faced with an impossible situation?

The totality of it all according to what is written by John in 1 John 4:17 is that as Jesus is so are you now in the world.

> *Herein is our love made perfect, that we may have boldness in the day of judgment: because as he is, so are we in this world.*
> **1 John 4:17**

With all these possibilities do you still believe that there can be any situation that can make you apprehensive or that you should be apprehensive about? Definitely you can see that as a truly born-again Christian in Christ, no situation warrants your being stressed up at all about it.

No situation warrants your having any form of anxiety because you have what it takes to be above any situation that you can ever come across. As a truly born-again Christian the manifold wisdom of God is now available to answer to you so that you can demonstrate these to the principalities and powers in heavenly places. According to 1 Corinthians 1:24 Christ is the wisdom of God and the power of God. Christ is living in you therefore you now have the wisdom of God living in you.

> *But unto them which are called, both Jews and Greeks, Christ the power of God, and the wisdom of God.*
> **1 Corinthians 1:24**

Living a supernatural life (Volume 3)

Therefore with this manifold wisdom of God, and the power of God, who is Christ now living in you it is expected that you should be demonstrating the power of God to the principalities and powers in heavenly places. That is the position that you are supposed to be according to what God told us through Apostle Paul in Ephesians 3:10. You cannot have this wisdom of God answering to you and still be held in bondage by any situation. When He answers to you all problems must vanish.

> *To the intent that now unto the principalities and powers in heavenly places might be known by the church the manifold wisdom of God,*
> **Ephesians 3:10**

SPEAK TO THAT SITUATION

You can have whatever you say if you will only believe it. That is what Jesus made us to see in Mark 11:23-24 by what He said. Therefore in any situation that you may find yourself, which is contrary to you it is possible for you to speak out and superimpose the situation that you really want upon that.

> *For verily I say unto you, That whosoever shall say unto this mountain, Be thou removed, and be thou cast into the sea; and shall not doubt in his heart, but shall believe that those things which he saith shall come to pass; he shall have whatsoever he saith.*

Faced with an impossible situation?
Therefore I say unto you, What things soever ye desire, when ye pray, believe that ye receive them, and ye shall have them.
                              Mark 11:23-24

He said in the Scriptures above, *"------and shall not doubt in his heart---."* Therefore it all starts from your heart, which is mainly your mind. If you believe those truths that have been written about your new identity and you start to proclaim all such truths about you that are listed in **Chapters 2-6** of this book the people around you who are not of the Heavenly Kingdom and even those who are, but who do not know their true position as citizens of the Kingdom will start to feel very uncomfortable around you. They will begin to say that you are proud and that you are boasting.

But do not let that disturb you because you are free to boast in the Lord. Boasting in the Lord is permitted. That is what God made us to know through King David in Psalm 34:2. He said,

"My soul shall make her boast in the LORD: the humble shall hear thereof, and be glad."
                              Psalm 34:2

They will not only start to tell you that you are boasting they will feel so uncomfortable around you that they will start to even persecute you. But that should not deter you one bit because their persecution cannot change who you are, what you are, what you have, what you can do and where you are. Their persecution can do you nothing. In fact, rejoice when you are so persecuted because it will become a testimony for you.

Living a supernatural life (Volume 3)

In fact, if you really know who you now are their persecution will only help to strengthen you the more. Whatever anybody may say or do cannot change your identity in Christ one bit. It cannot add to or remove from what you are, who you are, what you can do, what you have and where you are. It is what you think of yourself that really matters.

You must realize that it is the truth that you know that has set you free. They do not know the truth so they are still in bondage. Remember also that most of the time they will persecute you because they are actually envious of you. They are envious of your confidence. When they start to persecute you just remember that Jesus said as written in John 15:20 written below that you will be persecuted. He said,

> *"Remember the word that I said unto you, The servant is not greater than his lord. If they have persecuted me, they will also persecute you; if they have kept my saying, they will keep yours also."*
>
> **John 15:20**

Therefore you should expect persecution. Even when God uses you to heal their sick ones and to wrought miracles that they can see they will still persecute you because as you can see in John 5:16 they did the same thing to Jesus Christ.

> *And therefore did the Jews persecute Jesus, and sought to slay him, because he had done these things on the sabbath day.*
>
> **John 5:16**

Faced with an impossible situation?

Whatever people may do to you just make sure that you never allow them to take you out of focus from your identity in Christ. You must never allow anything to distract you and plant doubts in your mind concerning whom God says that you are and what God says that you are. Similarly you must not allow anything to take you away from where God says that you are. I want to emphasize this so that you may note that when people oppose you it does not mean that what God has said about you is not true. That should even strengthen your resolve. They are opposing you because what you are proclaiming about yourself makes them uncomfortable. They have always seen you as being the same as them but now you are telling them that you are totally different from them. Therefore they are bound to become uncomfortable. You are not only saying that you are totally different from them you are now telling them that you belong to a different Kingdom from them, which is superior to the kingdom where they are. You cannot expect them to be comfortable with that because deep down in them something will be telling them that what you are saying may be true. The nature of man is such that man does not want anybody to be in a better position than he is.

For example, when you tell them that you are a king, as written by John in Revelation 5:10, by all standards you are saying that you are actually superior to them. That will irritate them because they just cannot comprehend what you are saying. But you are not only a king you are the son of the King of kings. You are not only a lord you are the son of the Lord of lords.

Living a supernatural life (Volume 3)

And hast made us unto our God kings and priests: and we shall reign on the earth.
Revelation 5:10

You are a son of the Almighty God. That is what we can see from what is written in 1 Timothy 6:14-15 bearing in mind that Christ is the King of kings and the Lord of lords. That should make them mad.

That thou keep this commandment without spot, unrebukeable, until the appearing of our Lord Jesus Christ:

Which in his times he shall shew, who is the blessed and only Potentate, the King of kings, and Lord of lords;
1 Timothy 6:14-15

In the Kingdom of God where you now are, all its citizens are kings and all its citizens are lords. Whom will you tell that to who will not feel that you are claiming superiority over him? That is just too intimidating for anybody who is not of that Kingdom therefore you should expect people to oppose you when you start to confess and manifest who you are in Christ.

To top it all when you now also tell them that you are a god as is written, that to them will be absolute blasphemy. But never mind no matter how anybody feels about you it will not change who you are in Christ, what you are in Christ, what you have in Christ, what you can do in Christ and where you are in Christ.

Faced with an impossible situation?

No matter who may not be pleased with your confessions or who may be opposing you, if he is not a born again Christian you have a superior heritage to his own and you are a king. Your heritage in Christ is a *fate accompli.*

In any case you should know that people are opposing you because they do not know who you really are anymore. If they know who you are they will not oppose you. The people that opposed Christ when He came to this earth opposed Him because they did not know who He really was. Therefore do not be surprised when they oppose you. They are opposing you because as written in 2 Corinthians 5:17 you are a new creature and therefore totally different from whom they thought you to be. They can see that there is something different about you but they don't know what it is. The you that they used to know was dead and buried. You are now a new creature in Christ. How can you get them to understand that?

> *Therefore if any man be in Christ, he is a new creature: old things are passed away; behold, all things are become new.*
> **2 Corinthians 5:17**

They cannot understand this because it can only be discerned spiritually and they are trying to reason it out with their senses. But according to what God said through Paul in 1 Corinthians 2:14 such can only be discerned by those who are spiritual. The carnal man will know that there is something different about you but he just will not be able to understand what it is and why. He may even start to think that you are crazy.

Living a supernatural life (Volume 3)

> *But the natural man receiveth not the things of the Spirit of God: for they are foolishness unto him: neither can he know them, because they are spiritually discerned.*
>
> **1 Corinthians 2:14**

Whatever challenge the opposition may pose to you don't ever give up on meditating upon and confessing these attributes that constitute your new identity in Christ. You must be persistent in the meditation upon and the proclamation of all the attributes so that they can manifest physically and become clear to all. It is then that your profiting will appear for all to see. That is what we are told by Apostle Paul in 1 Timothy 4:15.

> *Meditate upon these things; give thyself wholly to them; that thy profiting may appear to all.*
>
> **1 Timothy 4:15**

Once you can do that you will not find any situation impossible or daunting anymore. You will not have any worry or anxiety about any situation. As a new Covenant saint you should realize that the position in which you are in Christ is unassailable. You are far above all situations that you can ever come across. You have been given the weapons with which to keep them under control should in case they seek to intimidate you. Did any situation intimidate Christ? Did Christ find any situation impossible to deal with? If your answer to these questions are NO then you should know that the same Christ who is now your life according to Paul in Colossians 3:4 is living in you and now wants to express Himself through you.

Faced with an impossible situation?
When Christ, who is our life, shall appear, then shall ye also appear with him in glory.
Colossians 3:4

If that is true then you must rest assured and know that there is no situation that can intimidate you any longer. That is why it is written in Colossians 1:27, *"Christ in you the hope of glory"*.

To whom God would make known what is the riches of the glory of this mystery among the Gentiles; which is Christ in you, the hope of glory:
Colossians 1:27

When you see your new status in Christ the thought of weakness, poverty, powerlessness, helplessness, failure and lack of ability will no longer have a place in your mind.

You will start to see yourself with God's ability, with God's strength, with God's power and with God's wisdom. Therefore you will find yourself positioned in a very strong, irresistible, overpowering, commanding and overwhelming position against all your enemies and their antics. They will no longer intimidate you.
Let me ask you this question.

After going through this Chapter do you still believe that any situation can intimidate you as a born-again Christian? Do you believe that you can find any situation impossible?

Living a supernatural life (Volume 3)

If you still do then it means that you are yet to understand your new relationship and standing with God and your new position as a believer recreated in Christ. You do not know yet the authority that you now have to use the Name of Jesus and the Word of God to control the situations around you. In that case I will advice you that you read again and meditate upon what is written in **Chapters 1-6** of this book so as to know who you really are now in Christ. For you as a born-again Christian there can be no situation that you should see as an impossible situation because you are not the one to face the situation with your power but it is God that will fight every battle for you. Definitely you must believe that if God is the One that is going to fight your battles then it is obvious that you can never lose any battle. Do you not believe that God is capable of winning every battle? If you are faced with a situation that you consider to be an impossible situation then it must mean that you have considered it and you believe that God will not fight the battle for you. In that case you are making God a liar.

Why do I say this? I say this because God Himself promised to fight your battles. I repeat here again what He said which we had looked at previously. Look at what He said in 2 Chronicles 20:17 written below.

> *Ye shall not need to fight in this battle: set yourselves, stand ye still, and see the salvation of the LORD with you, O Judah and Jerusalem: fear not, nor be dismayed; to morrow go out against them: for the LORD will be with you.*
> **2 Chronicles 20:17**

CHAPTER 14

YOU MUST BE BORN AGAIN

Now that you have read this book up to this point, I want you to know that what I have written in this book is just a tip of the iceberg of the power that is available to you once you are born again. What I have shared with you in this book is how to make sure that this power is demonstrated in your life once you are born again. If you can imbibe what is written in this book and act accordingly, your life will never be the same again. It will revolutionize your life. But as you can see it all starts with your being born-again.

If you have not believed Christ and accepted Him as your Saviour, you can see what you have been missing. But it is also quite possible that you may be saying that those things that you have read in this book cannot be true because they may not make sense to you. This is so because you cannot possibly understand these things using your innate, inborn or natural senses and knowledge. However, God has also recognized that until you become saved these will be foolishness to you because the things of God are spiritually discerned. That is what God has told us through Paul the Apostle written in 1 Corinthians 1:18-19 and also in 1 Corinthians 2:14.

Living a supernatural life (Volume 3)

For the preaching of the cross is to them that perish foolishness; but unto us which are saved it is the power of God.

For it is written, I will destroy the wisdom of the wise, and will bring to nothing the understanding of the prudent.
1 Corinthians 1:18-19

But the natural man receiveth not the things of the Spirit of God: for they are foolishness unto him: neither can he know them, because they are spiritually discerned.
1 Corinthians 2:14

That is why God is calling you today. Therefore if you are hearing the still small voice of God calling on you today to believe in Christ and accept Him as your Saviour, do not say, "No" to that voice because it is God Himself talking to you. Jesus said to the people who questioned Him in John 6:44 that it is not possible for anyone to come to Him unless God the Father draws that person to Him.

No man can come to me, except the Father which hath sent me draw him: and I will raise him up at the last day.
John 6:44

You have probably been living a life that has little or no meaning to you. Take a bold step today to move into this new life in Christ. Do not delay today. Seize this opportunity to come to Jesus.

You must be born-again

It is a great opportunity for you to also become a son of God, an opportunity to have a Father-son relationship with the Lord God who is the creator of the entire universe. It is an opportunity for you to also become a partaker of God's divine nature. It is an opportunity for you to share in God's power and demonstrate God's power to the world. That you should have His power and demonstrate it to the world is God's plan for your life.

I know that you have seen and you know many people who call themselves Christians and who have accepted Christ as their Saviour but who do not have this power of God demonstrated in their lives. Yes! This is true, but this is so because most people who have accepted Christ as their Saviour lack this knowledge and do not know that they have this power available to them. Even many of those that do know this do not know how to get this power demonstrated in their lives. So, even after they became born-again Christians, they continue to live their normal natural life buffeted about by the devil and his forces, unable to demonstrate the power of God or the supernatural life that is now their portion. God Himself wants us to recognize this truth. That is why He said through the Prophet Isaiah in Isaiah 5:13 and through the Prophet Hosea in Hosea 4:6 that His people are destroyed and gone into captivity because of their lack of knowledge.

> *Therefore my people are gone into captivity, because they have no knowledge: and their honourable men are famished, and their multitude dried up with thirst.*
> **Isaiah 5:13**

Living a supernatural life (Volume 3)

My people are destroyed for lack of knowledge: because thou hast rejected knowledge, I will also reject thee, that thou shalt be no priest to me: seeing thou hast forgotten the law of thy God, I will also forget thy children.

Hosea 4:6

It is a lack of knowledge that has not allowed such Christians to demonstrate the power of God in their lives. But you now know better. Having read this book, you have now been given the foundation knowledge that God wants you to have of the power that is made available to you once you become a born-again Christian and you also now know to some extent what you require to, and how you can, demonstrate this power in your life. You can no longer be stranded or tormented by the enemy.

Knowing these therefore, I know that you will not like to miss the opportunity to demonstrate this type of power that we have talked about in this book in your life.

However, as I have earlier said, this power can only be made available to you after you have accepted Jesus Christ as your Saviour and get born again.

You must have been told before that you have to change, clean up yourself and leave those things that you have been doing, which do not make your life compatible with a Christian life before you can be saved or become a born-again Christian.

You must be born-again

But I want you to know that this is not a pre-requisite for your being saved or born-again. Once you receive Christ into your life, the change will come. God Himself will be the One who will clean you up. He will give you a new heart and a new spirit. He will also give you His Spirit who will guide you and direct you into all truths. Once you have this Spirit, your desires will change and the change in your attitudes and orientation will follow.

The process of accepting Jesus Christ as your Saviour is not difficult. It is actually a very simple thing. Just follow the four instructions listed below.

1. Accept that you are a sinner because we are all sinners before God. God Himself made this known to us through Paul in Romans 3:23 and also through Apostle John in 1 John 1:8.

   For all have sinned, and come short of the glory of God;
   Romans 3:23

   If we say that we have no sin, we deceive ourselves, and the truth is not in us.
   1 John 1:8

2. Confess your sins genuinely with a contrite heart and believe that God has forgiven you of those sins. God Himself has told us through John that if we confess our sins He is faithful and just to forgive us our sins and to cleanse us from all forms of unrighteousness. That is what He told us through Apostle John in 1 John 1:9.

Living a supernatural life (Volume 3)

If we confess our sins, he is faithful and just to forgive us our sins, and to cleanse us from all unrighteousness.

1 John 1:9

3. Believe in your heart that Jesus Christ died for your sins and that God raised Him up from the dead. Confess this with your mouth. Then accept that Jesus Christ is the Lord and that He is your Saviour and confess this with your mouth also. Finally believe and confess with your mouth that as a result of this your confession with your mouth of His death for your sins and His resurrection you have now received your salvation as God made us to know through Apostle Paul in Romans 10:9-10.

That if thou shalt confess with thy mouth the Lord Jesus, and shalt believe in thine heart that God hath raised him from the dead, thou shalt be saved.

For with the heart man believeth unto righteousness; and with the mouth confession is made unto salvation.

Romans 10:9-10

4. Finally, pray out loud with your mouth and from the depth of your heart the prayer written below.

"My Father who is in Heaven, I have read your Word and I have heard what you have spoken to me. I desire to give my life to you today.

You must be born-again

I now confess to you that I am a sinner and ask that you forgive me my sins and cleanse me from all my unrighteousness. I know that having confessed my sins and asked you to forgive me; you have forgiven me and cleansed me from all my sins. Father, give me the strength of will not to go back to those sins.

I believe in my heart and I now confess with my mouth that Jesus Christ died for my sins and that you raised Him up the third day from the dead. I have confessed this my belief with my mouth, I also confess Him to be my Lord and Saviour therefore I now believe that I am born-again because your Word says so.

Thank you Father for giving me this free salvation. Thank you Jesus for offering yourself to save me from my sins. Thank you Holy Spirit for coming to live in me to direct me from now on.

I pray in the Name of Jesus Christ. AMEN"

Now that you have made the above confessions and prayed the above prayer from the depth of your heart, the Word of God says that once you do this you are saved and you have become a son of God. I can now boldly tell you that you are now a born-again child of God. I therefore welcome you into the family of God and into the Kingdom of God. You are now a member of that Kingdom. You have to believe this and move forward from this point on in faith. Your interaction with God can only be on the basis of faith in His Word. That is the only way you can please Him. He told us in Hebrews 11:6 that without faith we cannot please Him.

> *But without faith it is impossible to please him: for he that cometh to God must believe that he is, and that he is a rewarder of them that diligently seek him.*
> **Hebrews 11:6**

Therefore start going from now on in faith by what the Word of God says. He has said that you are now saved and born-again, therefore believe and have the faith that you are now saved and that you are born-again. Remember also that faith speaks out what it believes. Therefore speak out what you believe and let others know that you are now saved.

Because you have made the above confessions of your faith in Christ, in addition to your new birth, the Word of God also says that:

You are now a new creation.
You have now been given the gift of righteousness.
You are now a son of God and an heir of God.
You are now a temple of God.
The Holy Spirit of God now lives in you.
You are now a king and priest unto God.
You are now an ambassador for Christ.
You now have the mind of Christ.

From this point on, the above statements are all true of you. Therefore believe these, start speaking them out and acting accordingly. They are not only true of you but all the other attributes discussed in *Chapter 2 – Chapter 6* of this book will all become a reality in your life as you grow in the faith. From now on follow the four steps listed below.

You must be born-again

1. Stop seeing by sight. Stop acting based on what you see, on what you feel, on what you hear, on what you taste, on what you smell, and on what you think. Let all your actions be based on faith in what the Word of God says.

2. Stop basing your actions on facts but on the truth of the Word of God.

3. Find a Bible believing place of worship near to you that you can join so that you can be having fellowship with other Saints of God where you can be fed with the Word of God from time to time.

4. Read the Bible, which is the Word of God often to find out more in particular read ***Chapters 2 to 6*** and continue to make the confessions in these Chapters. These are now true for you. They are all yours in Christ.

As you continue to do these you will be growing from strength to strength in faith and in the Word. You will then become a vessel of honour to be used by God for this end time.

If you want more information on what has just happened to you and what you have now become with this new birth then read the companion book series to this book series written by the same author titled, ***"You are a New Creature" Volumes 1,2,3 and 4.***

Living a supernatural life (Volume 3)

If you have just accepted Christ as your Saviour through the reading of this book or you find the book useful and have seen or learn new things that can help your Christian life's journey or help you concerning the challenges that you have the author will like to hear from you so that you can gain more from his experience and others can also gain from your own experience. Contact the author to share your testimonies. The author Pastor Olumbo also holds from time to time healing and counselling seminars. Please contact the author to find out when the next healing and counselling seminar will hold at the following e-mail address or telephone numbers or both so that you can take advantage of this opportunity to know more about who you have just become or who you really are in-Christ:

michaelolumbo@outlook.com
or
+234 816 526 5668
+234 802 310 3275

I look forward to hearing from you.

THE OTHER VOLUMES OF THIS BOOK SERIES

In *Volume 1* we showed what the make-up of man is. We showed that man is basically created as a spirit being and therefore ought to be more sensitive to the spiritual things, which are unseen than he is to the physical things that are seen. Then we talked about a law of the spirit, which is operating in man's life on a continuous basis and, which most men have not taken cognizance of. This law is very important in the scheme of things and any man that wants to live a supernatural life here on earth must not only be very conversant with the law but must also make use of it. We tried to show you that it is not only possible but also essential to live a supernatural life right now here on earth and we believe that to a great extent we were able to do this. Every Christian, nay every human being needs the information that is in this book to be able to live as God created man. This book can be considered to be an explanation of *The Great Secret* that people did not know which was claimed to have been discovered some years ago. *The Secret* has always been an open *Secret* which has been made available for thousands of years but which have not been really understood until recently. It is well explained in this *"Living a Supernatural Life"* book series In particular read *Volume 1* of this series if you want to know this *Secret.*

In *Volume 2* we showed with proof the truth that as a born-again Christian you are really a supernatural being. We then looked at how as a supernatural being you can release the supernatural into your life.

Living a supernatural life (Volume 3)

We discussed the role that the Name of Jesus plays in the release of the supernatural and showed that the Name of Jesus is the major key for the release of the supernatural. We then showed that there are specific instructions left by Jesus Christ as to how to use His Name for the release of the supernatural and we showed that these instructions have been misinterpreted by many modern day Christians. We looked at the power that is in that Name of Jesus Christ and showed how that power can best be harnessed for the release of the supernatural by looking at the specific instructions given by Jesus as to how to use His Name. From His instructions we saw that His Name can be used to ask and receive from the Father and to get miracles done by Jesus Himself.

Even though the Father and Jesus are One and the same (Just two different manifestations of the same God), the method of using the Name of Jesus to receive from God manifesting as the Father is different from the method of using it to get God manifesting as Jesus to do miracles, signs and wonders. We discussed how to use the two methods as well as the mistakes in our current approach. We again showed in *Volume 2* that the supernatural is in your mouth because your mouth is the vehicle through which the supernatural is delivered. One of the major reasons why many Christians fail in their effort to live the supernatural life is that they expect that whatever commands they give to have immediate manifestation. We showed that it is the fulfillment that is immediate but the manifestation may take some time.

Further in *Volume 2* we also listed some of the things that you must be and that you must do if you want to successfully live a supernatural life. Those things that we have listed here are not by any means all that you have to do but these will go a long way to getting you there. One major requirement for any Christian wanting to live in the supernatural is that such a Christian must know how to pull down the strong holds that Satan will try to build in his mind from time to time. Satan will bombard the mind of such a Christian with all kinds of thoughts that can become strong holds if they are not pulled down.

You must pull down Satan's thoughts that he attempts to establish as strong holds in your mind before they can take root. How to do this is discussed in detail with examples *Volume 2*

In *Volume 4* we discuss two of the major requirements for living a supernatural life here on earth. These are the Holy Spirit and a willing mind. The roles that both the Holy Spirit and the mind play in living a supernatural life are examined in detail. The ways to submit to the Holy Spirit and harness the mind so as to live in the supernatural realm are also discussed. Finally we look at the various hindrances and obstacles that must be avoided if one is to live in this miracle realm.

OTHER BOOKS BY THE SAME AUTHOR

You Cannot Be Barren Series

Barrenness is a disease which can be very painful to whoever suffers from it. Yet the pain is difficult to express. The shame barrenness brings can lead to a deplorable life which makes the person become isolated. While trying to solve this problem you will meet with all kinds of trials and insults. As a Christian you need not go through all these problems.

You Cannot Be Barren book series is written to uplift the minds of every individual who is suffering from dearth in all human aspects, be it fruitfulness, or any other pressing needs. The book series makes you understand that barrenness is not of God and that every trial and tribulation has its expiration if only one is born-again.

The Book ***You Cannot Be Barren*** is written in six volumes and they are written to show you how you can conquer barrenness.

In Volume 1 we discussed in a simple way the various causes of barrenness looking first at what medical sciences say about the human reproductive system. We also look at what they say about the human reproductive process and about barrenness and its causes.

Then we looked at what the Word of God has to say about the causes of barrenness, giving the root cause as mainly spiritual even though it manifests physically. We showed how important it is not to have a sin-complex but a righteousness-complex if one is to approach God for the solution to the barrenness challenge. One must also be God-conscious, and God-focused if one is to solve the barrenness problem based on the Word of God. We also discussed briefly some of the things that the Word of God gives as the main causes of barrenness. These include sin, lack of forgiveness, taking the Communion unworthily and what one eats or drinks.

In Volume 2 we discussed the Covenant rights that you have to ask for healing from barrenness as a Christian. We first looked at your rights to healing as a result of the Covenant and showed that you have an unquestionable right as provided by God for your deliverance from anything that may be causing you to be barren. We discussed the terms of the Covenant that you must fulfill if you are to be able to claim your rights via the Covenant as well as how to use the Word of God to claim those rights. What we have done is to make sure that by the time that you would have gone through the *Volume 2* you would have gotten such a good understanding of the Covenant to the extent that there will be no doubt in your mind that it is your right to be fruitful and nothing can stop your fruitfulness.

In Volume 3 we looked at your New-Birth rights to being fruitful in detail. With your new-birth we showed that both spiritual and physical healing has been packaged with your salvation.

Living a supernatural life (Volume 3)

Not only that, we also showed that as a result of your new-birth God's life was imparted to you. With this God's life that was imparted to you we showed that if you are conscious of this new life, which you now have which is God's life then it is impossible for any disease that can lead to barrenness or unfruitfulness to attack your body and inhabit it or win against you.

Our aim in *Volumes 2 and 3* is to try to develop and increase your faith to the point where you can see yourself in the light of the Scriptures by discussing your and proving your covenant rights and your new-birth rights to fruitfulness.

In Volume 4 After discussing how important your confessions are and how to stand firm we looked at the various ways that the enemy uses to attack people with barrenness and give the Scriptures that can be used in confessions against it in each case. For each case we also gave sample Scripturally-based confessions that you can use. If you truly believe in your confessions and have processed them through meditation long enough for them to become revealed words of God to you embedded in your spirit then getting over any form of barrenness will be very easy for you. You will not have to struggle with barrenness.

In Volume 5 we discussed the various reasons why people don't generally receive their healing from diseases and in particular from barrenness. You will do well to look at these so that your healing will not be hindered.

Finally **in the** *Volume 6* of this, ***"You Can Not Be Barren"*** book series we looked at and discussed the various barrenness strong holds of the devil that he usually builds in the minds of the people who suffer from this scourge of barrenness. We looked at how these strong holds are developed in the mind in stages and discussed the Word of God to use to counter the strong holds at each stage.

REFERENCES

BROWN R. 1987. *Unbroken Curses.* New Kensington: Whitaker House.

CLARK J. 2003. *Exposing Spiritual Witchcraft.* Florida: Spirit of Life Publishing.

Grace Notes. *Bitterness.* Website. http://www.realtime.net/~wdoud/topics/bitterness.html. 20 August 2013

HICKEY M. 1987. *Breaking Generational Curses.* Oklahoma: Harrison House.

KENNETH E. HAGIN 1979. *What to do when Faith seems weak and Victory lost.* Kenneth Hagin Ministries.

NORI D. 1999. *Breaking Generational Curses.* Shippensburg: Destiny Image Publishers.

OLUMBO M. F. 2005. *Living A Supernatural Life. Volume 1.* Lagos: The Apostolic Church LAWNA Printing Press.

OLUMBO M. F. 2008. *Living A Supernatural Life. Volume 2.* Lagos: Extra Time Communications Ltd.

ORAL ROBERTS 1987. *When you see the invisible You can do the impossible.* Destiny Image Publishers Inc.

SHERMAN D. 1990. *Spiritual Warfare: How to live in Victory and Retake the Land. Seattle:* YWAM Publishing.

TOM MARSHALL 1977. *Free Indeed.* Sovereign World Publications.

WRIGHT H.W. 2005. *A More excellent way Be in Health.* Pleasant Valley Publications

INDEX

A parable of freed slaves	532
A parable of Mortgaged house	576
A parable of the rich man and his son	607
Angels can be dispatched to help you	632
Are you abiding in Christ?	701
Are you fighting in the faith or sense arena?	701
Are you not looking at things seen?	678
Are you opening your mouth wide?	690
Are you sick?	547
Are you struggling with sin?	651
Are you sure your prayer was heard?	680
Are you walking by faith?	676
Building a sound Scriptural image	521
Did you ask according to God's will?	687
Did you pray in hope and not in faith?	692
Did you pray with faith in Jesus Name?	693
Did you use Jesus's Name correctly?	694
Do you have iniquity in your heart?	690
Do you know you are righteous?	681
Even death cannot win against you	640
Even death has no power over you	598
Faced with an impossible situation?	719
Follow the footsteps of Christ	510
Following the footsteps of Jesus	33
Four steps to accepting salvation	755
Get the right Self Image	44
God is above you	305
God is around you	306
God is behind you	303
God is in front of you	301
God is in you	306

God is underneath you	304
God loves you	735
God now sees you as righteous	683
God uses our imagination	522
God's blessing covers both wealth and health	566
Healing is packaged with your salvation	547
Healing power should flow out of you	585
Healing the sick	538
Ignorance is Satan's weapon	542
Is your disease genetically inherited?	596
It is a choice	528
Jesus called God His Father	37
Jesus is interceding for you	715
Jesus said He was the bread from Heaven	38
Jesus said He was the Living Bread	38
Jesus said He would raise the dead	37
Jesus said He would shortly go back	39
Jesus's death solved the sin-sickness problem	452
Not sure of answer to your prayer?	675
Nothing can hold you in bondage	728
Nothing can hurt you anymore	738
Prayer of confession to salvation	756-757
Regaining one's captivities	531
Reviving dead destinies	532
Sanctification gives you power over sin	657
Sickness is not a chastening of the Lord	449
Sickness is not a persecution from God	447
Sickness is not an affliction from God	446
Sixteen Benefits of righteousness for you	115
Speak to that situation	742
The Blessing of Abraham are yours	49
The Holy Spirit will help you to pray	713
The more intense the sickness the better	594
The more severe the better	634
The Word has the power to fulfill	530

Living a supernatural life (Volume 3)

These are what I can now do in-Christ	458
These are what I have in-Christ	359
This is what I am in Christ	153
This is where I am in-Christ	498
This is who I am in-Christ	76
Tormented by affliction	613
What are these rivers of living waters	584
What does it mean to be sanctified?	652
What will you do about these?	501
What you are in Christ	79
What you can do in-Christ	373
What you have in-Christ	161
What you see is what you get	526
When you ask you will receive	679
Where you are in-Christ	463
Who you are in Christ	47
Why are people still praying for healing?	581
Why ask for what you already have?	604
You already have what you are praying for	600
You are a beloved of the Lord	88
You are a child of Abraham	47
You are a child of Light	62
You are a citizen of the Kingdom of God	93, 613
You are a citizen of the Kingdom of God	93
You are God's anointed	95
You are God's chosen	99
You are the salt of the earth	100
You are a light	62, 100
You are a god	72, 722
You are a king and priest unto God	66
You are a light in the world	619
You are a member of the Body of Christ	85
You are a new creature	79
You are a saint	90

You are a son of God	64, 721
You are a spirit-being	55
You are a sweet savour of Jesus Christ	147
You are a Temple of God	50
You are a temple of God	615
You are a victor	58, 134
You are an ambassador for Christ	135, 591, 707
You are an embodiment of power	505
You are an heir of God	128
You are an heir of God	705
You are anointed of God	616
You are born of God	52
You are buried with Christ	483
You are far above all things	486
You are far above any affliction	646
You are far above any disease	574
You are far above that situation	729
You are far from oppression	494
You are hidden in God	311
You are holy	125
You are in God's family	490
You are in the Kingdom of God	463
You are in the Light	491
You are light	62
You are more than a conqueror	639, 727
You are near to God	492
You are no longer a stranger to God	618
You are one Spirit with Christ	83
You are peculiar	146
You are resurrected with Christ	483
You are sanctified	256, 651
You are seating together with Christ	485
You are sent as Jesus was sent	708
You are sent to walk in victory	740
You are supposed to be shining	620

Living a supernatural life (Volume 3)

You are the just	103
You are righteous	111
You are to shine more and more	621
You are to walk by faith	628
You can bind and loose anything	408
You can command any affliction	629
You can do all things	386
You can do anything that you can think	405
You can do greater works in the New Covenant	416
You can do signs and wonders	399
You can do the works that Jesus did	419
You can get everything you prayed for	696
You can have knowledge of the truth	435
You can hear God's voice	440
You can impart the gifts of the Holy Spirit	423
You can keep sin under subjection	430
You can live in divine health	443
You can live in perpetual victory	401
You can make requests in Jesus's Name	441
You can move any mountain	393
You can now honestly serve God	373
You can open people's spiritual eyes	381
You can say no to death	425
You can see the invisible	438
You cannot inherit a disease	596
You don't even need to pray for healing	571
You don't have to carry diseases anymore	451
You dwell in-Christ	479
You have a building of God	165
You have a Comforter	168
You have a goodly heritage	227
You have a mouth and wisdom	630
You have a quickened body	240
You have a regenerated spirit	202

You have a royal priestly office	270
You have ability to overcome temptation	321
You have absolute security in Christ	195
You have all things that pertain to life	230
You have already won the battle	635
You have an assurance of protection	733
You have been delivered from all oppression	642
You have been healed already	569
You have better promises	349
You have divine health and healing	263
You have enriched knowledge	200
You have eternal life	174
You have freedom	178
You have God with you always	298
You have God working in you	623
You have God's divine protection	188
You have God's love	332
You have life	174
You have light and understanding	337
You have power above your enemies	624
You have power over sins	657
You have power over that of the enemy	316
You have reconciliation with God	185
You have redemption in Christ	278
You have sanctification	256
You have spiritual weapons of warfare	339
You have strength	292
You have the abundant life	280
You have the divine nature	207, 724
You have the glory that Jesus had	324
You have the greater One in you	273
You have the keys of the Kingdom	166, 643, 709
You have the Laws of God in your heart	201
You have the marks of Jesus Christ	161
You have the measure of faith	247

Living a supernatural life (Volume 3)	
You have the mind of Christ	243, 544, 724
You have the Name of Jesus	346
You have the power of God in you	214
You have the power of God	621
You have the power to bind or loose	732
You have the power to cast out devils	625
You have the righteousness of Christ	254
You have the rights to use the Name	698
You have the support that Jesus had	325
You have the weapons to fight with	627
You have victory over the world	232
You must be born-again	751
You must contend for your rights	507
You must focus your mind on this	592
You need the Word and the Blood	660
You no longer have the spirit of fear	734
You should be oozing out rivers of living waters	583
Your anointing is higher than old covenant saint	717
Your body is a habitation of God	593
Your healing is already inside you	594
Your life is hid with Christ in God	645
Your victory is already assured	726

www.ingramcontent.com/pod-product-compliance
Lightning Source LLC
Chambersburg PA
CBHW071932220426
43662CB00009B/890